PHILOSOPHY

*An Introduction to
the Central Issues*

PHILOSOPHY

An Introduction to the Central Issues

CHARLES LANDESMAN

Hunter College of the City University
of New York

HOLT, RINEHART AND WINSTON

New York   Chicago   San Francisco   Philadelphia
Montreal   Toronto   London   Sydney
Tokyo   Mexico City   Rio de Janeiro   Madrid

Publisher: **John Michel**
Acquisitions Editor: **Nedah Abbott**
Project Editor: **Melanie Miller**
Production Manager: **Robin B. Besofsky**
Design Supervisor: **Gloria Gentile**
Text Designer: **Mary Ann Joulwan**
Cover Designer: **Gloria Gentile**
Cover Computer Art: **Dr. E. P. Miles, Jr.**

Library of Congress Cataloging in Publication Data

Landesman, Charles.
    Philosophy : an introduction to the central issues.

    Bibliography: p.
    Includes index.
    1. Philosophy—Introduction.   I. Title.
BD21.L27   1984   100   84-4640

ISBN 0-03-063801-1

CBS COLLEGE PUBLISHING
Holt, Rinehart and Winston
The Dryden Press
Saunders College Publishing

Copyright Acknowledgments

A. J. Ayer, from *Language, Truth and Logic*. Reprinted by permission of Victor Gollancz Ltd.

Brand Blanshard, from *Nature of Thought*. Reprinted by permission of George Allen & Unwin (Publisher) Ltd. and Humanities Press Inc.

Søren Kierkegaard, from *Concluding Unscientific Postscript*. Translated by David F. Swenson and Walter Lowrie. Copyright © 1969 by Princeton University Press. Reprinted by permission of Princeton University Press.

Karl Marx, from *Capital I*. Reprinted by permission of International Publishers Co., Inc.

Karl Marx and Friedrich Engels, from *Selected Works*. Reprinted by permission of The Copyright Agency of the USSR.

Robert Nozick, from *Anarchy, State, and Utopia*. Copyright © 1974 by Basic Books, Inc. Reprinted by permission of Basic Books, Inc.

John Rawls, from *A Theory of Justice*. Reprinted by permission of Harvard University Press.

Bertrand Russell, from *The Problems of Philosophy*. Reprinted by permission of Oxford University Press.

For Arlyne

CONTENTS

PREFACE

The aim of this text is to introduce the central issues of philosophy. Intended for use in college-level courses that offer a general introduction to philosophy, the text can accommodate instructors who wish to organize a course around topics of contemporary significance as well as those who want to introduce ideas drawn from the history of philosophy. It can also be used in introductory courses that emphasize ethics, the theory of knowledge, or metaphysics, for the materials included constitute a basic introduction to these areas. Students at both two-year and four-year colleges will find the text accessible. In writing it, I have also kept in mind the needs of the general reader who desires to become familiar with the central issues of philosophy without the benefit of formal instruction.

The text is clear and readable and can be understood by anyone with a high-school education. It is also hoped that the style is interesting and lively; philosophy is filled with fascinating questions—and fascinating attempts at answering those questions— and a satisfactory text should keep the reader alert and interested. To make reading easier, I have tried to avoid technical jargon as much as possible; the meanings of those terms that are used are explained in the glossary that occurs at the end of each chapter.

Because philosophy has a long history and encompasses an enormous range of topics, not everything can or should be covered in an introductory text. I have selected those topics that most philosophers would agree represent the fundamental issues of modern philosophy. A student who has mastered these topics will have learned what is of greatest importance in the field and will have acquired an excellent basis for further study.

The text is organized to maximize flexibility in its use. It begins with an introductory chapter that explains what philosophy is and why it is worth studying. The remaining eight chapters are divided into three parts. Part I is an introduction to moral and political philosophy. Part II introduces two main areas of metaphysics: the philosophy of mind and the philosophy of religion. Part III discusses basic issues in the theory of knowledge, including empirical and a priori knowledge. Because each part is self-contained, the parts may be read in any order. Thus, instructors who prefer to begin the study of philosophy with the theory of knowledge can start with Part III. Instructors who prefer to begin with metaphysics can start with Part II, and can have their students read its two chapters in either order. If a briefer course is desired, any part may be omitted without loss of continuity.

Except for the introduction, each chapter begins with a preview of the issues and problems that will be discussed and ends with a glossary; a list of additional readings, drawn primarily from the history of philosophy, that can be used for further study; and a set of questions for thought and discussion. These questions were designed with several purposes in mind. They can serve as the basis for classroom discussion. They can be given as written assignments that will encourage the student to become actively involved with the problems presented in the chapter. Finally, they can serve as a source of topics for essays and research papers that the instructor may wish to assign.

The text has an unusual feature: its appendices. The first appendix presents the fundamentals of logic. Many instructors would like these fundamentals included in an introduction to philosophy, for logic is an integral branch of philosophy that has greatly influenced its development in the twentieth century. It is convenient to use the language and the concepts of logic to analyze, discuss, and evaluate philosophical arguments (or any argument, for that matter), and the first appendix is designed to satisfy this need. Its use is optional, and it may be read at any point.

The second appendix is concerned with philosophical research and writing. Instructors generally require their students to write papers, and students tend to feel lost trying to complete them. My aim is simply to provide some commonsense advice about writing a paper. The appendix discusses such basic matters as how to find a topic, how to organize a paper, and how to document its findings.

Throughout this text, it has been my intention to combine readability with depth. Some texts give many topics superficial coverage; others treat each topic in depth, but the result is too difficult for all but the best-prepared students. I have tried to make the text easy to read while giving each topic sufficient depth so that students feel that they have learned something substantial. I have tried not merely to talk about philosophy but also to communicate what it is like to philosophize, to come to grips with a problem and to think it through.

Now for the acknowledgments. I would like to thank Erica Landesman for her help with the biographical inserts. I have had many useful discussions with Howard Kahane and Arlyne Landesman on the teaching of philosophy that have influenced the style and content of this book. Norman Care, Arthur Collins, Arlyne and Jennifer Landesman, James Muyskens, David Rosenthal, Steve Spielmen, and various anonymous reviewers have read some or all of the manuscript and have offered many suggestions that I have incorporated. Finally, I would like to thank my students at Hunter College who have persisted in asking the questions that I have tried to clarify in this book.

Chapter 1

UNDERSTANDING PHILOSOPHY:
An Introduction

Philosophy and Its History

In this text, you will learn about some of the major questions that have preoccupied philosophers from the beginning of Western philosophy in the ancient world to the present day—questions that are hence among the enduring questions of the history of philosophy. You will become familiar with the answers that various philosophers have given to them and, I hope, you will be encouraged to devise answers of your own. Thinking people have been fascinated by these questions for centuries. It is very likely that you have considered some of them yourself. Thus, you have probably been philosophizing for some time now without realizing it. Everyone who thinks seriously about life's meaning and purpose, everyone who wants to get to the bottom of things, is a philosopher at heart.

Western philosophy originated in the Greek world in the sixth and fifth centuries B.C. The term *Western* here refers to philosophy as it has evolved in Europe and, much later, in the United States and in other countries that inherited a European culture. This book will focus almost exclusively on the philosophical problems and issues as they emerged from this culture. Non-Western civilizations such as India, China, Japan, and the Islamic nations have rich philosophical traditions as well, but the study of these traditions is a major undertaking in itself and cannot be included in the limited space of this volume.

The word *philosophy,* derived from the Greek, means literally the love of wisdom. Thus, the philosopher is not necessarily someone who is already wise, but someone who seeks wisdom seriously. One of the first great Greek philosophers, Socrates, said that the unexamined life is not worth living; the pursuit of wisdom thus consists in trying to find out, consciously and critically, what makes life worthwhile. Socrates was not content with an uncritical allegiance to existing ways of life, for they are usually adopted unreflectively through the influence of culture and tradition. Perhaps ways of life better than the traditional ones can be discovered through rational discussion that will expose unthinking prejudices and reveal more desirable alternatives.

It is customary to divide the history of philosophy into three main periods: ancient, medieval, and modern. In ancient philosophy, in the thought of Socrates, Plato, Aristotle, and others, we see the beginning of a critical and rational discussion of fundamental philosophical issues that threw into question the cultural and religious assumptions of the ancient world. Medieval philosophy was primarily concerned with fusing the main ideas of Christianity into a comprehensive world view that could be defended against criticism. Two of the greatest names of medieval philosophy were St. Augustine, who lived in the early years of the medieval period (in the fourth century A.D.) and St. Thomas Aquinas, who lived near its end (in the thirteenth century). In the modern period, which began in the sixteenth century and continues into the present, philosophers have sought to come to terms with the theories of nature developed by Galileo, Newton, Darwin, and Einstein, to mention just a few major scientists. How do human values fit into the world as revealed by science? Can science and religion coexist? Does life have a meaning and purpose, or is it, in Shakespeare's words, "a tale told by an idiot, full of sound and fury, signifying nothing"? Some of the important figures of modern philosophy whose ideas we shall discuss are Descartes, Locke, Hume, Kant, Marx, and Bertrand Russell.

In this book, the approach to the main questions that have been raised by philosophers since the time of Socrates is topical rather than historical. Each chapter is devoted to a major topic or theme, and the questions that have been asked about it are discussed systematically. The ideas of the great philosophers of the past will be introduced when they can help clarify the topic being discussed.

The Main Branches of Philosophy

As we survey the history of philosophy, we find that certain major themes occur over and over again. The study of philosophy has customarily been divided into several branches of philosophy: *ethics, metaphysics,* and *epistemology.*

Philosophical ethics—or *moral philosophy,* as it is sometimes called—probably began with Socrates' attempt to discover the meaning of his own life and, in general, the conditions that make life worth living. "How ought one to live?" is the question that he made the main issue of ethics. Ethics, then, is an attempt to understand the relation between what *is* and what *ought* to be. Each of us has certain interests and goals, and we live our lives accordingly. In ethics we consider whether we can evaluate life as we are actually living it according to a rationally justifiable conception or ideal of how it ought to be lived. Are we entitled to pursue our own individual interests or must we subordinate them to moral obligations? And if moral obligations do bind us, how are they to be known and verified? Chapters Two and Four take up these and related questions.

We are not isolated individuals; we are all members of groups—familial, social, and political. Ever since the time of Plato and Aristotle, philosophers have been interested in the relation of the individual to the groups to which he belongs. In particular, they have focused on political groups, examining what relationship ought to exist between the individual and the state or governing authority. How much does the individual owe to the state and to the other members of his political community? How much is the state required to benefit the individual citizen? That part of ethics that is concerned with the proper organization of collective life is called *social and political philosophy* and is discussed in Chapter Three.

Human life is part of a much larger reality about which philosophers have been speculating from the very beginning. That branch of philosophy that discusses reality as a whole is called *metaphysics*. Some of its main problems are presented in Part Two, as well as in Part Three. The world presents us with an amazing variety of objects, events, and experiences. Does some unifying factor underlie this variety? The world appears to us in various guises. But what are things really like—is the world anything like the way it appears to us through our senses? The contrast between *unity* and *variety* and between *appearance* and *reality* are two of the major themes in the history of Western metaphysics. Metaphysics is also concerned with determining what sorts of things exist. Besides bodies, are there minds? Besides physical nature, is there a God? The question of the relation of the mind to the body will be considered in Chapter Five, and the question of the existence of God will be the theme of Chapter Six.

To find out what the world is really like as distinct from its superficial appearances, we need to investigate what we can *know* of the world and what the nature and extent of human knowledge is. *Epistemology,* or *the theory of knowledge,* takes up these issues. We generally assert that our senses provide us with our basic knowledge of the world. Yet we acknowledge that our senses can be deceptive and that knowledge must be based on rational thought. Moreover, our senses cannot directly inform us about the world as described by science, a world that encompasses particles too small to see and vast extents in time and space. So it appears that both sense perception and reason are distinct sources of human knowledge. Throughout the history of philosophy, there is a basic disagreement about knowledge between the *empiricists*—philosophers like Aristotle and Hume who believed that sense perception is the foundation of human knowledge—and the *rationalists*—philosophers who emphasized that reason functions independently of the senses to yield knowledge. Part Three discusses the problem of knowledge by taking as its central theme this disagreement between empiricists and rationalists.

Philosophy, Science, and Religion

If metaphysics studies the nature of reality, you are probably wondering how it differs from science. Don't the natural sciences purport to tell us what the natural world is like? Don't the social sciences provide us with knowledge of the human world? And if metaphysics tells us about the human mind and its relation to the body, how does it differ from pyschology? If it inquires into the existence of God, how does it differ from religion? These questions are all perfectly legitimate.

In fact, philosophy was not sharply differentiated from science until quite recently. Thus, in the fourth century B.C. Aristotle wrote treatises on physics, biology, astronomy, and psychology as well as on metaphysics, ethics, and epistemology. In the seventeenth century, Descartes made important contributions to mathematics and physics as well as philosophy. Not too long ago physics was called natural philosophy. Psychology only recently became a discipline distinct from philosophy; the American philosopher William James is as well known for his contributions to psychology as he is for his contributions to philosophy.

Nor was religious thought, or what we today call theology, always sharply distinguished from philosophy. In the Middle Ages, for example, the writings of St. Augustine and St. Thomas Aquinas were considered to be just as significant to theology as to philosophy.

In recent times, philosophy has become separate in practice from science and religion. This is reflected in the organization of most colleges and universities, in which philosophy is taught in a separate department. But what is the basis of this separation? This is not an easy question to answer, for philosophers themselves disagree about the nature of philosophy and its relationships to other human activities.

The Nature of Philosophy

One of the best descriptions of philosophy I have ever heard was given by a student who had just completed his first philosophy course. He said, "Philosophy goes back to square one." He meant that philosophy deals with our most fundamental conceptions of the world and of human life. In all our activities, whether they be scientific or religious or artistic, whether they involve work or play, we take certain fundamental ideas for granted. These ideas are the basic assumptions we use to guide our conduct and interpret our experience. For example, scientists assume that by observing the world through their senses, they can gain knowledge of it. Theologians assume that there is a God and that the Bible accurately conveys God's nature and will. In everyday life, we often assume that we know how to distinguish right from wrong.

The most characteristic feature of philosophy is that it attempts to identify and examine assumptions such as these to determine whether or not they are true. Does sense perception reveal the world as it really is? Can there be a reliable source of information about God? How can we distinguish between right and wrong conduct? Most of our assumptions are conveyed to us early in life. Our minds are thus stocked with ideas before we acquire the ability to think critically and hence assess them. And until we have assessed them critically, these assumptions are really just prejudices. In this text, we shall regard philosophy as the criticism of the basic assumptions that guide the conduct of our lives. This is what Socrates had in mind when he said that an unexamined life is not worth living. To examine our lives is to examine the fundamental ideas that influence us and that determine how we conduct ourselves and who we become.

Criticism is a way of examining ideas: We first clarify an idea to see what it really says and then determine what arguments support our adopting it and what arguments support our rejecting it. In doing so, we are going back to square one and becoming more rational in the process.

Although philosophy considers whether relying on faith or dogma or authority is legitimate, it is not itself based on these things. It is based on argument, on giving reasons. In fact, an important part of philosophy—one that is explained fully in Appendix I—is *logic,* which tells us how to distinguish good arguments from bad. In criticizing ideas, philosophers have always relied on logical theory to help them evaluate the reasons given in support of an idea. In philosophy, the only idea that we are entitled to accept is one that has withstood searching criticism.

Because philosophy deals with our most basic ideas, there is little consensus or agreement among philosophers about which ideas are correct. In the natural sciences, there is usually agreement for at least some time on at least the major theories of the various disciplines. Thus, most biologists today accept some current version of Darwin's theory of evolution. Scientists can agree on major theories because they agree on the methods of gathering data and of confirming theories. But philosophers try to get behind the arguments of scientists and others to determine what reasons can be used to validate them. Thus, you should not expect here an account of the ideas that philosophers today agree on. What will be emphasized is what they disagree about and the reasons for their disagreement. There are no final answers in philosophy, nor should any be expected. After all, philosophy is only about 2,500 years old. That is too short a time to settle any questions of real significance that take us back to square one.

The Uses of Philosophy

"What is the point of studying philosophy?" you may well ask. Why bother with going back to square one? What value does it have? When you have finished this book, you may be able to provide your own answers to these questions. In the meantime, here are some suggestions.

Aristotle said that by nature all men desire to know. But not all knowledge enables us to reach some practical goal. Sometimes we want to get to know something just to satisfy our curiosity. Some things are worth knowing about for their own sake. Such reasoning impells most philosophers, and scientists as well. Sometimes their theories have practical applications. More often they do not. But philosophers gain satisfaction by arriving at a theory that can withstand criticism and that answers a question they have been wondering about.

Before we study philosophy, our ideas are mere prejudices, unthinking assumptions, irrational beliefs. We don't even think about doubting them; they are second nature to us. Without philosophy, we are like prisoners in a dark cave who think they are perceiving reality as it really is and do not realize that they have no grounds for interpreting their experiences as they do. Philosophizing is, as Plato emphasized, like being released from such a prison. We become liberated from the gentle (and sometimes not so gentle) tyranny of everyday life. New possibilities of life and thought emerge. What had seemed inevitable now appears to be contingent. So philosophy brings us a kind of freedom and power by giving us a sense of the openness of life. It melts rigid thought patterns and make us more receptive to our experiences.

Someone once said that philosophy bakes no bread. If this means that its practical consequences are seldom immediate and direct, then this is true. But after all, our ideas influence our actions and our assumptions provide the framework for our ideas. So a philosophical critique of one's assumptions that causes new ideas to emerge imperceptibly changes the general course of one's life. For example, most of the ideas that lie behind the political, legal, and educational institutions of the modern world were first formulated by philosophers. So although philosophy's influence is seldom direct and immediate, it is often indirect, imperceptible, and of lasting importance.

Part I

ETHICS AND SOCIETY

Chapter 2

SOURCES OF MORAL VALUE

PREVIEW

We are frequently faced with practical decisions about what we ought to do, and we often wish there were criteria for distinguishing right conduct from wrong. If there were, we could use them to determine how we ought to act. Philosophical ethics is that part of philosophy that proposes such criteria. In this chapter, we shall consider various criteria that have been proposed. We shall first consider religion to see whether it is a satisfactory source of moral value and shall find that our consideration poses certain critical questions that call for philosophical reflection. We shall then consider the life and ideas of Socrates, the Greek philosopher who initiated a critical approach to ethical issues.

One of the questions that Socrates posed was whether we should consider only our own good (**egoism**) or also the good of others (**altruism**) in making our practical decisions. We shall first discuss the merits of egoism, which could be described as selfishness erected into a philosophy. We shall then devote the remainder of the chapter to considering the two main theories of modern philosophical ethics that tell us how the good of others should be considered when making practical decisions: the utilitarianism of Bentham and Mill and the categorical imperative of Kant. Both these theories offer criteria for making decisions that are still used today by private individuals and public officials.

Philosophical Ethics

PROBLEMS OF CONDUCT

Problems of conduct concern how some person or group of persons *ought* to act in a given situation. "What ought I to do?" is the question we ask when we are uncertain how to act. In many cases, what one is uncertain about is what is good for oneself. Questions about what college to attend, what profession or occupation to enter, what food to eat, what physician to consult, and what book to read are generally concerned with the good or advantage of the individual asking the question. A person who is concerned about his or her own good and takes steps to secure it is *prudent*.

Not all problems of conduct are limited to a concern for one's own good, however. When other persons are affected by what one does, then their good and their interests must be considered. The problem then acquires a *moral,* or *ethical,* dimension. For example, take the case of a young unmarried woman who finds herself pregnant and wonders whether or not to undergo an abortion. There are prudential questions that she needs to resolve, for example, would it be good for her to have the child? But other issues are involved as well. Does the fetus in her womb have any rights that need to be respected? Must the good of the prospective father be taken into account? When the good of others is involved, the issue becomes ethical.

The problem whether or not to obtain an abortion is one of individual morality. Moral problems acquire social and political dimensions when groups of individuals and the government are involved. Take the case of a person convicted of murder. Should the judge sentence him to death, to life imprisonment, or to a shorter term in prison? Or should he release him immediately to return to his home and family? Whatever the judge decides to do, he is acting in the name of the government and the citizens of his political jurisdiction. What right has the government to punish anyone? And if it does have that right, how severe can the penalty be? These are moral questions that are also political and legal in nature because they involve the government and its system of law. Take income tax as another example. When the government imposes an income tax, it requires the citizens to turn over some of their earnings to the government for public purposes. The income that is taxed is generally earned by hard work, and the citizens who earned it would prefer to spend the money on themselves and their families. What right does the government have to take income from individuals against their will?

Questions of punishment and taxation concern what the government is entitled to do to individuals. Individuals can also ask what they are entitled, and what they are *not* entitled, to do to their government. For example, many young men believed that the war in Vietnam was unjust and that the government should discontinue it. Upon receiving notice that they were about to be drafted into the armed forces of the United States, these young men faced a dilemma. Should they obey orders and fight in what they considered an unjust war? Should they become conscientious objectors? Or should they escape to another country to avoid the draft?

THE ROLE OF PHILOSOPHICAL ETHICS

Philosophical ethics, or *moral theory,* seeks to understand the nature of moral problems and to find rational methods for resolving them. Of course, people already have ways of deciding what they ought to do. Perhaps the pregnant woman will decide to have an abortion because she feels that her interests deserve to take priority. The judge may sentence the murderer to death because he feels that this is the punishment that is deserved. A young man may flee the country rather than fight in a war he objects to as unjust. These are all moral judgments. Individuals begin acquiring the capacity to make such judgments in childhood; moral education is as much a part of education as learning reading, writing, and arithmetic. Thus, in their relations with family and friends, at school, at church, and at play, children learn precepts that help them resolve moral problems. "Keep your promises," "Honor your father and mother," and "Obey the law" are examples of moral precepts inculcated at an early age. Such precepts, applied unreflectively and automatically in making decisions, form the content of a person's *habitual morality*. For the most part, moral behavior is the result of standard habits of response and ingrained forms of conduct. In many cases, we do not even think about what we ought to do; we simply allow our habits to take charge.

Occasionally our moral habits turn out to be inadequate as guides to conduct. For example, in recent years new techniques have been invented that help keep people with certain diseases alive. Consider the machines that are used to cleanse the blood of individuals who have experienced kidney failure. Suppose there are fewer machines than there are people who need them. How are the machines to be apportioned? Who is to live and who is to die? Since people do not customarily have to cope with this situation, the precepts that they have learned will probably not be decisive in resolving this problem.

There are also times when one's habitual precepts conflict. Take the case of a physician who is asked by a dying patient for a drug with which to kill himself. What should the physician do? She may believe that it is wrong to commit suicide and that she has an obligation to keep her patients alive as long as possible. Yet she may see no value in prolonging the suffering of a dying patient and may in fact wonder whether it is inhumane to do so. Certain of her principles motivate her to withhold the drug; others incline her to offer it.

When habitual morality cannot resolve a problem, the individual is forced to reflect on it consciously. This is the beginning of the development of *reflective morality*. Old habits and traditions no longer suffice. Perhaps new rules need to be developed to take care of novel situations. When our old precepts are in conflict, we must decide which one takes priority over the others. From reflective morality evolves *philosophical ethics,* for when we consider moral problems, fundamental questions about the nature of moral principles and their justification are inevitably raised. To answer such questions, we must develop a moral theory that accounts for the nature of morality from a philosophical perspective.

Many disciplines have made important contributions to the study of moral phenomena. Psychologists have investigated the moral development of children and have tried to explain the emergence of such feelings as guilt and shame. Anthropologists have investigated the moral codes of primitive peoples. Sociologists have investigated how moral precepts are embodied in the workings of social institutions. Biologists have investigated the emergence of morality and of altruistic forms of behavior in the course of human evolution. Though philosophers welcome the contributions of all these disciplines, they view moral phenomena differently than scientists do. They wonder which precepts we ought to adopt, whether any forms of conduct are really right, and if so what makes them right. They ask how an ethical decision can be justified and what justification means. When a young man decides to evade the draft, is his decision correct? When a young women decides to obtain an abortion, is she doing the right thing? What is the difference between right and wrong? What precepts should we adopt? How shall we go about making up our minds on moral issues? These are the main questions of philosophical ethics.

Ethics and Religion

THE TEN COMMANDMENTS

In most cultures throughout most of human history, religion has been a major source of established morality. Religion is a social institution, and one of its most important functions has been the support of those forms of conduct that have been thought essential for the survival of the group. In some religions, God and his agents on earth are represented as moral teachers who instruct their peoples in the essentials of right and wrong conduct. God is thus seen as favoring some types of conduct and disapproving of others. In one of the most famous passages of the Old Testament, God is represented as issuing commandments to the people of Israel, gathered at the foot of Mt. Sinai:

> I am the Lord thy God, which have brought thee out of the land of Egypt, out of the house of bondage. Thou shalt have no other gods before me. Thou shalt not make unto thee any graven image, or any likeness of any thing that is in heaven above, or that is in the earth beneath, or that is in the water under the earth. Thou shalt not bow down thyself to them, nor serve them: for I the Lord thy God am a jealous God, visiting the iniquity of the fathers upon the children unto the third and fourth generation of them that hate me; And showing mercy unto thousands of them that love me, and keep my commandments. Thou shalt not take the name of the Lord thy God in vain; for the Lord will not hold him guiltless that taketh his name in vain. Remember the sabbath day, to keep it holy. Six days shalt thou labor, and do all thy work: But the seventh day is the sabbath of the Lord thy God: in it thou shalt not do any work, thou, nor thy son, nor thy daughter, thy manservant, nor thy maidservant, nor thy cattle, nor the stranger that is within thy gates: For in six days the Lord made heaven and earth, the sea, and all that in them is, and rested the seventh day: wherefore the Lord blessed the sabbath day, and hallowed it. Honor thy father and thy mother: that thy days may be long upon the land which the Lord thy God giveth thee. Thou shalt not kill. Thou shalt not commit adultery. Thou shalt not steal. Thou shalt not bear false witness against thy neighbor. Thy shalt not covet thy neighbor's wife, nor his manservant, nor his maidservant, nor his ox, nor his ass, nor any thing that is thy neighbor's.[1]

When issuing the Ten Commandments, God tells the children of Israel why they should obey him. He has brought them out of their bondage in Egypt. Therefore, they should respect his power and show gratitude for their freedom. He is superior to all other gods and hence exceeds them in authority. Moreover, he is capable of punishing

[1]Exod. 20:2–17.

those who disobey him. Some of the commandments he issued belong to the moral codes of almost all peoples, no matter what their religion. That we should honor our parents and refrain from stealing or commiting adultery or bearing false witness are universal requirements accepted throughout the world. Others, such as the requirement that no work be done on the Sabbath or that no graven images be made, are more closely connected to Judaism.

ABRAHAM AND JOB

In the Old Testament, God is portrayed as exercising his authority in unusual ways. In one of the most memorable of all stories, God says to Abraham:

> Take now thy son, thine only son Isaac, whom thou lovest, and get thee into the land of Moriah; and offer him there for a burnt offering upon one of the mountains which I will tell thee of.[2]

God is commanding Abraham to kill his only son, whom he knows Abraham loves dearly. Moreover, he provides no reason at all to Abraham for requiring this enormous sacrifice of him. Without asking any questions, Abraham prepares to carry out God's will. He carries his son to the mountain and prepares to kill him.

> And Abraham stretched forth his hand, and took the knife to slay his son. And the angel of the Lord called unto him out of heaven, and said, Abraham, Abraham: and he said, Here am I. And he said, Lay not thine hand upon the lad, neither do thou any thing unto him: for now I know that thou fearest God, seeing thou hast not withheld thy son, thine only son from me.[3]

It turned out that God was only testing Abraham to see whether he would follow his command without hesitation. Abraham clearly passed the test.

Another famous test of a man's faith is portrayed in the story of Job, an upright and God-fearing man. God is represented as boasting to Satan how fine a man Job is. Satan responds that if Job were to be deprived of his riches and his family, he would turn against God and curse him. God agrees to put Job to the test by depriving him of the things he values most. Once this happens, Job refuses to criticize or condemn God, but he does not accept his misfortunes silently. He discusses them with his friends, searching for a way to explain them. What did he do wrong? "Teach me, and I will hold my tongue: and cause me to understand wherein I have erred."[4] Job believes that it would be reasonable for God to penalize him only if he had done some wrong, for God is supposed to be good.

As Job looks around him, he sees no justice. A good man like him is made to suffer, yet the wicked prosper. "Wherefore do the wicked live, become old, yea, are mighty in

[2]Gen. 22:2.
[3]Gen. 22:10–12.
[4]Job 6:24.

power?. . . . Their houses are safe from fear, neither is the rod of God upon them."[5] If the world were indeed ruled by a just and benevolent God, should not the righteous prosper and the wicked suffer? But it is the wicked who prosper while the righteous suffer. Toward the end of the story, God finally responds to Job's questions:

> Then the Lord answered Job out of the whirlwind, and said, Who is this that darkeneth counsel by words without knowledge? Gird up now thy loins like a man; for I will demand of thee, and answer thou me. Where wast thou when I laid the foundations of the earth? Declare, if thou hast understanding. Who hath laid the measures thereof, if thou knowest? or who hath stretched the line upon it? Whereupon are the foundations thereof fastened? or who laid the corner stone thereof; When the morning stars sang together, and all the sons of God shouted for joy?[6]

In effect, God responds that it is not proper for such a weak and ignorant creature as man to question the actions of a supremely powerful God. Cowed, Job surrenders his search for understanding and repents:

> Then Job answered the Lord, and said, I know that thou canst do every thing, and that no thought can be withholden from thee. Who is he that hideth counsel without knowledge? therefore have I uttered what I understood not; things too wonderful for me, which I knew not. . . . I have heard of thee by the hearing of the ear: but now mine eye seeth thee. Wherefore I abhor myself, and repent in dust and ashes.[7]

The story has a happy ending. God returns to Job his wealth, his health, and his loved ones, and he lives in prosperity and happiness to a ripe old age.

The stories of Abraham and Job represent individuals submitting to God's power. Job, however, manages to raise some interesting questions. He wants to know *why* he should submit. God refuses an explanation, saying that submission without understanding is required of man. Nevertheless, the story of Job raises the question of how the existence of evil can be reconciled with the existence of a good and just and powerful God. If there is a God, then why does he permit so many bad things to happen? Why didn't he create a better world? This famous problem of evil shall be considered in some detail in Chapter Six.

THE RELATIONSHIP BETWEEN ETHICS AND RELIGION

This brief excursion into the Old Testament illustrates that ethics and religion are in some ways related. First, religion frequently attempts to enforce ethical precepts by backing them up with the authority and power of God. In effect, some parts of the Old Testament say to the people: "You should obey these rules because they were com-

[5]Job 21:7–9.
[6]Job 38:1–7.
[7]Job 42:1–6.

manded by a powerful and good God who knows what he is doing and has your good at heart. If you disobey these rules, God will find you out and punish you severely."

Second, a religion often enforces rules that are unique to it, such as the requirement that the children of Israel not work on the Sabbath. In this way, certain rituals become embedded in the moral code, and reflection and analysis are required to distinguish them from universally valid ethical precepts applicable to all people at all times.

Third, according to some religions, God insures the eventual triumph of good over evil: No matter how bad things get, good will win in the end. As we have seen in our discussion of Job, this idea raises the philosophical question of why God permits evil to exist at all.

Religion does not appeal to fear of punishment alone in order to direct human conduct. In some places in the Bible it is said that people should act out of love—love of their fellow beings and love of God—rather than out of fear and of blind submission to authority. The famous Twenty-third Psalm says

> The Lord is my shepherd; I shall not want. He maketh me to lie down in green
> pastures: he leadeth me beside the still waters. He restoreth my soul: he leadeth
> me in the paths of righteousness for his name's sake. Yea, though I walk through
> the valley of the shadow of death, I will fear no evil: for thou art with me. . . .

God is here represented as a shepherd who provides comfort and security for those who believe in him. Even death is not to be feared, for the existence of God assures the believer that death brings no evil. The emotional import of this psalm is not one of fear and trembling but of tranquillity and contentment.

Religion, then, can motivate us to act a certain way. But how do we know which way is the right way? How can we distinguish whether certain commands we are enjoined to follow are right or wrong? The mere fact that something is commanded by a religious authority does not make following that command automatically right. We must turn now to philosophy to see whether it can provide an answer to these questions.

The Approach of Socrates

THE ROLE OF THE GODS

Around the time that the story of Job was being compiled, Socrates (469–399 B.C.) was pursuing his ethical inquiries in Athens. Socrates did not write any philosophical treatises. As far as we know, he never wrote a thing. But as he wandered through Athens, he would strike up conversations with the people he happened to meet. In these conversations, or dialogues, he would ask questions about various ethical concepts and would then point out drawbacks to the answers he received. Our knowledge of the thoughts and conversations of Socrates comes mainly from the writings of Plato, who knew him personally and was deeply affected by his ideas and conduct.

One of Plato's dialogues tells of a conversation between Socrates and a man called Euthyphro. Socrates has gone to the law courts one day to reply to an accusation; there

SOCRATES
(469–399 B.C.)

Even though Socrates left no writings, he was one of the most famous and influential philosophers of ancient Athens. Most of what we know of his life and thought is contained in the dialogues of Plato and the *Memorabilia* of Xenophon. Even as a young man he seems to have acquired a reputation for intellectual distinction. According to Plato's account of his life and trial, when Socrates was forty he was pronounced the wisest man in Greece by the oracle at Delphi. Socrates then set out to determine whether the oracle was correct and if so, what it meant to possess wisdom. According to Plato, he spent his time engaged in philosophical discussions with a variety of Athenians at various locations in and around Athens. In 399 B.C. he was brought to trial for corrupting youth and for religious heresy. His execution is described by Plato in the *Phaedo,* and an interpretation of the trial and conviction of Socrates is offered in the *Apology.* According to Plato's *Crito,* Socrates refused to try to escape from prison because he thought it would be wrong to break the laws of the city.

he has met Euthyphro, who also has legal business to transact. It turns out that Euthyphro is about to prosecute his own father for killing one of his workmen. The workman had killed one of Euthyphro's slaves, and the father had captured him, bound him, and thrown him into a ditch until he could decide what to do with him. The man died of neglect. Euthyphro's father is naturally indignant with his son for prosecuting him, claiming that it is impious for a son to prosecute his own father. But Euthyphro thinks that he understands the concept of piety better than his father. Socrates uses this chance meeting to consider the nature of piety.

Euthyphro begins by arguing that it is not impious to prosecute his father because Zeus, the best and greatest of the gods, was said to have punished his father, Cronos. (Remember that at the time of Socrates, the Greek religion was polytheistic. While **monotheism** accepts only one god, **polytheism** accepts many gods.) But Socrates' attitude toward the Greek religion was somewhat skeptical. Unlike Euthyphro, he found it difficult to accept as literally true the old stories of the gods, and so he did not agree with Euthyphro's argument that he was entitled to do to his father what Zeus did to his.

To settle the matter, Socrates asks Euthyphro for a definition of piety. He wants to know what piety is—what characteristics are common to all acts of piety—so that he will have a means of determining what acts are pious and what acts impious. Euthyphro offers the following as his definition: "Piety, then, is that which is dear to the gods, and impiety is that which is not dear to them."[8] In the course of examining this definition, Socrates makes an important point about morality:

> SOCRATES: Come then and let us examine what we are saying. That thing or person which is dear to the gods is pious, and that thing or person which is hateful to the gods is impious, these two being the extreme opposites of one another. Was not that said?
>
> EUTHYPHRO: It was. . . .
>
> SOCRATES: And further, Euthyphro, the gods were admitted to have enmities and hatreds and differences?
>
> EUTHYPHRO: Yes, that was also said.
>
> SOCRATES: And what sort of difference creates enmity and anger? Suppose, for example, that you and I, my good friend, differ about a number; do differences of this sort make us enemies and set us at variance with one another? Do we not go at once to arithmetic, and put an end to them by a sum?
>
> EUTHYPHRO: True.
>
> SOCRATES: Or suppose that we differ about magnitudes, do we not quickly end the differences by measuring?
>
> EUTHYPHRO: Very true.
>
> SOCRATES: And we end a controversy about heavy and light by resorting to a weighing machine?
>
> EUTHYPHRO: To be sure.
>
> SOCRATES: But what differences are there which cannot be thus decided, and which therefore, make us angry and set us at enmity with one another? I dare say the answer does not occur to you at the moment, and therefore I will suggest that these enmities arise when the matters of difference are the just and unjust, good and evil, honorable and dishonorable. Are not these the points about which men differ, and about which when we are unable satisfactorily to decide our differences, you and I and all of us quarrel, when we do quarrel?[9]

Socrates points out that for many questions, we have procedures that assure us of arriving at an answer. For example, we have procedures for settling disagreements about number; by adding or subtracting, multiplying or dividing, we can resolve such disagreements easily. Similarly, disagreements about the size or weight of things can be settled by measuring and weighing. But when we come to ethical disagreements, we do not seem to have such a procedure. There is no simple, accepted method for settling questions about right and wrong conduct. Therefore, says Socrates, moral disagreements often lead to quarreling among the parties to the dispute.

Socrates finally rejects Euthyphro's definition of piety as what is pleasing to the gods. The trouble with this definition is that in the traditional stories the gods themselves are portrayed as disagreeing with one another about right and wrong conduct. Because actions that some gods approve are rejected by other gods, the same action will be both pious and impious.

---

[8]Plato, *Euthyphro* 6, Jowett translation.
[9]Ibid., 7.

Socrates' criticism of Euthyphro's definition reveals that monotheism is superior to polytheism in at least one respect. When there is only one god, the possibility of there being conflicting moral precepts is much reduced, though it is not eliminated entirely because different precepts could be ascribed to the same god. For example, the God of the Old Testament at times favors an ethic of retribution; evildoers are to be punished to the extent that they have caused harm. At times the God of the New Testament favors an ethics of nonviolence and forgiveness; a victim is supposed to "turn the other cheek." But in polytheism, because there are numerous moral authorities, there is *always* a strong likelihood that there will be differing opinions about what human beings are obliged to do.

ETHICS AND THE WILL OF THE GODS

To meet Socrates' criticism, Euthyphro adopts a new definition: An action is pious if *all* the gods approve of it, and it is impious if they *all* disapprove of it. Socrates then asks a most interesting question. "The point which I should first wish to understand is whether the pious or holy is beloved by the gods because it is holy, or holy because it is beloved of the gods."[10] In other words, does the gods' approval of something make it pious, or do they approve of it because it is pious independent of their approval?

When this question is formulated in more general terms, the relation between ethics and religion is illuminated. Does approval of a god or gods make something right to do, or do the god or gods approve of things because they are right independent of their approval? For example, in most religions, the killing of innocent people is judged to be wrong. Why is it wrong? Is it wrong simply because God disapproves of killing? Is it wrong simply because God commanded people not to kill one another? If God changed his mind and commanded people to kill one another, would that conduct then become right? If one answers "Yes" to these questions, one is close to adopting the point of view of Job.

According to Thomas Hobbes (1588–1679), it is God's power that justifies his commands. This is how Hobbes understands the story of Job:

> The *power* of God alone without other helps is sufficient *justification* of any action he doth. That which men make amongst themselves here by pacts and covenants, and call by the name of justice, and according whereunto men are accounted and termed rightly *just* or *unjust,* is not that by which God Almighty's actions are to be measured or called just, no more than his counsels are to be measured by human wisdom. That which he does, is made just by his doing it; just, I say, to him, though not always just in us. . . . When God afflicted Job, he did object no sin unto him, but justified his afflicting of him, by telling him of his *power*. . . . God cannot sin, because his doing a thing makes it just, and consequently, no sin.[11]

---

[10]Ibid., 9–10.
[11]Thomas Hobbes, "A Letter to the Lord Marquis of Newcastle," in *Body, Man, and Citizen: Selections from Thomas Hobbes,* ed. Richard S. Peters (New York: Collier Books, 1962), pp. 252–253. (This letter is dated 1652.)

For Hobbes, the mere fact of God's laying down a certain rule of conduct makes that rule just or valid. Another way of stating this view is that a rule of conduct or a course of action is *fully justified* by the fact that God has commanded it. Thus, Abraham's journey to kill his son was fully justified by the mere fact that God commanded it. God's authority becomes the basis of ethics.

This view, adopted by both Euthyphro and Hobbes, has two major difficulties. First, it cuts off our examination of ethics earlier than is warranted. To justify a moral rule, we must try to understand how it functions in human life. What would human life be like if we followed this rule? What would it be like if we followed some quite different rule? These questions are relevant to deciding whether or not the rule is justified. But appealing to God's power and authority as the basis for morality makes these questions unnecessary.

Second, this view makes God appear to be unreasonable. When someone orders you to do something, you surely believe that he should be prepared to provide you with a reason for doing it. An order without reasons to back it up is lacking in its justification. In some cases, the person giving the order may think that he is under no obligation to justify it to those who must obey it. A military commander, for example, may believe that the soldiers under his command should obey him blindly. Nevertheless, even if he is not obliged to *state* his reasons, he should *have* reasons. And these reasons should show how following his order will accomplish something of value. But according to Hobbes, God's merely commanding something justifies it. Even if what is commanded accomplishes nothing at all, it would still be justified. This seems to make human beings the victims of the arbitrary will of God.

Socrates, however, asserts that the gods are reasonable and that their mere approval of something is not what makes it pious or holy. After considering several other unsuccessful definitions, Socrates brings his discussion with Euthyphro to a close without having reached a firm conclusion about the nature of piety. The absence of a firm conclusion is not unusual in the dialogues that Plato wrote about Socrates. Many of the dialogues explore problems that resist neat solutions. But this does not mean that Socrates has nothing to teach us about philosophy. As portrayed by Plato, his life exemplifies a particular mission and ethical orientation that has influenced individuals ever since his death. Let us look at how he lived his life and met his death.

SOCRATES' LIFE AND MISSION

When he met Euthyphro, Socrates was visiting the law courts because he was required to answer the charge that he was guilty of leading the young men of Athens astray and of rejecting the official gods. Some time later, he was actually brought to trial on these charges. In the *Apology,* Plato describes Socrates' trial and his speech to a jury of 501 Athenian citizens, in which he tried to explain his preoccupation with questions about human conduct.

Socrates claimed that the charges brought against him resulted from the long-standing prejudice of a group of his fellow citizens. This prejudice originated when Socrates' friend Chaerephon asked the oracle at Delphi whether there was anyone wiser than Socrates. The oracle replied that no one was wiser. Socrates was puzzled at the oracle's

---

PLATO
(427–327 B.C.)

Plato was born and lived in Athens. As a young man he was a friend and pupil of Socrates. About 387 B.C., Plato founded the Academy, an institute for the study of philosophy and science. He worked there for the rest of his life. His writings take the form of dialogues in which he dramatizes a wide range of philosophical discussions. Socrates is the chief character in most of Plato's dialogues. In his *Apology,* Plato recounts the trial of Socrates, and his *Phaedo* tells us of the hours just preceding Socrates' death. Many of Plato's writings have survived. The most famous and influential is the *Republic,* which contains his account of the just society and his famous criticisms of democracy. Another dialogue, *Theaetetus,* is a major contribution to the theory of knowledge. Plato is generally regarded as the greatest of all philosophical writers. A good one-volume translation of all of Plato's known writings is *The Collected Dialogues of Plato,* ed. Edith Hamilton and Huntington Cairns (Princeton: Princeton University Press, 1961).

---

answer because he felt that he possessed little or no knowledge of any topic. How, then, could he be the wisest of all men?

To discover whether the oracle's statement was true, Socrates went about searching for someone wiser than he. He wandered about Athens questioning the people he met, just as he had questioned Euthyphro about piety. He found that everyone he questioned claimed to possess much wisdom about public affairs, religion, moral conduct, and other matters but that when put to the test they all turned out to be ignorant. Socrates concluded that he was the wisest of men only in the sense that he alone was aware of how ignorant he really was.

> But the truth is, O men of Athens, that God only is wise; and by his answer he intends to show [through the oracle] that the wisdom of men is worth little or nothing; he is not speaking of Socrates, he is only using my name by way of illustration, as if he said, He, O men, is the wisest, who, like Socrates, knows that his wisdom is in truth worth nothing. And so I go about the world, obedient to the god, and search and make enquiry into the wisdom of anyone, whether citizen or stranger, who appears to be wise; and if he is not wise, then in vindication of the oracle I show him that he is not wise; and my occupation quite absorbs me, and I have no time to give either to any public matter of interest or to any concern of my own, but I am in utter poverty by reason of my devotion to the god.[12]

---

[12]Plato, *Apology* 23, Jowett translation.

In his search for a man wiser than he, Socrates succeeded in deflating the claims to wisdom of the people he met. This made them indignant and angry, and they wished to be rid of him. In addition, many young men enjoyed hearing Socrates cross-examine their elders and ultimately prove them to be ignorant. Finally, as we noted in our presentation of the conversation with Euthyphro, Socrates' questions could lead to doubts about the validity of the official religion. The charge against him, Socrates claimed, was a trumped up charge designed to rid Athens of his embarrassing questions. But because of his influence upon the youth and his skepticism about the traditional stories of the gods, Socrates was perceived by those in power as a genuine threat to the stability of the Athenian state.

One of Socrates' most important ideas is that one should always adopt the moral point of view in making up one's mind about how to behave.

> Some one will say: And are you not ashamed, Socrates, of a course of life which is likely to bring you to an untimely end? To him I may fairly answer: There you are mistaken: a man who is good for anything ought not to calculate the chance of living or dying: he ought only to consider whether in doing anything he is doing right or wrong—acting the part of a good man or of a bad.[13]

Socrates did not fear the consequences of his actions. He believed that the only thing that deserves consideration is whether or not our actions are right. Even death did not make him afraid, for he believed that "no evil can happen to a good man, either in life or after death."[14] Moreover, Socrates refused to conform to public opinion when he judged that the values of the public were unreasonable or bad. The only thing that a person should be concerned about is the improvement of his soul, not death, or reputation, or wealth, or any other external good:

> If you should say to me, Socrates, this time . . . you shall be let off, but upon one condition, that you are not to enquire and speculate in this way any more, and that if you are caught doing so again you shall die;—if this was the condition on which you would let me go, I should reply: Men of Athens, I honor and love you; but I shall obey God rather than you, and while I have life and strength I shall never cease from the practice and teaching of philosophy, exhorting any one whom I meet and saying to him after my manner: You, my friend—a citizen of the great and mighty and wise city of Athens—are you not ashamed of heaping up the greatest amount of money and honor and reputation, and caring so little about wisdom and truth and the greatest improvement of the soul, which you never regard or heed at all? And if the person with whom I am arguing, says: Yes, but I do care; then I do not leave him or let him go at once; but I proceed to interrogate and examine and cross-examine him, and if I think that he has no virtue in him, but only says that he has, I reproach him with undervaluing the greater, and overvaluing the less.[15]

[13]Ibid., 28.
[14]Ibid., 41.
[15]Ibid., 29.

Socrates says that if the Athenians should decide to put him to death, they will not easily find another stinging fly like him who will undertake to arouse their sluggish minds and thoughtless souls.

Because of his defiant attitude, he was convicted by a vote of 281 to 220. It was the custom then for persons convicted of crimes to suggest their own penalty. Socrates says that for his great service to Athens he should receive what he deserves—namely, free meals—so that he can continue his quest for wisdom undisturbed by physical wants. He refuses to promise that he will hold his peace in return for mild punishment:

> To discourse about virtue, and of those other things about which you hear me examining myself and others, is the greatest good of man. . . . The unexamined life is not worth living.[16]

His contemptuous attitude toward the conventional opinions of the jury led to a death sentence. Difficult as it may be to believe, Socrates preferred death to a life in which he would be prevented from continuing his search for wisdom.

In the *Phaedo,* Plato dramatizes the famous death scene:

> Crito made a sign to the servant, who was standing by; and he went out, and having been absent for some time, returned with the jailer carrying the cup of poison. . . . Then raising the cup to his lips, quite readily and cheerfully Socrates drank off the poison. And hitherto most of us had been able to control our sorrow; but now when we saw him drinking, and saw too that he had finished the draught, we could no longer forbear, and in spite of myself my own tears were flowing fast. . . . Socrates alone maintained his calmness; What is this strange outcry? he said. I sent away the women mainly in order that they might not misbehave in this way, for I have been told that a man should die in peace. Be quiet then, and have patience. When we heard his words we were ashamed, and restrained our tears; and he walked about until, as he said, his legs began to fail, and then he lay on his back, according to the directions, and the man who gave him the poison now and then looked at his feet and legs; and after a while he pressed his foot hard, and asked him if he could feel; and he said, No; and then his leg, and so upwards and upwards, and showed us that he was cold and stiff. And he felt them himself, and said: Crito, I owe a cock to Asclepius; will you remember to pay the debt? The debt shall be paid, said Crito; is there anything else? There was no answer to this question; but in a minute or two a movement was heard, and the attendants uncovered him; his eyes were set, and Crito closed his eyes and mouth. Such was the end . . . of our friend; concerning whom I may truly say, that of all the men of his time whom I have known, he was the wisest and justest and best.[17]

So ended Socrates' life.

Even though he left no writings of his own, Socrates was one of the first great moral philosophers. He searched for wisdom, but it is difficult to determine whether he found

---

[16]Ibid., 29.
[17]Plato, *Phaedo* 117–118, Jowett translation.

it; the writings of Plato contain no systematic set of views about morality that we are justified in attributing to Socrates. His importance to moral philosophy is that he exemplifies the transition from traditional to critical morality. Socrates refused to accept the traditional views of human conduct uncritically. He refused to conform to the will of public opinion, raising questions that the defenders of traditional morality could not answer. But he offered few answers of his own.

Morality and Self-Interest

THE CONFLICT BETWEEN JUSTICE AND SELF-INTEREST

In Plato's greatest work, the *Republic,* Socrates is shown confronting one of the most interesting and pressing of all the problems that philosophical ethics must resolve. In Book II, some of Socrates' friends point out to him that it is often inconvenient and sometimes even imprudent to do what is right and just. Thus, what morality requires of a person is often contrary to his self-interest; people of good will must often do what is harmful to themselves. Socrates himself had to face this problem. As a result of doing what he thought was right—pursuing wisdom uncompromisingly—he lost his life. Socrates did not envision any conflict between morality and self-interest because he had faith that nothing bad could happen to a good person. Indeed, one of the traditional functions of religion has been to assure us that there is no conflict between morality and self-interest, when it is correctly understood. But if we put aside this religious guarantee, the conflict often appears.

Socrates' friends also point out that not only do good people sometimes find their interests threatened, but wicked people often prosper. People who are careful to keep up appearances may be able to disregard moral principles and still attain a prosperity that is the envy of others. Doesn't this show that it is better to be unjust and appear just than it is to be just?

This problem is illustrated in the *Republic* by the story of the ring of Gyges. Gyges was a shepherd who came upon a ring that caused him to become invisible when it was turned on his finger in a certain way. Taking advantage of his power to become invisible, Gyges seduced the queen of Lydia, killed the king, and became king himself. Gyges was unscrupulous, so we should not be surprised at his conduct. But suppose that a just person was given the ring of Gyges. Wouldn't he behave in the same way? Wouldn't he try to obtain good things for himself at the expense of others? If so, then clearly the just man remains just only because he fears the consequences of being unjust; he fears the penalties and the dishonor that exposure would bring. But if he could avoid these unpleasant consequences, the just man would act as wickedly as the unjust man. Consider this from a personal perspective. Suppose that you find a way of cheating on an examination without getting caught. What would you do? If you decide to cheat, then you are no better than the unjust man. Perhaps the only reason that you have not acted unjustly up to the present time was your fear of getting caught.

EGOISM AND ALTRUISM

According to *ethical egoism,* whenever there is a conflict between what an individual wants to do and what the moral rules of his society say he ought to do, then he is entitled to have his way. All conflicting claims are to be settled in favor of the individual. According to *ethical altruism,* the individual must consider the good of others as well as his own good. He must sometimes disregard his own self-interest to do what is right.

Egoism and altruism are primarily theories about what individuals are entitled to do when confronted with a conflict between personal interest and the interest of others. But these theories have a psychological dimension. *Psychological egoism* claims that individuals are motivated exclusively by self-interest; they will always choose what they think is best for themselves. A person may mistakenly do something to harm himself, but he will never choose to do so on purpose. He will always aim at achieving his own good. *Psychological altruism* claims that individuals are capable of acting with a view toward realizing the good of others. When there is a conflict between his own good and the good of others, a person is usually capable of choosing to realize the good of others even though he may suffer inconvenience or harm as a result.

EGOISM AND ALTRUISM AS THEORIES OF MOTIVATION

Psychological egoism states that, when actions are voluntary, people invariably pursue what they consider their own good. Although *philosophical egoism* offers various accounts of the good that each person seeks, it most frequently describes the goal of all human endeavor as happiness or pleasure. People love themselves best of all; the pursuit of individual happiness is thus their main activity and self-love the sole motive of all voluntary action.

One argument for egoism is based upon our everyday observations of how human beings actually behave. We note that the vast majority of human actions are intended either to achieve some personal benefit or to rid the agent of some discomfort or pain. Why, for example, do you get out of bed in the morning? You do so because you calculate that the benefits to be obtained from being up and about, from going to work or to school, exceed the comfort of lying all day in bed. After eating most people go the washroom and brush their teeth. Why? Because they calculate that the discomfort of brushing is less than the discomfort of the toothaches they will eventually experience if they fail to brush. Most of the actions of everyday life seem to be the result of a cost-benefit analysis in which the individual chooses the action that maximizes his own personal benefit and minimizes his costs.

People sometimes seem to act for the benefit of others. Examples are not hard to find; they include giving to charity, helping a sick friend, and making sacrifices for one's children. The egoist claims, however, that a closer analysis of these ostensibly altruistic actions will show that they are not really altruistic at all. We give to charity because of community pressure or to still the pangs of guilt. We help a sick friend in the hope that in the future assistance will be rendered in return. We make sacrifices for our children because of the pleasure that we take in their success. One must agree with the egoist that many altruistic actions are performed for selfish reasons.

A second argument for egoism is based upon an analysis of human motivation. Suppose a person is acting to benefit another. What causes him to act in this way? The cause cannot be the future benefit to the other person, for that does not yet exist and whatever motivates the action must be something that now exists in the mind of the agent. What causes him to act is his present desire for the future good. As John Locke (1632–1704) has written: "The greater good, though apprehended and acknowledged to be so, does not determine the will until our desire, raised proportionably to it, makes us uneasy in the want of it."[18] What motivates action, says Locke, is the uneasiness of desire. When there is some good that I realize I lack, I am made uneasy by the fact that I lack something that is necessary to my happiness. This uneasiness causes me to desire the absent good. It follows, therefore, that whenever I act voluntarily, I act to satisfy my own desire. The egoist concludes that since satisfying one's desire is the underlying motive of all voluntary actions, each person acts for his own good.

A CRITICISM OF PSYCHOLOGICAL EGOISM

The first argument is not sufficient to establish the validity of psychological egoism. Egoism claims that *all* conduct is motivated by self-interest; arguing that much of it is so motivated fails to prove the case. Furthermore, David Hume (1711–1776) argued that common observation establishes the truth of altruism and refutes egoism.

> The most obvious objection to the selfish hypothesis is that, as it is contrary to common feeling and our most unprejudiced notions, there is required the highest stretch of philosophy to establish so extraordinary a paradox. To the most careless observer there appear to be such dispositions as benevolence and generosity; such affections as love, friendship, compassion, gratitude. These sentiments have their causes, effects, objects, and operations, marked by common language and observation, and plainly distinguished from those of the selfish passions. And as all this is the obvious appearance of things, it must be admitted, till some hypothesis be discovered, which by penetrating deeper into human nature, may prove the former affections to be nothing but modifications of the latter. All attempts of this kind have hitherto proved fruitless.[19]

The most common observation, says Hume, is that human beings are moved by love and gratitude as well as by self-love. It would take a strong argument to establish self-love as the only motive, and Hume claims never to have found one.

There is another commonsense argument against egoism. A person who follows his desires without reflection or thought may sometimes act contrary to his self-interest. For example, he may eat or drink too much and thus cause himself to become ill or out of sudden anger do something rash and hence lose a valuable friendship. Acting on the principle of self-love is not the same as acting so as to satisfy our desires. Our desires

---

[18]John Locke, *An Essay concerning Human Understanding* (London: George Routledge and Sons), II.xxi.35. (This book was first published in 1690.)
[19]David Hume, *Enquiry concerning the Principles of Morals,* in *Hume's Enquiries,* ed. L. A. Selby-Bigge (Oxford: The Clarendon Press, 1972), p. 298. (This book was first published in 1751.)

must themselves be examined to determine whether or not their satisfaction will bring harm. It is a matter of common experience that we do not automatically follow our desires but first consider the consequences of following this alternative or that. Locke points this out when he says: "For the mind having in most cases, as is evident in experience, a power to suspend the execution and satisfaction of any of its desires, and so all, one after another, is at liberty to consider the objects of them, examine them on all sides, and weigh them with others. In this lies the liberty man has."[20] If a person can control desire to achieve his own good, there is nothing to prevent him from controlling desire so as to bring about the good of others. If a person can choose whether or not to pursue this or that desire, it would appear that he can choose whether to pursue a selfish or an altruistic desire.

The second argument offered by psychological egoism—which says that because all voluntary actions are motivated by desire, individuals always act to bring about their own satisfaction—is based upon a fallacious use of the word *satisfaction*. This word can have two meanings. In one sense of the word, a person achieves satisfaction when he gains pleasure from getting what he wants. For instance, a person gets satisfaction from eating oysters when he gets pleasure in eating them. Clearly, one does not always get satisfaction in this sense from obtaining what one wants; one may have wanted to eat oysters very badly but have failed to get pleasure from eating them because of indigestion, because of their poor quality, or because it turned out that one did not like oysters that much after all. In the second sense of the word, one satisfies one's desire simply when one gets what one wants. If a person wants oysters, then his desire is satisfied if he gets them. Whether or not he gains pleasure from them is another matter.

Let us now return to the argument that because all voluntary actions are motivated by desire, individuals always act to bring about their own satisfaction. This would seem to imply that a supposedly altruistic action is actually accomplished to achieve pleasure for the doer. But if *satisfaction* is meant in the second sense, this argument merely says that when a person acts from desire, he acts to obtain what he wants. An altruist can accept this by pointing out that one of the things a person may want is the good of others. This meaning of *satisfaction* thus fails to support egoism. When egoism is formulated using the first meaning, Hume's argument shows that it is not true.

A CRITICISM OF ETHICAL EGOISM

Having found that psychological egoism is probably false, let us consider ethical egoism, which says that an individual is always entitled to choose his own good whenever there is a conflict between it and the good of others. The first point to make is that our existing moral rules do not require that individuals always sacrifice their own good to that of others. We do not have to give all our money to charity, or even a great deal of it. We are often entitled to seek personal enjoyment even though there are others who could benefit from our attention. In fact, if a person did not have the right to take care of his own good most of the time, others would not be required to act altruistically toward

---

[20]Locke, *Essay,* II.xxi.47.

him some of the time. It is because a person's own good is morally valuable that others are obliged to respect it.

A moral issue does, however, arise when a person cannot obtain something he wants for himself without violating some rule that requires him to benefit or to avoid harming others. For example, if you have promised to pay a debt by a certain time, then you are morally obliged to return the money even if you still need it for yourself. If you are driving a car, you are obliged to avoid injuring pedestrians who are in your way even though you will be made late for an appointment. Thus, many of our moral rules require us to respect the good of others even if this means that some sacrifice of our own good is required. The ethical egoist replies that one is never morally obliged to obey these rules when it is inconvenient to oneself.

To clarify this issue, we must recognize that the term *moral rule* has at least two different meanings. In one sense a moral rule is a rule of conduct that belongs to the moral code of a group of individuals. In this way, we speak of the moral rules of the Chinese or of the American Indians or of the French. There is no implication that the rule is correct; it is just an accepted rule. In fact, a rule that we may reject with horror, such as the practice of killing and burying a widow beside the body of her dead husband, is nevertheless a moral rule in this usage. In the second sense, in speaking of a rule as a *moral* rule, we imply that it is correct and that we are morally obliged to obey it.

If the egoist uses the term *moral rule* in the second sense, then his theory is self-contradictory. For he would then be saying that whenever a person is morally obliged to do something that benefits others at some cost to himself, then he is not obliged to do it. We can thus dismiss this version of egoism.

For the egoist's view to be plausible, the ethical egoist should argue as follows: "I realize that most of the members of my society accept a certain set of rules as binding upon their conduct. I understand that if I too should accept these rules, then I will often be inconvenienced. But I see no reason to recognize these rules as binding upon my conduct. Why should I ever do anything inconvenient to myself?" In this formulation, the egoist presents himself as a skeptic regarding the rules accepted by his society. He wonders whether these or any other rules are valid. To refute this version of egoism, we must be able to show that certain rules are valid and hence binding upon everyone's conduct. The question of the validity of moral rules will be taken up in Chapter Four.

There is another version of egoism that does not rest upon skepticism. The egoist argues as follows: "I admit that there are certain valid rules that are binding upon me as well as upon others. But I also understand that I have a right to pursue my own happiness. If, on some occasion, a moral rule that I accept requires me to sacrifice my happiness, then since I am permitted to do the things that will make me happy, I see no reason to follow the rule." For example, consider the individual who is about to be drafted into the army to fight in a war that he considers to be just. He may recognize that he has an obligation to join the army, but he also has a right to pursue his own happiness, which a stay in the army would interrupt. Why should he sacrifice his happiness to do as he is obliged? We have here a case of a conflict within our rules. One rule gives him the right to do something; another rule forbids him from doing the very same thing. The egoist argues that in such cases the individual's claim to happiness

> **EGOISM AND ALTRUISM**
>
> As theories of motivation:
>   psychological egoism
>   psychological altruism
> As theories of conduct:
>   ethical egoism
>   ethical altruism

always has priority. To grapple with this version of egoism, we need an account of moral conflict. What steps should we take to resolve conflicts among our rules?

Teleological and Deontological Ethics

Our discussion of ethical egoism has raised two basic questions. The first one is, How can we determine what conduct is right? This question has both a practical and a theoretical aspect. From the practical standpoint, we are often in doubt about the right thing to do. Is it right for the pregnant woman to have an abortion or for the judge to sentence the convicted murderer to death? To settle such practical issues, we need a method or criterion that tells us how to distinguish right from wrong. But even when we are not in doubt, the question is nevertheless theoretically interesting. Suppose you are inclined to accept the morality that you were taught as a child or that your friends and associates follow. Even if you are not in doubt about which rules are correct, you may nevertheless want to know what makes them correct and what makes the rules you reject incorrect. Thinking about your own morality may begin to raise doubts in your mind about the validity of its rules.

The second basic questions is, How can we resolve conflicts among the rules that we accept as correct? If a person has the right to pursue his own good and is also required to respect the good of others, what is he to do when these two things conflict? Almost every existing system of moral rules leads to conflicts of this sort in particular cases. Thus, we need some way of telling which of the conflicting alternatives we should adopt.

Various answers to these questions have appeared in the history of ethical theory. It has become customary to classify the theories under two main heads: **teleological** ethics and **deontological** ethics. To understand how these two approaches differ, we must notice that we apply two major types of evaluation to things and actions. First, we say of actions that they are morally right or wrong, morally required or forbidden. This type of evaluation makes use of the concept of what is *right*. Second, we say of many things and circumstances that they are *good* or *desirable*. For example, we speak of a good book, a good film, a good wine, a good game of chess, a good job, a good party, and so forth. The *right* and the *good* are among the basic concepts we employ to appraise and judge the value of things, objects, actions, and events.

A teleological theory of right conduct says that what makes an action right or obligatory or morally required is that it brings about more good than alternative courses of action. An action is right, then, to the extent that it is an efficient way of bringing about as much good as possible. For example, suppose you are thinking about whether or not to visit a sick friend in the hospital. Your friend would enjoy the visit; it would do him good. On the other hand, it is snowing; the hospital is far off; you would really prefer to stay at home by the fire. What should you do? According to a teleological theory, you should determine which course of action would do the most good. If the good you would bring to your friend by visiting him exceeds the good you would gain for yourself by staying at home, then the right thing to do is to pay him a visit.

Deontological theories disagree with this approach, arguing that some actions that bring about the most good may nevertheless be morally vicious. Suppose, for example, that the political leader of a totalitarian country believes that he can advance the welfare and the overall good of most of his people by killing those who are very ill or very old or very crazy or otherwise dependent upon the attention and care of others. By killing this small number of people, the dictator thinks that he is thereby freeing society's resources, and the lot of the remainder of the population will improve. Even if more good can be accomplished by following the dictator's plan, it is natural to respond by saying that it would nevertheless be wrong to kill these people. To do so would violate their right to life, and violating one of their basic rights is a grave injustice. One who accepts a deontological ethics says that what is right cannot be completely defined as what leads to the good. Such values as justice and human rights determine the difference between right and wrong conduct.

All teleological theories have in common the claim that the test of right conduct is based upon the good that the conduct achieves. Different accounts of the nature of the human good distinguish one teleological theory from another. In the remainder of this chapter we shall explore one main teleological theory—**utilitarianism**. The teleological approach will be contrasted with the deontological approach, as exhibited by Kant's ethics.

Hedonism

The most common version of teleological ethics is based upon **hedonism**, according to which the good is identified with pleasure. Philosophers such as Epicurus, John Locke, Jeremy Bentham, and John Stuart Mill were all hedonists. We must be careful to avoid a common error in interpreting what the hedonist says. Sometimes the theory is identified with the advice: "Eat, drink, and be merry, for tomorrow we die." This advice suggests that the only things in life that are worthwhile are the physical pleasures— eating, drinking, and sex. But none of the great hedonists in the history of philosophy would have agreed that human beings should live for physical pleasures alone. They rejected this idea for two reasons. First, they agreed that there were other kinds of pleasure than the physical. One should seek physical pleasure in only moderate amounts, leaving room for the other kinds. Second, they agreed that a wise and rational person should take his whole life into consideration and refrain from sacrificing his future good to pursue physical pleasures in the present. One can ruin one's health by immoderate eating and drinking and thus destroy the possibility of gaining pleasure in the future.

Although hedonists used the term *pleasure* to designate the human good, it suggests too narrow a conception of what they had in mind. Terms such as *happiness* and *welfare* and *satisfaction* better indicate the hedonist's conception of good; these terms do not suggest that the good is limited to physical pleasures. For many hedonists, the absence of pain and suffering is just as valuable as the actual presence of pleasure.

A kind of hedonism is represented in this brief poem by Emily Dickinson:

The heart asks pleasure first,
And then, excuse from pain;
And then, those little anodynes
That deaden suffering;

And then, to go to sleep;
And then, if it should be
The will of its Inquisitor,
The liberty to die.

Most physical pleasures are really pleasant sensations of the body. The pleasures of eating lie in the sensations of taste and smell that come as a result of putting food into one's mouth, chewing it, and swallowing it. The physical pleasures of sex lie in the sensations that are aroused by the stimulation of the various erogenous zones of the body. There are other pleasant sensations, such as those that arise from scratching an itch or from taking a hot bath.

There are other forms of pleasure. Consider, for instance, the things you like to do. If you like to swim or play chess or study for a philosophy examination, then these things usually give you pleasure. There are pleasures of appreciation, or aesthetic pleasures, that come from looking at paintings, listening to music, reading poetry, or contemplating the beauties of nature. Pleasure can also come from comfort; you can simply feel comfortable even though you are not experiencing any particular sensations or engaged in any activity. There are pleasures that come from learning, from satisfying one's curiosity. The social pleasures come from friendly human relationships. There is the pleasant feeling you have when things are going well and life is satisfactory on the whole. For the hedonist, happiness is a mixture of these various pleasures in a proportion that reduces conflict among them and that allows for a life that is pleasant throughout. Different mixtures may be appropriate for different persons depending upon their preferences, their physical condition, and their physical and mental capacities. For the hedonist, the good life is the happy one, the one that contains as much pleasure as possible throughout.

Utilitarianism

UTILITARIANISM AND HEDONISM

Hedonism is a theory about the nature of the human good. It says that something is good for its own sake, or *intrinsically good,* if and only if it is pleasant. All other goods are means of obtaining pleasure; these are *instrumental goods.* For example, a visit to the dentist to repair some decaying teeth would hardly be considered a pleasure by anyone (except, perhaps, the dentist). But by repairing your teeth, you reduce the amount of pain you will experience in the future and thereby increase your capacity for pleasure. What the dentist does to your teeth qualifies as an instrumental good; it has utility. Utilitarianism is an ethical theory that takes utility as the criterion of right conduct. It says that an action is right if it tends to produce more pleasure and less pain than any alternative course of action. It says that right conduct is conduct that tends to maximize pleasure and happiness.

The clearest and most consistent utilitarian among the great philosophers was Jeremy Bentham (1748–1832). His major interest lay in encouraging the reform of the English legal and political system. His writings encouraged the growth of democratic and liberal tendencies within English politics. Bentham felt that the utilitarian approach would reduce reliance upon custom and transform institutions into means for increasing the general happiness, or the welfare of the people.

JEREMY BENTHAM
(1748–1832)

Bentham was one of the founders of the utilitarian tradition in English philosophy. Although he studied law, he spent most of his life developing his political and legal philosophy and constructing schemes for the improvement of the English legal and political system. As a reformer and advocate of democratic ideals, he became the intellectual leader of a group of influential thinkers and political activists known as the philosophical radicals. Bentham believed that all laws and institutions should be evaluated according to their contribution to the greatest happiness of the greatest number. He opposed reliance upon custom and tradition. The best introduction to his system is his *Introduction to the Principles of Morals and Legislation* (1789).

With these practical concerns in mind, Bentham formulated the *principle of utility*.

By the principle of utility is meant that principle which approves or disapproves of every action whatsoever, according to the tendency which it appears to have to augment or diminish the happiness of the party whose interest is in question: or what is the same thing in other words, to promote or oppose that happiness. I say of every action whatsoever; and therefore not only of every action of a private individual, but of every measure of government. By utility is meant that property in any object, whereby it tends to produce benefit, advantage, pleasure, good, or happiness, (all this in the present case comes to the same thing) or (what again comes to the same thing) to prevent the happening of mischief, pain, evil, or unhappiness to the party whose interest is considered: if that party be the community in general, then the happiness of the community: if a particular individual, then the happiness of the individual.[21]

Note that the principle of utility is altruistic rather than egoistic. In determining which action is right, an individual must consider all those concerned, not just himself. For Bentham, individuals are morally equal; no one is entitled to prefer his own good over the good of anyone else. Each person is obliged to seek not just his good or the good of those who belong to his race or class or religion or country, but rather *the greatest good of the greatest number*.

The principle of utility applies not only to the individual actions of private persons but also to the actions of the government and in particular to the laws that the legislature approves. When a private individual faces a moral dilemma, he must consider all the individuals who will be affected by what he does; he must consider all of them equally; and he must select that alternative which maximizes the pleasure and minimizes the pain of all concerned. When a legislator is considering whether or not to vote for a law, he must consider whether that law, if generally followed, would increase the welfare or happiness of the citizens to whom it applies.

It is important to realize that for Bentham the principle of utility applies to animals as well as to human beings. Animals are capable of feeling pleasure and pain, and their feelings must be taken into account. We are thus obliged to avoid inflicting needless suffering upon animals. If one decides to inflict harm upon animals to achieve some human good, as in a medical experiment, the good obtained must outweigh the harm inflicted. A human being is not permitted to cause pain in nonhuman animals for any trivial satisfaction. The principle of utility requires humans to act with kindness and compassion toward all forms of sentient life.

BENTHAM'S FELICIFIC CALCULUS

According to utilitarianism, an individual is obliged to choose that alternative course of action which maximizes pleasure and minimizes pain. But how is one to judge whether one quantity of pleasure is greater or less than another? If I should be faced with the option of visiting a sick friend or remaining at home, how am I to judge whether the pleasure my friend receives from the visit is greater or less than the pleasure I will receive by remaining at home? Or how can I judge that the pleasure I receive from eating beef outweighs the suffering caused by the confinement and slaughter of cattle?

---

[21]Jeremy Bentham, "An Introduction to the Principles of Morals and Legislation," in *The Utilitarians* (Garden City, New York: Anchor Press, 1973), chap. 1, par. 2–3. (This book was first published in 1789.)

To make judgments about the quantity of pleasure, Bentham offered a method that is often called the **felicific calculus**.

To understand Bentham's method, let us imagine that a person must decide between alternatives A and B. His first step is to compare the pleasures resulting from A with those resulting from B. Bentham lists several points of comparison.

> To a person considered *by himself,* the value of a pleasure or pain considered *by itself,* will be greater or less, according to the four following circumstances:
> 1. Its *intensity.*
> 2. Its *duration.*
> 3. Its *certainty* or *uncertainty.*
> 4. Its *propinquity* or *remoteness.*[22]

Bentham here says that any two pleasures may be compared in four different ways. First, one pleasure may be preferable to another because it is more *intense.* Thus, the pleasures of sexual intercourse may be preferable to those of a walk in the country because the former are stronger and more stimulating than the latter. Second, if pleasures are alike in intensity, then one pleasure may be preferable to the other because it lasts longer. Thus, if *duration* is the criterion, eating two slices of pizza would be preferable to eating only one because it prolongs the pleasures of eating. Third, even if two pleasures have the same intensity and duration, one pleasure may nevertheless be preferable to the other if the likelihood of its occurring is greater. For example, if it is more likely that under existing circumstances I will be able to obtain a slice of pizza than an oyster, then the first pleasure is to be preferred to the second. According to this criterion of *certainty* or *uncertainty,* a person should always choose the more likely good, if all other things are equal.

The fourth point of comparison is more controversial than the other three. Bentham says that, all things being equal, the pleasure that occurs sooner is to be preferred to the one that occurs later. Assuming that the pleasures of consuming a slice of pizza and an oyster are equal in other respects, if I can have the pizza now or the oyster later, I should choose the pizza. This point is controversial because it conflicts with another rule of rational choice that says that each moment of a person's life is of equal worth and that mere differences in time cannot justify a preference. "Rationality implies an impartial concern for all parts of our life. The mere difference of location in time, of something's being earlier or later, is not in itself a rational ground for having more or less regard for it."[23] Of course one may prefer the earlier to the later pleasure on the ground that the earlier one is more likely to occur than the later one. If the later pleasure lies well in the future, one may not live to enjoy it. But this is to use the criterion of certainty or uncertainty, not that of propinquity or remoteness.

Bentham suggests two additional criteria for evaluating pleasures and pains: *fecundity* and *purity.* A pleasure is fecund if it tends to produce pleasures of the same kind. For example, the pleasures that you obtain from learning something that you want to

---

[22]Ibid., chap. 4, par. 2.
[23]John Rawls, *A Theory of Justice* (Cambridge: Harvard University Press, 1971), p. 293.

know tend to promote subsequent learning—and hence subsequent pleasure—and thus are fecund. A pleasure is pure if it is unlikely to produce a pain. Thus, the pleasures of listening to music are pure because they seldom cause suffering whereas the pleasures of gorging oneself on rich food are impure because of the indigestion that may follow.

Thus far I have presented those criteria that apply when only one person is concerned. When others are involved, be they animals or humans, there is a seventh criterion, *extent*. The greater the number of individuals who experience the pleasure, the greater is its value.

Bentham tells us that in considering which action to perform, we should calculate all the pleasures and all the pains likely to follow from each alternative. We should then use these seven criteria to determine the value of each pleasure and pain. For each alternative course of action, we should calculate the sum of the values of all the pleasures and pains involved. We should then subtract the pains from the pleasures. The result gives the degree of goodness of each alternative. That alternative should be chosen which yields the greatest amount of good.

Bentham throughout assumes that it is always possible to compare pleasures and to make the necessary calculations. It is true that in everyday life we often make rough estimates of the amounts of pleasure and pain that a given course of action will cause. If I did not believe, for instance, that going to the dentist would cause less pain in the long run than is caused by not going, I would have no reason to go. Even when several persons are involved, we often make rough estimates of greater and less pleasure or pain. For example, John may enjoy the music of Mozart more than does Tom. Or we may have evidence that the pain that John suffered in undergoing surgery was not as great as the pain endured by Tom. We make such comparisons quite often, using as evidence the actions, gestures, and speech of the individuals concerned.

But there are other situations in which making such calculations is much more difficult. For example, suppose the government decides to tax every citizen one dollar to pay for the life-saving machines used by a few individuals with kidney failure. Can we say that the pain caused to the citizens by the tax is outweighed by the reduction in pain for the users of the machines and their families? Does it really make any sense to try to determine the total quantity of pain caused by this tax? Some philosophers have claimed that even in such cases we can and should make rough estimates. Others have insisted that when one is thinking about large numbers of individuals, as the legislator does, then it makes no sense to apply the felicific calculus. The question of the measurement of pleasure has always been one of the most controversial aspects of utilitarian ethics.

MILL'S VERSION OF UTILITARIANISM

John Stuart Mill (1806–1873) was greatly influenced by Bentham's ethical theory and political hopes. Yet Mill believed that by emphasizing the importance of intensity and duration in determining the value of a pleasure, Bentham attributed too much value to the lower physical pleasures and not enough value to the higher intellectual, social, and aesthetic satisfactions. Mill wanted to move away from the quantitative to the qualitative assessment of pleasure. He wanted to be able to say that "it is better to be a human being dissatisfied than a pig satisfied; better to be Socrates dissatisfied than a fool satisfied." Consequently, he claimed that pleasures differed from each other not only in quantity but also in quality.

> It is quite compatible with the principle of utility to recognize the fact that some kinds of pleasure are more desirable and more valuable than others. It would be absurd that, while in estimating all other things, quality is considered as well as quantity, the estimation of pleasures should be supposed to depend on quantity alone.[24]

Suppose that one goes to the store to buy some apples and finds that a small number of high-quality apples costs the same as a large quantity of low-quality apples. A person who enjoyed good apples would prefer quality to quantity and would settle for fewer but better apples. Mill says that one should do the same for pleasures. It may very well be the case that a life of eating, drinking, and sex contains more pleasure than a life spent pursuing scientific truth. A pig may experience more pleasure than Socrates. Nevertheless, says Mill, one should prefer the life of Socrates to that of a pig. One should choose quality over quantity.

But what is the criterion of quality? How can one tell which of two pleasures is the better? Mill answers:

> If I am asked what I mean by a difference of quality in pleasures, or what makes one pleasure more valuable than another, merely as a pleasure, except its being greater in amount, there is but one possible answer. Of two pleasures, if there be one to which all or almost all who have experience of both give a decided preference, irrespective of any feeling of moral obligation to prefer it, that is the more desirable pleasure. . . . From this verdict of the only competent judges, I apprehend there can be no appeal. On a question which is the best worth having of two pleasures, or which of two modes of existence is the most grateful to the feelings, apart from its moral attributes and from its consequences, the judgment of those who are qualified by knowledge of both, or, if they differ, that of the majority among them, must be admitted as final. And there needs be the less hesitation to accept this judgment respecting the quality of pleasures, since there is no other tribunal to be referred to even on the question of quantity.[25]

Here, Mill offers personal preference as the basis for assessing pleasures according to quality; one pleasure is superior to another if those who have experienced both prefer it. Mill was convinced that the higher intellectual pleasures would be judged superior to the physical pleasures if this test were used.

A difficulty in Mill's theory can best be understood by considering the case of the apples. A person who eats apples regularly and who consumes many different varieties will be a better judge of the quality of apples than one whose experience is limited; wide experience allows the former to become acquainted with those features of apples that

[24]John Stuart Mill, *Utilitarianism* (New York: The Liberal Arts Press, 1953), pp. 8–9. (This essay was first published entire in 1863.)
[25]Ibid., pp. 9–11.

make some superior to others. It is his ability to give reasons for an apple's superiority that convinces others that he is a qualified judge. But this is not the case with pleasure. If you asked someone to judge why pleasure A is superior to pleasure B, then according to Mill's test, there is nothing he can say. A is not superior in any other respect then its being preferred. Thus, the person cannot justify his preference by giving a reason other than that he likes A better then B. Mill's introduction of qualitative considerations into the evaluation of pleasure does not clarify the basis of choice.

RULE AND ACT UTILITARIANISM

Another modification of Bentham's system introduced by Mill has received considerable discussion in recent years. Bentham often writes as if we are supposed to consider only the specific consequences of the particular alternative courses of action. But this can lead to unacceptable choices. Suppose that John has borrowed some money from Tom, and the time has come for him to repay his debt. John would like to keep the money for himself but Tom insists that the debt be paid. If we consider only the particular alternatives of paying or not paying the debt, it may turn out that the benefit to John of keeping the money slightly outweighs the benefit to Tom of its being returned. Yet, barring unusual circumstances, we would think that John had a moral obligation to discharge his debt. It would appear, then, that right conduct is not necessarily the conduct that leads to the greatest happiness. It seems that some obligations should be honored even if the overall happiness is diminished.

Mill saves utilitarianism by pointing out that in most cases the principle of utility should be applied not to the particular case but to the general rule that is applicable to the particular case. In the case of John's debt there already is an applicable rule, namely, that individuals should discharge their debts. If John should repudiate his debt, he would then be committing himself to the general rule that individuals are permitted to repudiate their debts when it is convenient to do so. Which rule should John follow? According to Mill, one should ask oneself this question: What would happen if each rule was generally followed? If people generally paid their debts, then individuals with savings that they were not using would be willing to lend money to those who needed it. People would benefit by this practice, which tends to stimulate various forms of economic activity. If, on the other hand, people generally repudiated their debts, those with savings would be unwilling to lend money to those who needed it; capital would lie idle and many beneficial activities would be impeded. We can see how the principle of utility helps us to choose among moral rules; it tells us to adopt that rule which, if generally followed, would lead to greater happiness for a greater number than any other feasible rule.

The principle of utility is applicable to particular cases when existing rules are in conflict. Suppose, for example, that although Tom wanted his money back, he had no great need for it; John, on the other hand, needs it to pay for a lifesaving operation on one of his children. John is faced with a dilemma. Should he discharge his obligation to Tom and return the money, or should he do his duty to his child and provide the operation? Two rules that are generally acceptable—"Pay your debts" and "Take care of your children"—lead to conflicting results in this situation. What should John do?

Mill recommends that John apply the principle of utility directly to his problem. If paying for the operation would lead to greater happiness in the long run, he would be entitled to repudiate his debt.

> If utility is the ultimate source of moral obligations, utility may be invoked to decide between them when their demands are incompatible. Though the application of the standard may be difficult, it is better than none at all; while in other systems the moral laws all claiming independent authority, there is no common umpire entitled to interfere between them; their claims to precedence one over another rest on little better than sophistry, and, unless determined, as they generally are, by the unacknowledged influence of consideration of utility, afford a free scope for the action of personal desires and partialities. We must remember that only in the cases of conflict between secondary principles is it requisite that first principles should be appealed to. There is no case of moral obligation in which some secondary principle is not involved; and if only one, there can seldom be any real doubt which one it is, in the mind of any person by whom the principle itself is recognized.[26]

For Mill, a situation involving ethical choice has the following components: a rational agent considering which course of action he should choose, several secondary principles of obligation that the agent already accepts and is trying to put to work to solve his problem, and the supreme principle of morality—the principle of utility—which stands above the secondary rules as the means of judging them. The function of the supreme principle is to determine which secondary ones are valid and to determine what action to select when the valid secondary rules lead to conflict.

Because Mill insists that the principle of utility is primarily applicable to secondary rules, his type of theory is called *rule utilitarianism*. A theory which says that the principle of utility is applicable to particular actions rather than to rules is called *act utilitarianism*. As we have seen, the principle argument for rule versus act utilitarianism is that the former is more consistent with our sense of moral obligation. Of course, those who favor act utilitarianism can reply that our sense of obligation is defective and that it is therefore not legitimate to appeal to it.

CONCEPTS OF UTILITARIANISM

Hedonism: The value of an action is determined by the amount of pleasure it produces.

Felicific calculus: Bentham's method of measuring the value of an action.

Act utilitarianism: A particular action is right or wrong according to the amount of pleasure it produces compared with alternative actions.

Rule utilitarianism: A particular action is right if the rule that applies to it produces more pleasure when generally followed than alternative rules.

---

[26]Ibid., p. 27.

MORAL CONSCIOUSNESS

The disagreement between rule and act utilitarianism reflects a broader disagreement over the nature and function of ethical theory. According to one view, an ethical theory is valid if it provides a correct account of our sense of moral obligation or, more broadly, our moral consciousness. Suppose that the content of our moral consciousness can be described by a set of rules or principles that we would accept upon reflection. The best ethical theory would then be the one that most accurately records and explains the content of our moral consciousness. As we saw, act utilitarianism would lead us to perform actions that our moral consciousness repudiates, whereas rule utilitarianism would repudiate such actions. It therefore provides a better explanation of the considered moral judgments that we actually make. According to this view, to test an ethical theory, we should find out to what degree the judgments it says we should make square with the judgments we do make upon reflection and thoughtful consideration.

According to another view, our moral consciousness consists merely of our current habits and prejudices and has no particular authority. It may turn out that the best ethical theory would require us to change our established patterns of thinking and to adopt new criteria of conduct. Moralists such as Plato and Bentham have adopted this reformist viewpoint. For them, ethical theory does not just describe and explain our existing forms of thought but also prescribes new and better ones.

PROBLEMS WITH HEDONISM

Remember that utilitarianism has two components: the notion that only pleasure and the absence of pain are good for their own sake or intrinsically good and the notion that right conduct is that which tends to maximize the good. The first component is hedonism. According to hedonism, while many different things can be means to obtaining some intrinsic good, only pleasure and the absence of pain are good in themselves. By pleasure is meant pleasant experience. The objects and states of affairs that provide such experiences are merely means to obtaining what is intrinsically good. Apart from being experienced they have no intrinsic value at all. Thus, a beautiful tree is not something whose existence is good for its own sake; it is something that we want because we enjoy looking at it.

Many moral philosophers have claimed that there are things other than pleasure that are good for their own sake. Some philosophors have even said that it is not pleasure but something else that is intrinsically good, such as love or power or self-realization. Others have claimed that there are numerous goods, that many different things can be good for their own sake. For example, Aristotle (384–322 B.C.) wrote:

> And there are many things we should be keen about even if they brought no pleasure, e.g. seeing, remembering, knowing, possessing the virtues. If pleasures necessarily do accompany these, that makes no odds; we should choose these even if no pleasure resulted.[27]

[27]Aristotle, *Nicomachean Ethics* (London: Oxford University Press 1966), 1174a4–8.

Other examples of things that have been mentioned as intrinsic goods are knowledge, friendship, the realization of one's talents or potential, life, beauty, and so forth. Even though utilitarians have usually interpreted pleasure broadly including in it any sort of satisfaction to be found in experience, their theory has been criticized as having too restricted a conception of the good. Many other things, it has been said, can be good besides pleasant experiences. Many things other than pleasant experiences are valuable, and many things would be valuable even if they were never experienced. A beautiful tree is an example of something that might be thought to be good for its own sake, even if no human being were ever to see it.

Let us first consider the claim that knowledge is something that is intrinsically good. You can possess knowledge even when you are not thinking of what you know. For example, you can know that $2 + 3 = 5$ even if you are not thinking about it. Knowledge can exist without its being consciously experienced or enjoyed. Is mere knowledge something good for its own sake? I think not. There are many things that I have no interest at all in knowing. I have no interest in knowing how many pennies I have in my pocket, how many grains of sand there are in the Sahara Desert, how tall Clark Gable was, and so forth. There are many facts that are too trivial or too dull to bother about. Cluttering one's mind with such facts may interfere with achieving more important goals. We want to know only those facts that are important or interesting or useful. But this means that knowledge is at best an instrumental good, not something good for its own sake.

Perhaps the realization of one's talents is an intrinsic good. Consider the individual who has the potential to become a fine violinist. Isn't there something valuable for its own sake in a talented person's developing her potential? I do not think that the hedonist would be moved by this argument. After all, if a person had the potential to become a successful burglar, we would not agree that there is any positive value in realizing that potential. The hedonist argues that what makes it good to realize a talent is that the talent is useful to human beings. What makes it good for the talented violinist to realize her potential is not that there is some intrinsic good in standing on a stage scraping a bow over some strings but that in doing so she is providing pleasure to her listeners.

An argument against hedonism was developed by the English philosopher G. E. Moore (1873–1958) in the following passage:

> Let us imagine one world exceedingly beautiful. Imagine it as beautiful as you can; put into it whatever on this earth you most admire—mountains, rivers, the sea; trees, and sunsets, stars and moon. Imagine all these combined in the most exquisite proportions, so that no one thing jars against another, but each contributes to increase the beauty of the whole. And then imagine the ugliest world you can possibly conceive. Imagine it simply one heap of filth, containing everything that is most disgusting to us, for whatever reason, and the whole, as far as may be, without one redeeming feature.... The only thing we are not entitled to imagine is that any human being ever has or ever, by any possibility, *can,* live in either, can ever see and enjoy the beauty of the one or hate the foulness of the other. Well, even so, supposing them quite apart from any possible contemplation by human beings; still, is it irrational to hold that it is better that the beautiful world should exist, than the one which is ugly? Would it

not be well, in any case, to do what we could to produce it rather than the other? Certainly I cannot help thinking that it would.[28]

Remember that there are no human beings living in that beautiful world, so there is no one to enjoy it. Similarly, there is no one to suffer in the ugly world. Even so, Moore thinks that it would be better if the beautiful world existed than the ugly one. And so he draws the conclusion:

> If in any imaginable case you admit that the existence of a more beautiful thing is better in itself than that of one more ugly, quite apart from its effects on any human feeling, . . . then we shall have to include in our ultimate end something beyond the limits of human existence. I admit, of course, that our beautiful world would be better still, if there were human beings in it to contemplate and enjoy its beauty. But that admission makes nothing against my point. If it is once admitted that the beautiful world *in itself* is better than the ugly, then it follows, that however many beings may enjoy it, and however much better their enjoyment may be than it is itself, yet its mere existence adds *something* to the goodness of the whole: it is not only a means to our end, but also itself a part thereof.[29]

The beautiful world, Moore argues, is intrinsically good quite apart from any pleasure a human being or animal would take in it.

The hedonist has two responses to Moore. First, he would point out that one's preference for the beautiful world over the ugly is influenced by the thought of the pleasure that the one would give us and the pain that the other would evoke. Without these thoughts of pain and pleasure, what reason could there be to prefer the one over the other? For example, suppose that the ugly world is pervaded by an incredibly foul odor. Why should the existence of that odor be a reason for that world not to exist? Why should the existence of a fragrant odor be a reason for the existence of the beautiful world? Isn't what makes the foul odor bad the fact that we would hate to smell it? Isn't what makes the fragrant odor good that we would enjoy smelling it? It is our pains and pleasures, says the hedonist, that causes these odors to be either good or bad. If we completely ignore the pain it would cause us, there is nothing wrong with a foul odor.

Second, the hedonist argues that the very meaning of beauty involves reference to human pleasure. What makes an object beautiful is that it exemplifies a certain pattern and form; for example, the beauty of a tree consists of its particular shape and color and size as it appears in a certain setting. But why do we call that pattern beautiful rather than some other? We do so because that pattern provides pleasure. "Some particular forms or qualities . . . are calculated to please, and others to displease" says David Hume. "Though it be certain that beauty and deformity . . . are not qualities in objects, but belong entirely to the sentiment, . . . it must be allowed, that there are certain qualities in objects which are fitted by nature to produce those particular feel-

---

[28]G. E. Moore, *Principia Ethica* (Cambridge: The University Press, 1962), pp. 83–84. (This book was first published in 1903.)
[29]Ibid., pp. 84–85.

ings."[30] The goodness of a beautiful object, then, is not intrinsic but instrumental; it consists of a pattern that tends to arouse pleasure and enjoyment in a human viewer.

Another argument against hedonism claims that we cannot separate the pleasure from the activity that arouses it. The pleasures of sadism, for instance, are so tied up with sadistic action that they cannot be distinguished from it. The pleasures of looking at a beautiful painting are so intimately connected to the act of looking at the painting that one cannot really distinguish them from the act. We even identify and describe the various enjoyments by referring to the actions that elicit them. How else can we describe the pleasures of the sadist except by saying that they are what the sadist feels as he pursues his sadistic activities? It would follow that instead of pleasure being the criterion of the goodness of an activity, it is the goodness of an activity that makes the accompanying pleasure good. So argues Aristotle:

> Now since activities differ in respect of goodness and badness, and some are
> worthy to be chosen, others to be avoided, and others neutral, so, too, are the
> pleasures; for to each activity there is a proper pleasure. The pleasure proper to a
> worthy activity is good and that proper to an unworthy activity bad. . . . But the
> pleasures involved in activities are . . . so hard to distinguish from them that it
> admits of dispute whether the activity is not the same as the pleasure. . . . As
> activities are different, then, so are the corresponding pleasures.[31]

The hedonist replies that this argument rests upon a confusion. It is true that we usually name the pleasures we feel by using the names of the corresponding activities, that is, the pleasures of playing tennis, of swimming, of looking at pictures, and so forth. And it is also true that the particular feel of the pleasure is often bound up with the nature of the activity. The pleasures aroused by swimming, for instance, are connected with feeling wet and moving horizontally whereas the pleasures of tennis are related to the physical exertion of running about and swinging one's arms. Nevertheless, the pleasure is one thing and the activity another, for the activity can exist without the pleasure. We can swim and receive no pleasure from it; we can play tennis and hate every moment of it; we can look at a beautiful painting and find no enjoyment therein. Because the pleasure is something that is separate from the accompanying activity, it is possible to evaluate it in its own right. It is pleasure, insists the hedonist, that gives value to the activities, not the activities that give value to the pleasure.

Thus, utilitarianism is not refuted by arguments aimed at its hedonistic component. A reasonable and satisfactory reply can be given to every argument so far offered. Of course, the opponent of hedonism may nevertheless insist that there are things he prefers for their own sake quite independently of the pleasure that they arouse. He might claim, as did Moore, that if there were a beautiful tree that no one ever saw, it would be better that it exist than that it not exist. The hedonist may respond that he fails to understand

---

[30]David Hume, "Of the Standard of Taste," in *Essays, Moral, Political and Literary* (London: Oxford University Press, 1971), pp. 238–240.
[31]Aristotle, *Ethics,* 1175b24–38.

how anything can have value independently of its effect upon human experience. His opponent may then counter that to him some such things are valuable none the less simply because he prefers them. Although this impasse may be impossible to resolve, it does not mean that the hedonist must yield to his critics.

PROBLEMS WITH THE IDEA OF MAXIMIZING THE GOOD

The criticisms of utilitarianism investigated so far have endorsed a teleological ethics but disagreed with Bentham and Mill on the nature of the good to be sought. Utiliarianism can also be criticized from the standpoint of deontological ethics. This criticism rejects any attempt to explain moral obligation in terms of maximizing the good of the individuals involved. According to this approach, it is wrong to sacrifice the lives and interests of particular individuals merely to advance the welfare of the majority. Individuals have *rights*, and it would be unjust to disregard these rights.

To better understand this approach, consider the practice of deliberately murdering human beings as a form of religious sacrifice. Earlier in this chapter, I told the story of Abraham, who was ordered by the god of Israel to sacrifice his only son, Isaac. In the mythology of ancient Greece, the great king Agamemnon was required to sacrifice his daughter Iphigenia to propitiate the gods. But few societies have engaged in human sacrifice to the extent of the Aztecs in Mexico. Thousands of prisoners of war, slaves, and selected youths and maidens were killed by the Aztec priests.

What was the purpose of these sacrifices? It has been suggested that their purpose may actually have been rational. Since the bodies of those who were slaughtered were later eaten, it has been argued that the sacrifices were used to provide an inexpensive form of protein necessary to maintaining a healthy diet in an area whose resources were depleted because of excessive population growth.[32]

This speculation about the underlying purpose of Aztec cannibalism suggests the following idea. If we are to adopt the utilitarian morality according to which human welfare is the basis of moral choice, then in some circumstances it may be right and proper to sacrifice the lives or well-being of a few persons to assure the welfare of the great majority. It may be right and proper to permit cannibalism if it turned out to be an efficient means of assuring adequate nutrition. On utilitarian grounds, human sacrifice for nutritional purposes may be ethical.

Many philosophers have argued that utilitarianism—and for that matter, any teleological ethics—is wrong because it allows the end to justify the means. They have argued in favor of a deontological approach which, they believe, would not allow undesirable means to be employed to achieve a desirable end. In the remainder of this chapter, we shall explore the most famous of all deontological systems, that of the illustrious German philosopher Immanuel Kant (1724–1804).

[32]Marvin Harris, *Cannibals and Kings, The Origins of Cultures* (New York: Random House, 1977), p. 110.

The Ethics of Kant

THE CATEGORICAL IMPERATIVE

Kant believed that when we say that a person ought or ought not to do something, we are issuing a *command,* or *imperative.* For example, one way of formulating the moral requirement that you ought not steal is by uttering a sentence in the imperative: "Don't steal!" Thus, judgments about what we should or should not do are best understood by classifying them as imperatives.

IMMANUEL KANT
(1724–1804)

Kant was born in Königsberg, Germany. He became a professor of logic and metaphysics at the University of Königsberg in 1770. Kant led an uneventful life, but his ideas transformed the course of philosophy and indeed of thought in general. His three major works are the *Critique of Pure Reason* (1781), which contains his theory of knowledge and his criticism of traditional metaphysics; the *Critique of Practical Reason* (1788), in which he presents his ethics and his defense of freedom of the will; and the *Critique of Judgment* (1790), in which he discusses the topics of beauty and purpose. His *Prolegomena to any Future Metaphysics* (1783) is a briefer version of his first critique, and *The Fundamental Principles of the Metaphysics of Morals* (1785) is a briefer account of his ethics. The most readable translation of the *Critique of Pure Reason* is by Norman Kemp Smith (New York: St. Martin's Press, 1965). An excellent collection of Kant's ethical writings is *Critique of Practical Reason and Other Writings in Moral Philosophy,* trans. Lewis White Beck (Chicago: University of Chicago Press, 1950).

Imperatives, says Kant, are of two kinds. "If you want to get cool, then open the window" is a **hypothetical imperative.** It says that should getting cool be your purpose, then opening the window is the means to attain it. A hypothetical imperative is always of the form: "If you want such and such, then do so and so." Kant argued that the imperatives of morality are not hypothetical. For example, suppose that you are offended by the fact that a good friend has deliberately lied to you. You tell her that she ought not to have told you a lie. If she replies that she lied because she *wanted* to deceive you, you would probably not consider that an acceptable excuse at all. What she said might give her reason for lying, but it would not be acknowledged by you as a good reason, as one that justified the lie. In a situation of moral choice, says Kant, what you should do does not depend upon what you want or upon what is convenient to you. No matter what people want, they still should not lie or steal or commit murder or break promises to obtain it. Thus, morality is not founded upon the particular ends that a person has chosen, and morally sound action does not consist merely in adopting means to those ends. Moral imperatives are unconditional, or **categorical.** The categorical imperative is an absolute command that certain actions be done and others not be done. It says "Do such and such!" or "Don't do such and such!"

We are now in a position to understand why Kant rejected utilitarianism. An ethics whose goal is the pleasure of human beings cannot be based upon categorical imperatives. At best it can yield hypothetical imperatives of the form "If you want to become happy, or if you want others to become happy, then you should do such and such." Another reason why Kant rejected utilitarianism is that whereas morality gives absolutely definite and certain commands, what brings happiness and pleasure is uncertain and indefinite. "The notion of happiness is so indefinite that although every man wishes to attain it, yet he never can say definitely and consistently what it is that he really wishes and wills."[33] An ethic of happiness, says Kant, cannot provide clear-cut principles of conduct. "We cannot therefore act on any definite principles to secure happiness, but only on empirical counsels, for example, of regimen, frugality, courtesy, reserve, etc., which experience teaches do, on the average, most promote well-being. . . . The problem to determine certainly and universally what action would promote the happiness of a rational being is completely insoluble."[34]

UNIVERSALITY AS THE TEST OF MORAL OBLIGATION

If morality consists of categorical imperatives, how can I know when I am faced with a genuine and binding categorical imperative? In other words, how can I test a moral principle to see whether it is valid? Kant's main idea can best be understood by considering an example of the type that he himself analyzed. Suppose Susan needs to borrow money, which she knows she will be unable to pay back. But unless she promises to repay the loan by a certain time, she will not be eligible to receive it. Would it be right for her to borrow the money anyhow and make a false promise to repay it? If she followed only her own desires and her own conception of her welfare, she would borrow the money. But the question is whether borrowing it under false pretenses is right. Susan has a reason or motive for lying and taking the money. Kant called a person's reason the **maxim of the action.** In Susan's case, the maxim is that when an individual is in need of money, she should borrow it and promise to repay it even though she knows that she will be unable to repay it.

Kant contends that to test a maxim one should ask what it would be like if people in general were to act upon it. Susan should ask herself what it would be like if this maxim were to become a universal law binding upon everyone. Suppose that everyone were

[33]Immanual Kant, *Fundamental Principles of the Metaphysic of Morals,* trans. Thomas K. Abbott (New York: The Liberal Arts Press, 1949), p. 35. (This book was first published in 1785.)
[34]Ibid., pp. 35–36.

permitted to do as Susan considers doing. Kant argues that if the maxim were universalized, a kind of contradiction would occur.

> Then I see at once that it could never hold as a universal law of nature, but would necessarily contradict itself. For supposing it to be a universal law that everyone when he thinks himself in a difficulty should be able to promise whatever he pleases, with the purpose of not keeping his promise, the promise itself would become impossible, as well as the end that one might have in view in it, since no one would consider that anything was promised to him, but would ridicule all such statements as vain pretenses.[35]

If all individuals were to act upon this maxim, making false promises whenever it was convenient to do so, then no one would believe anyone else's promise and hence the practice of making promises would be destroyed. The contradiction is that once the maxim is universalized and put into practice, the very action that it presupposes—the action of making promises—would cease to be possible.

The test for determining which maxims are permissible as valid principles of action is formulated by Kant in his famous categorical imperative: *"Act only on that maxim whereby thou canst at the same time will that it should become a universal law."*[36] This is known as the **universalization test.** When universalized, certain maxims result in a kind of contradiction or conflict; these maxims, then, represent wrong conduct. Other maxims yield conduct that is free from conflict and contradiction and hence represent morally permissible actions.

RESPECT FOR PERSONS

There is another fundamental aspect to Kant's ethics. Let us consider the idea of universalization from the standpoint of the individual who is deliberating about her future actions. Should Susan make the false promise? If she considers only her own advantage, then she should, for she has nothing to lose. But instead she asks what it would be like not merely if she acted in this way but if individuals in general were to adopt this line of conduct as a rule. By universalizing the maxim, an individual can no longer consider herself, her interests, her advantage as the primary and decisive factors. She must consider the interests of all other persons. What would it be like if everyone were to act in this way? In particular, suppose someone were to act toward her in the way she is proposing to act toward others. Suppose someone were to borrow money from her and make a false promise to repay it. She would not accept the notion that others are entitled to act toward her as she is proposing to act toward others. Therefore, the action is forbidden. She cannot treat herself as an exception to the general rules that she has adopted. She must be disinterested.

The test of universalization therefore requires us to treat persons as *morally equal.*

[35]Ibid., p. 40.
[36]Ibid., p. 38.

Whatever differences there are among rational individuals in ability, religion, race, character, and so forth, it is morally required that the interests of each person be taken into account. Each person should act as if he were legislating for everyone. According to utilitarianism, the interests of a minority may be sacrificed to maximize the total happiness. But Kant counters that the interests of the minority should receive just as much consideration as those of the majority. Accordingly, Kant provides a formulation of the supreme principle of morality that emphasizes the idea of moral equality: "So act as to treat humanity, whether in thine own person or in that of any other, in every case as an end withal, never as means only."[37]

The idea that all persons should be treated as ends in themselves implies that they should not be thought of merely as objects that can be manipulated for one's own purposes. There is a limit to what you can do to another person. For each person possesses *rights*, the violation of which is morally prohibited. Thus, Kant's ethics implies a strong conception of human rights. Embodied in this conception is the idea of moral equality: all individuals have certain rights in common, and in pursuing one's own goals one must take care not to violate the rights of others. One must show respect for persons.

Let us amplify this view by considering the following case. Suppose that you are on a train and the conductor takes your ticket and provides you with a receipt. He is performing a certain function. The job he does may at some future time be performed by a machine. We can look at the conductor as a kind of machine whose purpose is to get a certain job done. If we look at human beings functionally—that is, we look at them in terms of the jobs they do and the roles they fill—we are thinking of them as means to various human ends. Thinking of them this way suggests that they are no more than machines and thus can be treated any way that we wish. Kant's claim that persons are ends and not mere means implies that although persons perform functions and fill roles, there is another, more fundamental aspect to their nature. They are subjects with certain basic rights that place limits on how they can be treated by others. The conductor, for example, is not a machine; he is a human being with feelings and needs and interests that demand to be respected. Each person is morally required to respect the interests of others just as he expects others to respect his interests.

AUTONOMY

Kant emphasized a further consequence of the universalization test. When applying the test of universalization to our own maxims, we each arrive at certain moral principles such as "Never make a false promise." These principles have been created by us as we consider which of our maxims can become universal laws. Thus, in our own moral thinking we are like legislators who lay down laws binding upon ourselves and others. Kant calls this "the idea of *the will of every rational being as a universally legislative will*."[38] Because each rational being is a universal lawgiver, he has **moral autonomy.** This

[37]Ibid., p. 46.
[38]Ibid., p. 48.

means that no person is morally required to obey any will but his own. Each person gives laws to himself and is not subjected to the authority of any other person.

Kant sees a close connection between the idea of moral autonomy and the notion that each person is an end in himself. Because individuals are autonomous, they are capable of free choice and of determining the course of their own lives. Thus, they do not exist as means to satisfy the interests and purposes of others; they are ends in themselves. Kant bases his view that there are certain basic rights applicable to all persons on the idea that persons are alike in being morally autonomous. Because they are required to obey no laws other than those that they give to themselves, they have a special dignity. For Kant, the dignity of man is founded upon his moral autonomy.

> **KANT'S CATEGORICAL IMPERATIVE**
>
> 1. Universalization test for right action
> 2. Moral equality of persons
> 3. Moral autonomy of persons

CRITICISMS OF KANT'S ETHICS

In devising his universalization test, Kant is widely appreciated as having hit upon something fundamental. This test represents a basic aspect of what is involved in thinking morally about our conduct toward others. In rejecting those maxims that cannot be universalized, we are effectively taking into account the interests of others. Universalization thus seems to be a prerequisite of any morally valid rule. Kant, however, does not seem to think of his test merely as a prerequisite. In certain passages he seems to consider it to be the sole test. He suggests that the only thing that needs to be done is to universalize our maxims to determine whether a contradiction results.

It has often been pointed out that universalization fails as the sole test. To see why, let us consider one of Kant's own examples. He considers a man who possesses a certain talent but who would rather pursue a life of pleasure than develop it. Is he morally entitled to pursue pleasure rather than to develop his abilities? Kant admits that there is no contradiction in individuals letting their talents lie idle while they pursue a life of ease and pleasure. But he adds that a person "cannot possibly *will* that this should be a universal law of nature, or be implanted in us as such by a natural instinct. For, as a rational being, he necessarily wills that his faculties be developed, since they serve him, for all sorts of possible purposes."[39] Kant's argument seems quite artificial. He concedes that there is no direct contradiction in not developing one's own talents. He then introduces without explanation the thought that a rational being necessarily wills that his powers be developed. But he fails to explain why such development is implied in the fact of being rational.

[39] Ibid., p. 40.

John Stuart Mill added to this criticism the suggestion that Kant really presupposed a utilitarian ethics. After quoting Kant's universalization test, Mill remarks:

> But when he begins to deduce from this precept any of the actual duties of morality, he fails, almost grotesquely, to show that there would be any contradiction, any logical (not to say physical) impossibility, in the adoption by all rational beings of the most outrageously immoral rules of conduct. All he shows is that the *consequences* of their universal adoption would be such as no one would choose to incur.[40]

Mill appears to accept the test of universalization, but he argues that it needs to be supplemented by utilitarian criteria. In considering any particular course of action, we should ask: "What would be the consequences if this course of action were generally followed?" If the consequences are good on the whole, then the action is obligatory. If they are bad on the whole, then the action is forbidden. By adding utilitarian criteria to Kant's universalization test, we thus derive a form of rule utilitarianism.

This criticism highlights a weak point in Kant's ethics. Kant does not make clear what he means by a contradiction. Certainly Mill is correct that if the notion of a contradiction is taken in its strict sense, universalization does not yield the full range of obligations that Kant endorses. But taken in a looser sense, this notion has the consequence of making the test inapplicable or so imprecise as to be useless.

There is, however, a different way of interpreting the universalization requirement. An individual, let us suppose, is obligated to act on only those maxims he is willing to universalize. He is willing to universalize a maxim when he would be willing to accept a world in which individuals were required to act as the maxim stipulates. In particular, he would be willing to live in a world in which others act toward him just as he is proposing to act toward others. For example, is it right for me to make a promise to repay a loan that I have no intention at all of keeping? Even if there is no strict contradiction in making false promises, I would not want to live in a world in which individuals were morally permitted to make false promises to me and to those I care about. I would not endorse as a general principle the legitimacy of false promises.

This interpretation of the universalization requirement partly satisfies Kant's theory. First, universalization tells me to act consistently with my principles; it says that I should not act in a way that I could not endorse as a general principle for all persons. Second, by requiring that actions be based upon general principles applicable to everyone, I am acknowledging the basic moral equality of all persons. Third, because each individual must choose his own principles by asking what kind of world he would be willing to accept, the idea of moral autonomy is endorsed.

But this *personalistic form of universalization* differs from Kant's version in one important respect. It allows the possibility of different individuals arriving at different principles without there being any way of reconciling their differences. Given what I would be willing to accept as general forms of conduct, I may decide upon certain principles that you would not be willing to accept. Whereas Kant sought for an objective

[40]John Stuart Mill, *Utilitarianism* (New York: The Liberal Arts Press, 1953), p. 4.

morality valid for all rational beings, personalistic universalization results in a set of principles relative to the values of the individual. Of course, it may turn out that all individuals have the same values; their principles of action will therefore be the same. But this is quite unlikely.

Furthermore, personalistic universalization may have results that are in serious disagreement with our moral consciousness. For example, suppose Hitler were asked to universalize the policies that he followed toward the European Jews. One might ask him, "If you were Jewish, would you be willing to be sent to a concentration camp and murdered in a gas chamber?" Hitler's irrational hatred of the Jews was so intense that he might have been able to say with sincerity that he would be willing to suffer these injuries if he were Jewish. Perhaps he would be willing to have the policies that he applied to others applied to himself as well. Thus, personalistic universalization fails as an ethical criterion when we consider whether it conforms to our moral consciousness.

A graver criticism of Kant's ethics was formulated by the German philosopher Arthur Schopenhauer (1788–1860). For Kant, morality is essentially an imperative or law that commands certain actions which constitute duties or moral requirements. Schopenhauer agreed with the following idea, formulated by John Locke: "But what duty is, cannot be understood without a law, or supposed, without a lawmaker, or without reward and punishment."[41] Locke here claims that for anything to be a duty or obligation, it must be a law. And for there to be law, there must be a lawmaker and there must be rewards and punishments to enforce that law. Locke added that since the adherence to or violation of moral laws is usually not rewarded or punished in this life, the existence of moral laws presupposes an afterlife and a god to enforce them.

Schopenhauer draws from Locke's ideas the following implication about Kant's theory of duty:

> If we put Ethics in an imperative form, making it a Doctrine of Duties, and regard the moral worth or worthlessness of human conduct as the fulfilment or violation of duties, we must remember that this view of Duty, and of Obligation in general, is undeniably derived solely from theological morals, and primarily from the Decalogue, and consequently that it rests essentially and inseparably on the assumption of man's dependence on another will which gives him commands and announces reward or punishment.[42]

Schopenhauer is here claiming that Kant's ethics presupposes a religious or theological point of view according to which morality consists of the commands of God, who rewards those who do his will and punishes those who violate it.

If Schopenhauer is correct, Kant must abandon the idea of moral autonomy. Individuals receive duties from a transcendent lawmaker instead of legislating them themselves. Moreover, the commands of morality cannot be considered categorical imperatives.

---

[41]Locke, *Essay,* I. iii. 12.
[42]Arthur Schopenhauer, *The Basis of Morality,* trans. Arthur Broderick Bullock (London: Swan and Sonnenschein, 1903), pp. 34–35. (This book was first published in 1840.)

> Every obligation derives all sense and meaning simply and solely from its relation
> to threatened punishment or promised reward. . . . What ought to be done is
> therefore necessarily conditioned by punishment and reward; consequently, to use
> Kant's language, it is essentially and inevitably hypothetical, and never, as he
> maintains, categorical. . . . A commanding voice, whether it come from within, or
> from without, cannot possibly be imagined except as threatening or promising.
> Consequently obedience to it, which may be wise or foolish according to
> circumstances, is yet always actuated by selfishness, and therefore morally
> worthless.[43]

If the only reason for my being obliged to do something is that my failure to do it will
cause me to be punished, then the obligation is hypothetical, not categorical. It says:
"If you wish to avoid such and such a punishment, then do so and so." There can be no
categorical or unconditional moral obligations, says Schopenhauer.

In his own ethics, Schopenhauer rejected the idea of obligation or duty. For him the
foundation of ethics lay in compassion or concern for the good of others. The only case
in which an action has moral worth is "when the person . . . by what he does, or omits
to do, simply and solely regards the weal and woe of another, and has absolutely no
other object than to benefit him, by keeping harm from his door, or, it may be, even by
affording help, assistance, and relief. It is this aim alone that gives to what is done, or
left undone, the stamp of moral worth."[44] For Schopenhauer, the whole idea of moral
obligation should be discarded because it presupposes a certain religious view that in
his mind is untrue.

This type of criticism of Kant has been echoed in twentieth-century thought by G.
E. M. Anscombe:

> To have a *law* conception of ethics is to hold that what is needed for conformity
> with the virtues . . . is required by divine law. Naturally it is not possible to have
> such a conception unless you believe in God as a law-giver; like Jews, Stoics, and
> Christians. But if such a conception is dominant for many centuries, and then is
> given up, it is a natural result that the concepts of "obligation," of being bound
> or required as by a law, should remain though they had lost their root; and if the
> word "ought" has become invested in certain contexts with the sense of
> "obligation," it too will remain to be spoken with a special emphasis and a
> special feeling in these contexts. . . . The situation, if I am right, was the
> interesting one of the survival of a concept outside of the framework of thought
> that made it a really intelligible one.[45]

Like Schopenhauer, Anscombe proposes that we no longer use the notion of moral obligation because the religious context that makes it intelligible can no longer be assumed.
Instead, she proposes a return to an ethics that emphasizes the ideas of virtue and vice
or being a good or bad person.

Kant might reply to these criticisms by denying that his ethics presupposes a religious

[43]Ibid., pp. 32–33.
[44]Ibid., p. 168.
[45]G. E. M. Anscombe, "Modern Moral Philosophy," in *Ethics,* ed. Judith J. Thomsom and Gerald
Dworkin (New York: Harper & Row, 1968), pp. 192–193.

framework. It is true that for Kant a moral obligation is a command or imperative and hence presupposes the existence of someone who issues it—a lawgiver. The lawgiver is not, however, God but an individual person. As we have already emphasized, Kant sees persons as morally autonomous. Morality is a human creation in which human individuals lay down the law for themselves.

This reply leads to another problem in Kant's thought that cannot be easily resolved. How can a command that I give to myself (as well as to others) result in an unconditional obligation binding upon me? Why cannot I just release myself from the commands that I give to myself? Let us consider an example in which one person commands another to do something. A sergeant in the army orders one of the soldiers under his command to run ten times around the track. After some deliberation, he comes to realize that his command was unreasonable and tells the soldier that he does not have to follow the order. A person is entitled to release another from the commands he has issued. Consequently, if I order myself to do something, I can release myself from my own requirement at will. But if I can release myself from doing something at will, then I am certainly under no strict obligation to do it. Thus, Kant's notion of autonomy does not seem to be consistent with the idea that persons are subject to moral obligations that are unconditonal and categorical.

Summary

Philosophical ethics attempts to provide an account of our fundamental ethical ideas. Whereas religion has often helped motivate individuals to obey the moral code of their society, philosophy is not content with traditional or habitual ethics but adopts a critical perspective. It insists that obedience to moral law be given a rational foundation. In the thought of Socrates we see the beginning of a transition from a traditional, religion-based morality to philosophical ethics.

A major question in ethics is whether we should consider only our own good (egoism) or the good of others (altruism) in making moral decisions. Neither psychological nor ethical egoism seem to be adequate accounts of morality. Utilitarianism is an altruistic theory that requires individuals to seek the greatest pleasure or happiness for the greatest number. The English philosopher Jeremy Bentham emphasized a quantitative approach to the evaluation of pleasure whereas John Stuart Mill stressed a qualitative approach.

The utilitarian can successfully defend hedonism against criticism but has difficulty defending another aspect of utilitarianism: the question of measuring amounts of pleasure. In addition, utilitarianism may allow individuals to be treated as means to an end: the welfare of others. The ethics of Kant is an alternative point of view that insists that persons be treated as ends in themselves. Kant also developed the idea that the main test of a rule of conduct is whether or not it can be universalized without contradiction. The result is a moral imperative issued by the individual himself, who is morally autonomous. Kant's ethics is not without its problems. Universalization fails as the sole test of conduct, for when the notion of contradiction is strictly interpreted, not all obligations are covered, and when this notion is loosely interpreted, the test is too vague. A personalistic form of universalization, devised to avoid this problem, results in the possibility that different individuals will arrive at different principles. Finally, why should a person regard commands he himself has given as binding? The notions of moral autonomy and moral obligation are apparently inconsistent.

Glossary

Altruism: The view that we are obliged to achieve the good of others as well as of ourselves.

Categorical imperative: A command that is unconditional and independent of the desires of the individual. It says "Do such and such," whatever your personal preferences. For Kant, moral rules take the form of categorical imperatives.

Deontological ethics: A group of theories that deny that right conduct consists in maximizing good results and instead emphasizes the independent validity of the right over the good.

Egoism: Psychological egoism claims that the only motive of voluntary conduct is the desire for one's own good. Ethical egoism says that the individual is always entitled to prefer his own good over the good of others.

Felicific calculus: A method invented by Bentham to determine the value of an action by calculating the amount of pleasure it produces.

Hedonism: The idea that pleasure and the absence of pain are the only intrinsic goods.

Hypothetical imperative: A command that says that if you want to achieve a certain goal, then you ought to adopt a certain course of action as a means of achieving it. The action commanded depends upon the goal that is sought.

Maxim of an action: In Kant's ethics, the rule that constitutes an individual's reason for his action.

Monotheism: A type of religion that presupposes the existence of one and only one god.

Moral autonomy: In Kant's ethics, the idea that each individual gives laws to himself and hence is not subject to the authority of another.

Polytheism: A type of religion that presupposes the existence of a plurality of gods.

Teleological ethics: A group of theories that say that right conduct is that which brings about the greatest amount of good.

Universalization test: Kant's test of a morally right action. The test consists in reformulating the maxim of one's action in general terms. The action is permitted only if the universalized maxim is free of contradiction.

Utilitarianism: A teleological theory that uses as the test of right conduct the criterion of maximizing pleasure and minimizing pain. *Act* utilitarianism says that an action is right if its particular consequences are better than those of any alternative. *Rule* utilitarianism says that an action is right if it conforms to the best rule.

Further Reading

A good edition of Plato's writing is *The Collected Dialogues of Plato,* ed. Edith Hamilton and Huntington Cairns (Princeton: Princeton University Press, 1971). The life, death, and conversations of Socrates are presented in such dialogues as *Euthyphro,*

Apology, Phaedo, Ion, Symposium, Gorgias, and *Protagoras,* all contained in this book. The key work for Plato's ethics is the *Republic;* see also *Meno, Philebus,* and *Laws* for additional material on ethics.

An egoistic account of human nature and motivation is contained in Thomas Hobbes' *Leviathan* (Oxford: The Clarendon Press, 1967). For Butler's reply to Hobbes see Joseph Butler, *Five Sermons* (New York: Liberal Arts Press, 1950).

Traditional hedonism is best represented by the letters of Epicurus and by Lucretius' *De Rerum Natura,* both contained in *The Stoic and Epicurean Philosophers,* ed. Whitney J. Oates (New York: Random House, 1940). Aristotle's nonhedonist account of happiness is contained in his *Ethica Nicomachea,* trans. W. D. Ross (London: Oxford University Press, 1966).

Two classic statements of utilitarianism are Jeremy Bentham's *An Introduction to the Principles of Morals and Legislation* and John Stuart Mill's *Utilitarianism.* Both are contained in *The Utilitarians* (Garden City, N. Y.: Anchor Press, 1973). The major nineteenth-century statement of utilitarianism is by Henry Sidgwick, *The Methods of Ethics* (Chicago: University of Chicago Press, 1962). A recent debate over the merits of utilitarianism is contained in J. J. C. Smart and Bernard Williams, *Utilitarianism, For and Against* (London: Cambridge University Press, 1973).

An excellent contemporary example of the deontological approach is in Sir David Ross, *The Right and the Good* (Oxford: The Clarendon Press, 1930).

Kant's major ethical writings are collected in *Critique of Practical Reason and Other Writings in Moral Philosophy,* trans. and ed. Lewis White Beck (Chicago: University of Chicago Press, 1949). A contemporary attempt to combine Kant's universalization criterion with utilitarianism is R. M. Hare, *Moral Thinking* (Oxford: The Clarendon Press, 1981).

Questions for Thought and Discussion

1. Have you ever faced a problem that your habitual morality was unable to resolve? What did you do? How did your reflections on your problem proceed? Did you need to change your moral views to cope with it?

2. Compare the response of Abraham or Job and Socrates to their respective God or gods. In what respect, if any, is Socrates more reflective in his approach than Abraham or Job?

3. Discuss some of the different methods for resolving ethical disagreement that philosophers have offered or that you have discovered yourself. Give an example of an important disagreement on ethical issues and discuss which methods, if any, provide a satisfactory resolution.

4. Does God's approval of some form of conduct make it right? Do you agree with Euthyphro and Hobbes that God's will is the standard of right conduct?

5. Does your experience support the view that people are invariably motivated to satisfy their own personal good, as the egoist says?

6. What are the main difficulties in the idea that those actions are morally right that produce more good than the alternatives?

7. Do animals have moral rights? Is one morally permitted to experiment on animals or to slaughter them for food? Perhaps animals are just machines with no feelings at all. Would this make a difference in how we should treat them?

8. Do you find that either act or rule utilitarianism is consistent with your own sense of personal obligation? Would you repudiate a debt or break a promise if you could produce more good by doing so?

9. Think about G. E. Moore's beautiful and ugly worlds. Do you agree with him that the beautiful world is better than the ugly one even if no one experiences either? Does Moore succeed in refuting hedonism?

10. Is Kant's ethics really that different from rule utilitarianism?

11. Kant's ethics is often preferred to utilitarianism because it provides for a strong theory of human rights. Can utilitarianism find a place for such rights?

Chapter 3

JUSTICE AND SOCIETY

PREVIEW

We often speak of some societies as being just and others as being unjust or lacking justice in some fundamental way. How can we explain the difference between justice and injustice regarding societies? Different accounts of the nature and foundations of social justice are implied by the main ethical theories that we discussed in the previous chapter: utilitarianism and the ethics of Kant. In this chaper, we shall refer frequently to these two theories in considering the ethical foundations of social justice. After considering the nature of justice in general and the forms that it assumes in human society, we shall focus on two main questions: What is the basis of a just system of punishment? What is the basis of a just distribution of property and wealth?

The Nature of Justice in General

The term *justice* has various uses, and there are different types of conduct and circumstance that we call *just*. In one sense, the just person is one who recognizes and acts consistently with the *rights* of others. Some rights are embodied in the law; others have a moral status. The just person recognizes both the legal and moral rights of others and is careful not to violate them. Justice is thus related to the concepts of fairness and equality. A just person is fair to others and treats those in equal circumstances equally. He neither discriminates unfairly nor acts in a prejudiced manner. The just person is thus impartial.

In the broadest sense, then, the just person is the righteous person, the one who makes every effort always and everywhere to do the right thing, the one who always aims at doing as he ought. Perhaps what distinguishes justice from righteousness in general is that the just person gives each one his due. He gives to each what he merits or deserves. The idea of something being owed to someone probably originated in the practice of lending and borrowing money and other goods. But the notion of something's being due someone extends beyond economic remuneration. Someone may be owed gratitude or honor; he may merit reward or punishment.

Under this concept of justice as giving according to merit, there fall two main topics. First, there is the question of **retributive justice,** or punishment. If an individual does wrong, he may deserve punishment. The theory of punishment attempts to determine who deserves punishment and how much punishment is deserved. Second, there is the question of **distributive justice.** Every society has a system under which individuals obtain goods for their personal consumption. What are the criteria for a just distribution of goods?

Justice alone does not define morality. Compassion, for instance, is an important aspect of morality, as Schopenhauer has emphasized. The compassionate person may do things that are beyond the call of duty. But justice remains a central aspect of morality, and it merits further discussion.

The Theory of the Social Contract

The concept of justice is very complex indeed. To explore it more fully, I shall follow a method of analysis called the theory of the **social contract.** It has been used by various philosophers, including Hobbes, Locke, and Rousseau, but I shall focus on the version that Locke developed in his *Second Treatise of Government.* According to the theory of the social contract, government has been established in human societies by an agreement or contract among the members of each society to accomplish certain purposes. Many of the problems related to justice can be understood by examining the process of setting up a government and legal system and by identifying the difficulties that have to be overcome if justice is to be achieved.

Locke argued that there was a time when people lived without a government or any human authority to regulate their conduct. Even if his argument was incorrect—if there never was a time without some government—it is nevertheless interesting to ask what human life would be like if there were no governmental authority. Answering this question can reveal the very purpose and function of government and of the legal system that it establishes.

Without government, says Locke, human beings are in "a state of perfect freedom to order their actions, and dispose of their possesssions and persons as they think fit, within the bounds of the law of Nature, without asking leave, or depending upon the will of any other man."[1] This condition of perfect freedom Locke calls the **state of nature.** Even though the state of nature lacks a system of laws, the conduct of individuals should still be guided by the precepts of morality. These precepts Locke calls the law of nature, or **natural law:**

> The state of Nature has a law of Nature to govern it, which obliges every one:
> And reason, which is that law, teaches all mankind who will but consult it, that

[1]John Locke, *The Second Treatise of Government,* par. 4. (This book was first published in 1690.)

being all equal and independent, no one ought to harm another in his life, health, liberty, or possessions.[2]

The term *natural law* has a long history. Locke was not the first to use it. It has its roots in Greek philosophy and was used by philosophers during the Middle Ages. By calling the laws of morality *natural,* Locke meant to imply two things. First, a natural law differs from a law that is established by a legislature, by the courts, or by human agreement—called a **positive law**—in that it is not established by human beings. They do not create it but discover it. According to Locke, the most important law of nature is that one ought not to harm or injure another—destroy his life, injure his health, reduce his liberty, or intefere with his property in any way.

Second, by calling these laws natural Locke implies that the ordinary human being is capable of learning what they require of him. Each individual has a rational capacity enabling him to determine his rights and obligations. He does not need to rely upon authority or supernatural guidance. Even though these laws were laid down by God, man has been created by God with the capacity to discover them on his own.

The Transition to Government

THE INCONVENIENCE OF THE STATE OF NATURE

In the state of nature, each person has the right to defend himself and his property against those who violate his rights. Furthermore, each has the right to punish those who violate the laws of nature and the rights of others. Thus, in the state of nature the enforcement of the laws of nature is up to each individual. As Locke sees it, a great inconvenience results: Because each individual is a judge in his own case, there is no impartial authority to settle disputes. Each person decides when his rights have been violated and when he has the right to punish someone else. But since individuals are invariably prejudiced in their own favor, they tend to retaliate even when they are not justified in doing so. The absence of an impartial authority makes it very difficult to settle disputes. As a result, there is a great deal of conflict in the state of nature and an ever-present threat of war among individuals. For Locke, "civil government is the proper remedy for the inconveniences of the state of Nature, which must certainly be great where men may be judges in their own case."[3]

To form a government, those living in a state of nature must agree to give up their right to punish those who violate the laws of nature and to transfer their right to the political authorities:

> There only is political society, where every one of the members hath quitted this natural power, resign'd it up into the hands of the community in all cases that exclude him not from appealing for protection to the law established by it. And

[2]Ibid., par. 6.
[3]Ibid., par. 13.

thus all private judgment of every particular member, being excluded, the community comes to be umpire, by settled standing rules, indifferent, and the same to all parties; and by men having authority from the community, for the execution of those rules, decides all the differences that may happen between any members of that society, concerning any matter of right; and punishes those offences, which any member hath committed against the society, with such penalties as the law has established.[4]

THE RULE OF LAW

The key idea in understanding the transition from the state of nature to political society is the **rule of law.** Instead of disputes being decided by individuals who act as judges in their own case, the government lays down laws that are "settled standing rules, indifferent, and the same to all parties." Under government, no one is required to live under the arbitrary will of another person:

> But freedom of men under government, is, to have a standing rule to live by, common to everyone of that society, and made by the legislative power erected in it; A liberty to follow my own will in all things, where the rule prescribes not; and not to be subject to the inconstant, uncertain, unknown, arbitrary will of another man.[5]

For Locke, political freedom presupposes the rule of law. To be governed by laws and not by men means that the political authorities are bound to act in accordance with general rules established by a legislative body in accordance with majority rule. The authorities shall have no discretion to decide cases according to their own personal wishes or interests.

The rule of law is part of justice according to which the members of the society are treated fairly and impartially. But it needs to be analyzed further. First, for there to be a rule of law, the legislature must establish laws applicable to everyone. No exceptions should be made for the rich and the powerful. Second, under the rule of law it is required that the administration of justice be fair. Even if the laws themselves make no unfair exceptions, it is not uncommon for judges and police and those who enforce the law to favor the rich and powerful over the poor and weak. A society displays *administrative justice* if those whose job it is to enforce the law act impartially and fairly, without fear or prejudice. A society embodies *justice under the law* if there are general rules applicable to all citizens and if those who administer justice apply the rules fairly.

If, however, the laws themselves are unfair, then even a society that embodies justice under the law may be unjust in other respects. Consider a society in which segregated school systems are legal. The rules apply to everyone; everyone is required to attend school only with members of his own race or religion. Though these rules are applied impartially, they discriminate unfairly against certain individuals and groups.

[4]Ibid., par. 87.
[5]Ibid., par. 21.

EQUALITY AND DISCRIMINATION

To have a rule of law, not only must the laws be applied impartially but there must also be no unfair discrimination in the content of the laws themselves. Notice that it is only *unfair* discrimination that is not allowed. Fair discrimination is permitted. For example, the income tax laws in the United States are progressive in that those who earn more income are required to pay taxes at a higher rate. These tax laws thus discriminate against those who earn more and discriminate in favor of those who earn less. But the legislators who established the progressive income tax believed that this discrimination was justified and that individuals ought to pay taxes according to their ability to pay.

What, then, is unfair discrimination? Why are the progressive tax laws thought to be fair whereas racially segregated public schools are condemned as unfair? To begin with, equality is, as we have noted, a basic component of justice, and one of the most important types of equality is **formal equality,** in which like cases are treated alike. For example, if two individuals of similar background and in similar circumstances commit the same crime, they should receive the same sentence. It would be a violation of the principle of formal equality to impose a harsher penalty upon one because of, say, race. Similarly, it would be a violation of formal equality to pay the members of one sex more for doing the same job under the same conditions.

When are cases alike and when are they different? Every situation is unique, differing from all others in some respects. How can we tell which differences matter and which do not? In our society we think that differences in race or religion or gender should not affect employment and educational opportunities. But differences in ability are thought to matter. Why does ability matter but not race or religion or sex? The answer generally given is that the only differences that matter are those that are relevant to the case at hand. Differences in ability *are* relevant to career opportunities; they provide good reasons for discrimination. But differences in race, religion, and sex do not provide good reasons for discrimination in employment or in wages and hence are not relevant. For example, the only good reasons for denying someone the position of dean of the college must be based upon the expected quality of his or her work. Race or sex or religion need have nothing to do with how someone functions on that job, and using any one of them as the basis of discrimination is wrong for two reasons. First, it means the denial of opportunities to people for reasons that have nothing to do with their qualifications. Second, this unjustified denial of opportunity harms those who are discriminated against by denying them benefits they otherwise would have earned and by displaying disrespect for them as persons.

If racial or religious or sexual discrimination is so obviously unjust, why do people engage in it in the first place? What is the source of prejudice? There is no simple answer. In some cases, people have developed irrational hostilities toward a given race or religion because of things that they were told while they were growing up. For example, hostility to Jewish people may result from a child's being taught that the Jews were responsible for the crucifixion of Jesus. Prejudice against certain races and ethnic groups is often encouraged by the widespread practice of making derogatory remarks about their intelligence or ability. Prejudice against women is often based upon the traditional notion that women operate best when they stay home, keep house, and rear children. Sometimes unjustified discrimination is used to maintain a system of economic exploitation, as occurs in societies characterized by slavery or male domination. There can be various motives for treating equals unequally, for violating the precept of formal equality. Prejudice seems to come easily to human beings and has been responsible for some of the most awful crimes in history.

It is an interesting question whether utilitarianism can account for the principle of formal equality. If we treat equal cases equally, will that always lead to the greatest happiness for the greatest number? It is really very difficult to say. The Aztec system of human sacrifice was obviously a violation of formal equality, among other things; prisoners of war were no more qualified to be murdered and eaten than anyone else. Yet it is not obvious that the pains outweighed the benefits. Often, we have no way of telling what does and does not maximize happiness. For instance, enslaving a minority may lead to great happiness for the majority. As a result of the system of slavery, the men of ancient Athens were liberated from physical toil and permitted the time and leisure to create works of art, systems of philosophy, dramas, and poems that have provided enjoyment to countless numbers of persons ever since that time. The results may have been beneficial on the whole. It is thus unlikely that utilitarianism can explain the great offence involved in violations of formal equality.

Kant's principles provide a better justification of formal equality. When an individual is denied an opportunity because of race or religion or gender, his or her interests have been neglected for no good reason. Such violations of formal equality represent a lack of respect for the persons injured and a failure to regard their interests and well-being equally. They may feel like victims rather than like persons, as if they were mere things unworthy of respect. When formal equality is violated, people are not being treated as ends in themselves.

Punishment

LOCKE'S ACCOUNT OF PUNISHMENT

According to Locke, as long as people live in the state of nature, each is entitled to punish those who violate the laws of nature. When government is introduced, the authorities assume the function of punishment. For Locke, punishment has several purposes. First, a person who injures someone is likely to be a threat to other innocent persons. By imprisoning or killing him, the innocent are protected. In addition, punishing someone who breaks the law sets an example for others who may be tempted to break the law as well, thereby functioning to deter individuals from causing harm. Thus, the practice of punishing those who violate the laws of nature finds its rationale in the protection of the innocent and in the deterrence of others from committing like crimes.

As far as the amount of punishment is concerned, Locke formulates the following general principle:

> Each transgression may be punished to that degree, and with so much severity as will suffice to make it an ill bargain to the offender, give him cause to repent, and terrify others from doing the like.[6]

The amount of punishment should be determined by what is necessary for protection and deterrence. In particular, a murderer may be justifiably punished by the death penalty:

> Every man in the state of Nature, has a power to kill a murderer, both to deter others from doing the like injury, which no reparation can compensate, by the example of the punishment that attends it from every body, and also to secure men from the attempts of a criminal, who having renounced reason, the common rule and measure, God hath given to mankind, hath by the unjust violence and slaughter he hath committed upon one, declared war against all mankind, and therefore may be destroyed as a lion or a tiger, one of those wild savage beasts, with whom men can have no society nor security.[7]

For Locke, a murderer is like a savage beast. Just as a beast that threatens humans may be destroyed, so may society punish a murderer with death.

UTILITARIAN THEORIES OF PUNISHMENT

Locke's theory of punishment is essentially utilitarian. Utilitarianism claims that punishment is justified because of its allegedly beneficial results. In general, when a person is punished, he suffers pain or some form of unhappiness. Because pain is always bad, according to the utilitarian, the practice of punishment can be justified only if its benefits outweigh the harm it causes. Utilitarians agree with Locke that protection and deterrence are two of the important benefits that punishment provides. The amount of punishment should never be greater than is necessary to satisfy these purposes. The greater the degree of protection and deterrence that a society requires to provide security and a sense of safety, the greater is the severity of the punishment that is permitted.

In addition to protection and deterrence, utilitarians often include reform or rehabilitation as a third purpose of punishment. Because Locke suggests that punishment should be sufficient to make the criminal repent of his crime, he would have acknowledged this purpose as well. The general aim of rehabilitation is to bring about changes in the criminal that will make his continuing a life of crime less likely. One form of rehabilitation is moral reform in which the criminal comes to regret having done wrong and vows not to do so in the future. Or the criminal may have found punishment so distasteful that he agrees to abjure crime just to avoid being punished again. Often programs of rehabilitation are designed to equip the prisoner with the skills and attitudes necessary for him to earn an honest living and become a useful member of society.

[6]Ibid., par. 12.
[7]Ibid., par. 11.

RETRIBUTIVE THEORIES OF PUNISHMENT

The utilitarian approach to punishment has often been severely criticized. Its basic difficulty is that it ignores the most fundamental rationale for punishment, namely, that because of his crime, the criminal *deserves* to suffer. According to *retributive theories of punishment,* a society is justified in inflicting the pain and suffering of punishment only if it is judged that a criminal deserves this treatment. Justice means giving each person what he deserves, and the degree of punishment deserved is determined by determining the individual's degree of guilt. Thus, punishment is just only to the extent that it is inflicted upon those who deserve it and to the extent to which they deserve it. The problem with the utilitarian approach is that it justifies inflicting suffering upon individuals without regard to merit.

For example, society may decide to punish a minor crime such as pickpocketing with a severe penalty to deter others. Although giving a life sentence to a pickpocket may be justifiable on utilitarian grounds, so severe a penalty for so minor a crime would be unjust, according to the retributivist. F. H. Bradley (1846–1924) provides a clear formulation of the retributivist view:

> Punishment is punishment, only where it is deserved. We pay the penalty, because we owe it, and for no other reason; and if punishment is inflicted for any other reason whatever than because it is merited by wrong, it is a gross immorality, a crying injustice, an abominable crime, and not what it pretends to be. We may have regard for whatever considerations we please—our own convenience, the good of society, the benefit of the offender; we are fools, and worse, if we fail to do so. Having once the right to punish, we may modify the punishment according to the useful and the pleasant; but these are external to the matter, they cannot give us a right to punish, and nothing can do that but criminal desert.[8]

Bradley claims that although the degree of punishment may be modified according to utilitarian considerations, we are not entitled to use the expected benefits of punishment to do an injustice to a criminal.

Kant himself thought that a retributive approach is implied by his basic ethical theory:

> Judicial punishment can never be used merely as a means to promote some other good for the criminal himself or for civil society, but instead it must in all cases be imposed on him only on the ground that he has committed a crime; for a human being can never be manipulated merely as a means to the purposes of someone else and can never be confused with the objects of the law of things. . . . He must first be found deserving of punishment before any consideration is given to the utility of this punishment for himself or for his fellow citizens. The law concerning punishment is a categorical imperative, and woe to him who

---

[8]F. H. Bradley, *Ethical Studies* (Oxford: The Clarendon Press, 1952), pp. 26–27. (This book was first published in 1876.)

rummages around in the winding paths of a theory of happiness looking for some advantage to be gained by releasing the criminal from punishment or by reducing the amount of it.[9]

For Kant, it would be in violation of the supreme principle of morality—that individuals should never be treated merely as means to someone else's purposes—to base one's treatment of the criminal on the expected social benefits of a certain punishment. To treat the criminal as a person, as an end in himself, it is necessary to give him just as much as he deserves, no more and no less.

Because the criminal is a person, he is entitled to receive what his conduct is worth. This is justice. And this means that if he has committed murder, he must die. Thus, Kant writes:

> If, however, he has committed murder, he must die. In this case, there is no substitute that will satisfy the requirements of legal justice. There is no sameness of kind between death and remaining alive even under the most miserable conditions. And consequently there is also no equality between the crime and the retribution unless the criminal is judicially condemned and put to death. But the death of the criminal must be kept entirely free of any maltreatment that would make an abomination of the humanity residing in the person suffering it. Even if a civil society were to dissolve itself by common agreement of all its members (for example, if the people inhabiting an island decided to separate and disperse themselves around the world), the last murderer remaining in prison must first be executed, so that everyone will duly receive what his actions are worth. . . .[10]

Because the criminal is required to receive the same type of treatment that he has inflicted, the murderer himself must be killed. If he were allowed to remain alive, says Kant, then he would be receiving less than he deserved and an injustice would be done both to him and to his victim.

CRITICISMS OF RETRIBUTIVE THEORIES

From the utilitarian point of view, the retributive approach has major faults. First, retribution could be regarded as merely a form of revenge, and revenge is a primitive and uncivilized response to crime. Of course, the retributivist can reply by denying that revenge and retribution are the same. Whereas retribution is applied in proportion to what the criminal deserves, revenge is not limited by any such consideration. A person may seek vengeance by harming someone who does not deserve punishment at all. For example, a man may kill the innocent children of his enemy. This may be revenge, but it is not justice. Moreover, whereas revenge is a private action inflicted by the one who thinks himself wronged, retributive punishment is meted out by the judicial arm of the government, which is supposed to decide impartially the penalty that justice requires.

[9]Immanuel Kant, *The Metaphysical Elements of Justice,* trans. John Ladd (Indianapolis: Bobbs-Merrill, 1965), p. 100.
[10]Ibid., p. 102.

Second, the utilitarian can find no positive value in retributive punishment. Remember that for the utilitarian the only thing that is good in itself is pleasure, and the only thing that is bad in itself is pain. Because punishment involves inflicting pain, it is considered bad in itself. The harm that the criminal caused is also bad. The utilitarian cannot understand how adding one bad thing (punishment) to another bad thing (the crime) yields something good (justice). The addition of bad to bad can only lead to what is bad. The retributivist replies that normally when a bad thing is added to a bad thing the result is usually bad. But he adds that in those cases in which someone deserves having something bad happen to him, the result is something good in itself, namely, justice. The retributivist argues that there are things intrinsically good and bad other than pleasure and pain. Justice, for example, is an intrinsic good, and injustice an intrinsic bad.

A third major criticism of the retributivist approach is its unintelligibility. For the utilitarian, the very idea of moral desert is problematic. Some utilitarians have doubted that human beings have free will; this has led them to wonder whether people are ever to blame for their conduct. The question of free will will be considered in Chapter Five. But putting aside the question of free will and responsibility, the utilitarian wonders whether one can ever really tell whether another person deserves pain and how much pain he deserves. The utilitarian points out that we can tell how much protection and deterrence will result from a certain level of punishment. Determining the causal influence of various forms and degrees of punishment is a matter of social observation. But what sort of observation can reveal how much punishment is truly deserved? What methods can be used to verify statements of the form "Person A deserves penalty D"? We can tell that penalty D will provide others with a certain degree of protection from person A. But, from an observational point of view, the idea of desert seems mysterious.

To this argument the retributivist replies that often we do make judgments about merit, that such judgments can be discussed and criticized, and consequently are possible and can be made by the ordinary person with such intellectual equipment as he possesses. People generally agree that a pickpocket deserves a lesser penalty than does a murderer because petty theft is a less severe crime. We are able to rank both crimes and penalties in order of severity and then match a penalty to a crime. There may, of course, be an element of imprecision and arbitrariness in fitting the punishment to the crime. The German philosopher Georg Wilhelm Friedrich Hegel (1770–1831) emphasized this point:

> Reason cannot determine, nor can the concept provide any principle whose application could decide whether justice requires for an offence (i) a corporal punishment of forty lashes or thirty-nine, or (ii) a fine of five dollars or four dollars ninety-three, four, etc. cents, or (iii) imprisonment of a year or three hundred and sixty-four, three, etc. days, or a year and one, two, or three days. And yet injustice is done at once if there is one lash too many, or one dollar or one cent, or one week in prison or one day, too many or too few.[11]

---

[11]G. W. F. Hegel, *Philosophy of Right,* trans. T. M. Knox (Oxford: The Clarendon Press, 1958), p. 137. (This book was first published in 1821.)

But this imprecision, says Hegel, should not make us hesitate to apply punishment. "This vacillation must be terminated, however, in the interest of getting something done, and for this reason there is a place . . . for contingent and arbitrary decisions."[12]

CAPITAL PUNISHMENT

Both utilitarian and retributive theories may be used to defend capital punishment, or the death penalty, but most contemporary criticisms use utilitarian arguments. The penalty acceptable to utilitarianism depends upon the facts of the case. If the death penalty deters, then that is an argument in its favor. If it fails to deter, then that is a reason to oppose it. Critics claim that the death penalty does not in fact deter others from committing murder. Retributivists, however, tend to favor the death penalty whether or not it deters because execution seems to them a particularly fitting penalty for the taking of human life.

Some opponents of capital punishment argue their case upon quite a different ground—the existence of a right to life. They argue that no one, and in particular no governmental authority, has the right to take the life of a human being. Most modern ethical theories incorporate the right to life as one of the fundamental human rights. If there were no such right, then governmental authorities would lack the right to defend their citizens from attack by criminals and invaders. But it is implausible to argue that no one can ever have a valid reason for taking the life of another. Most ethical theories agree that a person or a society is entitled to take a human life if doing so is a necessary means of defending the life of an innocent person.

Opponents of the death penalty point out that executing a murderer is not a necessary means of protecting the lives of others. Keeping the murderer locked up in prison provides protection without violating the right to life. Though the utilitarian may argue that it is cheaper to execute a murderer than to maintain him at public expense for a long period of time, some opponents of the death penalty argue that the right to life is so fundamental that it should not be violated for purely economic reasons, particularly when the cost of maintaining the life of a murderer represents a negligible sacrifice for the average citizen. It would seem then that retributivism offers the best argument for the death penalty and that the appeal to the right to life is the firmest basis for opposing it.

Property

Our discussion has suggested that to determine whether a society is just, we must find out the extent to which individuals in it live under the rule of law, the extent to which they are treated in accordance with the principle of formal equality, and the extent to which the methods of punishment are fair and reasonable. Another important feature of a just society is that the procedure it employs to distribute property, wealth, and wages among its citizens is fair. We turn now to the topic of distributive justice.

[12]Ibid.

There is a difference between possession and property. If I lend you my pen, then even though you have it in your possession, it still remains my property, not yours. If you rent a house from someone, you are not its owner even though you occupy it. It is not your property. When a person owns something as distinct from merely possessing or occupying it, then he has a right to the use of it and a right to decide what is to be done with it. Because I own this pen, I can use it for writing, I can lend it, I can give it away, and I can throw it away. The concept of property implies the idea of a right to the exclusive use of something. This use may be limited in various ways. I am not entitled to use an object to break the law. For example, it would be illegal for me to use my pen to forge a check. In addition, society may decide to place various restrictions on the ways people use property. Zoning regulations, for example, may prevent businesses from building factories in residential areas. And even if I operate a factory in a permitted area, I may be required to take care that no pollutants spill into adjacent streams.

What first comes to mind when one thinks of property is generally the *personal goods* that individuals consume or use. Examples include food, clothing, housing, tools, and so forth. But not all consumables are property. The air we breathe is not owned by anyone, though in principle, it could become property. The government could decide that it owns the air and that it will tax individuals for the use of it. The tax could be proportional to the amount of air that an individual breathes. That we might someday purchase air from the government or from some individual or group that has appropriated it may be a fanciful idea, but it does emphasize the point that the underlying motive for imposing property rights upon a commodity is its relative scarcity. Because the air we breathe is not (yet) scarce, it is not necessary to restrict its use by the imposition of property rights.

Public goods are items of property that are owned by the government or by society. A public park, an aircraft carrier, a highway, and the Washington Monument are public goods that are made available for use by various arrangements. A public park, for instance, is normally available for anyone's use during the time it is open. An aircraft carrier can be used only by members of the armed forces authorized to perform certain tasks. A highway can be used by anyone willing to pay the toll, or if it is not a toll road, by any vehicle except those in restricted classes such as trucks over a certain weight.

Other items of property do not imply the rights of consumption and use. For example, a person may own shares of stock in a corporation. Although a shareholder in a corporation may be thought of as one of its owners, he does not have the right to consume any of the goods that the corporation manufactures or to use any item that the corporation owns. Just because I own stock in General Motors, I am not entitled to drive a new Chevrolet home for my use or to take my place on the factory assembly line. The ownership of stock gives me the right to vote at meetings of shareholders, to receive dividends should they be issued, and to buy and sell stock on the market. A teacher who has received tenure may be thought to own his or her job. A person who contributes to a pension plan may be thought to own an annuity that he or his survivors will receive in the future. Some of the most important forms of property in the modern world are *intangible goods* of these kinds.

Liberal Individualistic Theories of Property

LOCKE'S THEORY

Disputes about the best way to distribute property among the members of society are among the major sources of social conflict in the modern world. Debates among advocates of capitalism, socialism, and communism partly represent disagreements over theories of distribution. Many issues in American politics concern "who gets what, when, how."[13] Our present interest lies in the moral dimension of these issues, and the question we will now consider is, What forms and methods of distribution are just? I shall begin by presenting Locke's theory of property. This is a version of what is often called *the liberal theory of property*. In the history of modern Europe and the United States, **liberalism** has been that political orientation which has emphasized the value of personal liberty. The liberal approach to questions of distributive justice recommends methods of distribution designed to maximize personal liberty. In recent American politics, the term *liberalism* has acquired a new meaning, referring to welfare policies that favor the redistribution of wealth to the poor and underprivileged. Even though there is historical continuity between the older and the more recent forms of liberalism, we need somehow to resolve the terminological ambiguity. To do so, I shall refer to the older liberalism as **individualism** and the new form as **welfare state liberalism.**

For Locke, one of the primary functions of government is to protect property. "Government has no other end but the preservation of property."[14] Remember that, according to Locke, the functions of government are determined by those inconveniences in the state of nature that government was introduced to remedy. The insecurity of property and the fact that it was difficult to settle disputes about property without force were among the major inconveniences.

Locke thought that God created the earth for the use and enjoyment of all humankind. Thus, the initial problem for Locke is to understand how an individual acquires the right to appropriate and consume particular items from the common stock of goods. What right does an individual have to appropriate for his own use and consumption what belongs to everyone? Locke founds his *theory of original acquisition* on labor:

> Though the earth, and all inferior creatures be common to all men, yet every man has a property in his own person. This no body has any right to but himself. The labour of his body, and the work of his hands, we may say, are properly his. Whatsoever then he removes out of the state that Nature hath provided, and left it in, he hath mixed his labour with, and joined to it something that is his own, and thereby makes it his property. It being by him removed from the common state Nature placed it in, hath by this labour something annexed to it, that excludes the common right of other men. For this labour being the unquestionable property of the labourer, no man but he can have a right to what

---

[13]See Harold D. Lasswell, *Politics: Who Gets What, When, How* (New York: World Publishing Co., 1968).
[14]Locke, *Second Treatise*, par. 94.

that was once joined to, at least where there is enough, and as good left in common for others.[15]

Locke assumes that there is an exception to the general rule that all things are originally held in common. Each individual owns his own labor, his capacity to work. Labor is not part of the common stock of goods. Therefore, no individual in the state of nature is accountable to others for the use of his labor. Locke then argues that because each owns his own labor, whatever items he removes from the common stock by his own labor are his to consume. If a person picks an apple from a tree, then because he acquired it by his own efforts, the apple becomes his. Similarly, a person comes to own land by farming it.

Locke argues that there are limits to what a person is entitled to appropriate from the common stock of goods. First, Locke assumes that the state of nature contains a surplus of goods and that there is no shortage in what is essential for life. He then states that appropriation may continue as long as there is enough left for others. Leaving enough for others is protection against someone's monopolizing the stock of any good. Second, one can appropriate only as much of an item as one can use without any spoilage or waste. If I want to eat three apples and only three apples, then I may pick no more than three from the tree. Man has no right to spoil what God has created. Nature exists for man's use.

According to the method of original acquisition, because people's appetites and their ability to consume are approximately equal, the amount of goods owned by each individual will also be approximately equal. Inequality arises, says Locke, from the invention of money:

> That the same rule of propriety, (viz.) that every man should have as much as he
> could make use of, would hold still in the world, without straitning any body,
> since there is land enough in the world to suffice double the inhabitants had not
> the invention of money, and the tacit agreement of men to put a value on it,
> introduced (by consent) larger possessions, and a right to them.[16]

Money leads to justifiable inequality because individuals can acquire an unlimited amount of money without violating the rule against spoilage. Money is a good that does not spoil. It usually exists in the form of a metal such as gold or silver, which can last indefinitely.

Another reason why this inequality is justified, according to Locke, is that men have consented to it:

> Men have agreed to disproportionate and unequal possession of the earth, they
> having by a tacit and voluntary consent found out a way, how a man may fairly
> possess more land than he himself can use the product of, by receiving in
> exchange for the overplus, gold and silver, which may be hoarded up without
> injury to any one, these metals not spoiling or decaying in the hands of the

[15]Ibid., par. 27.
[16]Ibid., par. 36.

possessor. This partage of things, in an inequality of private possessions, men have made practicable out of the bounds of society, and without compact, only by putting a value on gold and silver and tacitly agreeing in the use of money. For in governments the laws regulate the right of property, and the possession of land is determined by positive constitutions.[17]

The value of money is determined by human agreement. For example, that I can use a dollar bill to purchase a given quantity of goods depends upon the fact that individual buyers and sellers place a certain value on the dollar. In itself, a dollar bill has little or no value. Its buying power is the result of a tacit understanding among those who participate in production and exchange. Locke assumes that because the value of money rests upon consent, then men have also consented to all the inequalities that flow from the use of it. But this justification of inequality is unconvincing. It is not true that individuals always agree to all the consequences of what they have agreed to. If, after observing how an agreement has worked out, the participants conclude that the results have been disastrous, they may very well reconsider their original understanding.

A CONTEMPORARY THEORY OF PROPERTY

A contemporary version of Locke's theory of distributive justice has been developed by Robert Nozick.[18] He is concerned not so much with the question of how property is originally acquired as with the question of the justice of the transfer of property from one individual to another. A good deal of economic activity consists of property transfer. If I buy something from you, then I transfer some of my money to you and you transfer a commodity to me. This kind of property transfer is an economic exchange. There are other kinds. A thief may rob me and thus transfer my money into his pocket. The state may tax me and transfer my money into the pocket of some other citizen. The question is to distinguish between just and unjust transfers.

For Nozick, as for all individualist approaches generally, those transfers are just which are the results of voluntary agreements among individuals. Consider, for instance, the standard case of buying and selling. If I go into a store to buy some oranges, then in effect I have formed an agreement with the proprietor to transfer some of my money to him in exchange for the oranges. I get the oranges; he receives the money; we both agreed to the transaction. Consider again the standard labor contract. A person owns a business and needs someone to work for him. I am able and willing to work in this business. The employer and I strike up a bargain according to which I shall work for a certain length of time and shall recieve a specified salary in return. There are other kinds of voluntary exchanges. I may give something to someone as a gift. My wife may agree to pay some of my expenses. I may gamble and win money or I may receive interest from a bank account or returns on an investment. In each case, the transfer of money or goods is voluntary.

A voluntary transfer of money or goods from one person to another is just. For Noz-

---

[17]Ibid., par. 50.
[18]Robert Nozick, *Anarchy, State, and Utopia* (New York: Basic Books, 1974), chap. 7.

ick, if a group of people have acquired everything that they own justly, then the distribution that results from a series of subsequent voluntary transfers is also just. For example, suppose three individuals start off with $1,000 of goods and money each. After a series of voluntary transactions with each other, person A has $500, person B has $750 and person C has $1,750. Perhaps A gave $500 to C and B gave $250 to C. Or perhaps C invented a product that A and B purchased. The resulting inequality is just. "Whatever arises from a just situation by just steps is itself just."[19]

For individualism, a nonvoluntary transfer violates the rights of individuals. A nonvoluntary transfer is one in which an individual is forced against his will or without prior agreement to yield some of his property to another. If a thief steals the wages that I have justly earned, he violates my right to do as I will with the money. If the government forces individuals to pay some of their earnings in the form of taxes, it violates their right to use their income as they choose. According to the individualist, if people are left alone to engage in production and exchange in whatever ways they choose, there will arise substantial inequalities in wealth. These inequalities arise naturally as a result of differences among human beings. Some people work harder than others or are more intelligent or more prudent or are luckier. If the inequalities are the consequences of just transfers and exchanges, there is nothing morally wrong with them. Economic equality is not a fundamental value for individualism.

Other theories of justice have condemned the large inequalities that exist in modern society as unjust. The individualist concedes that those that result from unjust practices such as monopoly, fraud, conquest, and other forms of aggression are indeed unjust. But if they are not the result of unjust practices, if they are merely the result of basic human differences, then they cannot be justifiably condemned. In fact, for the individualist, it is not possible to reduce these inequalities without interfering with the liberties and rights of the members of society. The only way for these inequalities to be reduced is for the government to take wealth from those who have more and distribute it to those who have less. But, says the individualist, if those who have more obtained their wealth in a just manner, then they are morally entitled to what they have. Thus, it would be a violation of their rights to appropriate their property and give it to others.

Let us consider how the individualist view applies to the governmental policy of using taxes to support social programs. In modern capitalist societies, it is often asserted that the government should foster equality of opportunity. According to this view, even though individuals end up with different amounts of wealth, they ought to have approximately equal opportunities to acquire wealth for themselves. It is therefore necessary for the government to develop various social arrangements that enable those at the bottom of the economic ladder to compete with those who are better off. In practice this means that the government provides benefits in the areas of education, health, and family assistance to bring the opportunities of the poor up to the level of the middle and upper classes. The government provides these benefits by taxing the earnings of all the people and then distributing the taxes in various ways to some of the people. Nozick claims that such efforts violate people's rights:

[19]Ibid., p. 151.

> The major objection to speaking of everyone's having a right *to* various things such as equality of opportunity, life, and so on, and enforcing this right, is that these "rights" require a substructure of things and materials and actions; and *other* people may have rights and entitlements over these. No one has a right to something whose realization requires certain uses of things and activities that other people have rights and entitlements over.[20]

If equality of opportunity can be achieved only by forcibly taking from individuals wealth they have justly acquired, then this form of equality can be achieved only at the cost of injustice and a violation of people's rights.

Nozick goes on to criticize the basic mechanism that the modern state uses to redistribute wealth—taxation. "Taxation of earnings from labor is on a par with forced labor," he writes.[21] It takes a certain number of hours for a person to earn the money that the government takes away from him in taxes. For Nozick, the government's taking this money is no different in principle from forcing him to work that number of hours for another person. For example, if it takes one hundred hours for a rich man to earn the money that is used to send a poor man to college for one year, then the rich man is being forced against his will to work one hundred hours for the poor man. The government's role in the transfer of the money merely disguises the fact that the transfer is equivalent to forced labor. For the individualist, there is as much a violation of an individual's rights when the rich man is forced to work for the poor as when the poor man is forced to work for the rich man.

For individualism, the moral structure of society is best understood by reference to the concept of a moral right. First, all individuals have certain natural rights, such as the right not to be a victim of aggression and the right to protect themselves against it. Second, individuals acquire rights over particular items of property as a result of their voluntary actions and agreements. The function of government is simply to protect these rights. Any attempt by government to provide other benefits to individuals is unjust because it entails violating the rights that the government is obligated to protect.

Economists and politicians often justify this individualist theory of justice not by reference to rights but to efficiency. The economic system that arises as a result of voluntary actions and agreements is a free market system (sometimes called **capitalism**) in which individuals can buy and sell goods and labor as they choose; it is recommended for its productive efficiency. But for many philosophers the key issue is one of ethics, not of economics. According to the liberal theories of Locke and Nozick, even if the free market system were not efficient, it would still be morally required as the only one that is consistent with the rights of individuals.

For Nozick, the foundation of the individualist theory of rights is found in the ethical theory of Kant. For both Nozick and Kant the rights of individuals represent constraints on what one person is entitled to do to another. "Side constraints upon action reflect the underlying Kantian principle that individuals are ends and not merely means; they may not be sacrificed or used for the achieving of other ends without their consent. Individ-

[20]Ibid., p. 238.
[21]Ibid., p. 169.

uals are inviolable."[22] No individual can be used just to benefit some other person. There is no supreme social good for which individuals can be sacrificed:

> Why not . . . hold that some persons have to bear some costs that benefit other persons more, for the sake of the overall social good? But there is no *social entity* with a good that undergoes some sacrifice for its own good. There are only individual people, different individual people, with their own individual lives. Using one of these people for the benefit of others, uses him and benefits the others. Nothing more. What happens is that something is done to him for the sake of others. Talk of an overall social good covers this up. . . . To use a person in this way does not sufficiently respect and take account of the fact that he is a separate person, that his is the only life he has. *He* does not get some overbalancing good from his sacrifice, and no one is entitled to force this upon him—least of all a state or government that claims his allegiance (as other individuals do not) and that therefore scrupulously must be *neutral* between its citizens.[23]

Nozick here rejects the utilitarian principle that it may be proper to sacrifice the interests of some persons to bring about a social good. There is no such thing as the good of society over and above the good of the individual people who make up society. To sacrifice an individual for the good of society is really to sacrifice his interests in favor of the interests of some other person or group of persons. Whether the person performing the sacrifice is an Aztec priest or an official of the Internal Revenue Service, the victim is nevertheless being treated unjustly.

The Radical Critique of Liberal Individualism

Individualism emphasizes the value of liberty. It was developed in the seventeenth, eighteenth, and nineteenth centuries to provide a philosophical basis for the new political and economic systems that were emerging from the feudal past. Both democracy and capitalism needed a moral backing, and individualist theories of justice succeeded in providing one. The individualist argues that you cannot have both liberty and equality in wealth. As we saw in Locke and Nozick, to reduce the inequalities in society means interfering with people's liberty.

Radicalism, on the other hand, stresses equality. The radical argues that you cannot have genuine liberty without reducing the existing inequalities, for inequalities in wealth inevitably lead to inequalities in power. The result is that a class of wealthy individuals oppresses and exploits the working class. People with wealth can control political institutions even in a democracy. They can see to the passage of legislation that maintains their privileged position while suppressing attempts by the workers to improve their lot. For the radical, the liberty that the individualist makes so much of is simply the liberty

---

[22]Ibid., pp. 30–31.
[23]Ibid., pp. 32–33.

of the workingman to work in one dehumanizing factory or other and the liberty of the owners of the means of production to use the power of the state for their own benefit.

Radicalism has taken many forms in the past 150 years, and radicals have differed among themselves as to how equality should be achieved. For some, wealth should be distributed according to how hard a person has worked. For others, a person should receive according to his needs. Others claim that income should be determined by the quality of labor. Others would emphasize the quantity of labor, the number of hours worked. But no matter how they differ, radicals generally reject the large inequalities that are thought to divide society into two classes, the rich and the poor.

Many radicals have been **socialists;** they have recommended that industry be owned and controlled by the public in the public interest and not by private individuals seeking a profit for themselves. Others have rejected socialism on the grounds that it leads to a powerful and oppressive government bureaucracy. The tyranny that has resulted from the imposition of socialism in Russia has served as a warning to radicals about what can happen when the state becomes extremely powerful. Some of those who reject socialism favor **anarchism.** This is the view that hopes that government will disappear entirely and that economic activity will be conducted by the voluntary cooperative efforts of individuals. Other radicals have become **democratic socialists;** they are suspicious of the power of the state but believe that the public ownership of the means of production can avoid tyranny if it is tied to democratic political controls.

The radical theory that I shall present in this chapter is the set of ideas developed by Karl Marx and Friedrich Engels in the mid–nineteenth century. Although neither Marx nor Engels has as well-developed an ethical theory as Kant and Mill, their criticisms of capitalist society frequently make use of certain ethical ideas. Marx is the most respected and the most frequently cited theoretician of the radical tradition. His ideas have had greater influence in contemporary history than the ideas of any other social thinker.

Marxism and Justice

CAPITALISM

Unlike the individualist, Marx does not see society as merely a group of individuals pursuing their own personal goals and needing the protection of government to fend off aggressors. Society is, rather, a structure of classes contending with each other for wealth and power. Marx and Engels begin their famous *Manifesto of the Communist Party* with this theme:

> The history of all hitherto existing society is the history of class struggles.
> Freeman and slave, patrician and plebian, lord and serf, guildmaster and
> journeyman, in a word, oppressor and oppressed, stood in constant opposition to
> one another, carried on an uninterrupted, now hidden, now open fight, a fight
> that each time ended, either in a revolutionary re-constitution of society at large,
> or in the common ruin of the contending classes. . . . Our epoch, the epoch of the

bourgeoisie, possesses, however, this distinctive feature: it has simplified the class antagonisms. Society as a whole is more and more splitting up into two great hostile camps, into two great classes directly facing each other: Bourgeoisie and Proletariat.[24]

KARL MARX
(1818–1883)

Karl Marx, who wrote influential works in philosophy, economics, and sociology, was one of the founders of European socialism. He was born in Germany and received his doctorate in philosophy from the University of Jena. In Paris he met Friedrich Engels, who became his lifelong collaborator. In 1849 he went to London where he lived until his death. He devoted his life to an analysis and critique of the capitalist system and was deeply involved in various political movements aimed at overthrowing capitalism and replacing it with communism. His most famous work (written with Engels) is the brief *Communist Manifesto* (1848) in which he calls for the overthrow of capitalism. His major work is *Das Kapital* (three volumes published in 1867, 1885, and 1894), an extensive analysis of the economic foundations of the capitalist mode of production. A good selection of the major writings of Marx and Engels is *The Marx–Engels Reader,* ed. Robert Tucker (New York: W. W. Norton and Co., 1978).

As the bourgeoisie increases its economic power, it also acquires political power to such an extent that "the executive of the modern State is but a committee for managing the common affairs of the whole bourgeoisie."[25]

For the individualist, the government or state is a neutral mechanism designed to protect the individual and to help resolve disputes. For Marx, however, the government is necessarily a means of oppression. Political power is always seized by the dominant economic classes in society, who use it to further their own interests. The neutral state of the individualist can never be realized in practice. "Political power, properly so called, is merely the organized power of one class for oppressing another."[26] For Marx, the individualist theory of justice is an attempt by philosophers to rationalize the rule of the bourgeoisie. Its view of liberty and democracy is a misinterpretation of social reality designed to create a false consciousness of society so that the citizens will willingly accept a system of oppression. Marx uses the term **ideology** to refer to those theories

---

[24]Karl Marx and Frederick Engels, *Selected Works* (Moscow: Foreign Language Publishing House, 1950), I, 33–34.
[25]Ibid., p. 35.
[26]Ibid., p. 51.

whose function it is to create and sustain a false consciousness of social reality. The individualist theory of justice is an example of an ideology.

Marx's criticism of capitalism has many aspects. One of his major criticisms echoes the ethics of Kant:

> In proportion as the bourgeoisie, i.e., capital, is developed, in the same proportion is the proletarian, the modern working class, developed—a class of labourers, who live only so long as they find work, and who find work only so long as their labour increases capital. These labourers, who must sell themselves piecemeal, are a commodity, like every other article of commerce, and are consequently exposed to all the vicissitudes of competition, to all the fluctuations of the market. Owing to the extensive use of machinery and to division of labour, the work of the proletarians has lost all individual character, and, consequently, all charm for the workman. He becomes an appendage of the machine, and it is only the most simple, most monotonous, and most easily acquired knack, that is required of him.[27]

Because his labor is bought and sold on the market like any other commodity, the worker is thus treated as a commodity, as a thing rather than as a human being capable of a rich and dignified existence. For Marx, the market fails to treat persons as ends in themselves and thus alienates them from their humanity. If they are no longer needed, they are thrown out of work and left to starve. Recurring economic crises lead to prolonged periods of unemployment and reductions in wages. Because the division of labor requires each worker to perform a simple and repetitive task using a machine, work itself becomes monotonous and boring. In addition, the extraordinary length of the working day and the unsanitary conditions in the factory destroy the health and well-being of the workers.

Marx is particularly incensed by the long hours that men, women, and even very small children were forced to labor to earn their subsistence:

> But in its blind unrestrainable passion, its were-wolf hunger for surplus-labour, capital oversteps not only the moral, but even the merely physical maximum bounds of the working-day. It usurps the time for growth, development, and healthy maintenance of the body. It steals the time required for the consumption of fresh air and sunlight. It higgles over meal-time, incorporating it where possible with the process of production itself, so that food is given to the labourer as to a mere means of production, as coal is supplied to the boiler, grease and oil to the machinery.... The capitalist mode of production ... produces thus, with the extension of the working day, not only the deterioration of human labour-power by robbing it of its normal, moral and physical, conditions of development and function. It produces also the premature exhaustion and death of this labour-power itself. It extends the labourer's time of production during a given period by shortening his actual lifetime.[28]

[27]Ibid., pp. 38–39.
[28]Karl Marx, *Capital: A Critique of Political Economy,* trans. Samuel Moore and Edward Aveling (New York: International Publishers, 1967), pp. 264–265.

Whereas in some passages, Marx's criticism echoes the ethics of Kant, in passages like these there is a utilitarian aspect to his criticism. Capitalism harms the worker, physically and mentally. It is bad for his overall welfare.

SURPLUS VALUE

Marx's major criticism of capitalism is based upon his theory of **surplus value.** In a factory, the workers transform raw materials into a finished product. For example, in a spinning factory cotton is transformed into yarn. The finished product has more value than the raw materials. For Marx, the source of this value is the work that has been expended to create the finished product. Because the value of a commodity is determined by the labor used in producing it, the measure of that value is the time that it takes the worker to produce it.

> A use-value, or useful article, therefore, has value only because human labour in the abstract has been embodied or materialised in it. How, then, is the magnitude of this value to be measured? Plainly by the quantity of the value-creating substance, the labour contained in the article. The quantity of labour, however, is measured by its duration, and labour-time in its turn finds its standard in weeks, days, and hours. . . . That which determines the magnitude of the value of any article is the amount of the labour-time socially necessary for its production. . . . Commodities, therefore, in which equal quantities of labour are embodied, or which can be produced in the same time, have the same value.[29]

The labor power of the worker is itself a commodity that is bought and sold on the market. It too has a value just like any other commodity. What is the value of the worker's labor power? According to Marx, this value is determined by the amount of labor necessary to provide the worker with the means of subsistence. This value is represented by the wages that the worker receives.

Marx's main idea is that the value of the commodities that the worker produces in the factory is greater than the value of the commodities that he receives to support himself. This difference Marx calls surplus value.

> The action of labour-power, therefore, not only reproduces its own value, but produces value over and above it. This surplus value is the difference between the value of the product and the value of the elements consumed in the formation of that product, in other words, of the means of production and the labour-power.[30]

Let me illustrate the idea of surplus value by a simplified example. Suppose a worker labors in a spinning factory for fourteen hours on a given day, producing twenty pounds of yarn. The value of this yarn is measured by the fourteen hours that were needed to produce it. Suppose, however, that it takes only seven hours for other workers to produce the amount necessary to sustain this worker for one day and that he thus receives in the

[29]Ibid., pp. 38–39.
[30]Ibid., p. 208.

form of wages the monetary equivalent of seven hours' labor. The surplus value is represented by fourteen hours less seven hours, that is, seven hours. This means that the value that the worker creates is twice the value that he receives in wages. The surplus that he does not receive goes to the capitalist in the form of profits.

Marx thinks that the existence of surplus value is a form of exploitation, or unjust treatment. "The rate of surplus-value is therefore an exact expression for the degree of exploitation of labour-power by capital, or of the labourer by the capitalist."[31] The very system by which the owner of the means of production derives his profits exploits the worker. But why is surplus value unjust? A passage by Engels suggests the reasons:

> It was shown [by Marx] that the appropriation of unpaid labour is the basis of
> the capitalist mode of production, and of the exploitation of the worker that
> occurs under it; that even if the capitalist buys the labour power of his labourer
> at its full value as a commodity on the market, he yet extracts more value from it
> than he paid for; and that in the ultimate analysis this surplus-value forms those
> sums of value from which are heaped up the constantly increasing masses of
> capital in the hands of the possessing classes.[32]

Surplus value is unjust because the worker creates more value than he receives. It is also unjust because a substantial portion of the work he does is not paid for. Finally, it is unjust because someone who does not work in the factory receives a substantial amount of the value created by the worker in the form of profits. The general ethical principle underlying the claim that surplus value is exploitative is the requirement that individuals should receive the full value of what they produce by their labor. Surplus value may be interpreted as an example of unequal treatment and hence a violation of formal equality. Whereas the members of the working class must work to receive remuneration, surplus value makes it possible for the owners of the means of production to receive an income without doing any productive labor. But what ought to be relevant to the income one receives is how hard one works, as measured by the length of the working day. Thus, the owner and the worker are treated unequally for irrelevant reasons.

REVOLUTION

What is to be done? Marx does not believe that the capitalist system can be reformed. The degradation that the worker experiences is the result of the inexorable working out of economic forces: The worker is forced to create surplus value simply to live, and the capitalist is forced to accept surplus value as a condition of staying in business. For Marx, the evils of capitalism do not result from the unjust actions of bad people but are inherent in the system. Even if the workers' lot could be ameliorated by shortening the working day and improving conditions on the factory floor, the injustice of surplus value would still exist. This injustice will disappear only with the disappearance of capitalism itself.

[31]Ibid., p. 218.
[32]Marx and Engels, *Selected Works,* II, 124–125.

For these reasons Marx looks forward to a revolutionary transformation of society in which the capitalist mode of production will be replaced by communism. There will be a political revolution in which the working class takes power.

> Between capitalist and communist society lies the period of the revolutionary transformation of the one into the other. There corresponds to this also a political transition period in which the state can be nothing but *the revolutionary dictatorship of the proletariat.*[33]

It is not clear what Marx has in mind by his use of the controversial phrase "the dictatorship of the proletariat." Opponents of communism often refer to this phrase as evidence of the undemocratic aspect of Marxist theory. In any case, Marx was no friend to the state or to dictatorships and hoped that in the long run the state would wither away and finally disappear.

Immediately after the revolutionary transformation of capitalism into communism, the form of the distribution of commodities will change. The unjust form of capitalist distribution, which depends upon surplus value, will be replaced by the just form of communist distribution. Marx envisions two stages in this change. In the first stage,

> The individual producer receives back from society—after the deductions have been made—exactly what he gives to it. What he has given to it is his individual quantum of labour. For example, the social working day consists of the sum of the individual hours of work; the individual labour time of the individual producer is the part of the social working day contributed by him, his share in it. He receives a certificate from society that he has furnished such and such an amount of labour (after deducting his labour for the common funds), and with this certificate he draws from the social stock of means of consumption as much as costs the same amount of labour. The same amount of labour which he has given to society in one form he receives back in another.[34]

The aim of this first stage is to end surplus value. The distribution of commodities, however, is not one of perfect equality. Some workers will be able to work longer than others and will thus receive a greater number of items of consumption from the social stock.

> Further, one worker is married, another not; one has more children than another, and so on and so forth. Thus, with an equal performance of labour, and hence an equal share in the social consumption fund, one will in fact receive more than another, one will be richer than another, and so on. . . . But these defects are inevitable in the first phase of communist society as it is when it has just emerged after prolonged birth pangs from capitalist society.[35]

[33]Ibid., p. 30.
[34]Ibid., pp. 21–22.
[35]Ibid., pp. 22–23.

In the second stage these defects will themselves be abolished. Marx's description of the future is utopian in character:

> In a higher phase of communist society, after the enslaving subordination of the individual to the division of labour, and therewith also the antithesis between mental and physical labour, has vanished; after labour has become not only a means of life but life's prime want; after the productive forces have also increased with the all-round development of the individual, and all the springs of cooperative wealth flow more abundantly—only then can the narrow horizon of bourgeois right be crossed in its entirety and society inscribe on its banners: From each according to his ability, to each according to his needs![36]

In the second stage, the harsh conditions that made life so difficult for the worker under capitalism will be abolished, and work itself will become enjoyable rather than burdensome. Instead of being exploited, workers will have the opportunity to develop their talents and realize their potentials. In this stage, the problem of distributive justice will itself be abolished. Each individual will receive what he needs from an abundant productive system and will work according to his ability.

PROBLEMS WITH MARXISM

At least two main criticisms can be made of Marxism, each pertaining to an aspect of Marx's analysis of capitalism. First, Marx criticizes capitalism because of the degrading conditions under which the worker must earn his subsistence. He believes that these conditions cannot be significantly ameliorated under capitalism but that a new economic system, communism, must take its place. But, Marx's view that capitalism is not capable of significant internal reform has not been born out by recent events. The length of the working day has been significantly reduced. Conditions in the factory regarding health and safety have been improved. Child labor has been terminated. Free compulsory universal education has been successfully introduced. Unemployment insurance and welfare benefits have reduced the harm caused by losing one's job. Wages and living standards have increased significantly. Even though factory work is still monotonous, a much smaller percentage of the labor force is engaged in it. Of course, many problems remain to be solved in every capitalist society, but the nature of this economic system itself does not prevent reasonable solutions from being found and implemented. Moreover, the communist societies that have been founded since Marx's time have not been more successful than capitalism in ameliorating the sufferings of the worker.

The second major criticism pertains to Marx's theory of exploitation. Exploitation consists in the worker's producing more value than he receives, which is unjust. Thus, the very existence of profit is a form of injustice. But Marx's theory of value has serious difficulties. For Marx, the economic value of a commodity is determined by the quantity of labor used in producing it. But there does not seem to be an direct correlation between

[36]Ibid., p. 23.

value and price. A diamond may sell at a high price though very little labor is required to produce it. But if economic value is not reflected in the price of a commodity, what then is it? It seems something rather mysterious and unobservable. An alternative account of it is that it is simply what the commodity brings on the market. Thomas Hobbes expressed this view precisely:

> The *Value,* or Worth of a man, is as of all other things his Price; that is to say, so much as would be given for the use of his Power: therefore is not absolute; but a thing dependant on the need and judgement of another. An able conductor of Souldiers, is of great Price in time of War present, or imminent; but in Peace not so. A learned and uncorrupt Judge, is much Worth in time of Peace; but not so much in War. And as in other things, so in men, not the seller, but the buyer determines the Price. For let a man (as most men do), rate themselves at the highest Value they can; yet their true Value is not more than it is esteemed by others.[37]

According to Hobbes, the value of a thing is determined by the demand that others place upon it. The amount of labor that goes into producing a commodity will affect its value just as will any other cost of production. But labor is not the sole determinant of value, as Marx thought.

Even if one does not rely upon Marx's theory of value in questioning the justice of the capitalist system, cannot one argue on other grounds that profits are unjust? If a person makes a profit on an investment, the wealth that he thus accumulates is not the result of any work that he has performed. His profits are the result of the labor of others. Is this fair? Isn't it unjust for some individuals to gain income without work while others must labor hard and long for their daily bread? The traditional response to Marx by those who favor the capitalist system is that profit is necessary as an incentive to people's investing in a particular business; without the anticipation of a return on his investment, the individual who has money would have no reason to invest in the first place. It is argued that the importance of this incentive outweighs the apparent injustice of some people's gaining an income without having to work. This defence of profit implicitly concedes that any profit over and above what is necessary to encourage the optimum rate of investment is unjust. Therefore, it would be just to place limits on profit and to tax away the excess. In any case, Marx has not provided a persuasive critique of the capitalist system.

Individualism and Its Problems

Just as Marxism has been seen to exhibit several deep-seated flaws, so the classical individualist outlook also contains some serious problems. The individualist envisions two types of moral rights. One type consists of the natural rights that every person possesses to be free of agression and to punish those who engage in aggressive acts. The

---

[37]Thomas Hobbes, *Leviathan* (Oxford: The Clarendon Press, 1967), chap. 10, p. 67.

other type consists of those rights that individuals acquire over particular items of property as a result of voluntary transfers and agreements.

According to some ethical theories, the individualist's list of rights is too restricted. For example, suppose you are walking near a lake and you see a child fall into the water and cry for help. The child's plight is not the result of anyone's aggression. No one need be punished for harming the child. There is a life preserver near the shore. You are able to throw the life preserver to the child without any danger or great trouble to yourself. Doesn't the child have a right to your aid? And don't you have a moral obligation to provide it? It would seem that we do acknowledge a moral obligation to help others in distress when there is but slight inconvenience to ourselves. This suggests that individuals have rights in addition to the ones that the classical individualist would be willing to grant.

The principle of mutual aid can be applied to groups as well as to individuals. One of the traditional functions of government is to come to the aid of individuals in distress. Individuals caught up in emergency situations through no fault of their own—floods, earthquakes, fires, loss of job—have a right to aid from their government. This aid is financed through taxation, so its ultimate source is the members of society.

The principle of mutual aid can be justified on utilitarian grounds as leading to the greatest good for the greatest number. Kant also argues that to consider individuals as ends in themselves, we must not only refrain from inflicting harm on them but must help them to further their own interests:

> As regards meritorious duties towards others: The natural end which all men
> have is their own happiness. Now humanity might indeed subsist although no one
> should contribute anything to the happiness of others, provided he did not
> intentionally withdraw anything from it; but after all, this would only harmonize
> negatively, not positively, with *humanity as an end in itself,* if everyone does not
> also endeavor, as far as in him lies, to forward the ends of others. For the ends of
> any subject which is an end in himself ought as far as possible to be *my* ends
> also, if that conception is to have its *full* effect with me.[38]

For Kant, a person is obliged to consider the goals of others as if they were his own. This means at the very least that individuals have the right to the help of others when their existence or well-being is threatened by forces over which they have no control.

According to the individualist, political society is an association whose basic function is the protection of its citizens against aggression. But why must the function of government be defined so narrowly? After all, it is not written in the stars that providing protection is the only thing that government is equipped to do. Government can be given any function that is morally required. It is reasonable to consider political society as an association that also has the function of providing mutual aid. Anyone aware of how precarious human life can be would prefer to live in a society in which mutual aid as well as protection is an acknowledged function than in one in which only protection is recognized.

[38]Immanuel Kant, *Fundamental Principles of the Metaphysics of Morals,* trans. Thomas K. Abbott (New York: The Liberal Arts Press, 1949), p. 47. (This book was first published in 1785.)

John Rawls provides a rationale for mutual aid in these terms:

> A sufficient ground for adopting this duty is its pervasive effect on the quality of everyday life. The public knowledge that we are living in a society in which we can depend upon others to come to our assistance in difficult circumstances is itself of great value.... The primary value of the principle is not measured by the help we actually receive but rather by the sense of confidence and trust in other men's good intentions and the knowledge that they are there if we need them.[39]

The chief advantage of a society's accepting the principle of mutual aid lies in the sense of security that it fosters among the citizens. Having such security will enable the citizens to pursue their own goals with greater confidence than they would have if they were merely protected from aggression.

Nozick rejects the argument that individualism's conception of rights is narrow, arguing that a principle of mutual aid would be in conflict with existing rights:

> There are particular rights over particular things held by particular persons, and particular rights to reach agreement with others, *if* you and they together can acquire the means to reach an agreement.... No rights exist in conflict with this substructure of particular rights.... The particular rights over things fill the space of rights, leaving no room for general rights to be in a certain material condition.[40]

Suppose that as a result of an agreement with an owner of a business, you provide a service to that business and earn one hundred dollars. According to Nozick's theory of rights, you have the right to use the money as you wish. Suppose that the government decides to provide aid to various individuals and for that purpose imposes a twenty-five dollar tax on your earnings. That tax, says Nozick, violates your right to dispose of your income as you see fit. Thus, the government has no right to force citizens to provide aid to others. All mutual aid should be voluntary.

There is, however, an alternative approach to questions of distributive justice that would allow the government to tax earnings for purposes of mutual aid. According to this approach, the reason for there being rules for assigning property at all is to avoid disputes among those persons who wish to use or consume certain goods. For example, if both person A and person B wish to play on a certain piano at the same time, then the fact that A owns the piano settles without dispute who has the right to play it. The exact nature of the rules of property is determined by the legal system of the society. But whatever form the rules take, the ultimate criterion for the distribution of property is public utility. Thus David Hume writes:

> *What is a man's property?* Anything which it is lawful for him, and for him alone to use. *But what rule have we, by which we can distinguish these objects?* Here

---

[39]John Rawls, *A Theory of Justice* (Cambridge: Harvard University Press, 1971), p. 339.
[40]Nozick, p. 238.

we must have recourse to statutes, customs, precedents, analogies, and a hundred other circumstances; some of which are constant and inflexible, some variable and arbitrary. But the ultimate point, in which they all professedly terminate, is the interest and happiness of human society.[41]

Property is an instrument for the realization of social and individual purposes. It is these purposes that control the methods that individuals can use to acquire and dispose of items of property. Many such items—for example, stocks and bonds—could not even exist without a developed legal system. Thus, public purposes are prior to particular property rights.

L. T. Hobhouse (1864–1929), a British philosopher and sociologist who developed this approach to questions of property, writes:

The State organization is . . . the basis of security, therewith . . . of property itself. That consideration alone gives to the community the last word in declaring what rights of property it will recognize and on what terms. Ordinary thought is far too apt to conceive property as absolutely inherent in the individual and all taxation as a process of depriving him . . . of something which is unquestionably his own.[42]

Even though the purposes of society ultimately determine the rights of property, Hobhouse did agree with the individualist that private property is indispensable:

He who is wholly dependant on another for the opportunity of maintaining himself is also virtually devoid of freedom, of the means of guiding his own life and working out his own purposes in his own way.[43]

A good society would recognize many of the rights that the classical individualist defends. But a good society will also recognize the principle of mutual aid as necessary to provide security and mutual trust. The rights of classical liberal individualism are to be limited and defined by reference to new social purposes.

Justice as Fairness

THE ORIGINAL POSITION

In recent years, John Rawls has worked out a conception of justice—one that he calls *justice as fairness*—that attempts to reconcile the demand for equality made by the radical tradition with the demand for liberty and freedom from control made by individualism. He expounds a set of moral principles designed to regulate the basic institutions of any just society, arguing that social life is marked both by cooperation and

---

[41]David Hume, "Enquiry Concerning the Principles of Morals," in *Hume's Enquiries,* ed. L. A. Selby-Bigge (Oxford: The Clarendon Press, 1972), pp. 197–198.
[42]L. T. Hobhouse, *The Elements of Social Justice* (New York: Henry Holt and Co., 1922), p. 188.
[43]Ibid., p. 183.

by conflict and that these principles determine how conflicts are to be resolved and how the fruits of cooperative endeavor are to be distributed. These principles also serve as standards by which any given society may be criticized and judged.

In setting forth his principles, Rawls makes use of an idea that is drawn from Locke and from other philosophers who use the conception of a social contract. According to Locke, individuals in the state of nature agree to set up the institutions of government. This agreement is called the social contract. Rawls does not suppose that there ever really was a social contract drawn up in the distant past, as Locke thought. Instead, he considers a hypothetical situation. Suppose a group of rational persons who wanted to achieve their own goals were to meet and settle on a set of rules under which they would henceforth cooperate. The rules agreed upon in this, the hypothetical **original position,** would be worthy of general adoption because they had been freely chosen by rational individuals. These rules thus constitute the principles of social justice. The problem, then, is to identify which rules a group of representative rational individuals would agree to.

The next stage in Rawls's argument is to formulate the exact conditions under which such an agreement would be drawn up. Let us consider two persons, A and B. Suppose that A is rich and B is poor. Assuming that both are concerned only with their own interests, A would not agree to an equal division of goods. He would not agree to any division that would leave him with less than he already has. Because B wants as many goods as possible, he would have no reason to agree to any division of benefits in which he fails to receive more than he has. It looks as if no agreement is possible. According to Rawls, the reason for the failure to reach agreement is that A and B know their respective degrees of wealth and that A has no motive to provide benefits to B. Both A and B try to tailor the principles of justice to their own special circumstances. The rich try to maintain their advantages over the poor, and the poor try to obtain some of the wealth of the rich.

To avoid this impasse, Rawls suggests that the parties in the original position should ignore the differences among them and bargain as equals. To this end, he drops a **veil of ignorance** over the original position:

> Somehow we must nullify the effects of specific contingencies which put men at odds and tempt them to exploit social and natural circumstances to their advantage. Now in order to do this I assume that the parties are situated behind a veil of ignorance. They do not know how the various alternatives will affect their own particular case and they are obliged to evaluate principles solely on the basis of general considerations.[44]

The result of the veil of ignorance is that the parties in the original position no longer know any particular facts about themselves or others. They do not know whether they are rich or poor, strong or weak, intelligent or stupid. Thus, they are unable to tailor the principles of justice to their own particular circumstances. These principles, then,

[44]Rawls, *Theory of Justice,* pp. 136–137.

are those that would be chosen by rational, self-interested individuals coming to a unanimous agreement in a hypothetical original position in which they are ignorant of their particular circumstances.

THE DIFFERENCE PRINCIPLE

Among the principles that Rawls thinks would be chosen is one that he calls the **difference principle:**

> Social and economic inequalities are to be arranged so that they are both (a) to the greatest benefit of the least advantaged and (b) attached to offices and positions open to all under conditions of fair equality of opportunity.[45]

To understand the difference principle, let us see what would happen in the original position. Because the agreement must be unanimous and because each representative person wants as much as possible, no one would have any reason to agree to an arrangement in which someone else had more than he. It would appear, then, that the only terms on which they could agree would be an equal division of goods. Therefore, according to the difference principle, there is a presumption in favor of equality. To this extent, Rawls agrees with the demand for equality made by the radical tradition. But it may turn out that certain inequalities serve everyone's advantage, especially the advantage of those worst off. For example, inequalities can arise as a consequence of incentives offered to individuals to improve the overall productivity and efficiency of the economic system. These economic benefits spread throughout the whole system and improve everyone's circumstances, including those worst off. Rawls assumes that the individuals in the original position are not moved by feelings of envy; thus, they would have no objection to a person's having more than they provided that they benefit as well by this system of inequalities. It would be irrational for a person to deny himself the opportunity of obtaining more of what he wants just because the economic machinery that provides him with additional benefits leaves him worse off than some others.

Despite Rawls's concern for equality, he remains a liberal because he places liberty ahead of distributive equality. The principle that comes first in his theory of justice is the principle of equal liberty:

> Each person is to have an equal right to the most extensive basic liberty compatible with a similar liberty for others.[46]

In the original position, each representative person would need to consider the relative merits of liberty and equality. Each would realize that after a certain stage of economic well-being and security has been achieved, he and he alone would be best able to realize his own plan of life. Hence, none of the representative persons would agree to a society

---

[45]Ibid., p. 83.
[46]Ibid., p. 60.

in which they had to put themselves in the hands of others. Liberty should not be sacrificed to achieve equality or economic efficiency. Therefore, the principle of equal liberty will be placed ahead of the difference principle by those in the original position.

In its concrete application, the difference principle can lead to a society much like the welfare state systems in the United States and Western Europe:

> Suppose the law and government act effectively to keep markets competitive, resources fully employed, property and wealth (especially if private ownership of the means of production is allowed) widely distributed by the appropriate forms of taxation, or whatever, and to guarantee a reasonable social minimum. Assume also that there is fair equality of opportunity underwritten by education for all; and that the other equal liberties are secured. Then it would appear that the resulting distribution of income and the pattern of expectations will tend to satisfy the difference principle. In this complex of institutions, which we think of as establishing social justice in the modern state, the advantages of the better situated improve the condition of the least favored. Or when they do not, they can be adjusted to do so, for example, by setting the social minimum at the appropriate level.[47]

A reformed version of welfare capitalism would, then, satisfy the difference principle. Rawls does not deny that some versions of socialism would also satisfy it, but he does not discuss the possibility in any detail.

THE KANTIAN INTERPRETATION OF JUSTICE AS FAIRNESS

Rawls's theory of social justice draws on the ethics of Kant rather than that of utilitarianism. The problem with utilitarianism is that under certain circumstances, it would allow the welfare of some individuals to be sacrificed to secure the overall advantage of society. Individual persons would not, then, be inviolable. "Utilitarianism does not take seriously the distinction between persons."[48] Furthermore, the ideals of liberty and equality are not included in the primary principle of utilitarianism and thus may be violated when it is expedient to do so.

Rawls prefers the Kantian principle that individuals should be treated as ends and not merely as means:

> The difference principle explicates the distinction between treating men as means only and treating them also as ends in themselves. To regard persons as ends in themselves in the basic design of society is to agree to forgo those gains which do not contribute to their representative expectations. By contrast, to regard persons as means is to be prepared to impose upon them lower prospects of life for the sake of higher expectations of others.[49]

---

[47]Ibid., p. 87.
[48]Ibid., p. 27.
[49]Ibid., p. 180.

An example of a society in which people are treated as means is one in which the poor are used as cheap labor to operate the factories of the rich no matter what the cost to the poor's welfare. Under the difference principle, the laboring poor would be treated as ends because factories owned by the rich would be permitted only to the extent that the poor were thereby benefited. Rawls is thus attempting to work out the structure of a society that would satisfy Kant's categorical imperative.

PROBLEMS WITH JUSTICE AS FAIRNESS

Rawls's work is the most substantial effort in recent philosophy to develop an account of the principles of social justice. It has received a great deal of comment and criticism. Let us now examine two main criticisms that raise questions about the foundations of his thought.

The first criticism is a consequence of a conflict between Rawls's theory and individualism. Think of how the individualist would respond to the difference principle. He would claim that if a person works long and hard and through his industry and intelligence earns a substantial income, then he *deserves* what he has earned and no one, including the government, has the right to take it from him. We saw earlier that the notion of justice entails giving to each person what he or she deserves. Does not the person who earns his income through hard work deserve it? Does not the able-bodied person who earns less because he lacks industry or intelligence deserve his inferior position?

Rawls replies to this criticism by expressing doubt about the validity of the idea that those who are better endowed deserve more than those who are not so well endowed. Whether one is or is not industrious, whether one has or lacks intelligence or some useful and wanted skill, depends upon the capacities that one is born with and the abilities that circumstances and family life have encouraged. Thus, these differences among persons do not lead to differences in what is or is not deserved. "No one deserves his greater natural capacity nor merits a more favorable starting place in society."[50] Talent and ability are distributed according to a lottery that nature establishes. The person whom nature provides with the character and the ability to succeed in life does not deserve his success any more than someone at the bottom of the economic laddder deserves his ill fortune.

Instead of eliminating differences due to nature's lottery, Rawls recommends that society be so organized as to make use of them:

> The basic structure can be arranged so that these contingencies work for the good of the least fortunate. Thus we are led to the difference principle if we wish to set up the social system so that no one gains or loses from his arbitrary place in the distribution of natural assets or his initial position in society without giving or receiving compensating advantages in return.[51]

[50]Ibid., p. 102.
[51]Ibid.

According to Rawls, the advantages that result from the distribution by nature of various abilities among individuals should not be treated as the private possessions of these individuals but should be shared by all members of society. They are to be interpreted as common property:

> We see then that the difference principle represents, in effect, an agreement to regard the distribution of natural talents as a common asset and to share in the benefits of this distribution whatever it turns out to be. Those who have been favored by nature, whoever they are, may gain from their good fortune only on terms that improve the situation of those who have lost out.[52]

The assets of the better endowed should be treated, then, as a common asset. For example, suppose someone is a talented inventor. For Rawls, it is just an accident that this talent resides in him. If nature had worked differently, it might have resided in some other person. Society as a whole has the right to use the fruits of this talent to benefit the least advantaged.

But how does this response to individualism square with the Kantian morality that Rawls endorses? Does it not treat the better endowed as means to satisfy the interests of the poor and the disadvantaged? According to Kant, each individual is an end in himself and is entitled to pursue his own goals provided he respects the rights of others to do so as well. But the difference principle seems to allow that the liberty of some may be sacrificed to enhance the welfare of others. There seems to be a fundamental incoherence in the foundations of justice as fairness.

The second criticism raises the question whether the difference principle really would be chosen by representative individuals in the original position. Perhaps an aristocratic principle would be chosen instead according to which persons with ability, intelligence, and willpower would be favored. To avoid an aristocratic principle or anything like it, Rawls makes a certain assumption about the way individuals in the original position would make their choice. He assumes that they would be extremely cautious and would select a principle that would prevent the worst possibility from occuring. Thus, if I chose an aristocratic principle, I could be one of those with few talents who would be relegated to the bottom of the heap. So I would be cautious and choose the difference principle, for then, no matter how untalented or unintelligent I may be, I am guaranteed to benefit from the abilities of others. The difference principle is safer to choose than the aristocratic ideal. For Rawls, the principles of justice "are those a person would choose for the design of a society in which his enemy is to assign him his place."[53]

Rawls assumes, therefore, that the representative individuals in the original position would be extremely cautious when choosing. They are willing to lose a great good in order to be sure that they will not be afflicted with great evil. But this seems unreasonable. Real as opposed to imaginary persons in the original position may be willing to take greater risks. Perhaps the great achievements of human civilization depend upon a willingness to take chances rather than a policy of extreme caution. It seems as if

[52]Ibid., p. 101.
[53]Ibid., p. 152.

Rawls ascribes this cautious policy to his representative persons just so he can obtain the principles that he is committed to in the first place. Thus, the basic argument for the difference principle involves a very dubious assumption.

Summary

A central problem of philosophical ethics is to clarify the concept of justice. Justice is a complex concept assuming various forms, and perhaps the best way to examine it is to examine the theory of the social contract according to which individuals in the state of nature agree to establish a government for their mutual benefit. Disputes are no longer decided by individuals but by the rule of law. This rule requires that laws be applied impartially and that they not discriminate among persons for irrelevant reasons. Thus, one purpose of government is to assure justice in punishment. Examining the reasons for punishment reveals a clash between utilitarians, who see it as a means of protection, deterrence, and rehabilitation, and the retributivists, who see it primarily as a means of giving criminals what they deserve—namely, the pain and suffering they inflicted originally. Another aspect of justice is the distribution of goods. Distributive justice is concerned with the rationale for property rights and the criteria for a just distribution of wealth among the members of society. Liberal individualist theories of distributive justice emphasize the importance of voluntary transactions and are willing to accept the inequalities that result. Radical theories such as Marxism emphasize equality and the public interest over private profit. Justice as fairness is the view of Rawls that favors equal distribution except where inequalities benefit the least advantaged. These three main competing accounts of distributive justice were presented and their drawbacks explored in this chapter.

Glossary

Anarchism: A political theory which says that government is a source of oppression and should be abolished.

Capitalism: That organization of society according to which the means of production are owned by private individuals motivated to make a profit for themselves.

Democratic socialism: The belief that tyranny can be avoided if public ownership of the means of production is tied to democratic political controls.

Difference principle: A principle in Rawls's theory of justice as fairness according to which inequalities are justified only if they benefit the least advantaged.

Distributive justice: The principles regulating the just distribution of wealth.

Formal equality: A type of equality in which cases that are alike are treated alike and those that are different are treated differently.

Ideology: According to Marxists, a theory whose purpose is to create a false consciousness of the conditions of society.

Individualism: That form of liberal political philosophy which emphasizes the value of personal liberty and the autonomy of the individual.

Liberalism: See **Individualism** and **Welfare state liberalism.**

Natural law: In Locke's theory, the moral rules that can be known by all rational beings. Natural laws in this sense should be distinguished from the laws of nature that are discovered in science and describe the uniformities of nature.

Original position: In Rawls's theory of justice, a hypothetical situation in which representative persons are to choose principles of justice.

Positive law: The rules established by the legislative authority in various legal jurisdictions, such as the nation or the city.

Radicalism: Refers to various theories of society that emphasize the value of equality. Radicals generally are critical of the existing state of society, which they take as authorizing unjustified inequalities.

Retributive justice: The principles regulating the just methods of punishment.

Rule of law: A society is regulated by the rule of law when the laws are applied impartially and when they contain no unfair discrimination.

Social contract: In Locke's theory, the agreement by which individuals in the state of nature establish government.

Socialism: The view that the means of production should be owned and controlled by the public for the public interest and not by profit-seeking individuals or corporations.

State of nature: In Locke's theory, the condition of individuals who live without a government to enforce the laws of nature.

Surplus value: In Marx's economics, the extra value that is created by the working class beyond the value that is needed to maintain the workers' existence.

Veil of ignorance: In Rawls's theory, this is the condition of the individuals in the original position who are unaware of their particular circumstances and characteristics. Thus, they are unable to tailor their choice of the principles of justice to their own personal advantage.

Welfare state liberalism: A more recent version of liberalism that emphasizes the redistribution of wealth in favor of the poor and underprivileged as well as the value of freedom and personal autonomy.

Further Reading

The best edition of Locke's *Second Treatise of Government* is contained in *Two Treatises of Government,* ed. Peter Laslett (New York: New American Library, 1965). Laslett's introduction is particularly illuminating. Another important source of Locke's political philosophy is his *A Letter on Toleration,* trans. J. W. Gough (Oxford: The Clarendon Press, 1968). A good collection of essays about Locke's politics is Gordon J. Schochet, *Life, Liberty, and Property; Essays on Locke's Political Ideas* (Belmont, California: Wadsworth, 1971.)

The major accounts of justice in ancient philosophy are in Plato's *Republic* in *The Collected Dialogues of Plato,* ed. Edith Hamilton and Huntington Cairns (Princeton: Princeton University Press, 1971) and in Book V of Aristotle's *Ethica Nicomachea,* trans. W. D. Ross (London: Oxford University Press, 1966).

Two good collections of recent writings on justice are Frederick A. Olafson, *Justice* and Social Policy (Englewood Cliffs, New Jersey: Prentice-Hall, 1961) and Richard B. Brandt, Social Justice (Englewood Cliffs, New Jersey: Prentice-Hall, 1962).

The classic utilitarian theory of law is John Austin, The Province of Jurisprudence Determined (New York: Noonday Press, 1954). A contemporary critique and development of Austin's approach is H. L. A. Hart, The Concept of Law (Oxford: The Clarendon Press, 1961). Hart has also written on the problem of punishment in his Punishment and Responsibility (Oxford: The Clarendon Press, 1968).

A famous defense of classical liberal individualism is Herbert Spencer, The Man Versus the State (Baltimore: Penguin Books, 1969). Robert Nozick's position is contained in his Anarchy, State and Utopia (New York: Basic Books, 1968). An excellent defense of the capitalist system is developed by the economist F. A. Hayek, The Constitution of Liberty (Chicago: University of Chicago Press, 1960).

Two good collections of writings by Marx and Engels are Lewis S. Feuer, Marx and Engels: Basic Writings on Politics and Philosophy (Garden City, New York: Doubleday and Co., 1959) and Robert C. Tucker, The Marx–Engels Reader (New York: W. W. Norton and Co., 1978). Marx's major critique of capitalism is contained in Volume I of his Capital (New York: International Publishers, 1967).

John Rawls's major work is A Theory of Justice (Cambridge: Harvard University Press, 1971). A collection of articles about Rawls's theory is Norman Daniels, Reading Rawls: Critical Studies of "A Theory of Justice" (New York: Basic Books). Another approach to social justice that has elicited much recent discussion is Ronald Dworkin, Taking Rights Seriously (Cambridge: Harvard University Press, 1977).

Two important recent statements of liberalism are Isaiah Berlin, Four Essays on Liberty (New York: Oxford University Press, 1969) and John Dewey, Liberalism and Social Action (New York: Capricorn, 1963). An influential statement of the conservative position is in Michael Oakeshott, Rationalism in Politics (London: Methuen, 1962).

Two excellent histories of political philosophy are George H. Sabine, A History of Political Theory (New York: Henry Holt and Co., 1937) and John Plamenatz, Man and Society (London: Longmans, 1963, two volumes).

Questions for Thought and Discussion

1. Modern societies tend to consider discrimination on the basis of race, religion, and gender to be morally wrong. In the United States, it is a matter of public policy to prohibit such discrimination in employment, education, public accommodations, and other areas of life. What reasons can you give for regarding such discrimination as wrong? Should members of groups that have been discriminated against be given preference in jobs and other opportunities to compensate for past discrimination?

2. Now that you have studied the disagreement between utilitarians and retributivists concerning the justification of punishment, which position do you think has the stronger argument? Do you agree with the utilitarian that capital punishment is justified only if it has beneficial consequences on the whole without regard to what the individual may deserve?

3. The versions of liberal individualism formulated by Locke and Nozick presuppose a particular theory of human rights. What is their underlying view of rights? What reasons can be given for thinking that there really are such rights?

4. Are you convinced by Marx's criticisms of capitalism? If you are, how would you reply to the arguments for capitalism implied by liberal individualism? If you are not, what are the weak points of Marx's argument?

5. How would you assess the importance of merit in the distribution of wealth? Should a system of distribution give to each according to what he deserves? What do you think of Rawls's rejection of the very notion of merit as a basis for distributive justice?

Chapter 4

THE FOUNDATIONS OF MORAL CHOICE

PREVIEW

Why should I be moral? What if someone were to give reasons for thinking that I *ought* to do something that I do not want to do at all? Perhaps I would still prefer to pursue my own advantage instead of conforming to what is right. Is it possible to provide morality with a justification that would convince me or any other rational agent to subordinate our own good to its dictates? How are claims about what is moral justified? Can they be given a rational justification at all? Are moral values things we discover or things we choose? These are the main questions that we shall take up in this chapter. We shall consider various theories in modern philosophy put forth to explain how our values can be justified.

Ethical Disagreement

We often find ourselves in situations in which we have to decide what we *ought* to do, what course of action we *should* choose. In selecting one action from a set of alternatives, we normally do not think that our choice is arbitrary or willful or irrational. In most cases we are conscious of trying to base our choices upon reasons; we try to find good reasons for doing this rather than that. Reasoning whose goal is to help us decide what we ought to do is called **practical reasoning,** for it aims at practice or action. It is to be distinguished from **theoretical reasoning,** whose aim is to establish the truth of some proposition.

We often engage in discussions with others about what course of action should be taken regarding some practical problem. Such problems are usually issues that groups of people are interested in resolving, and they often succeed in generating controversy. What should be done with regard, say, to abortion or capital punishment or nuclear arms or the energy problem? These are topics that people disagree about. Disagreement about what ought to be done is an inherent and inescapable feature of human life.

There are innumerable reasons why people disagree about practical problems. But two general sources of disagreement are particularly important. People may disagree about what ought to be done because they have a different understanding of the facts. For example, one person may be opposed to capital punishment because he believes that executing convicted murderers fails to deter others from committing murder. But another may disagree and favor capital punishment because she thinks that it is a deterrent. Their disagreement stems from a disagreement about the facts, about whether or not capital punishment deters.

But people may be in agreement about the facts and yet still come to different conclusions because they differ in their values or moral principles. For example, two people may agree that capital punishment does deter and yet disagree about its morality. One may oppose capital punishment because he believes that it is always wrong to take a human life. The other may favor it on the grounds that one may be obliged to take the life of a guilty party to prevent further harm to the innocent. Thus, there can be disagreements about facts *and* about values.

Disagreements about facts can be settled by further investigation. Thus, we have a good general idea of how to go about resolving such disagreements even though it may be hard to do so in practice. But it is not so clear what we should do to settle disagreements about fundamental moral values. Is there some rational way to remove such disagreements, or is our choice of basic values ultimately arbitrary?

The "Is–Ought" Problem

Our understanding of the problem of justifying first principles of morality has been increased by an insight of David Hume:

> In every system of morality, which I have hitherto met with, I have always remark'd, that the author proceeds for some time in the ordinary way of reasoning, and establishes the being of a God, or makes observations concerning human affairs; when of a sudden I am surprized to find, that instead of the usual copulations of propositions, *is,* and *is not,* I meet with no proposition that is not connected with an *ought,* or an *ought not.* This change is imperceptible; but is, however, of the last consequence. For as this *ought,* or *ought not,* expresses some new relation or affirmation, 'tis necessary that it shou'd be observ'd and explain'd; and at the same time that a reason should be given, for what seems altogether inconceivable, how this new relation can be a deduction from others, which are entirely different from it.[1]

Hume points out that in the systems of moral philosophy that he has studied, he finds that the author first tries to establish certain facts, such as the claim that God exists. **Statements of fact** assert what is or is not the case and indeed are often formulated in

---

[1]David Hume, *A Treatise of Human Nature,* ed. L. A. Selby-Bigge (Oxford: The Clarendon Press, 1968), p. 469.

DAVID HUME
(1711–1776)

Hume was one of the British empiricists, along with John Locke and George Berkeley. He was born in Edinburgh, Scotland and attended the University of Edinburgh. His major philosophical work was *A Treatise of Human Nature* (1739), written when he was quite a young man. He complained that ''it fell *dead-born from the press*'' and did not receive the attention he thought it deserved. He later published a more popular account of his philosophical ideas in his *An Enquiry concerning Human Understanding* (1748) and *An Enquiry concerning the Principles of Morals* (1751). After some years as a tutor and then as the head of a library, he finally achieved the literary fame he desired with his various essays on ethical, political, and literary topics and with his *History of Great Britain.* His last contribution to philosophy was the posthumously published *Dialogues concerning Natural Religion.* As his death approached, he described himself in his brief autobiography as ''a man of mild dispositions, of command of temper, of an open, social, and cheerful humor, capable of attachment, but little susceptible of enmity, and of great moderation in all my passions.''

sentences whose verb is *is* or *is not*, such as "This man is in pain" and "This man is not in pain." Hume notes, however, that the author then proceeds to formulate **normative statements** using the verb *ought* and *ought not*, such as "Promises ought to be kept." Hume wonders how a normative statement can be derived from a statement of fact.

First principles of morality are generally formulated as normative statements, and it has been common in moral theory to attempt to derive these principles from certain factual assumptions. For example, from the supposed fact that God disapproves of murder, it is inferred that people *ought not* to murder one another. Or from the supposed fact that human beings desire happiness, it is inferred that people *ought* to aim at the greatest happiness for the greatest number. But Hume points out that normative statements express an idea not expressed by factual statements—the idea expressed by *ought*—suggesting that it is doubtful that moral first principles can be inferred by valid steps from factual statements. Therefore, if Hume is correct, the question "How can ethical principles be justified?" cannot be answered by saying that they follow from certain facts about the world or human nature.

If we follow Hume, we seem to be caught up in the following impasse. Moral first principles cannot be justified by deriving them from more fundamental moral principles because there are none more fundamental. And they cannot be justified by deriving them from the way the world or the way human nature is constituted because normative statements do not follow from statements of fact. So ethical first principles apparently cannot be justified. Where shall we go from here?

Reason and Sentiment

A **moral skeptic** is one who thinks that ethical principles cannot be justified. Although Hume's argument seems inclined in the direction of skepticism, Hume himself was not a skeptic. He believed in the reality of moral distinctions. For him, the main question was not to establish their reality but to understand their nature. And there are only two possible explanations thereof: Morality is founded either on reason or on sentiment:

> There has been a controversy started of late . . . concerning the general
> foundation of Morals; whether they can be derived from Reason, or from
> Sentiment; whether we attain the knowledge of them by a chain of argument and
> induction, or by an immediate feeling and finer internal sense; whether, like all
> sound judgement of truth and falsehood, they should be the same to every
> rational intelligent being; or whether, like the perception of beauty and
> deformity, they be founded entirely on the particular fabric and constitution of
> the human species.[2]

The distinction between virtue and vice can be established either by some kind of argument or by an appeal to human emotion. These are the alternatives as Hume understood them, and he opted for sentiment as the foundation of morality. But before examining his account, let us first consider the claim that moral principles are founded upon reason.

Intuitionism

THE ETHICAL INTUITIONISM OF THOMAS REID

Intuitionism is the name of a family of theories according to which the first principles of morals express self-evident truths. The familiar words of *The Declaration of Independence* that "We hold these truths to be self-evident, that all men are created equal, that they are endowed by their Creator with certain unalienable Rights, that among these are Life, Liberty, and the pursuit of Happiness" express an intuitionist point of view because they claim that certain ethical judgments are self-evidently true.

Thomas Reid (1710–1796), a contemporary of Hume, is responsible for formulating a particularly clear intuitionist theory. For Reid, statements about what a person ought to do express a relation between the person and the action that constitutes his duty.

> If we examine the abstract notion of Duty, or Moral Obligation, it appears to be
> neither any real quality of the action considered by itself, nor of the agent
> considered without respect to the action, but a certain relation between the one
> and the other. When we say a man ought to do such a thing, the *ought,* which

---

[2]David Hume, "An Enquiry concerning the Principles of Morals," in *Hume's Enquiries,* ed. L. A. Selby-Bigge (Oxford: The Clarendon Press, 1972), p. 170.

expresses the moral obligation, has a respect, on the one hand, to the person who ought; and, on the other hand, to the action which he ought to do.[3]

According to this analysis, the statement "John ought to keep his promise to Tom" represents a relation that holds between John and his action of keeping his promise to Tom.

What is this relation? Can an analysis or definition of it be provided? Reid replies that this cannot be done.

> Moral obligation is a relation of its own kind, which every man understands, but is, perhaps, too simple to admit of logical definition.[4]

Some of the notions expressed in language can be defined. For example, *triangle* can be defined as meaning a three-sided enclosed figure. Anything that can be so defined is a complex notion that can be analyzed into its component parts. Thus, the idea of a triangle includes the following components: being a figure, having three sides, and being enclosed. But, according to Reid, the idea expressed by "ought" is not complex. It is a simple idea and thus defies analysis. This does not mean, however, that it cannot be explained. Just as someone can explain the simple idea of red by pointing to red things, so one explains the simple idea of obligation by calling one's attention to situations in which a person is obliged to perform a particular action.

According to Reid's intuitionism, one can come to know the truth of moral first principles that state our obligations by the use of the *moral sense:*

> We are next to consider, how we learn to judge and determine, that this is right, and that is wrong. . . . Some philosophers, with whom I agree, ascribe this to an original power or faculty in man, which they call the *Moral Sense,* the *Moral Faculty, Conscience.* . . . By an original power of the mind, when we come to years of understanding and reflection, we not only have the notions of right and wrong in conduct, but perceive certain things to be right, and others to be wrong.[5]

Just as we apprehend colors through the sense of sight, so we apprehend moral obligation by means of a power of reason that is called the moral sense. The moral sense is part of the basic inborn intellectual equipment of the average human being. And just as one can perceive a color using the sense of sight without having to reason about it, one can perceive the truth of a moral first principle directly through the moral sense without having to employ any reasoning or inference:

> All moral reasoning rests upon one or more first principles of morals, whose truth is immediately perceived without reasoning, by all men come to years of

[3]Thomas Reid, "Essays on the Active Powers of Man," in *Philosophical Works,* ed. Sir William Hamilton, II, 588–589. (This book was first published in 1788.)
[4]Ibid., p. 589.
[5]Ibid.

> understanding. . . . The first principles of morals are the immediate dictates of
> the moral faculty. They shew us, not what man is, but what he ought to be.
> Whatever is immediately perceived to be just, honest, and honourable in human
> conduct, carries moral obligation along with it, and the contrary carries demerit
> and blame; and from those moral obligations that are immediately perceived, all
> other moral obligations must be deduced by reasoning. . . . He that will judge of
> the first principles of morals, must consult his conscience, or moral faculty, when
> he is calm and dispassionate, unbiassed by interest, affection, or fashion.[6]

In response to Hume's claim that normative statements cannot be deduced from statements of fact, Reid says that such a deduction is not necessary. Moral first principles are known directly without any need of deduction or inference.

> The first principles of morals are not deductions. They are self-evident; and their
> truth, like that of other axioms, is perceived without reasoning or deduction. And
> moral truths that are not self-evident are deduced, not from relations quite
> different from them, but from the first principles of morals.[7]

For Reid, normative statements are themselves a kind of factual statement. They state that an objective relation exists between persons and their actions and that this relation is perceived through the moral sense. Moral insight permits a knowledge of moral facts.

The difficulty that Hume discovered in deducing "ought" statements from "is" statements is rejected by Reid on the grounds that the justification of "ought" statements does not depend upon their being deduced from any other statements. Because they are self-evident, they are known through themselves and not through some other thing. For the intuitionist, the justification of first principles of any kind is not a matter of inferring a conclusion from the premises but a matter of observation. In ethics, the observation is of a special kind. It is performed not by a sense organ but by a power of the reason in much the same way as we observe the truth of "2 + 3 = 5."

The intuitionist claims that we are able to determine how we should act in a particular case by applying to it a self-evident rule. Thus, my decision to pay one hundred dollars to Jennifer may be based on the fact that I borrowed one hundred dollars from her, that I promised to repay her, and that it is self-evident that promises should be kept.

PROBLEMS WITH INTUITIONISM

The basic difficulty with the intuitionist approach is that there is a genuine basis for doubting the reality of the moral sense. The ordinary senses such as sight and hearing operate through a physical sense organ; the eye is the organ of sight and the ear of hearing. The existence of these organs is not in doubt. But through what organ does the moral sense operate? Through what means does a person observe moral relationships? The analysis of the human cognitive apparatus produced by modern psychology and

---

[6]Ibid., p. 591.
[7]Ibid., p. 675.

biology appears to leave no room for a moral sense. All observation is the consequence of the reception of physical stimuli by the sense organs such as the eyes, ears, skin, and so forth. If there is a moral sense, it must work in ways that we do not understand.

Intuitionism seems plausible because there are basic ethical principles of which we are strongly convinced and for which we can offer no argument or reason. It therefore seems plausible to say that these principles are self-evidently true. Critics, however, have pointed out that strong conviction is not the same thing as knowledge (see the analysis of knowledge in Chapter Seven) and consequently that the appeal to intuition may just be a mask for prejudice and dogma. From the fact that one is strongly convinced that killing is wrong, it does not follow that one *knows* that killing is wrong. Knowledge requires something more than strong conviction. Yet the intuitionist gives us no way of distinguishing knowledge from firm belief, no way of distinguishing justified ethical commitment from prejudice.

Sometimes intuitionists appeal to the universal judgment of humankind. The fact that everyone believes that killing is wrong is sufficient to establish that it really is wrong. To this argument, John Stuart Mill has replied:

> The universal voice of mankind, so often appealed to, is universal only in its discordance. What passes for it is merely the voice of the majority, or, failing that, of any large number having a strong feeling of which they cannot give any account, and which, as it is not consciously grounded on reasons, is supposed to be better than reasons and of higher authority.[8]

For Mill, the universal voice of humankind is just a myth. There are conflicting opinions on most major topics in ethics, and the appeal to universal intuition functions as a way of stopping argument and enforcing prejudice or fashion.

Most intuitionists have been **ethical pluralists.** This is because they believe that there are several basic principles of ethics such as "Killing is wrong," "Promises should be kept," and "Theft is wrong" and not merely one basic principle, as the utilitarians and Kant believed. A problem of pluralism is to determine what to do when there is a conflict among principles. For example, suppose a friend of yours gives you his weapons for safekeeping and exacts a promise from you to return them when he asks. In a fit of rage, he threatens to kill a perfectly innocent person and demands the weapons from you. If you keep your promise and return the weapons, you will aid him in killing an innocent person. If you refuse to return the weapons, you will be breaking your promise. You cannot act in accordance with both the principles "Killing is wrong" and "Promises should be kept."

To deal with this problem, the intuitionist W. D. Ross developed the concept of **prima facie obligation.** According to this concept, a valid moral principle does not state unconditionally what a person ought to do but indicates only what he should do provided that the action has no other features that would make it wrong to do. An action can be right given some of its features and wrong given others. Thus, the action of returning the

---

[8]John Stuart Mill, "Dr. Whewell on Moral Philosophy," *Collected Works* (Toronto: University of Toronto Press, 1969), p. 194.

weapons is right in the sense that it is done to keep a promise and wrong in the sense that it aids and abets a murder. A statement of prima facie obligation says that in one respect an action is right to do. But whether it ought to be done depends upon whether it has aspects that make it wrong to do.[9]

In a situation of moral conflict, intuition is to be used in the following way. First, it is used to identify the relevant principles of prima facie obligation. Then, if the principles conflict, it is used to determine which one has priority in the situation. Thus, in the case of the weapons, we would likely agree that the avoidance of killing has priority over the keeping of a promise. In explaining what to do in the case of moral conflict, intuitionists use the term *intuition* as the name of that faculty in us which makes us feel that one type of action is more urgent than another in a given situation. But the fact that this faculty in us is given a name should not convince us that we understand it. Intuitionism fails to provide any deeper understanding of our ability to achieve moral insight than the giving of a name.

Naturalism

THE MEANING OF ETHICAL TERMS

In ethics, the **naturalist** agrees with the intuitionist that moral judgments are statements of fact. But the naturalist does not believe that moral facts contain a special moral relation to be apprehended by the moral sense, as did Reid. The naturalist identifies these facts with ordinary items of everyday observation. For example, for Bentham, who was a naturalist in ethics, to say that an action is right simply means that it brings about the greatest happiness for the greatest number. Moral obligation is thus a causal property of actions; it is their tendency to cause pleasure. We can learn that an action is right by studying its consequences and observing whether it brings about more pleasure than its alternatives. No special moral sense is required. Naturalism is attractive to those philosophers who would like to consider morality a branch of science, much like psychology or sociology. If there is a science of morality, then decisions about what actions are right and what are wrong can be the product of scientific investigation, using the methods of science.

The first step in developing a science of morality would be to define the basic ideas of ethics in terms of characteristics that can be investigated by the scientific method. We can see how this works by using Bentham's utilitarianism as an example. We first define *right action* to signify any action that produces the greatest good for the greatest number. Next, we define the term *good* to mean pleasant; something is good just to the extent that it is pleasant. Using these definitions, we can determine whether or not an action is right just by studying its effects upon the feelings of individuals; are its effects pleasant? Such studies can be carried out by the methods of the social sciences. Naturalism in ethics can thus be interpreted as a claim about the meanings of the basic terms found in moral discourse, such as *good* and *right*. Naturalists may disagree about the

---

[9]W. D. Ross, *Foundations of Ethics* (Oxford: The Clarendon Press, 1939), pp. 84–85.

true meanings of these terms, but they agree that they represent features of objects that can be ascertained by the methods of the social sciences.

In Chapter Two, Socrates was shown to have claimed that in ethics there is no procedure for determining the correct answers to questions as there is in arithmetic and in other sciences. As a result, disagreements in ethics are often settled by quarrels or by violence rather than by rational methods of inquiry. Naturalism gives us the hope that ethical disagreements can be settled peacefully by the use of scientific techniques. Just as earlier ages hoped to find the foundations of ethics in religion, our age looks to science. Can ethical questions be reformulated as scientific questions?

PROBLEMS WITH NATURALISM

Now let us consider two major criticisms of the naturalist approach to ethics. The first criticism concerns the claim that ethical concepts can be defined in terms of characteristics that are observable and hence accessible to the scientific method. Let us take, for example, the definition of *good* to mean pleasant. Now, one can sensibly ask "Is what is good pleasant?" But if *good* means pleasant, then this question is really the same as the question "Is what is pleasant pleasant?" But certainly when one asks "Is what is good pleasant?" one is not just asking "Is what is pleasant pleasant?" Though the answer to the first question may be in doubt and hence may need justification, the answer to the second question is obviously "Yes."

Moreover, if *good* simply means pleasant, then someone who rejects hedonism and says that there are goods other than pleasure is simply contradicting himself. It would be like saying that not all pleasures are pleasant. But hedonism is a substantive thesis that cannot be proved or disproved merely by investigating the meanings of words. One may plausibly reject it without self-contradiction, and even if it should turn out to be true and all good things are pleasant, it does not follow that being pleasant is incorporated into the meaning of *good*.[10]

A second criticism is drawn from Hume and applies not only to naturalism but also to intuitionism and to any theory that regards ethical judgments as statements of fact.

> Since morals, therefore, have an influence on the actions and affections, it
> follows, that they cannot be derived from reason; and that because reason alone
> ... can never have any such influence. Morals excite passions, and produce or
> prevent actions. Reason itself is utterly impotent in this particular. The rules of
> morality, therefore, are not conclusions of our reason.[11]

According to Hume, the purpose of making a moral judgment is either to decide what to do or to advise someone else what to do. Moral judgments are practical, not theoretical. They do not merely assert facts but motivate people to act. For example, suppose I come to realize that I am morally obliged to repay a certain debt. In so realizing, I

---

[10]G. E. Moore developed this criticism in his *Principia Ethica* (Cambridge: Cambridge University Press, 1962), chap. 1. He called the error of defining ethical terms by referring to the observable features of things the naturalistic fallacy.

[11]Hume, *Treatise,* p. 457.

do not simply become aware of a certain fact in the world to which I may or may not be indifferent. Rather, I am prepared to take steps to repay the debt. Thus, moral awareness involves not merely noticing certain facts in the world but also a preparedness to act. For Hume, to have moral knowledge is to be motivated to act. He concludes that moral judgments are not statements of fact. They are representations of the feelings that cause us to make decisions. Both intuitionism and naturalism go wrong in interpreting moral judgments as a kind of theoretical statement. For the intuitionist they are like mathematical statements and for the naturalist they resemble statements in the social sciences. But theoretical statements do not motivate action, and therefore science is not the correct model of morality.

Ethics and the Emotions

THE SUBJECTIVISM OF HUME

Hume's view that the foundation of morality lies in the sentiments or emotions is called **subjectivism.** He assumes that morality must be founded either on reason or on sentiment. It cannot be based upon reason, as we have seen. Therefore, it must be based upon sentiment. Moral judgment is really a form of approval or disapproval arising in the emotions:

> But after every circumstance, every relation is known, the understanding has no further room to operate, nor any object on which it could employ itself. The approbation or blame which then ensues, cannot be the work of the judgement, but of the heart; and is not a speculative proposition or affirmation, but an active feeling or sentiment. . . . In moral decisions, all the circumstances and relations must be previously known; and the mind, from the contemplation of the whole, feels some new impression of affection or disgust, esteem or contempt, approbation or blame.[12]

A moral sentiment, says Hume, is active. This means that the person who feels the moral sentiment is fully prepared to act in accordance with it. A moral sentiment is also fully informed. This means that it arises after all the facts are known. Finally, a moral sentiment is impartial. It arises upon a disinterested survey of the situation:

> Nor is every sentiment of pleasure or pain, which arises from characters and actions, of that *peculiar* kind, which makes us praise or condemn. The good qualities of an enemy are hurtful to us; but may still command our esteem and respect. 'Tis only when a character is considered in general, without reference to our particular interest, that it causes such a feeling or sentiment, as denominates it morally good or evil.[13]

[12]Hume, *Enquiry,* p. 290
[13]Hume, *Treatise,* p. 472.

Consider Hume's example. If I think of an enemy of mine only from the point of view of my personal interests, since he stands in my way, I can only look upon his actions with disapproval. But I may think of him independently of any personal interest. In that case, I may find him admirable. Thus, a moral sentiment is one that is active, informed, and disinterested.

Reason, or the capacity for discovering facts, does have a limited role to play in forming a moral judgment. It tells us about the consequences of our actions and characteristics. But whether these actions are good or bad is to be determined by the sentiments:

> But though reason, when fully assisted and improved, be sufficient to instruct us in the pernicious or useful tendency of qualities and actions; it is not alone sufficient to produce any moral blame or approbation. Utility is only a tendency to a certain end; and were the end totally indifferent to us, we should feel the same indifference towards the means. It is requisite a *sentiment* should here display itself, in order to give a preference to the useful above the pernicious tendencies. This sentiment can be no other than a feeling for the happiness of mankind, and a resentment of their misery; since these are the different ends which virtue and vice have a tendency to promote. Here therefore *reason* instructs us in the several tendencies of our actions, and *humanity* makes a distinction in favour of those which are useful and beneficial.[14]

Human beings are capable of a certain feeling Hume calls humanity or benevolence. Humanity is a concern for the well-being of humankind in general; it involves an ability to identify with the good of others, which Hume calls sympathy. The function of reason is to identify those things that will either help or hinder human well-being. The function of sentiment is to approve of those things that help it and to disapprove of those things that hinder it. For Hume, a study of the foundation of the moral judgment not only finds that the judgment itself is grounded in sentiment but that it uses utilitarian criteria in pronouncing sentence upon actions and characteristics.

EMOTIVISM

A contemporary version of the view that morality is founded on sentiment is called the **emotive theory of ethics.** The emotive theory begins with an account of the meanings of the terms that appear in moral judgments, terms like *good, ought, duty,* and so forth. The emotivist agrees with the criticism directed against naturalism that ethical terms cannot be statements of fact. For example, *good* cannot mean pleasant because it is an open question whether or not everything pleasant is good. But the emotivist does not thereby conclude that ethical terms refer to simple indefinable nonnatural characteristics observable by a moral sense, as does Reid. The emotivist denies the existence of a moral sense. In rejecting the moral sense, the emotivist agrees with the naturalist.

The basic problem with both naturalism and intuitionism lies in assumptions common

---

[14]Hume, *Enquiry,* p. 286.

to them both. They both assume that moral judgments assert facts and that moral terms name qualities or relations that are observable either by the ordinary senses or by a moral sense. If we reject these assumptions, argues the emotivist, we will conclude that moral judgments are not statements of fact at all but expressions of feeling or emotion. If I say "Theft is wrong," I am expressing my disapproval of theft, not asserting some special fact about it.

> The presence of an ethical symbol in a proposition adds nothing to its factual content. Thus if I say to someone "You acted wrongly in stealing that money," I am not stating anything more than if I had simply said, "You stole that money." In adding that this action is wrong I am not making any further statement about it. I am simply evincing my moral disapproval of it. It is as if I had said, "You stole that money," in a peculiar tone of horror, or written it with the addition of some special exclamation marks. The tone, or the exclamation marks, adds nothing to the literal meaning of the sentence. It merely serves to show that the expression of it is attended by certain feelings in the speaker.[15]

Ethical terms, then, do not have cognitive meaning, as do words like *green* and *large* that name observable qualities and relations. Because ethical terms do not name any qualities or relations, the only kind of meaning they have is emotive meaning. Their characteristic use is to express the approval or disapproval of the speaker.

When a term is said to have emotive meaning, it must not be inferred that the term *names* the feelings of the speaker. When a person states that theft is wrong, he is not making the factual assertion that he disapproves of theft. The emotivist says that ethical judgments do not make any factual assertion at all. They are neither true nor false. But they do *express* feeling. This means that they are more like the expressions "Alas" and "Hurrah," which are used to evince disapproval and approval. For the emotivist, there is no such thing as moral knowledge or moral truth.

PROBLEMS WITH SUBJECTIVISM AND EMOTIVISM

A major criticism of both subjectivism and emotivism is that if they were true, we could not reason about ethics. Ethical judgments would be arbitrary, so there would be no point in arguing about them. We do, however, reason about ethical matters; we do argue about conflicting judgments. So emotivism and subjectivism have gone wrong somewhere.

One reply to this criticism is already implicit in Hume's presentation. All that the subjectivist or emotivist need point out is that the feelings that we have about certain actions are tied to factual beliefs about their consequences. Thus, I may initially disapprove of someone's refusing to return weapons that he held in safekeeping. But when I find that their owner has turned into a madman, my disapproval will turn into approval. It is certainly possible to engage in reasoning about the facts to which our feelings are tied. People can change their reaction to a situation if they are brought to

---

[15]A. J. Ayer, *Language, Truth and Logic* (London: Victor Gollantz, Ltd., 1946), p. 107.

see the facts in a new light. But, says the emotivist, ultimately there can be no reasoning about values or preferences.

Another more serious difficulty with the view that morality is founded upon feeling is that one can make a moral judgment without any discernible feeling or even despite a contrary one. I may, for example, agree that theft is wrong without having any particular feeling about it one way or another. I may be acquainted with a particular thief whose charm makes him lovable and whose daring I admire. Yet I nevertheless believe that he and his occupation are to be morally condemned. If I cannot find in me a particular emotion associated with a particular judgment, then it is implausible to think that the meaning of ethical terms consists in their evincing emotions.

Hume would reply that the feeling that is the basis of morality is cool and calm, not involved and passionate. Thus, it is easily missed and easily confused with a judgment of the reason. We may think we are making a judgment when all we are really doing is expressing a feeling. This reply makes us wonder how we can distinguish feeling from judgment. If one cannot find any observable differences between certain feelings and certain judgments, then what is the point of subjectivism?

MAIN THEORIES OF THE FOUNDATIONS OF ETHICS

Intuitionism: Ethical judgments are verified by a moral sense.
Naturalism: Ethical judgments are verified by observation.
Subjectivism and emotivism: Ethical judgments express sentiments and emotions.
Skepticism: Ethical judgments cannot be justified.

Rules

I began this chapter by raising the question, How are moral judgments to be justified? In twentieth-century moral philosophy, this issue has been linked to the question, What kind of meaning do moral judgments have? The question is thus one of language. When a moral judgment is formulated in words, what use of language is involved? According to intuitionists and naturalists, language is used to make statements of fact that can be either true or false and that can be shown to be true or false by intuition or observation. According to the emotivists, a moral judgment is not a statement of fact but uses language to express emotion and feeling. We have found difficulties with every one of these views. In the remainder of this chapter, I shall explore another view, called the rule theory, that says that moral discourse consists in the formulation and application of rules.

Moral principles are very much like rules. For example, upon entering a theater, it is common to find posted on a wall the announcement, "No smoking is permitted in this theater." This announcement is a use of words that formulates a rule against smoking in a certain place. Given the existence of such a rule, persons who wish to smoke are obliged not to, and everyone in the theater has the right to request smokers to discontinue smoking. A rule against smoking is, linguistically, similar to the moral rules against killing, lying, and the breaking of promises. Let us consider the hypothesis that moral principles and precepts can be interpreted as rules stating types of actions that are permitted, forbidden, or obligatory. In a singular moral judgment such as "John ought to repay his debt to Jane," a moral rule is applied to a particular case. The basic language of morals, then, is one in which rules are formulated and applied to specific situations.

One can adopt either an external or an internal standpoint toward rules.[16] The individual who speaks of rules from an external standpoint merely reports their existence or nonexistence. For example, if I am an inveterate smoker, I may wish to know whether I will be permitted to smoke in the theater. If the manager says "There is a rule against smoking," he is making the statement that such a rule exists. Someone who reports the existence of a rule from the external standpoint may not agree with the rule at all. The manager may be opposed to the prohibition because it discourages customers and still be able to report that there is such a rule. An anthropologist who is reporting on the rules of behavior of a culture quite different from ours need not agree with the rules whose existence he has discovered. If he reports, for example, that a certain tribe has a rule that a widow must be buried alive with the body of her dead husband, no one would think that he agreed with such a barbaric custom.

The individual who speaks of rules from the internal standpoint does not merely report their existence or nonexistence but expresses agreement with them and indicates a willingness to apply them to particular cases. Whereas the anthropologist who merely records its existence occupies the external point of view, individuals who accept and live by a certain moral code have adopted the internal standpoint. To illustrate the difference, consider the following two expressions:

(*1*) Widows must be buried alive along with the bodies of their dead husbands.
(*2*) Amanda is a widow whose husband is about to be buried.

A member of the tribe who accepted its customs and practices and who thus agreed with the rule formulated in (1) would be willing to draw the conclusion:

(*3*) Amanda should now be buried alive with the body of her dead husband.

Agreeing with the rule, he agrees with the conclusion expressed in (3). But an anthropologist may accept (1) as a report that there is such a rule in that culture without endorsing (3).

Individuals who adopt the external standpoint make *statements* about rules. For the anthropologist, (1) is a statement of fact, a way of reporting that such a practice exists in that society. But the member of the tribe who utters (1) is not making a statement but prescribing a rule that he endorses. Thus, the same words may be used to perform two quite distinct types of linguistic acts. The external standpoint uses statement-making language; the internal standpoint uses rule-endorsing and rule-applying language.

[16]H. L. A. Hart, *The Concept of Law* (Oxford: The Clarendon Press, 1961), p. 55.

This account of the language of morality does justice to certain aspects of the theories we have already discussed. Both intuitionists and naturalists claim that the expression of a moral principle is a statement of fact. The rule theory agrees that the formulation of a rule from the external standpoint states that there is such a rule in force in a certain place. The intuitionist claims that a moral principle is not reducible to a claim of empirical science. The rule theory agrees, for it says that the endorsement of a moral principle from the internal standpoint is not a scientific statement. The naturalist claims that ethical judgments are verifiable using the methods of science. The rule theory agrees that the question whether a rule exists in a certain group of people can be answered by observing their actions. The emotivist asserts that expressing moral principles indicates approval or disapproval of certain classes of actions. According to the rule theory, the endorsement of a moral principle from the internal standpoint expresses approval of the principle. The frequent absence of any feeling of approval or disapproval, which was noted as a difficulty with emotivism, is explained by the rule theory as being characteristic of rules described from the external standpoint. Finally, the rule theory can incorporate Hume's insight that when a person makes a moral judgment, he is thereby motivated to act. For when someone endorses a rule from the internal standpoint, he thereby indicates his willingness to act in accordance with it should the appropriate circumstances arise.

Moral Rules

The rule against smoking in a crowded theater does not qualify as a moral or ethical rule, as do the rules against killing or theft. Some rules are just customs; others are rules of etiquette; still others are laws. What distinguishes these from the principles, or rules, of morality?

One important characteristic of a moral rule is that those who accept it believe that people are required to live up to it. Following it is not optional, for the type of conduct it prescribes, permits, or forbids is thought to be too important to allow individuals to deviate from it. For example, the rules against murder and theft prescribe rights to life and property that are indispensable for a secure and orderly social life. A rule of etiquette, however, is optional. Whether one holds one's fork with the right or left hand is too insignificant to consider it an ethical matter.

A second characteristic of a moral rule is that it tends to be easily generalized and is thus widely applicable to many persons and situations. Thus, the rule against smoking in a certain theater fails to be a moral rule because, among other things, its applicability is restricted in time and place to this theater. As Kant argued, moral rules are universal in form and are applicable to all persons at all times and places. But though the rule against smoking is not itself a moral principle, its value can be explained in terms of morality. The reason to forbid smoking in a theater is that it endangers the health and safety of others, and there is a moral rule that forbids individuals to harm others.

Another characteristic of a moral rule is that it need not be the product of a specific act of legislation or judicial decision. Moral rules are more like customs than legal rules in this respect. A rule of law exists when it is passed by an authoritative legislative body or endorsed by a judge or court. A rule of morality, on the other hand, is apparent in the behavior of individuals and groups and does not require legislative or judicial enactment for its binding force.

David Hume saw that it is possible for groups of persons to come to agree on rules even though the rules are not established by an explicit decision:

> Thus two men pull the oars of a boat by common convention for common interest, without any promise or contract: thus gold and silver are made the measures of exchange; thus speech and words and language are fixed by human convention and agreement. Whatever is advantageous to two or more persons if all perform their part; but what loses all advantage if only one perform, can arise from no other principle.[17]

The rules that determine the value of money or the meanings of words did not arise through explicit agreement or legislation but evolved gradually as a part of human conduct. The rules of morality have a similar status. A moral rule may also become a law. For example, many criminal laws put into effect the moral rule that forbids violence. Most of the laws of our society are attempts to apply our morality to particular circumstances. But the validity of a moral rule does not depend upon its being a law. Some promises are not illegal to break even though it would be wrong to break them.

Another characteristic of moral rules is that they are ways of realizing certain basic human goals and interests. For example, all human beings have an interest in avoiding violence and harm. Hence, there is a moral rule forbidding individuals from harming one another. The existence of property helps resolve conflict concerning the use of items of consumption, and human beings have an interest in preserving the stability of possession. Hence, there are rules against theft and vandalism that serve to sustain the system of property. Our interest in sustaining forms of cooperation is advanced by rules forbidding the breaking of promises and of lying. Some moral rules serve to preserve and sustain important human groups that are indispensable for a satisfactory life for most people. Thus, the rule against adultery and the obligations of parents toward children help sustain the family. The obligation to obey the law helps sustain political society.

A rule, then, is of moral significance if it has some or all of these characteristics. Of course, there can be disagreement whether a rule is morally valid. For example, in some circles the rule against adultery no longer holds. Among politicians the rule against lying has never had much importance. Compare also the austere morality of the Puritans, which was based upon following a rigid set of rules, with the more liberal morality of the affluent middle class of twentieth-century America. But rules that have ceased to be respected among certain groups may be valid rules nevertheless.

Culture and Morality

Cultural relativism claims that moral rules arise out of the needs of particular cultures and that their validity is limited to the cultures in which they arise. This view can be

[17]Hume, *Enquiry*, p. 306.

stated in a weak or a strong form. In its weak form, it is a theory about the origin of morality; it says that morality arises out of cultural needs. In its strong form, it is a theory about the validity of morals. It says that a rule is binding upon a given individual if it is an accepted rule in his culture.

There is much to be said for the weak form of cultural relativism. Many rules do arise in the course of cultural evolution. Let me give as an example Marvin Harris's speculations about the origin of the taboo against eating pork found among certain Middle Eastern peoples. He indicates certain general principles that explain taboos on the consumption of animal flesh:

> Cultures tend to impose supernatural sanctions on the consumption of animal
> flesh when the ratio of communal benefits to costs associated with the use of a
> particular species deteriorates. . . . Animals that have high benefits and low costs
> at one time, but that become more costly later on, are the principle targets of
> supernatural sanctions.[18]

According to Harris, "pig raising incurred costs that posed a threat to the entire subsistence in the hot, semiarid lands of the ancient Middle East." The climate was not good for raising pigs, and their diet had to be supplemented by grains that could have been used for human consumption. The taboo against eating pork was a technique that a culture devised for suppressing the temptation to raise and consume a costly form of animal life.[19] Groups that accept this taboo tend to believe that their members must adhere to it; whether or not to include pork in one's diet is not optional for them.

Whatever the merits of Harris's particular explanation, certainly the existence of some firmly held rules of behavior can be explained by the particular circumstances in which a culture evolves. One difficulty with this weak form of cultural relativism, however, is that some rules of morality do not originate in cultural evolution but are invented by individuals. For example, the rule against retribution—against returning harm with harm—is ascribed to Socrates in some of Plato's writings and is advocated by Jesus in the New Testament. The cultural relativist may reply that his theory is not concerned with who first discovered a principle of conduct but how such principles become accepted among large groups of people. In this form, the weak version of cultural relativism claims that moral rules come to be accepted because of the needs of the culture.

Once its basic concepts have been sufficiently clarified, the weak version of this theory can be tested by the methods of the social sciences. The strong form offers a criterion of moral validity. To find out whether or not a rule is binding upon a certain person, you must examine his culture to see if the rule is generally accepted. If it is, then he is obliged to follow it. In its strong form, cultural relativism is not a scientific theory that can be tested by sociologists and anthropologists but a normative claim about how people *ought* to behave.

One main problem with this criterion is that it counsels mere conformity and discourages critical thinking. It dictates that what I am obliged to do is what is done.

---

[18]Marvin Harris, *Cannibals and Kings: The Origins of Cultures* (New York: Random House, 1977), p. 131.
[19]Ibid., pp. 132–133.

Ethics is identified with custom. A critical thinker, on the other hand, does not blindly follow the customs of the country. He subjects them to analysis and criticism to determine whether or not they are correct. If a rule is widely accepted in my society, I should consider it carefully and give due weight to the fact that others who are as intelligent and wise as I accept it. But if, upon reflection, I find serious defects in it, I am not obliged to go along.

Another difficulty with the strong form of cultural relativism is that it offers no guidance when there is disagreement among the people. For example, in our society many thoughtful and intelligent people disagree about the morality of abortion. While some strongly favor it, others bitterly oppose it. We cannot discover which position is correct merely by finding out which has the largest number of adherents.

Justification and Critical Morality

By the time each of us begins to think critically about ethical problems, a set of moral values has already been instilled in us through our relations with our family, our friends, our teachers, and other members of society. Initially, then, justification in ethics consists of applying the moral values we already have to particular cases: I find that I ought to repay a debt because I accept the rule that debts ought to be repaid. Then I begin to think critically about the rules that I accept. I begin to wonder why I should continue to accept them, and I try to find a rationale for the rules themselves. Do they serve the fundamental human interests and needs that are the underlying basis of morality? Why is there a rule for the repayment of debts? Because without it all sorts of commercial and other transactions could not occur. Why should people keep their promises? Because if they did not, they would cease to trust and rely upon one another.

In trying to relate rules to fundamental interests, I may come to reject some of them. For example, someone who accepts the pork taboo may become convinced by Harris's arguments about its origin and conclude that because the conditions under which the taboo was rational no longer hold, there is no longer any reason to maintain it. Or I may find that the factual presuppositions under which I accepted certain rules are incorrect. For example, I may have opposed divorce because I was convinced that God commanded married people to stay together. Later, I may come to believe that God did not issue such a command, or that there is no God, or that God never issues commands at all.

Other circumstances cause me to question my existing moral rules. Situations may arise that are not covered by any rules that I already accept. For example, I may have no rule that tells me how to resolve the question of abortion. Should I extend the rule against taking a human life to a fetus? In other situations, things that I have hitherto taken for granted may suddenly present me with an ethical problem. I have always been a meat eater. A visit to a slaughter house may cause me to wonder whether it is right to take the lives of animals to consume their flesh. In still other situations, the rules that I already accept may come into conflict with one another, leaving me to wonder how I should resolve this inconsistency in my moral system. For example, if I favor both political freedom and economic equality and if I find that the attempt to foster equality tends to squelch freedom, then I must decide which value takes precedence. To deal with such novel problems, I may have to extend and revise old rules or invent new ones. As I invent, revise, extend, and order my rules, I appeal to the fundamental interests that the rules are supposed to serve. I justify a change in my moral code by showing how the change better serves a human need or furthers a basic interest.

Morality and Human Interest

That a particular action should be done is justified by an appeal to the agent's moral rules. That a general rule ought to be followed is justified by showing that if people in general follow it, certain fundamental needs and interests are served. There can, however, be disagreements about what needs and interests *should* be served. For example, are the needs of human beings only to be served or are those of animals to be included? Does one have an obligation to avoid human suffering only or does the suffering of animals count as well? Are the utilitarians correct in thinking that the only interest that counts is the desire for pleasure? Or shall we agree with Kant that respect for persons takes priority? The fundamental values in terms of which the rules of morality are themselves justified may also be questioned.

Questions about these fundamental values cannot be settled by an appeal to these values themselves. Can they be settled at all by rational means? To answer a question by rational means is to give a reason favoring one answer over the alternatives. But what reason can be given favoring fundamental values? Because the values are fundamental, there is logically no more fundamental value to appeal to. At this point, rational analysis may give way to commitment. The fundamental values that morality serves cannot be *proved* to be correct. Rather, they are *chosen* or accepted in light of our total available knowledge and experience. These values are products of choice and commitment, as well as of reason and science.

In actual discussion about what ought to be done, however, we seldom, if ever, arrive at the point where rational analysis gives way completely to commitment. Further discussion is always possible. The nature of the values to which we are committed may need to be clarified. We may come to doubt the relation between these values and the rules of our moral code. New experiences may alter our understanding of them. Finally, we may decide to revise the values we are committed to after reflecting upon their consequences. Thus, even though commitment plays a crucial role in the formation of a critical morality, the commitment is related in a variety of ways to the exercise of our rational capacities.

Why Should I Be Moral?

Let us return to the problem that was raised in Chapter Two. Why should *I* regulate my conduct according to rules that serve fundamental human values? Why should *I* adopt a moral standpoint at all? Perhaps I should do as I please in every situation and not subordinate my own goals to those of humankind generally. There are various answers to these questions. First, because almost all human beings have been raised and educated within a community, they have already internalized their community's system of moral rules. Thus, from a psychological standpoint, it is not easy to put aside the rules of one's community because, in the process of individual development, they have become one's own rules. Acting against the rules that have been internalized will lead one to suffer from a guilty conscience. In addition, if one breaks the rules and is found out, one will be scorned and hated by others. So a refusal to adopt the moral point of view of one's community can lead to unhappiness for two reasons: guilt and loneliness.

Suppose, however, that a person does not have a very strong conscience and that he can find a way to break the rules without anyone's ever finding out. Remember Plato's story of the ring of Gyges in Chapter Two? What can be said to him? No strict proof, I think, can convince the amoralist. The argument that one should subordinate one's own personal interest to humanity's fundamental values will not convince someone who is not concerned about realizing these values in practice, who lacks sympathy for others, and who believes that he can get away with breaking the rules anyway. There is, however, something that can be done, namely, we can create institutions and systems of education that will encourage the members of society to obey our considered rules of morality.

Summary

This chapter is concerned with the justification of moral judgments. How can one settle disagreements about moral principles? Can one derive a normative judgment from a statement of fact? Is morality based upon reason or sentiment? Intuitionism claims that moral principles can be established by a direct rational insight, using the moral sense. The basic difficulty with this view is that the existence of a moral sense can be questioned. For naturalism, moral principles can be verified by ordinary sense observation. Naturalism offers the hope that ethics can be founded upon science, but it founders on the difficulty of defining ethical concepts in terms of observables. Hume offered the idea that morality is founded on sentiment. His view has been called subjectivism. Emotivism is a contemporary version of Hume's subjectivism. It says that the ethical judgments express the feelings of the speaker. The basic difficulty with emotivism is that moral judgments may be made in the absence of feelings of approval or disapproval. It was then suggested that the language of morals neither states fact nor expresses emotion but consists in the formulation and application of rules. Rules may be formulated from either an external or internal standpoint. Speaking from the external standpoint merely describes a rule; speaking from the internal standpoint endorses it. Moral rules are non-optional, general, independent of legislative enactment or judicial decision, and are ways of realizing basic interests and values. The claim that they are relative to culture has the difficulty that mere conformity to the customs of one's society is not a valid criterion of right conduct. Particular actions are justified by reference to general rules, and general rules can be justified by reference to fundamental values. But the fundamental values are selected by thoughtful commitment rather than proved to be correct by reason.

Glossary

Cultural relativism: The view that the criterion of right conduct is conformity to the rules of one's culture.

Emotivism: The view that ethical judgments express the feelings or emotions of the speaker.

Ethical pluralism: The view that there is more than one fundamental principle of morality.

Intuitionism: The theory that the fundamental principles of ethics are self-evident truths apprehended through the moral sense.

Moral skepticism: The view that the fundamental principles of ethics cannot be justified.

Naturalism: A type of ethical theory that claims that the fundamental principles of ethics can be verified by sense observation and established by the scientific method.

Normative statement: A statement about what ought to be done as distinguished from a *statement of fact* about the way things are.

Practical reasoning: Reasoning in which individuals try to determine which actions they should perform. It is distinguished from *theoretical reasoning,* whose goal is not action but the discovery of truth.

Prima facie obligation: An act is prima facie obligatory if it possesses characteristics that tend to make it the right act to do. It may, however, possess other characteristics that make it wrong to do.

Subjectivism: The view that morality is founded on human feeling or emotion.

Further Reading

David Hume's account of the foundations of ethics is contained in book III, part 1 of his *A Treatise of Human Nature,* ed. L. A. Selby-Bigge (Oxford: The Clarendon Press, 1968) as well as in chapter 1 and Appendix I of his "An Enquiry concerning the Principles of Morals" in *Hume's Enquiries,* ed. L. A. Selby-Bigge (Oxford: The Clarendon Press, 1972). Book II, part 3, sect. 3 of the *Treatise* contains Hume's famous discussion of the view that reason is the slave of the passions and that reason by itself cannot motivate action.

Versions of intuitionism are contained in Thomas Reid, "Essays on the Active Powers of Man" in his *Philosophical Works,* ed. Sir William Hamilton, volume II; G. E. Moore, *Principia Ethica* (Cambridge: Cambridge University Press, 1962); H. A. Prichard, *Moral Obligation* (Oxford: Oxford University Press, 1968); and W. D. Ross, *Foundations of Ethics* (Oxford: The Clarendon Press, 1939).

Naturalism is well represented in the writings of John Dewey. See his *Human Nature and Conduct* (New York: Random House, 1930), and *Theory of the Moral Life* (New York: Holt, Rinehart and Winston, 1960). See also Ralph Barton Perry, *General Theory of Value* (Cambridge: Harvard University Press, 1926).

The classic account of emotivism is in Charles L. Stevenson, *Ethics and Language*

(New Haven: Yale University Press, 1944). A brief presentation is in A. J. Ayer, *Language, Truth, and Logic* (London: Victor Gollantz, Ltd., 1946), p. 107.

Some important contemporary treatises on the foundations of ethics are Kurt Baier, *The Moral Point of View* (New York: Random House, 1965); Alan Donagan, *The Theory of Morality* (Chicago: University of Chicago Press, 1977); J. N. Findlay, *Values and Intentions* (London: George Allen and Unwin, 1968); William Frankena, *Ethics* (Englewood Cliffs, N. J.: Prentice-Hall, 1963); R. M. Hare, *The Language of Morals* (Oxford: The Clarendon Press, 1952); J. L. Mackie, *Ethics: Inventing Right and Wrong* (New York: Penguin Books, 1977).

Questions for Thought and Discussion

1. The Declaration of Independence declares that certain truths are self-evident, especially truths concerning inalienable rights. What assumptions about our ethical knowledge fits the Declaration? Can these assumptions be defended by argument?

2. What are the main differences between intuitionism and naturalism? Do you agree with their common assumption that ethical judgments assert facts and are not merely expressions of feeling? What is the difference between asserting a fact and expressing a feeling?

3. Is there any important difference between Hume's subjectivism and the emotive theory of ethics?

4. Consider some major ethical disagreement that you have been involved in and determine how the different approaches to the foundations of ethics would try to settle it.

5. Some philosophers have adopted a kind of moral relativism according to which a society's morality is determined by its laws and hence is relative to its legal system. Can moral principles be distinguished from laws? Can this form of relativism be defended?

6. Are there any really important differences between subjectivism and cultural relativism?

7. Have you ever wondered why you should be moral? If the ring of Gyges ever came into your possession, would you act as Gyges did? Would you have a sufficient reason for not acting as he did?

Part II

THE HUMAN CONDITION

Chapter 5

MIND AND FREEDOM

PREVIEW

What is the place of human beings in nature? Are we just one more animal alongside the others or do we in some way transcend our biological heritage? In our discussion of this issue, we shall raise and consider three fundamental questions.

First, how is the human mind, the instrument of thought, related to the human body? In particular, what is the relationship between mind and brain? Are they one and the same thing or is the mind in some way distinct from the brain?

Second, given that human beings are persons, what does it mean to be a person as distinct from a thing or object? Here we shall consider the important question, What constitutes a person's identity?

Third, given that human beings make choices and are held accountable for them, is freedom possible? In particular, if every event is caused by a previous event in accordance with the laws of nature, how can humans be said to have the freedom to act in accordance with their will?

Life and Mind

When we are quite young, our curiosity about the world is aroused, and we quickly become aware of the difference between living and nonliving things. A rock, a grain of sand, and the moon are examples of nonliving material substances. Plants and animals are the primary examples of living things. Essentially, living creatures are distinguished from lifeless substances by their need for nutrition and their ability to grow and reproduce. A lifeless thing like a rock does not need to consume food; nor can it grow or produce new rocks. Among animals (and human beings are included as a kind of animal) we find evidence of mind and intelligence. First, animals are capable of experiencing sensations like pains, itches, tingles, aches, stings, pricks, tastes, feelings of warmth and cold, and so forth. This fundamental capacity is called **sentience.** The importance of sentience is that it alerts the animal to things in its environment that can sustain or threaten its health and life. Second, animals are capable of some form of *sense perception.* Through the use of the five senses, human animals become directly aware of the world about them. Sense perception is thus a form of *awareness* of the world. Other forms of awareness common among the higher animals are *memory,* which is the capacity to retain information about the past; *expectation,* which is the capacity to anticipate the future; and *imagination,* which is the capacity to form images of our own creation.

Human beings differ from other animals in that their thoughts are not necessarily tied to the particular events yielded by sense perception or memory but can range throughout the actual universe and through imaginary worlds as well. Whereas the thoughts of other animals are apparently restricted to particular events in their environment, human beings can initiate trains of thought about events they have never experienced. The historian reflects on events that occurred in the far past. The physicist studies the properties of particles too small to be observed by the human senses. The theologian wonders about the fate of humankind and about God. Human thought is thus free of direct environmental constraints. The term **intellect** has often been used to indicate this capacity for unconstrained thought.

Though animals may lack human intellectual capacities, they may possess other virtues that make them superior to humans in certain respects. In these lines from the poem "Song of Myself," Walt Whitman celebrates the life of animals:

> I think I could turn and live with animals, they are so placid and self-contained;
> I stand and look at them long and long.
> They do not sweat and whine about their condition;
> They do not lie awake in the dark and weep for their sins;
> They do not make me sick discussing their duty to God;
> Not one is dissatisfied—not one is demented with the mania of owning things;
> Not one kneels to another, nor to his kind that lived thousands of years ago;
> Not one is respectable or industrious over the whole earth.

Humans and some other animals also have the capacity to act deliberately and intentionally, a capacity generally called **will.** Human action itself does not always occur as a direct response to an environmental stimulus. Often a motive is reached after deliberation. Prior to acting, we often form intentions to pursue a purpose or goal, and our conduct is guided by our formed intentions.

Another major capacity of humans and many animals is indicated by the term *emotion.* Joy, sadness, anxiety, anger, depression, serenity, love, and so forth are emotions that color our experience of the world and influence our actions and values.

The intellect, the will, and the emotions are the states of mind that indicate an awareness of the world. Thinking—the exercise of intellect—always embodies an awareness of something thought about. An individual's intentions contain a reference to the goal sought. Emotions often contain a reference to an object; one is angry at someone or fearful of something or grateful to someone. Awareness of the world permeates our mental life.

It is sometimes said that the distinguishing feature of the mind is **consciousness.** This term, however, is ambiguous. Sometimes it is used to mean sentience, or bodily feeling. In this sense, even the lowest animals have consciousness, whereas plants probably lack it. At other times, *consciousness* is used to mean awareness. Thus, a person who is in a deep sleep or who has been knocked out is described as being unconscious, and he regains consciousness when his capacities for thought and perception are able to be exercised. Whether this second sense of the word distinguishes mental from physical states is in part a verbal question. If we wish to classify bodily feelings as mental states, since feelings do not necessarily imply any awareness of the world, then not all mental states imply consciousness. But even if consciousness is not invariably present in states of mind, it is a central feature of the mind and is an essential aspect of the kind of mind that human beings have.

The characteristics that distinguish animal life from plants and nonliving things can be summed up in the statement that animals and humans possess minds whereas these other things do not. But what sort of thing is a mind? How are minds related to various material things and processes? In particular, how is the mind related to the brain and nervous system of an animal?

Mind and Self

The first person singular pronoun *I* is a very peculiar word. It is the only word in the English language that has in its standard use the following characteristic: When different speakers utter it, they are necessarily referring to different things. Any other word can be used by different speakers to talk about the same thing. Even the first person plural pronoun *we* can be used by different speakers to refer to the same group; two members of the same committee who both said "We decided to do such and such" are using *we* to indicate the same group. But when I utter the word *I,* I am referring to me. When you utter it, you are referring to you. Each person using *I* is naming a different thing, namely, the self or the person using *I.*

The self, then, is that which is signified by the word *I* in English and by the first person singular pronoun in other languages. What is the self? How is it related to the mind? How is the self related to the body?

Try the following experiment. Just point to your own body. That's all that is being asked. I doubt that any of you found this a difficult thing to do. None of you had to spend much time, I am sure, figuring out which of the various human bodies in your proximity is yours. But how do you know which body is yours?

Suppose someone were to challenge you to explain why the body you pointed to is yours rather than someone else's. I think that you could give the following reply. First, your body is the one whose feelings you feel. There is only one body whose itches, pains, aches, and tingles you feel, and that one is yours. You do not feel the pains in my body, and I do not feel the pains in yours. I do not suffer with your toothache and you do not groan over my backache. You do not scratch my itches and I do not scratch yours.

Second, your body is the one from which you perceive the world. You see through a certain set of eyes and hear through a certain pair of ears. The body to which these eyes and ears belong gives you a perspective from which the world is perceived. And finally, your body is the one by which you act and do things. The arm that rises when you decide to raise your arm, the legs that move when you decide to walk, and the tongue that wags when you decide to talk belong to your body just by virtue of the fact that your body is the one whose arms, legs, and tongue respond directly to your will.

There is, then, an intimate connection between the self and its body. Can the self be identified with the body? Is a person nothing more than his or her body? We have reason to believe that however close the connection, the self should be distinguished from the body. Some of you may have read a story by Franz Kafka called "The Metamorphosis."[1] In this story, Gregor Samsa awakes in the morning to find that he has been transformed into a gigantic insect. He had gone to sleep the night before with his own human body and now finds that he inhabits the body of a bug. Imagine something like that happening to you. Imagine that you awake, look in the mirror, and discover to your amazement that your body is entirely different from the way it was when you went to sleep. That this new body is yours will be established by the fact that it is the one in which you have feelings, from which you perceive the world, and which responds directly to your will. We are able, then, to imagine changing our bodies. Thus, it is at least possible that the self is not to be identified with its body no matter how closely connected they are.

Not only can we imagine changing bodies, some theories assert that we actually do change them. According to the theory of reincarnation accepted by certain philosophers (e.g., Plato) and by certain religions (e.g., Buddhism), a person acquires a new body and a new life after the death of the old.

The idea of immortality, in which the soul survives death, also assumes that body and self are distinguishable. According to this view, after death the self separates from its body and continues to exist in a disembodied state. It is difficult to understand how such a separated self could feel, perceive, or act because these functions normally require the use of bodily parts. But if the self could exist in such a disembodied state, then it would be wrong to identify it with its body. Those philosophers who accept the idea of disembodied existence, commonly identify the self with the mind or soul of a person. Because of this historically influential identification, the question of the relation between self and body has become tied to the question of the relation between mind and body.

Mind–Body Dualism

ARGUMENTS FOR DUALISM

Mind–body dualism is the theory that the mind or self is a distinct being from the body. According to this theory, my mind and my body are numerically different; my mind is one thing, my body another. The most influential statement of mind–body dualism in

---

[1]"The Metamorphosis" is included in *Selected Short Stories of Franz Kafka,* trans. Willa and Edwin Muir (New York: Modern Library, 1952).

RENÉ DESCARTES
(1596–1650)

Descartes was born in the village of La Haye in France. He was educated by the Jesuits and spent several years traveling and in military service. He went to live in Holland, where he found the time to engage in scientific and philosophical research. He was invited to travel to Stockholm to present his philosophical ideas to Queen Christina of Sweden. It is said that because the queen insisted on having early lessons, Descartes lost his health, caught pneumonia, and died. He made important contributions to science and mathematics as well as philosophy and wished to apply mathematical methods to all areas of human knowledge. His major philosophical work is his *Meditations on First Philosophy*. Various criticisms of his ideas as presented in the *Meditations* together with his replies to his critics are contained in the *Objections and Replies*. The *Discourse on Method* presents Descartes' intellectual autobiography. His *Rules for the Direction of the Mind* contains his theory of knowledge. (A full presentation of Descartes' philosophy is contained in *The Philosophical Works of Descartes,* trans. Elizabeth S. Haldane and G. R. T. Ross (Cambridge: Cambridge University Press, 1972, 2 volumes).

modern philosophy was formulated by René Descartes (1596–1650) in his *Meditations on First Philosophy*. According to Descartes, the universe contains two distinct kinds of substances. On the one hand, there are material or physical bodies. A body is something that occupies space and that can be observed. Its essential attribute is extension. On the other hand, there are selves or minds. A self is something that can think; it is characterized by various forms of awareness; it is conscious. The essential attribute of the self is to be a thinking thing.

To establish the dualism of mind and body, Descartes argued that nothing could have both these essential attributes. If something were a thinking being, it could not be extended, and if something was an extended being, it could not think. It followed that the self could not be identified with its body. In developing this argument, Descartes used the idea that if things have incompatible properties, then they must be different. If x has the property P and y has the property $Q,$ and if P and Q are incompatible, then x and y are distinct. P and Q are incompatible if it is impossible for them to be possessed by the same object. Thus, red and green are incompatible because no object can be both red and green in the same places and at the same time. If x is red and y is green, we know that x and y are distinct.

Descartes thought that being extended in space is incompatible with being a thinking being. They are incompatible because whereas the existence of bodies can be doubted— even of one's own body—no one can doubt his own existence. When I think I see a material body, I may be mistaken. Since my senses often lead me into error, it is always possible that any body that I think exists does not really exist. Thus, I think I see a typewriter on which I am now typing. But I have "seen" this typewriter in my dreams, and for all I know, I may be dreaming. (See Chapter Seven for a detailed discussion of Descartes' doubting the existence of things.) On the other hand, I cannot doubt that I now exist. I realize that anyone who tries to doubt anything must exist as a precondition of his trying to doubt. Only existing things can doubt anything. Thus, the very attempt to doubt that I exist leads me to affirm my existence. It follows, thought Descartes, that the self possesses a characteristic that the body lacks, namely, that its existence is indubitable.

The notion of incompatibility has been widely used in the attempt to establish mind–body dualism. For example, consider this passage by the contemporary philosopher Brand Blanshard.

> That we really do mean something different by consciousness and bodily behavior is made clear again by the different attributes that we assign to them. We speak of an idea as clear or confused, as apposite or inapposite, as witty or dull. Are such terms intelligible when applied to those motions of electrons, atoms, molecules, or muscles, which for the behaviorist are all there is to consciousness? Can a motion be clear, or cogent, or witty? . . . These adjectives are perfectly in order when applied to ideas; they become at once absurd when applied to movements in muscle or nerve. . . . On the other side, movements have attributes which are unthinkable as applied to ideas. Movements have velocity; but what is the average velocity of one's ideas on a protective tariff? Movements have direction; would there be any sense in talking of the north-easterly direction of one's thought on the morality of revenge?[2]

The general strategy behind this argument consists in showing that characteristics possessed by mental phenomena such as ideas could not be possessed by physical phenomena such as motions of molecules, and vice versa.

In Lewis Carroll's *Through the Looking Glass,* the White Knight appears to be a dualist. He fell off his horse and rolled head first into a ditch; but that didn't stop him from talking:

"How can you go on talking so quietly, head downwards?" asked Alice, as she dragged him out by the feet and laid him in a heap on the bank.
 The Knight looked surprised at the question. "What does it matter where my body happens to be?" he said. "My mind goes on working all the same. In fact the more headdownwards I am, the more I keep inventing new things."

---

[2]Brand Blanshard, *The Nature of Thought* (London: George Allen and Unwin, 1948), I, 336–337.

A related type of argument supposes that we can directly observe the difference between mind and body. **Introspection** is the term generally applied to a person's observing what is going on in his own mind. C. J. Ducasse, another contemporary dualist, formulates an argument based upon what introspection allegedly reveals:

> What thought, desire, sensation, and other mental states are like, each of us can observe directly by introspection, and what introspection reveals is that they do not in the least resemble muscular contraction, or glandular secretion, or any other known bodily events. No tampering with language can alter the observable fact that thinking is one thing and muttering quite another; that the feeling called anger has no resemblance to the bodily behavior which usually goes with it; or that an act of will is not in the least like anything we find when we open the skull and examine the brain.[3]

Through introspection, says Ducasse, we become directly aware of our mental states, and we discover that they bear no resemblance to physical states.

Another important reason often given for accepting mind–body dualism is the claim that whereas physical phenomena are public, mental phenomena are private. Consider a physical object such as a rock. Both the rock and its characteristics can be observed by anyone in its vicinity who has normal vision. The rock is a publicly observable object. But mental phenomena are different. No one can observe my thoughts and feelings except me. Others can discover what is going on in my mind only if I reveal it through my speech or behavior. Each person, says the dualist, possesses a self-enclosed interior life inaccessible to others. This privacy of what is mental can be explained only on the assumption that there is a distinction between mind and body.

INTERACTION BETWEEN MIND AND BODY

Although claiming that the mind is different from the body, the dualist does not conclude that there is no communication between them. Descartes himself was a **two-sided interactionist.** He believed that events in the mind can cause changes in the physical world and that changes in the physical world can cause changes in the mind. For example, when I decide to raise my arm (a mental event), my arm rises (a physical change). And if an automobile is headed in my direction (a physical change), then I may decide (a mental change) to get out of its path. Other dualists have favored a one-sided interaction, claiming that physical events can cause changes in the mind but doubting whether the mind can produce changes in the body. This view is called **epiphenomenalism.** Still others have been skeptical about any form of interaction. "How can things so different as the mind and the body possibly interact?" they have asked.

For Descartes, the brain, or at least one part of it, is the principal point of contact between the mind and the body. Thus, for a person to raise his arm deliberately, the mind causes a signal to be sent from the brain to the muscle in the arm. The signal

---

[3]C. J. Ducasse, "Is Life after Death Possible?" in Paul Edwards and Arthur Pap, *A Modern Introduction to Philosophy* (New York: The Free Press, 1965), pp. 252–253.

causes the muscle to contract and the arm to rise. Yet even though the brain is the most important point of interaction, Descartes insists that the self is not located in the body merely as a pilot in a vessel. The union between the mind and the body is much closer than that. For instance, the mind does not merely notice changes that occur in the body but often feels them at the place at which they occur. Thus, a disturbance in the stomach is not just noticed intellectually but felt as a stomach ache. The existence of bodily sensations indicates that in some sense the mind is present throughout the body and not merely in the brain.

THE STATUS OF ANIMALS

The term *brute* was once used to refer to animals other than humans. Do brutes think? Do brutes have minds or souls? Descartes answered "No!" Brutes are merely machines incapable of rational thought. You may have a dog or a cat as a pet, and you may be under the impression that your pet occasionally thinks before it acts. For example, when I tell my dog, Piper, that I am going to give him his meal, he jumps up and looks as if he is thinking about the delicious feast that I am about to give him. But, according to Descartes, this impression is no more than an illusion. Piper is a machine that acts without any conscious awareness at all.

How can we tell that humans have minds whereas brutes do not? Descartes mentioned two tests for distinguishing machines from creatures with a mind:

> The first is, that they could never use speech or other signs as we do when placing our thoughts on record for the benefit of others. For we can easily understand a machine's being constituted so that it can utter words, and even emit some responses to action on it of a corporeal kind, which brings about a change in its organs; for instance, if it is touched in a particular part it may ask what we wish to say to it; if in another part it may exclaim that it is being hurt, and so on. But it never happens that it arranges its speech in various ways, in order to reply appropriately to everything that may be said in its presence, as even the lowest type of man can do. And the second difference is, that although machines can perform certain things as well or perhaps better than any of us can do, they infallibly fall short in others, by the which means we may discover that they did not act from knowledge, but only from the disposition of their organs. For while reason is a universal instrument which can serve for all contingencies, these organs have need of some special adaptation for every particular action. From this it follows that it is morally impossible that there should be sufficient diversity in any machine to allow it to act in all the events of life in the same way that reason causes us to act.[4]

According to Descartes, what distinguishes humans from machines is the fact that both human speech and human behavior can be adapted to the enormous variety of situations that each individual encounters, whereas the responses of machines are more rigid and

---

[4]René Descartes, "Discourse on Method," in *The Philosophical Works of Descartes*, trans. E. S. Haldane and G. R. T. Ross (Cambridge: Cambridge University Press, 1972), I, 116.

limited. This difference could only be explained by the presence of mind in humans and its absence in brutes and in machines.

Descartes was, of course, unaware of the great complexity of response of which modern machines are capable. For example, the modern computer can mimic a wide variety of human actions. In fact, there is no observable response that a human can accomplish that cannot in principle be accomplished by a machine even though it may be difficult in practice to build a machine for a given type of response. Thus, Descartes' test will not invariably distinguish beings with minds from those that lack them.

Criticisms of Dualism

CONTINUITY AND EVOLUTION

Mind–body dualism as Descartes stated it is no longer widely accepted among those in either philosophy or science who study the mind. One reason for its decline was the influence of the theory of evolution as formulated by Charles Darwin (1809–1882) in the middle of the nineteenth century. Darwin established that the higher and more complex forms of life evolved naturally from lower and more simple forms. In particular, the human animal evolved from lower forms and is as much a creature of nature as the other species. When we study evolution and animal behavior, we tend to find that as we pass from the simpler to the more complex forms of life we find continuities in structure, function, and behavior rather than sudden breaks. It seems implausible to claim that only humans can think and possess a mind whereas the remainder of the animal kingdom consists of mindless machines.[5]

A modern follower of Descartes might reply that if continuity is indeed required by the evidence, then we should conclude that animals have minds as well as humans. But that only raises a further problem. Where does mind begin? Do oysters have minds? Do bacteria? Do plants?

Because intelligence is something that is present in nature in various degrees in various species, and because, according to Descartes, mind or soul is either entirely present or entirely absent, the mind–body dualism of Descartes cannot plausibly explain the occurrence of intelligence by reference to the mind or soul.

EXPLANATORY STRUCTURE

Another criticism of mind–body dualism is based upon the fact that dualism is unable to provide detailed theoretical explanations of human behavior. Normally, when we wish to understand how and why a particular mechanism works, we take it apart to find out how its internal parts behave. And if, for one reason or another, it cannot be taken apart, we construct hypotheses about the workings of its internal parts. For example, to understand how a radio manages to transmit speech and music, we must learn how its

---

[5]Over a century before Darwin, the philosopher David Hume argued that "beasts are endow'd with thought and reason as well as men." See his *A Treatise of Human Nature,* ed. L. A. Selby-Bigge (Oxford: The Clarendon Press, 1951), p. 176.

various tubes and wires transform electrical impulses into sound waves. In biology, we think that we understand the behavior of plants and animals when we have grasped how their parts work together to produce the behavior in question. But, according to mind–body dualism, the soul is not a physical thing. It does not have physical parts that can be examined and studied. Therefore, explaining something by reference to the soul fails to provide the type of understanding characteristic of science.

In general, the attempt to explain observable phenomena by reference to hidden spiritual beings represents an early and relatively primitive stage in the investigation of nature. Primitive peoples ascribed spirits to stars and to trees. The creation of the world and various other events were explained as the workings of the gods. Even as late as the early twentieth century there was a trend in the biological sciences called vitalism that sought to explain the phenomena of growth and development as the outcome of spiritual forces. But as scientists learn more and more about the underlying physical mechanisms of observable phenomena, the temptation to couch explanations in terms of the activities of hidden spirits disappears. Similarly, as we learn more and more about the workings of the human nervous system and brain, there is less and less reason to explain human conduct by reference to the soul. The advance of the scientific understanding of human nature appears to make the dualistic hypothesis implausible.

CATEGORY MISTAKES

According to Gilbert Ryle, dualism is guilty of a certain type of logical error that he calls a **category mistake.** A category is a way of classifying or representing in language various aspects of reality. For example, a rock is a *thing* or *substance*. Its gray color is one of its *properties*. The fact that this rock is heavier than that one is a *relation* between them. The rock's rolling down the hill is an *event* or *occurrence*. The notions of substance, property, relation, and event are examples of categories. According to Ryle, Descartes and his followers allocated the mind to the wrong sort of category:

> The differences between the physical and the mental were thus represented as differences inside the common framework of the categories of "thing," "stuff," "attribute," "state," "process," "change," "cause" and "effect." Minds are things, but different sorts of things from bodies; mental processes are causes and effects, but different sorts of causes and effects from bodily movements.[6]

According to dualism, both minds and bodies are things or substances. We may be led by language to adopt this view because the word *mind* is a noun, and we tend to use nouns to classify substances. The use of *mind* as a noun is, however, primarily idiomatic. When a person says "I have something on my mind" one does not interpret him to mean literally that the mind is a thing on top of which lies his thoughts. We take what he says as a metaphor meaning that he is worried about something.

[6]Gilbert Ryle, *The Concept of Mind* (London: Hutchinson's University Library, 1949), p. 19.

For Ryle, it is a mistake to classify the mind as a substance. To talk about a person's mind is really just to talk about his behavior and the various ways that he is likely to behave:

> When we characterize people by mental predicates, we are not making
> untestable inferences to any ghostly processes occurring in streams of
> consciousness which we are debarred from visiting; we are describing the ways in
> which those people conduct parts of their predominantly public behavior. True,
> we go beyond what we see them do and hear them say, but this going beyond is
> not a going behind, in the sense of making inferences to occult causes; it is going
> beyond in the sense of considering, in the first instance, the powers and
> propensities of which their actions are exercises.[7]

For Ryle, the mind belongs to the categories of conduct and power. This means that when we speak of a person's mind, what we are really talking about is his conduct— the way he behaves—and his powers and abilities. Intelligence, for example, is usually taken as an important attribute of mind. For Ryle, when we say that someone is intelligent, we are not referring to a hidden characteristic of her soul. We do not need to postulate a "ghost in the machine." Instead, to say that a person is intelligent implies that her conduct is usually successful and that she has various abilities and powers to perform successfully over and over again.

OTHER MINDS

According to Descartes, brutes are merely machines lacking mind and intelligence. But each of us may well wonder whether other humans are not also mindless machines. How can I tell that you are not a robot but have a mind like mine? The answer that most dualists have offered is that each person learns about the minds of others by noting their resemblance to himself. For example, I cannot witness or feel the pains of another person. Suppose I see Tom kick Jack in the shin and hear Jack cry out in pain. Of course, I believe that Jack is experiencing a sharp pain in his leg. But what justifies my belief? It is that when a part of my body is struck, I feel pain and the pain makes me cry out. Because a similar thing happened to Jack, I infer that he has a similar feeling.

This kind of inference is sometimes called an argument from analogy. It is based upon the analogies, or resemblances, between different cases. For example, suppose you enter a room and find that it contains a large number of boxes that are exactly alike in size, shape, and color. Suppose also that in each box you open you find a shirt. It is natural to infer that the boxes you did not open contain shirts as well. This example resembles the inference that other people have minds. Just as you infer what is in the unopened boxes by means of their similarity in appearance to the opened ones, so you infer what is going on in someone else's mind by means of the similarity between what

[7]Ibid., p. 51.

happens to him and what he does to what you know at first hand, namely your own experience.

As critics see it, the main problem with this analogical argument for the existence of other minds is that it does not seem to satisfy the criteria for reliable analogical inferences. First, the larger the number of cases that you observe, the more reliable the conclusion that you draw. Thus, if you open only one box, your belief that all the unopened boxes contain shirts is much less probable than if you open several boxes and find that they all contain shirts. But in the case of the inference to the existence of other minds, you are restricted to your own case alone. So your conclusion has at best a very low degree of probability.

Second, an argument from analogy is more reliable when you have checked your inference and found it to be correct. Thus, I can check my hunch that this unopened box contains a shirt by opening it and looking inside. If I find my hunch to be correct, then the reliability of my next inference is increased. But in the case of other minds, I am forever prevented from checking to see whether my inference is correct. I cannot peer directly into another person's mind. There is no box that I can open to observe his mind at work. His mind, according to the dualist, is private and thus inaccessible to others.

Finally, the greater the degree of resemblance among the various cases, the more reliable an analogical argument will be. Thus, because all the boxes are exactly alike, my judgment about their contents is more probable than if they had been different in color or size or shape. But here again, the analogical argument for other minds fails, according to its critics. There are many differences between Jack and me. We differ in size, in weight, in the color of our hair and eyes, in our fingerprints, in our clothes, and so forth. Of course, you may think that none of these differences is relevant to the question whether or not Jack feels pain as I do. But how does one decide that a difference is not relevant except by using the analogical argument for other minds in the first place?

It seems, then, that if dualism were true, no one could ever know that another person had a mind or what was going on in it. Yet this consequence is unacceptable. We often have strong convictions about the thoughts and feelings of others, and we guide our own conduct accordingly. We find that some of our convictions are supported by evidence and others are disproved. Thus, to claim that we can never know another person's mind seems extravagant. It is a conclusion that we should accept only if, upon examination, all else fails. So now let us consider a different, more promising conception of mind—behaviorism.

Behaviorism

Behaviorism is a family of theories about the nature of the mind that attempts to compensate for some of the failures of dualism. There are various versions of behaviorism; all of them have in common the idea that the hypothesis of the soul is unscientific and that the mind consists not of unobservable processes but rather of the observable behavior and conduct of humans and animals.

The term **behavior** is ambiguous. Sometimes it refers to the observable actions of animals and humans. Other times it refers to any physical change going on inside or outside the body, whether or not it happens to be observable. In this broader sense, we speak of the behavior of the heart or of the brain. In the following discussion, I shall use the term in the narrower sense to indicate observable actions. Generally, psychology and the social sciences focus on behavior in this narrow sense, explaining its occurrence by reference to environmental forces affecting the organism. Thus, one of the leading behaviorists, the psychologist B. F. Skinner, claims that it is scientifically more fruitful to study human behavior as a function of environmental stimuli than to study it as the outcome of changes that occur in the nervous system and brain. Because we do not know very much about these inner changes, a rigorous science concerned with prediction and control will concentrate upon the environmental sources of behavior.[8]

An important reason for our examining the behaviorist approach is that many scientists and philosophers endorse **empiricism.** Empiricism is a theory of human knowledge that claims that all justified belief about the world must be grounded in observation. (See Part Three for an extensive discussion of the issues pertaining to empiricism.) Believing that such things as the soul or private mental states are inaccessible to observation, behaviorists claim either that there is no soul or that even if there is a private mental life, it is not the proper object of scientific study.

Some philosophical behaviorists claim that even our everyday talk about the mind is essentially behaviorist. They argue that for those words that refer to things and their properties to have meaning, they must have observable criteria as part of their meaning. Thus, to know the meaning of a word like *rock* or *elephant* implies knowing what sorts of observations would show that something is a rock or an elephant. Therefore, words referring to our mental life like *thinking, deciding,* or *feeling* can be applied in particular cases only if their use is governed by behavioral criteria. If there were no such criteria, we could not apply our vocabulary of the mind in a nonarbitrary way. How can I tell what Jack is feeling unless he expresses his feelings in his actions (including speech, which is a linguistic action)? Thus, there must be a tie between action and mind in the meanings of the very words we use to talk about the mind.[9]

Problems with Behaviorism

EXPLANATION

It is doubtful that behaviorism can provide an adequate account of how behavior itself is to be explained. Consider, for example, Skinner's point that there is no need to formulate hypotheses about inner states because behavior can be understood directly as a product of environmental forces impinging upon the organism. This approach resembles our everyday approach to certain complex mechanisms that we need to handle and control. When, for instance, you turn on the television set to a particular channel (stimu-

[8]B. F. Skinner, *Science and Human Behavior* (New York: Macmillan, 1953), p. 33.
[9]Gilbert Ryle's *The Concept of Mind* is an extended defense of this type of logical behaviorism.

lus), then, given the program listings as they appear in the newspaper, you can predict which program will appear on the screen (behavioral response). To predict and control the picture on the screen, you do not have to know very much about how a television set works.

But if we wish to gain a full understanding of why a certain picture appears when the knobs are turned in a certain way, it is necessary to understand what goes on inside the set. Similarly, to understand why certain stimuli produce certain forms of behavior, it is necessary to examine events occurring within the organism, that is, behavior in the broad sense. It is characteristic of our most advanced sciences—physics, chemistry, and biology—to be dissatisfied with observable uniformities and to try to understand the observable by reference to underlying physical processes and forces. All the advanced sciences are deeply theoretical. They go beyond empirical regularities to form theories and hypotheses about underlying causes.

In addition, in human existence few uniformities hold between stimulus and observable response. Suppose someone says, "It would be nice to have some oysters." This single stimulus will generate widely different responses among different individuals or on the part of the same individuals at different times. To understand how this same stimulus produces different responses, we would have to know what is going on in the mind or brain of each person. Thus, one person's response "I wouldn't care for any at all" may be explained by the fact that the thought of oysters fills him with nausea. Another's response "But the name of this month has no *r* in it" may be explained by his belief that oysters are unobtainable in months with no *r* in their names. These cases illustrate the point that in explaining behavior we often refer to such inner states as thoughts, feelings, and beliefs.

Behaviorism's faulty conception of explanation is probably due to its rather narrow view of the aim of science. As Skinner points out, if our aim is the prediction and control of behavior, it is plausible to see how much can be accomplished by restricting our attention to observable stimuli and responses. But if our aim is the understanding of behavior, then it is necessary to proceed to the underlying causes of the connections that we observe. Understanding something for its own sake is as valid a goal for intellectual endeavor as prediction and control. Pure science is not just a form of engineering.

INNER EXPERIENCE

Another problem with behaviorism is that inner experience does exist and no theory that denies it can be correct. Ryle, who is perhaps contemporary philosophy's most persuasive behaviorist, claims that the words we use to talk about the mind refer either to observable behavior or to powers and abilities. But this certainly seems wrong. For example, if you are paying close attention to these words as you read them (Wake up!), then something is now going on in you that may not be manifested in any outer behavior. This something is heeding or attending to what you are reading. Similarly, a thought or feeling may occur without any outer expression. Many terms of our mental vocabulary refer to events and processes that may, but need not, find expression in observable conduct.

An indication of our belief in the existence of inner experience is the fact that we often wonder what it is like for another person or an animal to undergo some particular experience. For example, a person innocent of sexual experience may wonder what it is like to have sexual intercourse. A man may wonder what it is like to be a woman, and a woman may wonder about the male experience. One may even wonder what it is like to be a dog or an elephant or even a bat.[10] Last winter, as the temperature plummeted toward zero, I noticed some ducks swimming in a corner of a near-by pond that was otherwise completely frozen over. I wondered what it was like to be a duck swimming in such cold water. In such cases one is not wondering simply about the behavior that is exhibited, for that can be perfectly familiar. One is wondering about the inner aspect of behavior, the inner experience of which the behavior is the outer expression. We return here to the idea that there is a private inner aspect to the lives of people and of some animals. And if there is such an aspect, behaviorism loses its plausibility.

BEHAVIOR

Another criticism of behaviorism is founded upon the very concept of behavior itself. Consider a simple action such as raising your arm to signal a turn. For you to succeed in signaling a turn, your arm must rise. But your arm can rise without your signaling at all. For example, if you raise your arm in a classroom, your action is not signaling a turn. It is also possible for your arm to rise without your having raised it. Someone else can raise it, or it can rise as a reflex action without your cooperation at all. Thus, your raising your arm to signal a turn cannot be identified simply with the fact of your arm's rising. Wittgenstein asked:

> When "I raise my arm," my arm goes up. And the problem arises: what is left over if I subtract the fact that my arm goes up from the fact that I raise my arm?[11]

Your action of your raising your arm consists of your arm rising plus something else. What is this something else?

First, not only did your arm rise; you raised it. Not only did your body move; you performed a genuine action. In addition, you acted with a certain purpose or intention. You raised your arm with the intention of signaling a turn. Two factors, then, seem to distinguish actions from mere movements of the body: An action involves the performance of something by an agent, a performance that is the expression of the agent's intention. Critics of behaviorism have argued that although the motions of the parts of the body such as the arms and legs are observable, neither the performance (or willing) of the deed nor the underlying intention are themselves observable to others, although through introspection they may be apparent to the agent himself. Behaviorism would be an intelligible theory provided that the behavior that is studied consisted merely of observable motions of the body. But such a conception of behavior leaves out two impor-

---

[10]Thomas Nagel, "What Is It Like to Be a Bat?" *The Philosophical Review* 83 (1974): pp. 435–450.
[11]Ludwig Wittgenstein, *Philosophical Investigations,* trans. G. E. M. Anscombe (New York: The Macmillan Co., 1968), par. 621, p. 161.

tant things: action and purpose. Thus, behaviorism surprisingly presupposes an inadequate conception of behavior.

Materialism and the Identity Thesis

Materialism is a philosophical outlook that denies the separate reality of mind and of mental and spiritual processes. According to the materialist, the only things that exist are material substances and their characteristics, relationships, and processes. Mind exists only as an aspect of matter. At this point you may want to reject materialism immediately, assuming that the criticisms directed against behaviorism must apply to materialism in general and that a return to mind–body dualism is the only alternative. Doesn't the reality of inner experience and consciousness, of action and purpose, compel us to return to Descartes' system, unsatisfactory though it is?

Certain materialists have argued that one can avoid returning to dualism by identifying the mind with the brain. The inner private experiences that the dualist emphasizes no doubt exist, but they are really events in the brain of the person having the experience. Events going on in a person's brain are not observable from the outside; they are within the organism. They are known to accompany inner experience. Why not simply identify inner experiences with their accompanying brain processes?

Let us examine this **mind–brain identity thesis** more closely. It says first that research into the relation between the mind and the brain tends to corroborate the hypothesis that there is an accompanying brain event for every mental event. For every thought or feeling or sensation that you have, there is a corresponding event in your brain, an electrical discharge in the nerve fibers. Let us call this assertion the **correspondence hypothesis.** Let M be some mental event. Then, according to the correspondence hypothesis, there is a brain event B that occurs whenever M occurs. There are no unattached mental processes. Each thought, feeling, and sensation that goes on inside you is married, so to speak, to an event in your brain or nervous system.

The next assertion that the identity thesis makes is that M does not merely accompany B; M really *is* B. The mental event M is nothing more than a brain process B. Consider this analogy. Whenever a flash of lightning occurs in the atmosphere, it is accompanied by an electrical discharge. Instead of asserting that the lightning is one thing and the electrical discharge another, different thing, scientists identify them. They say that lightning is nothing but its accompanying electrical discharge. In the same way, your thoughts and feelings do not merely accompany certain brain events; they *are* those brain events. For example, your thought about how delicious your breakfast was this morning is merely an electrical discharge in the nerves and cells of your brain.

When one thing regularly accompanies another thing, we sometimes identify them, as in the case of lightning. But in other cases we acknowledge that they are separate events that cannot be identified. For example, although smoke is regularly accompanied by fire, we never say that smoke *is* fire. Why, then, should we identify the mind with the brain? Why do we not rest content with the correspondence hypothesis and admit that brain events, though distinct from mental events, always accompany them? One reason often given by materialists is based on the current direction of science. Thus, J. J. C. Smart writes:

> It seems to me that science is increasingly giving us a viewpoint whereby organisms are able to be seen as physiochemical mechanisms: it seems that even the behavior of man himself will one day be explicable in mechanistic terms. There does seem to be, so far as science is concerned, nothing in the world but increasingly complex arrangements of physical constituents.[12]

Smart cannot bring himself to believe that consciousness constitutes an exception to the general materialist trend of scientific research and explanation.

Another reason for adopting the identity thesis is based on **Occam's Razor.** This is the principle, named after the fourteenth-century philosopher William of Occam, that one should accept the simplest theory compatible with the available evidence. Now, the evidence established by science that is relevant to the nature of mind is contained in the correspondence hypothesis. Both dualism, which says that the mind is different from the brain, and the identity thesis, which identifies them, are compatible with the correspondence hypothesis. The materialist argues that the identity thesis is a simpler theory and should be accepted for that reason. It is simpler because it claims that there is only one kind of event, the physical kind, whereas dualism asserts that there are two irreducible kinds: the physical and the mental.

Problems with the Identity Thesis

IMAGES

Images play an important role in human life. Very often when we are aware of something that turns out not to be a real, physical thing, we say that we have been conscious of an image. Images occur in dreams, in illusions, in hallucinations. They also occur as reflections in mirrors and other surfaces and as afterimages. I am sure that most of you have at one time or another perceived a visual afterimage. Stare for a few moments at a bright light and then look at a blank wall. You will very likely see an afterimage caused by the glare of the light. Whereas afterimages are relatively unimportant phenomena, they do represent a severe problem for theories of the mind. The problem can be expressed by the question, Where are afterimages located?

Suppose you are looking at a yellow afterimage. Where does it exist? It does not exist as a yellow patch on the wall on which it is projected because no one else can see it. It is a private object, inside you in some way. Is it in the retina of your eye? No, because there is no yellow patch in your retina at the time you are looking at the afterimage. Is it in your brain? Apparently not, for there is no yellow patch in your brain either.

---

[12]J. J. C. Smart, "Sensations and Brain Processes," in *Materialism and the Mind–Body Problem,* ed. David M. Rosenthal (Prentice-Hall, 1971), p. 54.

Because the afterimage is yellow, any place that contained it would have to contain a yellow patch.

How then does the identity thesis explain imagery? According to Smart, there are, strictly speaking, no such things as afterimages. He does not deny that people experience them. But images themselves do not exist, and our thinking that they do is a kind of illusion. They no more have to exist because people experience them than unicorns have to exist because people think of them. Moreover, the reason why people might experience a yellow afterimage in the first place is that although there is no yellow object they are seeing when they "see" a yellow afterimage, nevertheless something is going on inside them that resembles what goes on when they really do see something yellow. And this inner event is said by Smart and other materialists to be a brain process.[13]

Provided, then, that it is intelligible to deny the existence of images while at the same time affirming that there are experiences of them, imagery offers no great difficulty for the identity theory. Notice that the problem of images applies to dualism as well as materialism. Because yellow afterimages are extended in space and, for the dualist, the mind is an unextended substance, he cannot admit that they exist in the mind. That would imply that the mind is extended. But the dualist could make use of Smart's idea to solve his problem. He need merely add to Smart's exposition that the inner event that consists in the awareness of the afterimage is a mental process.

MEANING AND REFERENCE

Another problem for the identity thesis is raised by Blanshard's argument that we mean different things by consciousness and bodily behavior. Suppose, for example, that whenever I think about the mind–body problem, there exists an electrical discharge in the upper left-hand hemisphere of my brain. Yet the phrase "my thought about the mind–body problem" obviously has a different meaning from "an electrical discharge in the upper left-hand hemisphere of my brain." And if they mean different things, how can the events that they mean possibly be the same? Moreover, I can know what I am thinking about even though I am entirely ignorant of what goes on in my brain. How can something that I know about be the same as something about which I remain in complete ignorance?

The materialist's response to Blanshard relies on the distinction between the meaning of a term and its reference. This distinction was developed by the German logician Gottlob Frege (1848–1925). Consider the phrase "the Morning Star." This phrase has a certain meaning—namely, a star that appears in the sky in the morning hours—and it refers to the planet Venus. Now the phrase "the Evening Star" refers to Venus as well, even though the phrase has a different meaning. This example illustrates the general point that two terms can differ in meaning although they agree in reference. Similarly, although "flash of lightning" means something different from "electrical discharge in the atmosphere," nevertheless the event they both refer to is the same just because lightning is an electrical discharge in the atmosphere and vice versa.

[13]Ibid., pp. 61–62.

The same point is made by the identity theory for terms that refer to the brain and mind. Even though "my thought about the mind–body problem" means something different from "an electrical discharge in the upper left-hand hemisphere in my brain," the event that the first refers to is identical with the event that the second names. The difference between meaning and reference can also be used to explain how I can be ignorant of the brain event even though I have knowledge of my thought. The phrase "my thought about the mind–body problem" conveys as part of its meaning a certain feature of an event, namely, that the event is about the mind–body problem. The phrase "an electrical discharge in the upper left-hand hemisphere of my brain" conveys a different feature of the same event. Now, it is possible to be familiar with one feature of an event while remaining ignorant of another feature. Thus, for centuries, human beings were acquainted with the visual aspect of lightning as it flashed in the sky, but it was only recently that they have come to understand its underlying electrical nature. Similarly, each individual is acquainted with those aspects of his mental life that he can grasp from within. According to the identity thesis, scientific research has revealed that these same states of mind that are grasped from within also have a physical aspect delineated in the physiology of the brain and nervous system.

ASPECTS

This response to Blanshard's argument leads immediately to a much greater difficulty for the identity thesis. In his response, the advocate of mind–brain identity has conceded that mental events have a twofold aspect. The physical aspect is revealed by research into the brain and nervous system. The mental aspect is revealed directly to the individual by introspection. The physical aspect is public; it is just as accessible to others as it is to the person in whose brain the event is occurring. The mental aspect is private; it is accessible only to the individual himself.

The admission that there exists a double aspect to mental events transforms the identity thesis into a version of mind–body dualism. It is not a dualism of substances. The mind is no longer regarded as a separate thing. It is a dualism of aspects in which the mental aspect is distinct from the physical aspect. The mind, then, can be regarded as the inner private side of events and states of the brain. Even though this double-aspect theory is compatible with the identity thesis, it is not compatible with strict materialism. There is more to the world than physical things and processes. The world contains an irreducible mental aspect that escapes complete explanation in terms of the concepts of the physical sciences. The claim of J. J. C. Smart that "there does seem to be, so far as science is concerned, nothing in the world but increasingly complex arrangements of physical constituents" does not seem to be true.

In attempting to avoid this outcome, one advocate of the identity thesis has even gone so far as to argue that we should give up the idea that there is a private inner aspect to mental events. Mental events are brain events. They have a physical aspect, but belief in a mental aspect is a superstition on a par with belief in the existence of demons.[14]

---

[14]Richard Rorty, "Mind–Body Identity, Privacy, and Categories," in *Materialism and the Mind–Body Problem.*

Just as there is no place in the universe as understood by modern science for afterimages, so there is no place in it for the mental aspects of physical events.

It is possible that the universe contains nothing of mind or spirit. Any theory that is logically consistent expresses a possible world. But though it is possible, extreme materialism flies in the face of well-established facts. To say that there is no inner mental aspect to human life means that pains don't hurt, itches don't itch, thoughts are never about anything; it means that there is nothing that is like undergoing this or that experience. Though all this *may* be true, though the belief in mind *may* be a gross superstition, it *seems* on the face of it to be obviously false. And if it were true, there could be no such thing as the thought that it is true. The denial of mental aspects is a last-ditch effort to save extreme materialism. It flies in the face of many of our most common beliefs. It is, literally, unbelievable.

The advocate of the identity thesis may argue that if it is reasonable to deny the existence of afterimages, then it is also reasonable to deny the existence of consciousness and sentience as well. Now the argument against afterimages was based upon the fact that nothing in the world could serve to contain these images. Anything that contained a yellow afterimage would have to have a yellow patch in it. But neither the eye nor the brain nor the soul has a patch of the right color—or a patch of any color at all. But there does not seem to be the same difficulty with mental aspects. There does not seem to be anything about the inner side of human experience that makes it impossible for it to exist as an aspect of the brain and nervous system. This question about the compatibility of the physical and the mental has, however, been debated continuously from the time of Descartes to the present day, so we should not pronounce upon it dogmatically.

Emergent Materialism

The theory that seems best to fit the variety of facts and arguments that have been discussed in this chapter can be called **emergent materialism.** It states first that there is a distinction to be drawn between the mental and physical aspects of reality. Mind is not completely reducible to matter. To this extent, emergent materialism agrees with Descartes and the dualists. Second, it says that the mental aspect of reality emerges from and is causally dependent upon the physical aspect. Although mind is distinct from matter, it is nevertheless dependent upon it and its processes. This second claim seems supported by the results of modern science. Science seems more and more able to explain the behavior and functioning of living organisms through research into the details of the workings of their physical parts. In addition, the theory of evolution suggests that just as life emerged from and depends upon physical processes, so mind emerges from those living beings that have attained a certain degree of physical complexity.

Emergent materialism selects the best features of both dualism and the identity thesis. It agrees with dualism in asserting the existence of an inner private dimension to the self. It agrees with the identity thesis in claiming that this dimension is dependent upon physical processes for its existence and that it does not consist of a separate substance but merely of a distinguishable aspect of the workings of bodies.[15] Emergent materialism is an extremely general hypothesis about the nature of the mind that may be confirmed or possibly even refuted by further research in biology and psychology.

If, as emergent materialism asserts, there is an irreducibly private aspect to human life, then it is necessary to come to terms with the problem of other minds. Earlier I recounted some of the standard objections to the analogical argument for other minds on which dualists had traditionally relied. Emergent materialism needs to rely upon this argument as well to establish the existence of the private aspects of experience. For example, even if your pains are identical to processes in your nervous system, I cannot tell by purely physiological research into the physical aspects of the processes that they are indeed pains. To ascertain that you feel that private something that I call pain, I must infer it from physical processes that I can observe, such as your behavior. Can the objections to this inference be rebutted?

One difficulty regarding the analogical argument for other minds that has already been mentioned is that it is restricted to only a single case. But this criticism does not do justice to the argument. Although I can directly observe only my own inner life, I can do so on many occasions. I am not restricted to a single occurrence of a feeling or a thought but have my whole mental history to rely upon as the basis for the inference. Another difficulty was that there are many dissimilarities between me and others, and these dissimilarities weakened the inference. But if I am allowed to use my own experience as the basis for the inference to other minds, I can also use it to determine which differences are and which are not relevant. For example, I can discover that the fact that you and I have different fingerprints does not influence whether you will feel pain when kicked in the shin any more than it influences my feelings of pain. I can discover this by establishing that in my case the nerves responsible for my feeling pain are not hooked up in the right way to my fingerprints. I infer that the same holds for others. Once I have obtained a foothold for the inference to other minds by using my own experiences, I then discover that my judgments about the thoughts and feelings of others are often confirmed by their behavior and speech. My belief in other minds receives continuous support from the whole body of my experience of myself and others.

There was the final objection that a person cannot check the correctness of his inference by directly observing the private experiences of others. But if this is an objection to the analogical argument, it is an objection as well to a substantial amount of scientific inference. If I receive a shock upon touching a wire, given my knowledge of scientific theory I conclude that there is an electric current flowing through the wire. I cannot check my conclusion directly because neither I nor anyone else can actually see a flow of electrons. But I can check it in other indirect ways. Similarly, although I cannot directly observe the private aspects of others' experiences, I can check my judgments indirectly. For example, if upon hearing you yell loudly and seeing you hold your shin, I am still uncertain whether you feel a pain there, I can then ask you, or I can examine your leg to see if it is injured. Because many scientific theories refer to unobservable

---

[15]Whether or not the mental aspect can itself cause changes in the brain or is a mere epiphenomenon that has no causal power is a question to be decided by scientific investigation.

entities to explain observable phenomena, to object to indirect checks in the absence of direct observation would lead to discarding much of modern science.

> ### THEORIES ABOUT THE RELATION BETWEEN MIND AND BODY
>
> Mind–body dualism
> Behaviorism
> Mind–brain identity thesis
> Emergent materialism

Personal Identity

IDENTITY AND CHANGE

Thus far we have considered the question of the relation between the mind and the body. But what of the self? What sort of being is it that each of us names when we utter the word *I?* Descartes assumed without argument that the mind and the self are one and the same thing. For him, the self is an immaterial, unextended, mental substance.

Investigation into the nature of the self has been illuminated in subsequent philosophy by raising the question of personal identity. Like other types of things, a person can change and still retain his or her identity. One and the same person, Thomas Jefferson, wrote the Declaration of Independence and served as the third president of the United States. Despite all the changes that Jefferson underwent, he remained Thomas Jefferson nevertheless. Each of us undergoes radical changes throughout our lives. Did you ever see a picture of yourself as a baby? There is an immense difference between the way you were then and the way you are today. Yet you are the very same person as that baby. Of course, some changes are so great as to destroy personal identity. According to many philosophers, death entails the destruction of the self. After death, the self that once existed no longer exists. Jefferson's corpse is no longer to be identified with Jefferson. But many changes do not destroy identity. What then does identity consist in? According to Descartes, the identity of the self is explained as the persistence through time of the same mental substance. When a person refers at various times to himself using the word *I,* he is referring to the same mental substance.

PERSONAL IDENTITY AND CONSCIOUSNESS

Both John Locke and David Hume in different ways challenged Descartes' account of the self. According to Locke, personal identity is based not upon the persistence of the same substance, but upon *consciousness* or *memory.* Here is what Locke says:

> To find wherein personal identity consists, we must consider what "person" stands for; which, I think, is a thinking intelligent being, that has reason and reflection, and can consider itself as itself, the same thinking thing, in different

> times and places; which it does only by that consciousness which is
> inseparable from thinking, and it seems to me to be essential to it: it being
> impossible for anyone to perceive, without perceiving that he does perceive.
> When we see, hear, smell, taste, feel, meditate, or will anything, we know that we
> do so. Thus it is always as to our present sensations and perceptions: and by this
> everyone is to himself that which he calls "self"; it not being considered, in this
> case, whether the same self be continued in the same or diverse substances. For
> since consciousness always accompanies thinking, and it is that that makes
> everyone to be what he calls "self," and thereby distinguishes himself from all
> other thinking things; in this alone consists personal identity, i.e., the sameness of
> a rational being: and as far as this consciousness can be extended backwards to
> any past action or thought, so far reaches the identity of that person.[16]

As Locke explains his use of the term, consciousness is that capacity by means of which human beings are aware of their states of mind; when someone knows that he is thinking while he is thinking, that is the work of consciousness. Not only does consciousness reveal a person's states of mind to himself, it reveals them as belonging to himself. Thus, when someone is conscious of his own thinking, he not only knows that thinking is going on—that someone is thinking—he knows that *he* is the one doing the thinking. Consciousness not only tells us about our present thoughts and feelings but also about our past states of mind. Because any state of mind that I am conscious of belongs to me, any past state that I am conscious of belongs to a person identical to me.

Locke's theory of personal identity has the following interesting consequence. Suppose I am conscious of or remember having many of the experiences that Julius Caesar once did. Perhaps I remember leading a large army across the Rubicon. Perhaps I can remember how it felt to be stabbed by my best friend Brutus. It follows, according to Locke, that I *am* Julius Caesar. More accurately it follows that I am a person who was once identical with Julius Caesar. Even if Caesar's soul and body are different from my soul and body, I would still maintain my identity with Caesar just because I am conscious of having had his experiences.

In Locke's theory, reincarnation would be possible. It would be possible for a person to die and to continue to exist in a new body. Because, however, consciousness of my past is necessary for personal identity, if I do not remember a past existence, then I cannot claim to have had one.

One obvious difficulty with Locke's theory is that it does not seem compatible with the phenomenon of amnesia. As a result of some injury or mental trauma, a person may forget his whole past life. Yet, apparently, he does not thereby lose his identity. Locke tries to grapple with this problem in the following way:

> But yet possibly it will still be objected, "Suppose I wholly lose the memory of
> some parts of my life, beyond the possibility of retrieving them, so that perhaps I
> shall never be conscious of them again; yet am I not the same person that did
> those actions, had those thoughts, that I was once conscious of, though I have

---

[16]John Locke, *An Essay concerning Human Understanding* (London: George Routledge and Sons), II. xxvii. 9.

now forgot them?" To which I answer, That we must here take notice what the word "I" is applied to; which in this case is the man only. And the same man being presumed to be the same person, "I" is easily here supposed to stand also for the same person. But if it be possible for the same man to have distinct incommunicable consciousnesses at different times, it is past doubt the same man would at different times make different persons; which, we see, is the sense of mankind in the solemnest declaration of their opinions, human laws not punishing the mad man for the sober man's actions, nor the sober man for what the mad man did, thereby making them two persons; which is somewhat explained by our way of speaking in English, when we say, "Such an one is not himself, or is beside himself;" in which phrases it is insinuated as if those who now or, at least, first used them, thought that self was changed, the self-same person was no longer that man.[17]

Locke's solution depends upon a distinction he draws between the concept of a human being and the concept of a person. The criterion for the identity of a human being is his or her body. The same living body implies the same human being. Thus, our amnesiac is the same human being he or she was before the loss of memory. But because consciousness or memory is the identity criterion for persons, he or she is not the same person. The gap in memory constitutes a new personality. Locke would handle the phenomenon of multiple or split personality in the same way. If the same individual should exhibit several different personalities at different times, each with no recollection of the others, each personality constitutes a distinct person even though only one human being persists throughout this variety.

THE LOSS OF THE SELF

David Hume developed an additional criticism of Descartes' concept of self-identity. Hume was an empiricist. Thus, for him to accept something as real, it must be capable of being observed, either through the five senses or by introspection. But try as he might, Hume cannot discover the self among his particular experiences, or, as he calls them, his perceptions:

> For my part, when I enter most intimately into what I call *myself,* I always stumble on some particular perception or other, of heat or cold, light or shade, love or hatred, pain or pleasure. I never can catch *myself* at any time without a perception, and never can observe anything but the perception. When my perceptions are remov'd for any time, as by sound sleep; so long am I insensible of *myself,* and may truly be said not to exist. And were all my perceptions remov'd by death, and cou'd I neither think nor feel, nor see, nor love, nor hate after the dissolution of my body, I shou'd be entirely annihilated, nor do I conceive what is farther requisite to make me a perfect non-entity.[18]

[17]Ibid., par. 20.
[18]David Hume, *A Treatise of Human Nature,* ed. L. A. Selby-Bigge (Oxford: The Clarendon Press, 1968), p. 252.

When he looks within to try to find himself, all that Hume succeeds in observing are his experiences. The self that is supposed to remain the same throughout the changes in his perceptions cannot be found at all. There is no such thing, says Hume.

An individual person is nothing more nor less than the sum total of his experiences, or, in Hume's terms, a bundle of perceptions:

> [People] are nothing but a bundle or collection of different perceptions, which succeed each other with an inconceivable rapidity, and are in a perpetual flux and movement. Our eyes cannot turn in their sockets without varying our perceptions. Our thought is still more variable than our sight; and all our other senses and faculties contribute to this change; nor is there any single power of the soul, which remains unalterably the same, perhaps for one moment. The mind is a kind of theatre, where several perceptions successively make their appearance; pass, re-pass, glide away, and mingle in an infinite variety of postures and situations.[19]

If a person is nothing but a bundle of experiences, what ties the experiences together into a particular bundle? What distinguishes the experiences in the bundle that is *you* from those in the bundle that is *me?* What makes my experiences mine? What is the basis of my identity?

Hume answers these questions by modifying Locke's account of personal identity. He argues that both memory and causation are sources of personal identity:

> As memory alone acquaints us with the continuance and extent of this succession of perceptions, 'tis to be consider'd, upon that account chiefly, as the source of personal identity. Had we no memory, we never shou'd have any notion of causation, nor consequently of that chain of causes and effects, which constitute our self or person. But having once acquir'd this notion of causation from the memory, we can extend the same chain of causes, and consequently the identity of our persons beyond our memory, and can comprehend times, and circumstances, and actions, which we have entirely forgot, but suppose in general to have existed.... In this view, therefore, memory does not so much *produce* as *discover* personal identity, by shewing us the relation of cause and effect among our different perceptions.[20]

Our awareness of identity, says Hume, is due primarily to our memory. The experiences that we remember having are our own. But Hume understands the deficiencies of Locke's theory. Suppose that I remember seeing Mt. Mansfield when I was eighteen years old but forgot that I had seen Pike's Peak when I was twenty. Because for Locke consciousness or memory is necessary for personal identity, it follows that although I am now the same person as the eighteen-year-old who saw Mt. Mansfield, I am different from the twenty-year-old who observed Pike's Peak. This is an implausible result. Hume therefore concludes that although memory reveals many of our past experiences to us,

[19]Ibid., p. 253.
[20]Ibid., p. 262.

it is causation and not memory that makes them our own. What makes an experience mine is that it is related either as a cause or as an effect to the other experiences in my bundle. For Hume,

> the true idea of the human mind, is to consider it as a system of different perceptions or different existences, which are link'd together by the relation of cause and effect, and mutually produce, destroy, influence, and modify each other.[21]

Each person is a causal system. Memory discovers what belongs to the self. Causation tells us what it means for something to belong to the self.

DIFFICULTIES WITH THE BUNDLE THEORY

There are two serious difficulties with Hume's bundle theory of the self. First, he assumes that an experience or a perception can exist by itself, independently of something that has the experience. Our perceptions, he says, "may exist separately, and have no need of any other thing to support their existence.[22] But what can this mean? Suppose I hear a sound. Then according to Hume, the experience of hearing a sound can exist independently of me; there can be things like hearing sounds even though there is no one who is doing the hearing. It is difficult to know what to make of such a theory. Many philosophers have argued that it is as absurd to claim that there can be an unowned experience as to assert that there can be a color—say, yellow—without there being anything that has that color, or a shape—say, square—without anything of that shape.

Second, the idea that causality can account for personal identity will not work. It will not work for the simple reason that persons are not isolated systems. Your experiences will influence what the experiences of others will be. For example, suppose you are thirsty and you ask me for a glass of water. I hear your request and give you some water. An experience of yours, the feeling of thirst, is causally implicated in an experience of mine, my hearing certain sounds. The experiences or perceptions of distinct persons are linked together by the relation of cause and effect.

THE CONCEPT OF A PERSON

If a person cannot be identified with his body or his soul or the combination of the two or his experiences, what then is a person? P. F. Strawson has suggested a view that is more promising than the ones we have rejected. For him,

> the concept of a person is the concept of a type of entity such that *both* predicates ascribing states of consciousness *and* predicates ascribing corporeal

[21]Ibid., p. 261.
[22]Ibid., p. 252.

characteristics, a physical situation, etc. are equally applicable to a single individual of that type.[23]

To understand his theory, let us examine the views he rejects. A person is not to be identified solely with his or her body because a body as such has only physical characteristics and lacks states of consciousness or states of mind. Nor is a person to be identified solely with a soul or mind because although the mind possesses states of consciousness, it lacks physical characteristics. Nor is a person to be identified merely with the sum of his experiences, for that too would lack physical characteristics. A person is an entity that has both physical and mental characteristics. When John, who is six feet tall, is angry, the very same being who has the physical characteristic of being six feet tall also has the mental characteristic of being in a state of anger. Persons are, therefore, different from mere bodies and from disembodied souls. A person is a special type of entity that combines both physical and mental characteristics in a unity of its own.

This conception of a person reflects the ways that we talk about persons in everyday life. When I say that John is angry and is six feet tall, I am ascribing both a physical and mental characteristic to John. So John must be a being who is capable of possessing both. With regard to personal identity, this commonsense conception of the person emphasizes the role of the body. The reason is that the only way we have of identifying states of mind is to refer them to a certain person via his body. For example, I cannot pick out a particular state of anger except by referring it to the person whose anger it is, say John, and I can only pick out John by specifying where his body is. Our access to persons is based upon the observation of their bodies. So the identity of a person is constituted by the identity of his body.

But what about reincarnation or the possibility of changing bodies? Does not the fact that one can imagine oneself switching from one body to another imply that personal identity cannot consist just of bodily identity? This is a very difficult question to answer. Thinking about personal identity is similar to swinging on a swing. One moves ceaselessly from one position to another without ever being on firm territory. There are difficulties with almost every account. But let me suggest an answer. The commonsense concept of a person was developed to apply in everyday situations. In such situations, the identity of a person is constituted by the continuity of a living, functioning body. Situations arise, however, that deviate from the ordinary. There are, for instance, the phenomena of split personality and amnesia. These do not refute the commonsense concept. The victim of amnesia is still the same person; he has merely lost his memory. The victim of split personality is a single person who exhibits two or more personalities. As far as imaginary situations are concerned—situations in which we consider the possibility of changing our body or existing without a body at all—the commonsense concept has no application because it has been developed for ordinary rather than extraordinary circumstances. If it should happen that one of these imaginary situations should actually exist, then we may have to revise our concept of a person. But until its reality is established, our comonsense view best fits the circumstances of everyday life.

[23]P. F. Strawson, *Individuals: An Essay in Descriptive Metaphysics* (London: Methuen and Co., 1959), pp. 101–102.

Human Action

THE PROBLEM OF ACTION

Although a person knows his own mind directly by introspection, he knows about the mental and personal life of others only as they reveal themselves in their actions or behavior. A person's actions express and thus reveal his inner life, his thoughts, his emotions, and his intentions. In our discussion of behaviorism, we saw that the concept of an action is itself none too clear. An action is not just a physical movement of a part of the body. Often the same actions may be performed by quite different movements. For example, you may greet a friend by shaking her hand, by kissing her cheek, or simply by saying "Hello." Sometimes the same movement may constitute different actions. The same raising of your arm may in some circumstances constitute signaling a turn and in others asking for recognition from a teacher and in still others waving farewell to a companion.

There is yet another reason for differentiating actions from mere movements. In some movements that people make, they are not actually performing any action. Three examples of such movements come to mind. One consists of automatic changes in the body such as the blinking of one's eyes or the beating of one's heart. A second consists of reflex movements such as jerking one's leg when one's knee is tapped. A third consists of accidents as when one slips on a patch of ice and falls. An important characteristic of all these movements is that they are produced without the cooperation of the agent's will. They are not voluntary; they are produced without being intended or chosen.

To constitute an action, a movement must be produced by an agent intentionally or on purpose. It must be chosen or willed to realize the agent's goal or purpose. In other words, it must be voluntary, or free. In his actions, a human being displays a freedom that is absent in movements that are automatic or reflexive or accidental or forced.

Because it expresses an individual's will or intention or purpose, an action has a mental component. Thus, the study of human action is a branch of the philosophy of mind. But if actions entail or presuppose freedom of the will, one might well wonder how actions are possible. Are not the things we do caused to happen by events in our brain and nervous system? But if our actions are produced in this way, how can we be free when we act? Can freedom be reconciled with causality? Without freedom we cannot act, and we would then be indistinguishable from mere physical mechanisms. And if we are just mechanisms, how can it be that we ever *ought* to do anything? If there ever is any action that we *ought* to do, then it must be possible for us to choose to do it, to select it freely from the alternative courses of action we envisage. It is via the topic of freedom that the philosophy of mind addresses one of the major issues of ethics, whether the human being is ever morally obliged to do anything.

In the rest of this chapter, we shall consider the question of how freedom is possible. Now even when a person is acting freely, it is appropriate to ask why he acts as he does. We can ask for an explanation of his actions in terms of his intentions or motives or reasons. Let us turn to the topic of explaining actions as a first step in considering the possibility of freedom.

EXPLAINING ACTIONS

In one of Plato's most widely read dialogues, *Phaedo,* Socrates is portrayed sitting in prison awaiting execution. A few hours before his death, he speaks to his friends about such topics as the immortality of the soul and the nature of true wisdom. He mentions that when he was young, he was attracted to the writings of Anaxagoras, who said that the cause of everything that happens is mind rather than matter. But the writings of Anaxagoras proved to be disappointing.

> What expectations I had formed, and how grievously was I disappointed! As I proceeded, I found my philosopher altogether forsaking mind or any other principle of order, but having recourse to air, and ether, and water, and other eccentricities. I might compare him to a person who began by maintaining generally that mind is the cause of the actions of Socrates, but who, when he endeavoured to explain the causes of my several actions in detail, went on to show that I sit here because my body is made up of bones and muscles; and the bones, as he would say, are hard and have joints which divide them, and the muscles are elastic, and they cover the bones which have also a covering or environment of flesh and skin which contains them; and as the bones are lifted at their joints by the contraction or relaxation of the muscles, I am able to bend my limbs, and this is why I am sitting here in a curved posture.[24]

Why is Socrates sitting in prison? According to the method of Anaxagoras as presented by Socrates, the explanation is couched in terms of the movements of his bones and muscles, which cause his body to be in a sitting posture. An explanation of this kind, describing the causal interactions among the parts of a system, is called a **mechanical explanation.** A modern example of a mechanical explanation is explaining how an automobile starts by mentioning that gasoline is sprayed into the engine cylinders by the fuel injectors; the gasoline is then caused to explode, thus moving the pistons up and down, which causes the wheels to be turned.

Socrates was disappointed that Anaxagoras would have offered a mere mechanical account of why he is sitting in prison. For Socrates, the true explanation is not mechanical but is based on the fact that

> the Athenians have thought fit to condemn me, and accordingly I have thought it better and more right to remain here and undergo my sentence; for I am inclined to think that these muscles and bones of mine would have gone off long ago to Megara or Boeotia—by the dog, they would, if they had been moved only by their own idea of what was best, and if I had not chosen the better and nobler part, instead of playing truant and running away, of enduring any punishment the state inflicts. There is surely a strange confusion of causes and conditions in all this. It may be said, indeed, that without bones and muscles and the other parts of the body I cannot execute my purposes. But to say that I do as I do

---

[24]Plato, *Phaedo* 98, Jowett translation.

because of them, and that this is the way in which the mind acts, and not from the choice of the best, is a very careless and idle mode of speaking.[25]

The true explanation of why Socrates is sitting in prison awaiting execution rather than escaping to another part of Greece is that he has made up his mind to do what he thinks is best. It is better to obey the laws and accept death than to violate them by escaping. The mechanical explanation that Anaxagoras might have offered would at best state the physical conditions of his sitting there. What is missing is his purpose. An explanation of why a person acts as he does by reference to his purpose or reason is called a **teleological explanation.** According to Socrates, the proper method of accounting for human action is the teleological explanation.

THE SCOPE OF TELEOLOGICAL EXPLANATION

The scientific writings of Aristotle determined the direction of scientific research until the development of modern science in the sixteenth and seventeenth centuries. It was characteristic of Aristotle's approach to emphasize that purposes exist throughout all of nature. Here is a typical passage:

> Further, where a series has a completion, all the preceding steps are for the sake of that. Now surely as in intelligent action, so in nature; and as in nature, so it is in each action if nothing interferes. Now intelligent action is for the sake of an end; therefore the nature of things also is so. . . . If, therefore, artificial products are for the sake of an end, so clearly also are natural products . . . we come to see clearly that in plants too that is produced which is conducive to the end—leaves, e.g. grow to provide shade for the fruit.[26]

According to Aristotle, one can give a teleological explanation of any series of events in which the earlier events regularly lead to the later ones. The leaves of plants regularly provide shade for their fruit, thinks Aristotle. Therefore, the leaves grow to provide shade for the fruit.

It has been the general tendency in modern science to explain events in nature mechanically rather than teleologically. Thus, according to Newton's physical theories, the movements of the planets around the sun are explained not by the purposes of the planets, for they have none, but by the effects of the gravitational force that the sun and the planets exert on each other. Regular sequences of events are to be explained by impersonal laws of nature, not by assigning purpose to objects. Aristotle appears to be guilty of personification, that is, of attributing human characteristics to nature.

Is there anything to which we can assign purpose? In everyday situations, we still think it common sense to give teleological explanations of the actions of our fellow humans and of animals. True, Descartes denied that animals possess souls—he saw

---

[25]Ibid., 99.
[26]Aristotle, *Physics,* book 2, chap. 8, trans. R. P. Hardie and R. K. Gaye (Oxford: The Clarendon Press, 1970).

ARISTOTLE
(384–322 B.C.)

Aristotle was born in the small town of Stagira in Macedonia. As a young man, he went to Athens, where he studied under Plato at the Academy. He remained there for twenty years, devoting himself to the study of philosophy, mathematics, and astronomy, which were the main subjects of research at the Academy, and also to the biological and physical sciences. After extensive travel, he was summoned by Philip, King of Macedonia, to become tutor to his son, who later became Alexander the Great. Aristotle returned to Athens in 335 and started his own school called the Lyceum. He wrote on all the main branches of human knowledge, but many of his works have been lost. The works that have survived include important treatises on science and philosophy. His major philosophical works are *Metaphysics, Nicomachean Ethics, Politics, On the Soul (De Anima),* and *Posterior Analytics.* A good one-volume edition of the major philosophical works of Aristotle is *The Basic Works of Aristotle,* ed. Richard McKeon (New York: Random House, 1941).

them as machines governed by mechanical principles—and behaviorist psychologists prefer to apply mechanical stimulus–response principles even to human behavior, thus seeming to banish purpose from human endeavor. But our discussions of Descartes and of behaviorism have given us no reason to go along with these more extreme views. Let us then take it as established that it is legitimate to account for human conduct at least by reference to the purposes, goals, and intentions of human agents.

TELEOLOGICAL AND FUNCTIONAL EXPLANATION

The purpose of the heart is to circulate the blood. The purpose of the eyes is to help a person see. Are these examples of teleological explanations, not of human actions, but of the behavior of parts of the body? No! When we say that the purpose of the heart is to circulate the blood, only verbally does our explanation resemble a teleological one. We are not talking about purpose in the sense of intention. Circulating the blood is not the intention of the heart in pumping the blood into the arteries. The heart does not have purposes in the sense of intentions. It does have purposes in another sense, in the sense of *functions*. It is the function of the heart to circulate the blood.

It is necessary, therefore, to distinguish teleological from **functional explanations.** In a typical functional explanation, we show how a part of a system causes the system to maintain itself in a particular state or condition. By pumping, the heart causes the blood to circulate throughout the body, and this causes the animal to remain alive. There is no presumption that the heart has any intentions or goals. Even after the function of the heart is discovered, we still need a mechanical account of the heart's action: What causes it to pump the blood in the way that it does? Functional explanation is still employed in biology. Perhaps it was this sort of explanation that Aristotle had in mind when he said that plants grow leaves to provide shade for their fruit. Perhaps he simply meant that the function of leaves is to provide shade. If this interpretation is correct, his mistake lay not in the type of explanation he used but rather in his understanding of how leaves function. Leaves are food factories, not fruit shaders.

TYPES OF EXPLANATION

Mechanical: An explanation of an event in terms of the causal interactions among the parts of a system.

Teleological: An explanation of an action by reference to the agent's intention or purpose or reason.

Functional: An explanation of an event by reference to its function, i.e., by reference to the state of the system that the event sustains or maintains.

Free Action

THE PROBLEM OF FREEDOM

If a man is killed by a moving subway train, one of the first things that the police want to know is whether he fell or was pushed or whether he jumped in front of the train on purpose. Was his death voluntary or involuntary? What does it mean for an action to be voluntary, or free? This question is of great practical as well as theoretical interest. We tend to praise and blame, to bestow rewards and punishments, in cases in which a person's actions are free. If the driver of an automobile that has just struck and killed a pedestrian can show that it was an accident, that he did not do it on purpose, that he did not will it or choose it, then he will be able to deny responsibility and avoid judicial punishment.

In the history of philosophy, the problem of free will has been discussed in two distinct contexts. In medieval philosophy, the problem was associated with questions about the relation between humankind and God. God was thought to be omniscient, to know everything, and in particular to know every event in the future. But if God foreknows how an individual will act, then how can that action be free? If God knows that an action A will occur, then it is necessary that A will occur. But if it is necessary that A will occur, then it is necessary that the individual do A rather than something else.

St. Augustine (354–430) argued, however, that God's foreknowledge is compatible with human freedom. He considers the case of one human person predicting what another will do.

Your foreknowledge that a man will sin does not of itself necessitate the sin.
Your foreknowledge did not force him to sin even though he was, without doubt,

going to sin; otherwise you would not foreknow that which was to be. Thus, these two things are not contradictories. As you, by your foreknowledge, know what someone else is going to do of his own will, so God forces no one to sin; yet He foreknows those who will sin by their own will. . . . Your recollection of events in the past does not compel them to occur. In the same way God's foreknowledge of future events does not compel them to take place. As you remember certain things that you have done and yet have not done all the things that you remember, so God foreknows all the things of which He Himself is the Cause, and yet He is not the Cause of all the things He foreknows.[27]

If you know a friend well, you can often predict what he will do. For example, if you know that your friend has a strong dislike of getting wet, you can predict that he will carry an umbrella at the slightest chance of rain. But your knowing that he will take an umbrella does not cause or compel him to take it. In the same way, God's knowing what you will do neither causes nor compels you to do it. So God's omniscience does not deny human freedom and responsibility.

In modern philosophy, the context of the problem gradually shifted from religion to science. The success and growing prestige of science from the seventeenth century to the present has convinced many people that science has established the truth of **determinism.** A determinist is one who believes that every event has a cause and that all the changes and processes that occur in nature and in human life are governed by laws of nature. It is often argued that if determinism is true, then whatever a person does is caused ultimately by events over which he has no control. And this, it is said, is incompatible with his having free will. More recently, developments in the social sciences have intensified doubts about free will. The psychoanalytical theories of Freud, for example, have suggested that the conscious choices that people make are produced to a great extent by the unconscious part of their minds of which they are unaware. In any case, human action is now seen as part of the causal order of nature. We do not transcend nature; we are an integral part of it. How, then, can the will be free?

THE WILL

John Locke pointed out that the question whether a person's will is or is not free is improper or, at least, poorly framed. To speak of the will, says Locke, is to speak of a power that individuals possess. The will is the power of choice. Being a power, the will cannot itself be free or unfree. The proper question is whether the individual is free in his actions.[28]

For Locke, individuals exercise their will when they actually make a choice or decision. Locke used the term *volition* to refer to the inner mental act of choosing. A person is free in his actions when nothing prevents him from doing as he chooses, when nothing stands in the way of his volitions' bringing about his actions. For example, suppose I choose or decide to raise my arm. The inner decision to raise my arm is a volition. This

[27]St. Augustine, *On Free Choice of the Will*, trans. Anna S. Benjamin and L. H. Hackstaff (Indianapolis: Bobbs-Merrill, 1964), pp. 94–95.
[28]Locke, *Essay*, II. xxi. 14–15.

volition then causes my arm to rise. When nothing prevents the volition from causing my arm to rise, then I am free in that action. But suppose my arm is tied to my side so that no matter how hard I try, I cannot raise it. My volition in that case cannot cause my arm to rise. In that event, I am not free with respect to that action. A person, then, is free when nothing stands in the way of his doing what he wills. This is Locke's theory, and it is one of the most popular accounts of freedom that one finds in the philosophical literature.

LIBERTY AND NECESSITY

Thomas Hobbes developed a similar conception of freedom:

> Liberty, or Freedome, signifieth (properly) the absence of Opposition. . . . A Free-Man is he, that in those things, which by his strength and wit he is able to do, is not hindred to doe what he has a will to do.[29]

THOMAS HOBBES
(1588–1679)

Hobbes was born in the town of Malmesbury in England just as the Spanish Armada was approaching. He was raised by his uncle after his father fled from home as a result of his participation in a brawl outside church. After graduating from Oxford University, he became a tutor to the sons of several wealthy nobles. He fled England at the beginning of the English civil war and lived in Paris for about eleven years. With the restoration of the monarchy, he returned to England and spent the remainder of his long life writing books on philosophy and other subjects. His writings were vigorously criticized during his lifetime because of his materialism as well as his unorthodox views on politics and religion. His major work is *Leviathan* (1651), which contains a summary of his whole system written in an unusually direct and incisive style.

Hobbes was also a determinist. He believed that every event, including human actions and volitions, are causally necessitated by previous events. He accepted the view that liberty and necessity are not in conflict with each other and that an action can be both free and necessitated at the same time:

> *Liberty,* and *Necessity* are consistent: As in the water, that hath not only liberty, but a *necessity* of descending by the Channel; so likewise in the Actions which

[29]Thomas Hobbes, *Leviathan* (Oxford: The Clarendon Press, 1967), p. 161.

150

men voluntarily doe: which, because they proceed from their will, proceed from *liberty;* and yet, because every act of mans will, and every desire, and inclination proceedeth from some cause, and that from another cause, in a continuall chaine (whose first link is the hand of God the first of all causes,) they proceed from *necessity.* So that to him that could see the connexion of those causes, the *necessity* of all mens voluntary actions, would appeare manifest. And therefore God, that seeth, and disposeth all things, seeth also that the *liberty* of man in doing what he will, is accompanied with the *necessity* of doing that which God will, and no more, nor lesse. For though men may do many things, which God does not command, nor is therefore Author of them; yet they can have no passion, nor appetite to anything, of which appetite Gods will is not the cause.[30]

Hobbes's view that liberty and necessity are consistent is sometimes called **soft determinism.** It has several advantages that have led to its being widely adopted in contemporary philosophy.

First, soft determinism permits us to accept the idea that people can be held responsible for their actions and at the same time accept the insights of modern science regarding the causes of human behavior. For example, one can both hold a criminal responsible for his voluntary behavior and thus subject to punishment and yet agree that his crimes are precipitated by such social conditions as poverty and rootlessness. Soft determinism lets us have our cake and eat it too.

Second, soft determinism appears to be consistent with our commonsense conception of a free action. In our everyday judgments, we assume that an individual has acted freely if nothing has compelled him to act or has forced his hand. Yet at the same time we also agree that individuals who act freely or voluntarily or of their own free will have reasons or motives for their actions. But if a person acts for a reason, then, according to the determinist his action is caused. So common sense seems to admit that freedom and determinism are compatible.

A third virtue of soft determinism is that it allows the question whether or not a person is free to be decided by observation of his behavior and circumstances. If a person does something against the law and for which he can be punished, we want to know whether his act was voluntary. According to the account of freedom offered by Locke or Hobbes, we need to examine the circumstances of his actions to see whether anything forced or compelled him to act contrary to his choice. If he was free of external compulsion, then his action was free and he is responsible for it. Similarly, if someone refrains from doing as he ought, we need to examine the circumstances to discover whether some external impediment prevented him from acting as he willed. If there were no impediments to action, then he is responsible for his failure to act.

CAUSALITY AND COMPULSION

Despite these advantages, it is difficult to avoid the suspicion that there is some deep difficulty with soft determinism. How can freedom be compatible with necessity? If a

[30]Ibid., p. 162.

person's volitions are necessitated by events of which he is unaware or events not in his power, then isn't he compelled to act as he does? And if he is compelled, how can he be free? For example, suppose all the various relationships that a certain man enters into with women turn out to be disastrous for him. He wonders why this should keep happening. Before entering each relationship, he considers at length the qualities of the woman and how they might affect him in the long run. He never acts impetuously or thoughtlessly. Nevertheless, he makes one mistake after another. His life is in a shambles. After five years of psychoanalytical treatment, he discovers that his choice of partner had never been motivated by rational considerations, as he had thought, but were unconsciously determined by a desire for a woman like his mother. The outcomes of his search for an adult relationship with a woman were thus determined by his unconscious need for a mother. Even though he seemed to be making conscious rational choices, he was really compelled by unconscious forces beyond his control. Can such a person really be free?

An important advance in our thought about this issue was made by David Hume. Hume asked about the nature of causal necessity. Suppose that one event E_1 causes another event E_2. What is the relationship between them in virtue of which we say that E_1 necessitates E_2? We know, for example, that fire causes smoke. What justifies our belief? Hume pointed out that the mere fact that a particular occurrence of E_2 followed a particular occurrence of E_1 does not establish a causal pattern. If you take medicine and later your illness disappears, this does not prove that your cure was caused by the medicine. It could have been a coincidence. Perhaps you would have returned to health even if you hadn't taken the medicine. Furthermore, we cannot establish causal necessity merely by observing events and changes. All that observation teaches is that one thing follows another. We never observe any underlying linkages in virtue of which one thing necessitates another.

For Hume, what establishes the existence of a causal relation is the fact that whenever E_1 occurs, E_2 also occurs. Causality consists in the constant conjunction or correlation or uniformity that holds between E_1 and E_2. We believe that smoke is caused by fire not because this smoke accompanied this fire nor because we observed some special causal linkage between fire and smoke, but because we find that whenever there is fire, there is smoke.[31]

If Hume is correct, then we must distinguish between causal necessity on the one hand and compulsion on the other. For Hume, to say that the occurrence of E_2 is necessitated by the occurrence of E_1 means that E_2 has occurred whenever E_1 has occurred. Although fire causes smoke, fire does not compel the burning wood to give forth smoke. To speak of compulsion brings in the notion of the will of some human being. To say that a person was compelled to do such and such does not mean merely that he was caused to do it, but that he was caused to do it against his will.

Let us return to the case of the man whose relationships with women ended unhappily. If the diagnosis was correct, then we must admit that his choice of partner was

---

[31]For Hume's famous discussion of causality and its application to the problem of free will, see sects. 7 and 8 of his "An Enquiry concerning Human Understanding" in *Hume's Enquiries,* ed. L. A. Selby-Bigge (Oxford: The Claredon Press, 1972). (This book was first published in 1748.)

caused by certain unconscious motives. But it does not follow that his selection was forced on him against his will. Each partner was a woman he wanted and chose willingly. No compulsion was present at all. According to the soft determinist, the man's will was free. Freedom is consistent with causality.

THE EXISTENCE OF ALTERNATIVES

The critics of soft determinism present another important argument. Granted that the man was not forced to act against his will, yet one wonders whether he was really able to choose or to act differently from the way he did. An action is free, say these critics, not only if the action was in accordance with the individual's will but also if he could have acted otherwise. To be free with regard to some action A, I must be able to do something other than A. I am free to raise my arm only if it is open to me to keep my arm at my side. Freedom entails the existence of alternatives. If there is only one course of action available, then there are no alternatives and there is no freedom. But if my choices and my actions are causally necessitated, then what I do I must do, and I therefore have no alternatives. Thus, say the critics, soft determinism cannot be the correct account of freedom. Often critics who make this argument will go on to assert that there is a breach in the causal order and that freedom exists only because determinism is false. This position is called **libertarianism.**

Let us examine the problem in light of a specific example. Suppose John lies to Erica, thus doing something he ought not to have done. When Erica finds out, should she hold John responsible for his action? According to the libertarian, John is responsible only if it was open to him to refrain from lying. But if John's lie was caused by his volitions, and his volitions were caused by other events, and these other events were caused by still others, so that we go back in time to the first cause of the universe, then it was necessary that John lied. And if it was necessary and if he had no alternatives, then he cannot be held responsible. For the libertarian, for a person to be free with respect to an action A, it is not sufficient that he is not compelled to do A against his will. Another condition is required as well. And this condition is that his choice of A be uncaused.

Suppose a person is deliberating between various courses of action. Should he choose to do A or B? Let us say that he chooses A. According to the libertarian, if he is free in doing A, then it must have been open to him to have done B instead. And this means that he could have chosen to do B even if everything else had remained the same. John chose to lie to Erica. John is a man with a certain character and personality, with certain desires and goals, acting in a particular situation. Given all these conditions, John chose to lie. The libertarian says that if John were truly free and responsible, then he could have refrained from lying even if these conditions had not changed. But this means that the sum total of the conditions in which he was acting and choosing were not sufficient to cause him to lie. And this implies that his lie had no sufficient causal conditions. It was, in this sense, uncaused.

The libertarian, however, admits that John's lie was caused in another sense, for there is an ambiguity in the notion of causality. Suppose you come home one day to find the window of your bedroom broken. How did this happen? you wonder. If you find a brick lying on the floor near your window, you have discovered the cause of your misfortune.

The cause of the window's breaking was the impact of the brick. You have learned the cause in the sense of an antecedent event or condition that, in the circumstances, was sufficient to shatter your window. This form of causality is called **event causation.** You may not, however, be satisfied. You may want to know the cause in the sense of finding out who it was who threw the brick through your window. It was little Toby Diller. She threw it. You have now discovered the cause in a second sense; you have discovered the agent who did it. This type of causality is **agent causation,** or **agency** for short. The libertarian asserts that although free actions lack sufficient event causation, they do have agency causation. When John lies to Erica, although no event or set of conditions necessitated his choice, nevertheless John himself caused his choice to be made. John was the agent who acted, and in acting he brought about an event that was open to him not to do.

THE DENIAL OF FREEDOM

There is a serious difficulty in the libertarian position. How can we tell whether or not a person acted freely in doing what he did? For us to verify the existence of a free action, we would have to discover an action that was not caused by any previous events or conditions of the agent's circumstances. But because there are countless numbers of things going on, many of which are beyond our powers of observation, we can never be sure that none of them caused the choice. Think of all the things going on in a person's brain and nervous system at any given time. How can we tell that none of them caused his action? Kant, one of the major libertarians in the Western philosophical tradition, admitted that we can never know whether any given action is free. "Freedom . . . is a concept for which no corresponding example can be given in any possible experience."[32] But if we are thus ignorant of freedom, then we are never in a position to ascribe responsibility to persons for their conduct nor to distribute rewards and punishments, praise and blame. We would always doubt whether any ascription of responsibility was truly deserved.

It is possible to agree with the libertarian's claim that freedom entails a breach in the causal order and still maintain that determinism is true. The conclusion that one would have to draw is that there is no such thing as freedom. This is exactly the position of **hard determinism.** The hard determinist agrees with the libertarian analysis of the meaning of free will. He agrees that freedom implies that determinism is false. Instead of concluding, as the libertarian does, that freedom exists and consequently that determinism is false, he asserts that freedom does not exist and that determinism is true. The hard determinist is willing to live with unwelcome facts: Science tends to establish that human choices are caused either by events in the brain, the nervous system, the unconscious, or the environment of human agents. And if they are so caused, then no one can act in any way other than the way he in fact acts. No action is free, and no person is ever morally responsible for what he does. Hard determinism is indeed a tough-minded position.

[32]Immanuel Kant, *The Metaphysical Elements of Justice,* trans. John Ladd (Indianapolis: Bobbs-Merrill, 1965), p. 21.

Does this mean that no one can ever be praised or blamed, rewarded or punished? Must dangerous criminals be allowed to roam the streets? The hard determinist denies that these consequences follow from his position. The purpose of imprisoning a convicted criminal, he claims, is to protect the innocent. This purpose is still valid even if the criminal is not free and hence not morally responsible. After all, we would keep a dangerous tiger in a cage to protect ourselves even though we do not presume that the tiger is to blame in a moral sense for its desire to eat people. Furthermore, punishment, like praise and blame, is a practice that can cause changes in behavior. We praise someone for an action if we want to cause him to act similarly in the future. We blame him if we want to cause him to stop acting in that way. Seeing criminals punished will discourage others from committing more crimes. The hard determinist insists that the rationality of these practices does not presuppose any breaches in the causal order of things. Just the contrary. Unless the behavior of individuals can be causally influenced by praise and blame, reward and punishment, there would be no point to these practices. Unless determinism is true, human behavior could not be influenced, and these practices would lose their value.

CONCEPTIONS OF HUMAN FREEDOM

Libertarianism: Freedom entails a break in the causal order.
Soft determinism: Freedom and determinism are compatible, and determinism is true.
Hard determinism: Freedom and determinism are incompatible, and determinism is true.

THE IMPLICATIONS OF FREEDOM

The soft determinist can observe the argument between the libertarian and the hard determinist with a certain amount of detachment. He thinks that they both make an incorrect assumption. This assumption is presupposed in their analysis of what it means for a person to have alternatives and to be able to do other than what he does. According to the libertarian, an agent can do other than what he does even if all the antecedent conditions and events remain the same. Because the hard determinist agrees that this is what it means to have alternatives, he concludes that the belief that agents do have alternatives is mistaken. The soft determinist offers a different explanation of what it means to have alternatives. He claims that indeed John could have refrained from lying in the sense that he would have refrained if he had chosen not to lie. John can do as he chooses. He lied because he chose to. He could have told the truth if he had chosen. Freedom in general implies that individuals have alternatives in the sense that they would act differently if they were to choose differently. John is free not to lie in the sense that nothing in the circumstances necessitates that he will lie if he chooses not to.

The libertarian insists that the meaning of "He could have acted otherwise" is unconditional. Even if everything remained the same, it was open to him to choose differently.

The soft determinist asserts that its meaning is conditional; he would have acted otherwise *if* he had chosen a different course of action.

The libertarian now asks, Could he have *chosen* otherwise? The libertarian agrees that a person can do otherwise if he chooses otherwise. But what of the power of choice itself? If the person lacks the power to choose other than as he does, then his action is not free. The soft determinist replies with a conditional analysis of the power to choose otherwise: A person can choose other than he does provided he would have made a different choice if he had wanted to. The soft determinist claims that a person's choices are caused by his desires. If his desires were different, his choices would also be different. For the libertarian, however, freedom implies that the individual is not in the grip of his desires but has the power to choose a course of conduct in opposition to his desires. He may judge that what he would like to do is wrong or imprudent or otherwise faulty. No matter how strong his desires, he can rise above them by an effort of will that, according to the libertarian, represents a breach of causal continuity.

THE CURRENT STATUS OF THE DEBATE

Contemporary philosophy has still not resolved the debate between libertarianism, hard determinism, and soft determinism. The great strength of the libertarian position lies in its analysis of what it means to have alternatives and its insistence that in the moment of moral choice we can rise to the occasion and act in opposition to our desires and inclinations. Its major weakness lies in the fact that it is well-nigh impossible to ascertain whether or not an action is free. Until recently it was thought that a great defect of libertarianism was its rejection of determinism, for determinism had apparently been established by science. With the development of quantum mechanics, however, many physicists now believe that determinism is not true, that there is no exceptionless causal order, that, at the atomic level at least, unpredictable events often occur. Thus, libertarianism no longer runs counter to the scientific enterprise.

This debate involves both a question of fact and a question of meaning. The major question of fact is to ascertain the extent to which people's desires and other inner conditions represent sufficient conditions for their choices and actions. The major question of meaning is to settle upon a satisfactory account of what it means to have the power to act otherwise. The outcome of the debate will influence our conception of human action and of what it means to be a person who is both a part of nature and yet, unlike other forms of life, has a moral dimension to his existence. The question of human freedom is still being debated with vigor in contemporary philosophy.

Summary

What is the self? What is the mind? How is the mind related to the body? According to influential arguments advanced by Descartes and others, the mind is a thinking thing that must be distinguished from all extended things, including the human body. Mind and body are said to have incompatible characteristics. Many contemporary thinkers, however, are not inclined to accept this dualism. The theory of evolution, considerations about the nature of explanation, the concept of category mistakes, and the problem of other minds have been used to challenge mind–body dualism.

Consequently, many thinkers have adopted a behaviorist point of view according to which the mind consists of observable behavior and behavioral dispositions. Behaviorism, however, presupposes an inadequate conception of scientific explanation and cannot account for inner or private experience. In addition, the very concept of behavior itself seems to point to an inner private aspect.

The mind–brain identity thesis allows for the possibility of explaining behavior by reference to inner events in the brain and nervous system. Considerations about the direction of scientific research and of theoretical simplicity have been thought to favor this materialistic point of view. Although the identity thesis is able to deal with certain problems, especially the problem of the status of images, it seems to require an admission that brain events have an irreducibly mental aspect. And this is to admit a kind of dualism between mind and body. The theory that best fits the facts is emergent materialism, which represents a compromise between dualism and the identity thesis. Reflection on the question of personal identity also suggests a compromise with dualism: Whereas the identity of persons is based upon the identity of their bodies, nevertheless a person has mental as well as physical characteristics.

Human action is an expression of mind and presupposes freedom. But how is free action possible if man's behavior is caused by events in his body and environment? We explain actions by reference to the agent's intentions or purposes. But if determinism is true, how can an agent's intentions be effective? How can they produce actions that are free?

There are three major theories about free action and its relation to determinism: The soft determinist asserts that freedom is compatible with causal necessity; the hard determinist rejects the belief that they are compatible and denies the reality of freedom; and the libertarian also rejects their compatibility but denies the truth of determinism. Each position has its strengths and weaknesses, and contemporary philosophers are quite divided in their assessment of them.

Glossary

Agent causation or agency: The causation of an event by an agent, as when a person causes a window to break by throwing a brick through it.

Behavior: The observable actions of animals and humans.

Behaviorism: The belief that there is no more to the study of the mind than the study of the behavior and behavioral dispositions of animals and humans.

Category mistake: A type of error according to which something is allocated to the wrong category or classification. According to Ryle, Descartes' dualism is a category mistake.

Consciousness: Used to mean either sentience—the capacity for feeling—or awareness.

Correspondence hypothesis: The claim that for every mental event there exists a corresponding brain event.

Determinism: The view that every event is an effect of previous events according to the laws of nature.

Emergent materialism: A view that agrees with materialism that mind depends upon matter for its existence, but also partly accepts dualism when it says that events in the brain have a mental aspect.

Empiricism: The view that all justified belief about the world is based upon observation.

Epiphenomenalism: The view that whereas changes in the body are capable of causing changes in the mind, the mind is incapable of causing bodily changes.

Event causation: The causing of one event by another event, as when the impact of a brick upon a window causes the window to break.

Functional explanation: An explanation of an event by reference to its function, that is, by reference to the state of the system that the event maintains.

Hard determinism: The view that because determinism is true, there can be no such thing as free action.

Intellect: The capacity for thought.

Introspection: The awareness that a person has of his thoughts, feelings, and other events in his mind.

Libertarianism: The view that freedom implies that determinism is false, that there is a breach in the causal order of events.

Materialism: A philosophical approach that denies the separate reality of mind.

Mechanical explanation: An explanation of an event by reference to the causal interactions among the parts of the system in which the event occurs.

Mind–body dualism: The theory that the mind or self is a thing distinct from its body.

Mind–brain identity thesis: The theory that says that the mind and mental processes are identical with the brain and brain processes.

Occam's razor: The principle that one should accept the simplest theory among those compatible with the evidence.

Sentience: The capacity for feeling, for having sensations.

Soft determinism: The view that the existence of free action is compatible with the truth of determinism.

Teleological explanation: An explanation of an event that gives its purpose or the intention with which it was done.

Two-sided interaction: The view that the mind can influence what happens in the body and that the body can also influence what happens in the mind.

Will: The capacity for deliberation and choice.

Further Reading

Two readable general works on the philosophy of mind are Jerome A. Shaffer, *Philosophy of Mind* (Englewood Cliffs, New Jersey: Prentice-Hall, 1968) and the much longer C. D. Broad, *The Mind and Its Place in Nature* (London: Routledge and Kegan Paul, 1925). Some of the better anthologies are V. C. Chappell (ed.), *The Philosophy of Mind* (Englewood Cliffs, New Jersey: Prentice-Hall, 1962); Antony Flew (ed.),

Body, Mind, and Death (New York: Macmillan, 1964); Jonathan Glover (ed.), *The Philosophy of Mind* (Oxford: Oxford University Press, 1976); Donald F. Gustafson (ed.), *Essays in Philosophical Psychology* (Garden City, New York: Doubleday, 1964); and Stuart Hampshire (ed.), *Philosophy of Mind* (New York: Harper & Row, 1966).

Important arguments for dualism are included in Plato, *Phaedo;* Descartes, *Meditations on First Philosophy;* Arthur O. Lovejoy, *The Revolt against Dualism* (La Salle, Illinois: Open Court, 1955); and C. J. Ducasse, *Nature, Mind, and Death* (La Salle, Illinois: Open Court, 1951). The most influential contemporary arguments against dualism are contained in Gilbert Ryle, *The Concept of Mind* (London: Hutchinson's University Library, 1949), and Ludwig Wittgenstein, *Philosophical Investigations,* trans. G. E. M. Anscombe (New York: Macmillan, 1953).

For behaviorism, in addition to the writings of Ryle and Wittgenstein mentioned above, see B. F. Skinner, *Beyond Freedom and Dignity* (New York: Alfred A. Knopf, 1971), and Edward Chace Tolman, *Behavior and Psychological Man* (Berkeley: University of California Press, 1961). For a theory of language in opposition to behaviorism, see Noam Chomsky, *Language and Mind* (New York: Harcourt Brace Jovanovich, 1972).

Two major materialistic systems are Lucretius' great Latin poem, *De Rerum Natura,* an English translation of which is included in Whitney J. Oates (ed.), *The Stoic and Epicurean Philosophers* (New York: Random House, 1940); and Thomas Hobbes, *Leviathan.* For a general history see Frederick Albert Lange, *The History of Materialism,* trans. Ernest Chester Thomas (New York: Humanities Press, 1950). There are two good collections of recent papers on the mind–brain identity thesis: John O'Connor (ed.), *Modern Materialism: Readings on Mind–Body Identity* (New York: Harcourt, Brace and World, 1969); and David M. Rosenthal (ed.), *Materialism and the Mind–Body Problem* (Englewood Cliffs, New Jersey: Prentice-Hall, 1971).

A good collection on the topic of personal identity is John Perry (ed.), *Personal Identity* (Berkeley: University of California Press, 1975).

A fine general account of action is Alvin Goldman, *A Theory of Human Action* (Princeton, New Jersey: Princeton University Press, 1976). Two collections of contemporary articles are Norman S. Care and Charles Landesman (eds.), *Readings in the Theory of Action* (Bloomington: Indiana University Press, 1968); and Alan R. White, *The Philosophy of Action* (London: Oxford University Press, 1968). A good collection on teleological and functional explanation is John V. Canfield (ed.), *Purpose in Nature* (Englewood Cliffs, New Jersey: Prentice-Hall, 1966). Major papers on the topic of free will are included in Bernard Berofsky (ed.), *Free Will and Determinism* (New York: Harper & Row, 1966).

Questions for Thought and Discussion

1. Even if we agree that both humans and nonhuman animals possess minds in some sense, nevertheless there appear to be significant differences in their degree and type of mentality. What differences seem to you to be the most important? What similarities do you find? Do you agree with Descartes that nonhuman animals lack minds entirely?

2. Do you think that the mind–body dualism of Descartes can be successfully defended in light of the theories and explanatory practices of modern science? Is dualism a category mistake, as Ryle contends?

3. What conception of behavior or action is presupposed by the behaviorist conception of the mind? Is it a conception that is applicable to actual cases of human conduct? Can the behaviorist provide an adequate account of even the simplest of actions, such as raising one's arm?

4. How do we learn about what is going on in the minds of others? How do theories about the nature of the mind influence our view about our knowledge of other minds? Can you defend the idea of solipsism—the idea that you are the only being with a mind?

5. Hume says that when he reflects upon his experience and tries to find his *self,* there is nothing that he can identify as that self. Was he looking in the right place for the self? What is the self anyhow? What do you name when you use the word *I?*

6. How can people ever act freely if, as the determinist claims, actions are ultimately caused by events over which we have no control? Must we accept determinism? Has science proved it?

7. What exactly is the nature of the explanation we give when we explain why a person acted as he did? How does this type of explanation differ from the explanations we give of inanimate events?

8. What does it mean to say that although a person acted in a certain way, it was in his *power* to act in a different way? Discuss how different theories of freedom offer different accounts of the existence of alternatives in action.

Chapter 6

GOD, NATURE, AND THE MEANING OF LIFE

PREVIEW

Does life have a meaning? This is the main question we shall consider in this chapter. People have most commonly sought the meaning of life in religion, so most of the chapter will be concerned with the reasons for and against holding a religious belief. We shall consider at length the great question of the existence of God. How strong are the arguments intended to prove God's existence? How strong are those designed to prove that there is no God? If the arguments are not decisive, is there any other way to make up our minds about religion? Is there any alternative to religion that gives life a meaning? In discussing these questions, we shall refer to two of the main philosophical movements of the twentieth century: existentialism and naturalism.

The Meaning of Life

Many of the philosophical problems examined in this book require a searching analysis of concepts fundamental to our understanding of the world. It may seem as if philosophy is an impersonal inquiry into fundamental concepts analogous to other scientific inquiries in its rigor and objectivity. This conception of philosophy, although not inaccurate, is incomplete. For there is another type of problem of great concern to philosophy that is of personal significance to all thoughtful individuals: the problem of the meaning of life. Most of the great philosophical systems of the past attempted to explain the meaning of human life and of our relationship to reality as a whole. To use religious terminology, they were concerned with the salvation of souls, that is, with delineating the true purpose of human life and the ways and means by which individuals can realize it in their own lives.

We have all experienced situations in life that prompt us to ask, "What is it all about?" For example, some of you are considering what vocation to choose. You are concerned to select a profession or occupation that will provide you with a meaningful and satisfactory life. But what kind of life is meaningful and satisfactory? Should you choose a vocation that will require you to subordinate your own personal interests to the needs of others? Consider the missionary who leaves his family, friends, and country to help save the souls of peoples living in a distant country. Or should you be preoccupied with the pursuit of your own personal interests and pleasures? "You only live once," it is said. So perhaps you should live for yourself and your family and friends. Can one reconcile the competing demands of a life of service and a life of personal gratification? Is there any work to do in the world that is of any great value?

Even if you should be lucky enough to find a career of whose value you are convinced, there may come a time when it loses its charm. It may cease to be a source of happiness. The English philosopher John Stuart Mill (1806–1873) described a crisis that he lived through when he was a young man:

> It was in the autumn of 1826. I was in a dull state of nerves, such as everybody is occasionally liable to; unsusceptible to enjoyment or pleasurable excitement; one of those moods when what is pleasure at other times, becomes insipid or indifferent. . . . In this frame of mind it occurred to me to put the question directly to myself: "Suppose that all your objects in life were realized; that all the changes in institutions and opinions which you are looking forward to, could

---

JOHN STUART MILL
(1806–1873)

Mill was probably the most influential English philosopher of the nineteenth century. He made important contributions to ethics, political theory, logic, and economics. Born in London, he was a precocious child and was educated by his father. One of the philosophical radicals who attempted to put liberal and democratic ideals into practice, Mill earned his living by working in the examiner's office of the East India Company. He was strongly influenced by Harriet Taylor, whom he loved for twenty years until the death of her husband allowed them to marry. His life and ideas are recounted in his fascinating *Autobiography* (1873). Mill's theory of knowledge and his philosophy of logic is contained in his *System of Logic* (1843). His famous defense of liberty is presented in *On Liberty* (1859). *Utilitarianism* (1863) is his major work on ethics. His theory of democracy is contained in *Considerations on Representative Government* (1861).

---

be completely effected at this very instant: would this be a great joy and happiness to you?" And an irrepressible self-consciousness distinctly answered, "No!" At this my heart sank within me: the whole foundation of which my life was constructed fell down. All my happiness was to have been found in the continual pursuit of this end. The end had ceased to charm, and how could there ever again be any interest in the means? I seemed to have nothing left to live for.[1]

Mill became so unhappy that he even contemplated suicide. Today, under the influence of psychiatry, many people would interpret Mill's depression and breakdown as an indication of mental illness requiring some form of medical treatment. Mill, however, interpreted his mental crisis as a consequence of his loss of purpose in life. All his actions had gained their meaning by being related to the goals of social reform that he and his associates were seeking. But the goals had "ceased to charm."

> The sense of meaninglessness is wonderfully conveyed in this passage from Shakespeare's *Macbeth:*
>
> *To-morrow, and to-morrow, and to-morrow,*
> *Creeps in this petty pace from day to day,*
> *To the last syllable of recorded time;*
> *And all our yesterdays have lighted fools*
> *The way to dusty death. Out, out, brief candle!*
> *Life's but a walking shadow; a poor player*
> *That struts and frets his hour upon the stage*
> *And then is heard no more. It is a tale*
> *Told by an idiot, full of sound and fury,*
> *Signifying nothing.*

As he understood it, the problem lay in a flaw in human existence itself:

I felt that the flaw in my life, must be a flaw in life itself; that the question was, whether, if the reformers of society and government could succeed in their objects, and every person in the community were free and in a state of physical comfort, the pleasures of life, being no longer kept up by struggle and privation, would cease to be pleasures. And I felt that unless I could see my way to some better hope than this for human happiness in general, my dejection must continue; but that if I could see such an outlet, I should then look on the world with pleasure; content as far as I was myself concerned, with any fair share of the general lot.[2]

[1]John Stuart Mill, *Autobiography* (New York: Columbia University Press, 1924), p. 94. (This book was first published in 1873.)
[2]Ibid., pp. 102–103.

The flaw is that human happiness requires struggle and unhappiness as its prerequisite. We have all found enjoyment in something that we have achieved only as a result of great difficulty and labor. For example, in writing this book, I have experienced dejection because of the enormous amount of work involved, despair at the thought of the long road ahead, mental difficulty in finding the correct way of expressing my ideas, boredom with the endless revisions, and so forth. But I am sure that I shall be quite pleased when I finish. Every author achieves enormous happiness when he finally holds in his hand a copy of his newly published book. I am sure, however, that I would not feel such happiness had I completed this book in a few minutes just by voicing a few magic words. Suppose all I had to do was say "Shazam" to produce a new and original volume of philosophy. Although such volumes may be of interest to others, I would achieve no satisfaction in having produced it in this way. Things that come to us too easily have no capacity to provide satisfaction. If the social reformers have their way, thinks Mill, and eliminate discomfort and hardship from human life, then our very happiness would be threatened.

Mill overcame his mental crisis partly as a result of reading the poetry of Wordsworth:

> What made Wordsworth's poems a medicine for my state of mind, was that they expressed, not mere outward beauty, but states of feeling, and of thought coloured by feeling, under the excitement of beauty. They seemed to be the very culture of the feelings, which I was in quest of. In them I seemed to draw from a source of inward joy, of sympathetic and imaginative pleasure, which could be shared in by all human beings; which had no connection with struggle or imperfection, but would be made richer by every improvement in the physical or social condition of mankind. From them I seemed to learn what would be the perennial sources of happiness, when all the greater evils of life shall have been removed.[3]

From his reading of poetry, Mill learned that the happiness that is produced by the cultivation of the feelings and the appreciation of beauty will not be adversely affected even if the social reforms that Mill hoped for were achieved. The solution to Mill's crisis lay not in medicine but in deepening his understanding of the nature of human happiness.

The Problem of Death

Even if you should find a satisfactory vocation that, together with your relationships with family and friends, becomes a sure source of happiness, you may start to wonder about the permanent value of your life. You may realize that you will soon die and that your life and work will be forgotten. In having to come to terms with death, you may find that the happiness that you have been able to sustain thus far may lose its vigor and value.

[3]Ibid., p. 104.

The significance of the shortness of human life is well represented in this brief poem by Ernest Dowson called ''Envoy'':

> They are not long, the weeping and the laughter,
>   Love and desire and hate;
> I think they have no portion in us after
>   We pass the gate.
>
> They are not long, the days of wine and roses:
>   Out of a misty dream
> Our path emerges for a while, then closes
>   Within a dream.

In his short novel *The Death of Ivan Ilych,* Leo Tolstoy (1828–1910) tells of the life and death of a minor Russian official. Ivan Ilych was a man who lived his life in accordance with the values of his fellow officials and other members of his class and rank. In choosing a wife and in otherwise arranging his life, he was concerned to maintain his status in society. He became quite preoccupied with his work and found, after a while, that he ceased to enjoy life with his family. With his ambitions realized and his status secure, he found that his greatest pleasure was in playing cards.

One day he injured himself. The pain did not go away. He began to worry about his health and feared for his very life. As his fears increased, he discovered to his dismay that all the people around him—the members of his family, his friends, his colleagues, the doctors he visited—were profoundly indifferent to his fate. They were all intent upon avoiding unpleasant situations and conversations. His doctors maintained an official and distant attitude, the same attitude that he himself had assumed toward others in his work as an officer of the court. No one tendered him any genuine sympathy. He realized that he had to face his death all by himself:

> There was no deceiving himself: something terrible, new, and more important than anything before in his life, was taking place within him of which he alone was aware. Those about him did not understand or would not understand it, but thought everything in the world was going on as usual. That tormented Ivan Ilych more than anything. He saw that his household, especially his wife and daughter who were in a perfect whirl of visiting, did not understand anything of it and were annoyed that he was so depressed and so exacting, as if he were to blame for it. Though they tried to disguise it he saw that he was an obstacle in their path. . . .[4]

Ivan Ilych realized that as his own sufferings increased, he stood in the way of the happiness of others. No one cared about him: "The whole interest he had for other

---

[4]Leo Tolstoy, *Ivan Ilych and Hadji Murad* (Oxford: Oxford University Press, 1951), pp. 36–37.

people was whether he would soon vacate his place, and at last release the living from the discomfort caused by his presence and be himself released from his suffering."[5]

Others refused even to admit the fact that he was dying. They pretended that he was merely ill and would soon recover. This infuriated him, but he soon realized that they were displaying the same hypocrisy that he himself had so often practiced:

> The awful, terrible act of his dying was, he could see, reduced by those about him to the level of a casual, unpleasant, and almost indecorous incident (as if someone entered a drawing room diffusing an unpleasant odor) and this was done by that very decorum which he had served all his life long. He saw that no one felt for him, because no one even wished to grasp his position.[6]

The only person who offered him any consolation was his simple, healthy servant of peasant stock who took care of him in his final days. He came to realize that his whole past life was worthless because it was filled with vain social striving, mindless conformity, meaningless ambition, hypocrisy, and insincerity. Just as he was about to die,

> He sought his former accustomed fear of death and did not find it. "Where is it? What death?" There was no fear because there was no death. In place of death there was light.[7]

But what is this light that banishes death? Tolstoy does not tell us. He has given us a brilliant portrayal of how the values of everyday life, the strivings and concerns of the ordinary individual, fail to sustain the spirit in the face of death. But what shall we put in their place?

Platonism

In his dialogue *Phaedo,* Plato described the final hours of the life of Socrates before his execution. The causes of his imprisonment and his courage in the face of death were discussed in Chapter Two. In the beginning of the *Phaedo,* Socrates asserts that the true philosopher is one who searches after knowledge and wisdom. He then announces the apparent paradox that anyone who undertakes this search will actually look forward to death. Thus, rather than fearing death like the ordinary man, Socrates seems to anticipate it with pleasure.

Socrates defines death as "the separation of soul and body." When a person has died, "the soul exists in herself, and is released from the body and the body is released from the soul."[8] Before death, the soul dwells in the body. But the body, says Socrates, impedes the search for wisdom. The body causes the individual to spend his life seeking physical pleasures, the pleasures of eating, drinking, and sexual activity. But these dis-

---

[5]Ibid., p. 48.
[6]Ibid., pp. 51–52.
[7]Ibid., p. 73.
[8]Plato, *Phaedo,* 64, Jowett translation.

tract him from other, more important, pursuits. The true philosopher "would like, as far as he can, to get away from the body and to turn to the soul."[9]

Using Socrates as the vehicle for his ideas, Plato proposes a theory of forms or absolutes. (See Chapter Nine for a fuller discussion of this theory.) To achieve knowledge of the form or true nature of a thing, one must strive to put aside the information coming in through the bodily senses and simply think:

> And he attains purest knowledge of them [the forms] who goes to each with the mind alone, not introducing or intruding in the act of thought sight or any other sense together with reason, but with the very light of the mind in her own clearness searches into the very truth of each; he who has got rid, as far as he can, of eyes and ears and, so to speak, of the whole body, these being in his opinion distracting elements which when they infect the soul hinder her from acquiring truth and knowledge—who, if not he, is likely to attain to the knowledge of true being.[10]

The world of forms or of true being represents the nature of reality, the way things really are, and can be grasped only by the soul in separation from the body. It is no wonder, then, that the philosopher looks forward to death:

> If we would have pure knowledge of anything we must be quit of the body—the soul in herself must behold things in themselves: and then we shall attain the wisdom which we desire, and of which we say that we are lovers; not while we live, but after death; for if while in company with the body, the soul cannot have pure knowledge, one of two things follows—either knowledge is not to be attained at all, or, if at all, after death. For then, and till then, the soul will be parted from the body and exist in herself alone.[11]

Plato provides us with an intellectualist account of salvation. A person is saved just to the extent that he acquires the ability to apprehend the unchanging world of the forms. In the pursuit of this pure knowledge, the body and the changing world that is revealed to our senses stands as a continuing distraction that will finally be overcome by death.

For Plato, the life of the ordinary person is filled with falsehood and illusion. We think that the objects that are revealed to us in sense perception are real when in fact they are merely images of the true realities that are understood after death. The lover of wisdom may gain a glimpse of the unchanging world of forms in this life. In that case, he will be led to reject the values of everyday life in favor of the absolute Good that he has grasped with his soul. To his fellow citizens, he will seem eccentric, useless, and absentminded. Thus, Plato agrees with Tolstoy's negative appraisal of our everyday attitudes and concerns. For both of them, the values, the hopes and fears, the ambitions, the strivings, the pleasures and satisfactions of everyday life are to be rejected in favor of something else. For Plato, this something else is the life of the intellect, which

[9]Ibid.
[10]Ibid., 65–66.
[11]Ibid., 66–67.

searches after the true nature of reality. Plato would interpret the light that Ivan Ilych saw at the moment of his death as a glimmer of the unchanging world of forms.

In his argument, Plato assumes that a person is composed of a soul and a body and that after death the soul survives. The Platonic view of the world depends upon this assumption. If it should happen that the soul does not survive death or that there is no soul, then the form of salvation that Plato proposes would have no reality. In Chapter Five, I argued that the dualist theory of the self that Plato assumed and that Descartes many centuries later tried to demonstrate can no longer be defended. Consequently, Plato's interpretation of the meaning and significance of death is not acceptable as he formulated it. But, we must not dismiss his thought entirely. His criticisms of the mindlessness and vain strivings of everyday life are still powerful and convincing. And his idea that the pleasures of the body constitute distractions from the pursuit of such important goals as scientific knowledge and a rational understanding of the world is true. Bodily impulses need to be tamed and disciplined in the interests of higher values.

Theism

THE NATURE OF GOD

Theism is the name of a family of theories about reality, all of which assert the existence of God. **Atheism** is the view that there is no God, and **agnosticism** is the view that no one knows whether or not God exists and that we should therefore suspend our judgment. Theism is often offered as a solution to the personal problem of finding meaning in life. One's life has meaning, it is said, because it is part of a larger plan formulated by a divine being who has one's good at heart. Even though we are ignorant of the details of God's plan in creating the universe, we are assured, says theism, that each of us is playing a significant role in the unfolding of this plan and that human suffering has a purpose that will finally be revealed. Each person believes that his own life is of great significance. Each thinks of his life as a world of which he is the center. Each worries that after death his world will cease to exist. Theism agrees that the individual life is significant, and it tries to provide the individual with the consolation that his personal world may not, after all, be extinguished at his death. Theism tries to provide the assurance that Ivan Ilych found at the end that "there was no death. In place of death there was light."

There are many versions of theistic philosophy. In this chapter, we will discuss the conception of God that was developed in the Western philosophical tradition by a number of thinkers reflecting upon the Jewish and Christian religions. I shall call this conception *personal theism* because it conceives of God as a person with an intellect and a will analogous to the intellect and will of human beings. Personal theism makes the following statements about God. First, God created the universe and everything in it. In this respect, the God of personal theism differs from the god or gods of Greek philosophy, who were described as working upon matter that they did not create. The God of personal theism is not simply a worker who labors upon materials that are already there; he creates the very materials themselves, and he creates them out of nothing.

In *Genesis,* God is described as taking six days to complete his creation and resting on the seventh day. But some philosophers have argued that God is not only responsible for the beginnings of things, he also sustains and conserves the universe after it has come into existence. For example, Descartes wrote:

> For the whole time of my life may be divided into an infinity of parts, each of which is in no way dependent on any other; and, accordingly, because I was in existence a short time ago, it does not follow that I must now exist, unless in this moment some cause create me anew, as it were,—that is, conserve me. In truth, it is perfectly clear and evident to all who will attentively consider the nature of duration that the conservation of a substance, in each moment of its duration, requires the same power and act that would be necessary to create it, supposing it were not yet in existence.[12]

In this interesting argument, Descartes suggests a startling reversal of our commonsense attitude toward the things around us. Consider any object near you, say, the pencil on your desk. If that pencil were suddenly to disappear and go completely out of existence for no discernible reason, you would, I am sure, be shocked. According to our common-sense attitude, things continue to exist unless something causes them to go out of existence. Descartes, however, insists that this natural view is mistaken. The fact that something exists at one time does not provide any reason for its existing at any subsequent time. For your pencil to continue to exist, it is necessary for it to be acted upon by the same power that was required to create it from nothing in the first place. Descartes uses this idea to argue that God not only created the universe at the beginning of time but that he continues to sustain and to conserve it throughout time.

A second claim of personal theism is that God is perfectly and completely good. Whatever God wills or aims at is good, and whatever means he uses to achieve his goals are also good. There is no moral imperfection at all in God. Also, God is defined as completely powerful or omnipotent. He is able to do everything that is possible to do. Of course, there are some actions, such as squaring the circle or making two and four add up to eight, that are logically impossible for any being to perform.[13] Finally, according to personal theism, God is all-knowing or omniscient. There is nothing that escapes his apprehension. Even those thoughts and feelings that you are careful to keep to yourself are known to him.

LIFE AFTER DEATH

Many versions of personal theism assert that death is not the end of life but merely the end of a certain phase of life. They claim that the individual in some way survives death. According to some theists, after death the individual's soul survives separate from its

---

[12]Descartes, *Meditations on the First Philosophy,* III, trans. John Veitch
[13]According to some philosophers, God created the laws of logic and mathematics and is capable of changing them. Thus, he can do things that are logically impossible by modifying these laws and making them possible.

body, as Plato thought. This disembodied existence is the immortality of the soul. Others believe in the resurrection of the body. Accordingly, the dead shall come to life again either in their old bodies or in new ones provided by God. In Eastern religions, reincarnation is a popular conception of survival. The individual is given a new body, perhaps the body of a different kind of animal. Thus after death you may continue to exist as a tiger or as a spider. Neither reincarnation nor the resurrection of the body presuppose a separation of body and soul.

It is characteristic of personal theism that the particular way that one exists after death is influenced by the kind of life that one has led. A good person will reap the rewards of his or her goodness, and a bad person will be punished. The idea that each reaps what he sows is pictured graphically in Christianity's conceptions of heaven and hell. In Eastern religions, the individual's form of reincarnation depends upon his conduct in the preceding life. Someone who has been bad may be reincarnated as a particularly offensive bug. Most philosophical theists have been skeptics about the actual details of life after death. Although they have accepted the general idea that each will reap as he has sown, they usually profess no precise knowledge of the details.

In its attitude toward death, personal theism has provided consolation to those individuals who fear the extinction of their consciousness, who dread their lives' coming to a complete end. But because the bad person will have to pay for his misdeeds in some way, theism itself is a source of fear. Because no one is completely good in this life and since no one can be sure what standards God will use to judge the individual, each person is justified in being afraid of what will happen to him after he dies. The thought of suffering eternally in hell may cause as much anxiety as the thought of extinction. In any case, for the theist, the overall meaning of life is provided by each individual's particular place in God's plan. Just as a person may find it valuable to play a role in some large organization, so one may find one's life to be of value because God provides one with a role in that supreme organization, the universe.

Faith and Reason

What is the basis for a belief in God? According to some philosophers, arguments can be provided that prove that God exists and evidence can be provided that makes it probable that he exists. Other philosophers claim that faith is central to a person's belief. **Faith** is a belief that something is true based upon neither a proof of its truth nor evidence that directly makes its truth probable. St. Thomas Aquinas (1225–1274) argued that both faith and reason are necessary to develop a full and satisfactory knowledge of God:

> Some truths about God exceed all the ability of the human reason. Such is the
> truth that God is triune. But there are some truths which the natural reason also
> is able to reach. Such are that God exists, that He is one, and the like. In fact,
> such truths about God have been proved demonstratively by the philosophers,
> guided by the light of the natural reason.[14]

[14]St. Thomas Aquinas, *Summa Contra Gentiles,* trans. Anton C. Pegis under the title *On the Truth of the Catholic Faith* (Garden City, N.Y.: Doubleday, 1955), I.iii.2.

THOMAS AQUINAS
(1225–1274)

Thomas Aquinas was the founder of a system of thought that was declared by Pope Leo XIII in 1879 to be the official Catholic philosophy. He is the greatest figure in medieval scholasticism, a philosophical movement that sought to answer fundamental philosophical questions from a Christian point of view. His great achievement was to synthesize the philosophy of Aristotle with the doctrines of the Christian religion. He was born in Italy and as a young man entered the Dominican Order. Later, he became a professor of theology at the University of Paris. He spent several years in Italy as an adviser to the papal court and then returned to Paris. After his death, he was declared a saint of the Catholic Church. His major work is the *Summa Theologica,* which presents a systematic account of his philosophy and theology. An excellent selection from the writings of Aquinas is *Basic Writings of Saint Thomas Aquinas,* ed. Anton C. Pegis (New York: Random House, 1945, 2 volumes).

Certain basic religious truths can be established by reason. But those persons whose reason is incapable of following a complex argument should accept these truths on faith:

> The existence of God, and other like truths about God, which can be known by natural reason, are not articles of faith, but are preambles to the articles; for faith presupposes natural knowledge. . . . Nevertheless, there is nothing to prevent a man, who cannot grasp a proof, from accepting, as a matter of faith, something which in itself is capable of being scientifically known and demonstrated.[15]

But some truths, says Aquinas, cannot be known by the human intellect. Belief in these truths must be based upon faith, which means that the believer must have faith in the truth of certain ideas communicated by the Bible or by revelation.

But why should a person accept the statements made in the Bible or those made by Christian religious authorities rather than those in the sacred books of other religions or those made by skeptical or atheistic philosophers? Aquinas answers:

> For these "secrets of the divine Wisdom" (Job 11:6) the divine Wisdom itself, which knows all things to the full, has deigned to reveal to men. It reveals its own presence, as well as the truth of its teaching and inspiration, by fitting arguments; and in order to confirm those truths that exceed natural knowledge, it gives visible manifestation to works that surpass the ability of all nature. Thus,

[15]St. Thomas Aquinas, "Summa Theologica," trans. Anton C. Pegis, in *Introduction to St. Thomas Aquinas* (New York: Random House, 1948), part I, p. 2, art. 2.

there are the wonderful cures of illnesses, there is the raising of the dead, and the wonderful immutation in the heavenly bodies; and what is more wonderful, there is the inspiration given to human minds, so that simple and untutored persons, filled with the gift of the Holy spirit, come to possess instantaneously the highest wisdom and the readiest eloquence.[16]

It is the existence of miracles that is said to confirm the statements of revelation. The truth of these statements is confirmed by the occurrence of such events as miraculous cures that could not have happened had God not intervened in the usual course of nature to cause them.

One must be careful, however, to avoid a circular argument in appealing to miracles. In using miracles to confirm certain statements in the Bible, we are not entitled to appeal to those miracles that are described in the Bible as evidence, for it is the reliability of the Bible itself that is in question. For example, suppose we are trying to confirm the biblical claim that Jesus possessed divine authority. In the Bible, Jesus is portrayed as someone who is able to perform miraculous cures. But because it is the claims in the Bible that are in question, we cannot use certain of them—the miraculous cures—to confirm others—the special authority of Jesus. Rather, we must, if we are to establish the general reliability of biblical ideas, base our argument on something whose truth can be established independently of biblical belief.

Is theism an acceptable world view? We shall first discuss some of the main attempts to prove and to disprove the existence of God on rational grounds. Later, we shall reconsider the appeal to faith.

Arguments for God's Existence

THE FIRST CAUSE ARGUMENT

An argument that many philosophers have used to establish the existence of God is that God must exist as the first cause of all the other things and events in the universe. Thomas Hobbes has formulated this argument succinctly:

> For he that from any effect hee seeth come to passe, should reason to the next and immediate cause thereof, and from thence to the cause of that cause, and plunge himself profoundly in the pursuit of causes; shall at last come to this, that there must be (as even the Heathen Philosophers confessed) one First Mover; that is, a First, and an Eternall cause of all things; which is that which men mean by the name of God.[17]

Consider some event that we are now observing and call it A. The cause of A will be called B, the cause of B is C, the cause of C is D, and so forth. As we trace back these causes in time, says Hobbes, we at last arrive at a first cause, and that first cause is God.

[16]Aquinas, *Summa Contra Gentiles,* I.vi.1.
[17]Thomas Hobbes, *Leviathan* (Oxford: The Clarendon Press, 1967), p. 83)

There are many difficulties with this version of the first cause argument. First, Hobbes takes it for granted that every event has a cause. Thus, given any event we can trace backward in time a series of causes and effects. But this assumption is very difficult to establish in its own right. Even if the existence of an uncaused event would be astonishing, it would perhaps be no more astonishing than the existence of God.

Second, why must there be a *first* cause? Perhaps the chain of causes and effects extends backward to infinity. Of course, it is impossible for us to picture in our minds an infinite series of events extending backward in time. Nevertheless, we can give a precise definition of such a series: A series of events is infinite in the past if, for any event, there is always an earlier one. There is nothing in the first cause argument as stated by Hobbes demonstrating that there cannot be such an infinite series. But if there is such a series, then it has no first member and, hence, it has no first cause.

And if there is a first cause, it does not follow that it has the characteristics that the God of personal theism is supposed to have. For example, the God of personal theism is completely good, omnipotent, and omniscient. There is no reason why a first cause should have any of these attributes. According to certain cosmological theories that are widely accepted among scientists, the universe began with an enormous explosion. Even if this explosion turns out to be the first cause of all subsequent events, one would have no reason to call it "God." Moreover, although according to personal theism, there is only one God, there may be several series of events that begin with distinct causes. So this argument fails to establish the unity of God.

Some philosophers have interpreted the first cause argument so as to permit an infinite series of events extending backward in time. Let this series be represented by A, B, C, D, . . . where A is an event in the present and where there is no first member in time. Let the whole series be called S. Then, it is argued, the existence of S as a whole needs a cause. The whole sequence of events requires an explanation. Why does S exist rather than some other sequence of events? Why does S exist rather than no sequence at all? It is concluded that only a supremely powerful God can provide the necessary explanation.

In his *Dialogues concerning Natural Religion,* David Hume provided a searching criticism of this and other arguments. In response to the claim that the whole infinite series needs a cause, Hume argues:

> In such a chain, too, or succession of objects, each part is caused by that which preceded it, and causes that which succeeds it. Where then is the difficulty? But the WHOLE, you say, wants a cause. I answer, that the uniting of these parts into a whole, like the uniting of several distinct counties into one kingdom, or several distinct members into one body, is performed merely by an arbitrary act of the mind, and has no influence on the nature of things. Did I show you the particular causes of each individual in a collection of twenty particles of matter, I should think it very unreasonable, should you afterwards ask me, what was the cause of the whole twenty. This is sufficiently explained in explaining the cause of the parts.[18]

---

[18]David Hume, *Dialogues concerning Natural Religion* (Indianapolis: Bobbs-Merrill, 1947), pp. 190–191. (This book was first published in 1779.)

In the chain of events S, B causes A, C causes B, D causes C, and so forth. Each member of the series is caused to exist by an earlier member of the series. No member of the series lacks a cause. Therefore, says Hume, the question "What causes the whole series?" has already been answered. The cause of the whole consists of the causes of each part. There is no need to look outside the series to a personal God to discover its cause. There is no need for any outside cause at all. The first cause argument, then, is not a promising approach to establishing the existence of God.

THE ARGUMENT FROM DESIGN

The **argument from design,** sometimes called *the teleological argument,* is perhaps the most popular and most persuasive of the proofs for God's existence. It appeals to an aspect of reality—the harmony of nature—that philosophers and poets as well as ordinary human beings have felt can only be explained by reference to a supernatural cause. In his *Dialogues,* David Hume has one of the characters express a version of this argument:

> Look round the world: Contemplate the whole and every part of it: You will find it to be nothing but one great machine, subdivided into an infinite number of lesser machines, which again admit of subdivisions, to a degree beyond what human senses and faculties can trace and explain. All these various machines, and even their most minute parts, are adjusted to each other with an accuracy, which ravishes into admiration all men, who have ever contemplated them. The curious adapting of means to ends, throughout all nature, resembles exactly, though it much exceeds, the productions of human contrivance; of human design, thought, wisdom, and intelligence. Since therefore the effects resemble each other, we are led to infer, by all the rules of analogy, that the causes also resemble; and that the Author of nature is somewhat similar to the mind of man; though possessed of much larger faculties, proportioned to the grandeur of the work, which he has executed.[19]

The basic premise of the argument is that nature exhibits order or harmony. This means that the parts that make up the various living organisms are adapted to each other. Consider, for example, a plant, and note how its various parts perform different functions, all of which serve to keep it alive and flourishing. (See Chapter Five for a discussion of functional explanation.) Examine the human eye. Isn't it amazing how the parts of this complex and delicate structure are arranged to serve the purpose of enabling human beings to see?

In this respect, living organisms resemble the complex mechanisms that human beings deliberately design and construct. Consider a watch made by a watchmaker. All of its parts serve the function of enabling the watch to record the time accurately. We explain how such things as a watch come into existence by pointing out that they are created by human beings through the use of their intelligence. By analogy, then, we

[19]Ibid., p. 143.

infer that the living systems in nature that were not designed by humankind were designed and created by a different kind of being who used his intelligence in the process. This being is God. The existence of complex mechanisms whose parts are adapted to an end prove the existence of an intelligent designer. This is the argument from design.

Even if this argument does prove the existence of a supernatural intelligent being, it does not quite prove the existence of the God of personal theism. First, the argument does not establish that God created the universe from nothing. At best it shows that he is a workman who creates his machines out of materials that are already available, much as human workers do. Second, even if the argument proves that there is a powerful and knowledgeable God, it does not prove that he is omniscient and omnipotent and perfect in every way. The imperfections of nature, the occasional failures of adaptation, suggest that the designer of nature also has limitations. At best, the design argument can prove the existence of a finite god or of several finite gods, not the infinite God of personal theism.

The argument, however, does not even succeed in proving the existence of a finite god. For the proof to be successful it is not enough to say that systems exist in nature whose parts exhibit a high level of adaptation. It must also establish that the best explanation of how these systems come into existence is through design, that is, through the deliberate and purposeful activities of an intelligent being. Hume points out that nature contains examples of adaptive systems that are created without any apparent design:

> A tree bestows order and organization on that tree which springs from it, without knowing that order: an animal, in the same manner, on its offspring: a bird, on its nest: And instances of this kind are more frequent in the world than those of order, which arise from reason and contrivance.[20]

Of course, the theist can argue that a tree would be unable to produce another tree and an animal, another animal unless an intelligent agent was guiding the process. To this Hume replies that the theist is making a certain assumption. He is assuming that if no intelligent agent were guiding the process, then it would be improbable that systems exhibiting a high degree of adaptation would ever come into existence. But, says Hume, the existence of such systems would not be improbable because the only living beings that are able to survive are those that exhibit the ability to adapt to their circumstances.

> It is vain, therefore, to insist upon the uses of the parts in animals or vegetables, and their curious adjustment to each other. I would fain know how an animal could subsist, unless its parts were so adjusted? Do we not find, that it immediately perishes whenever this adjustment ceases, and that its matter corrupting tries some new form? It happens, indeed, that the parts of the world are so well adjusted, that some regular form immediately lays claim to this corrupted matter: And if it were not so, could the world subsist? Must it not dissolve as well as the animal, and pass through new positions and situations; till

---

[20]Ibid., p. 179.

in a great, but finite succession, it fall at least into the present or some such order?[21]

It is not surprising, says Hume, that existing things exhibit adaptation because if they did not they could not remain in existence. If the parts of the plant did not function to help the plant acquire nourishment, to manufacture food, and to foster reproduction, that species of plant would soon cease to exist.

Hume here anticipated an idea later developed by Darwin in his theory of evolution. Different species of plants and animals come into existence as a result of the workings of random causes. Only those species survive whose parts function harmoniously with one another to adapt the living organism to its environment. Therefore, one would expect all surviving species to exhibit adaptation even in the absence of design and intelligence in their origin. The theory of evolution of plants and animals has undercut the basic assumption of the argument from design, namely, that the activities of an intelligent being can best account for the existence of adaptation in nature.

THE ONTOLOGICAL ARGUMENT

One of the major defects of the two arguments that we have just considered is that neither establishes the existence of an infinite and perfect God. At best they succeed in confirming the existence of a finite god or gods, but, as we have seen, they fail to achieve even that modest goal. There is, however, one argument that would establish the existence of such a God, if it were sound. It is the **ontological argument.** It has been formulated in several different ways. I shall explain it as Descartes presented it in his *Meditations*.

When we consider certain ideas that are in our minds, we find that they have various implications. For example, upon reflecting on what it means for something to be a triangle, I discover that it must have its three angles equal to two right angles. This is what the idea of a triangle implies. In thinking of a square, I realize that it must have four equal sides. This is what the idea of a square implies. Now, says Descartes, I have in mind the idea of God, the idea of a supremely perfect being. When I examine the implications of this idea I find that it implies the idea of having every perfection. Because God is by definition a supremely perfect being, he has every characteristic that contributes to his perfection. For example, God is morally perfect and omniscient and omnipotent. He cannot lack any characteristic that is necessary for his perfection, any more than a square can lack the characteristic of having four equal sides.

The next step in the argument is really surprising. When we examine what is implied by the idea of a supremely perfect being, we find that that being must exist. For suppose he did not exist. Then we could think of a being even more perfect than him, namely, one who had all of his perfections and, in addition, existed. It follows that existence is a perfection in the sense that a being who lacks it fails to be as perfect as one who has it. Because God has all perfections, it follows that God also has the characteristic of existing. Thus, God exists.

[21]Ibid., p. 185.

We can sum up the argument by indicating its major steps:

Premise I: God is a perfect being.

This premise is simply a definition. At the outset of an argument, one is entitled to state what one means by certain words, and it is usually best to state their meanings in clearly and explicitly. Of course, others may use the same words to mean something different. For example, you may wish to use the word *God* in a way different from the way Descartes uses it in Premise I. That is your privilege. But Descartes is also entitled to use the word *God* to mean what he stipulates.

Premise II: Existence is a perfection.

This premise is justified on the grounds that something's failure to exist prevents it from being supremely perfect. Therefore, existence must be one of the characteristics that contribute to a thing's perfection.

From these two premises we can draw our first conclusion:

Conclusion I: God has existence as one of his characteristics.

According to the first premise, God is a perfect being and thus possesses every characteristic that contributes to a thing's perfection. According to the second, existence is one of those characteristics. Therefore, God has existence as one of his characteristics.

Conclusion II: God exists.

This is simply another way of stating Conclusion I. For instance, instead of saying that a rose has redness as one of its characteristics, I can more simply say that the rose is red. So Conclusion II is a simpler and less pretentious way of asserting Conclusion I.

IS THE ONTOLOGICAL ARGUMENT SOUND?

For centuries, philosophers have discussed the ontological argument. Although most of them have disagreed with it, they have also disagreed with one another as to what is wrong with it. Take Hume's criticism, for example. The ontological argument attempts to prove God's existence merely by analyzing the logical implications of the idea of God. Unlike the first cause argument or the argument from design, the ontological argument makes no reference at all to observable facts in reality. It is an a priori argument; this means that its premises and its conclusion are to be established independently of observation. Hume argued that one cannot deduce the existence of God a priori:

> There is an evident absurdity in pretending to demonstrate a matter of fact, or to prove it by any arguments a priori. Nothing is demonstrable, unless the contrary implies a contradiction. Nothing, that is distinctly conceivable, implies a

contradiction. Whatever we conceive as existent, we can also conceive as non-existent. There is no Being, therefore, whose non-existence implies a contradiction. Consequently there is no being, whose existence is demonstrable.[22]

Hume was convinced that *anything* can be conceived as not existing. For example, even though the book in which you are reading these words exists, its nonexistence is possible. It is possible, for example, that I had never made up my mind to write it. Whatever exists, says Hume, might not have existed. But according to the ontological argument, it is absurd that God might not have existed. God necessarily exists because his existence is implied by the very idea of God.

The problem with Hume's criticism is that it does not state exactly where the argument goes wrong. In the absence of a precise diagnosis of its failure, it is open to one who accepts it to reply that God is an exception to the general rule that anything that exists might not have existed. It can be argued that Hume is just wrong because at least one thing, God, exists necessarily.

Another criticism of the ontological argument was provided by Gaunilon, an eleventh-century Benedictine monk, in response to a version of the argument formulated by St. Anselm of Canterbury (1033–1109). Gaunilon said that an argument parallel to the ontological argument can be constructed that proves the existence of a perfect island. For an island that did not exist would be less perfect than one that did exist; therefore, the idea of a perfect island implies its existence just as the idea of God was said by Anselm to imply his existence. Because it is absurd to suppose that one can prove in this way the existence of a perfect island, it is likewise absurd to suppose that one can prove in the same way the existence of God.

Anselm replied to Gaunilon that the ontological argument is intended to apply only to beings that are perfect in every respect. An island, even one that is perfect as islands go, is not a being that is perfect in every respect and thus need not have every characteristic that contributes to its perfection. It can, therefore, be conceived not to exist.

A criticism developed by Kant is directed against Premise II. Kant argues that the premise assumes that existence is a characteristic of things on a par with other characteristics such as having four equal sides or having its angles equal to two right angles. But, argues Kant, existence is not a characteristic. Consider two things that are exactly alike except that one exists and the other is purely imaginary. For example, take a penny out of your pocket and lay it on the table. Now imagine a penny exactly like the one before you. Imagine it to have every characteristic that the one before you has. Kant claims that because the two pennies do not differ as pennies, the imaginary one has every characteristic that the real one has. But the imaginary one does not exist. So existence is not a characteristic.

Descartes would reply to Kant's argument that there is a genuine difference between the two pennies. It is a most important difference indeed, consisting in the fact that the first exists and the second doesn't. Given that existence is what distinguishes real from imaginary things, it is arbitrary to deny that existence is a characteristic. For like the other characteristics, existence is something that a thing may have or lack.

[22]Ibid., p. 189.

I do agree with Kant, however, that the weakest link in the argument is Premise II. It has never been clear to me why existence can make a thing more perfect and why something that lacks existence is on that ground alone less perfect than something that has existence. Of course, I admit that it would be better for other beings if a perfect being were to exist. If the God of personal theism exists, then this world is a much better place than I have thought it ever could be. So I hope that God does exist. But it does not at all follow that because it would be better for others if God existed that God himself would be better or more perfect if he existed.

In recent philosophy, there have been numerous discussions of the ontological argument. Because the argument derives such a strong conclusion from such weak premises and because it is so difficult to identify where it goes wrong, it is perennially interesting to the philosophic mind.

THE MORAL ARGUMENT

It is common to find personal theism defended by an appeal to morality. This defense can take several forms. According to one version, it is said that belief in God is necessary to cause people to be good and thus to maintain an orderly society. Thus, one of the characters in Hume's *Dialogues* says:

> Religion, however corrupted, is still better than no religion at all. The doctrine of
> a future state is so strong and necessary a security to morals, that we never ought
> to abandon or neglect it. For if finite and temporary rewards and punishments
> have so great an effect, as we daily find: How much greater must be expected
> from such as are infinite and eternal?[23]

The threat of punishment for wrongdoing implied in the religious conception of the survival of death is essential, it is said, to keep people in line. Hume, however, does not agree that religion is a particularly important support for conventional morality:

> The inference is not just, because finite and temporary rewards and punishments
> have so great influence, that therefore such as are infinite and eternal must have
> so much greater. Consider, I beseech you, the attachment which we have to
> present things, and the little concern which we discover for objects so remote and
> uncertain.[24]

Human beings tend to be shortsighted, preferring the goods of the present to those that lie in the distant future. For example, how many of you as you read this book are very much concerned whether your retirement pension will be sufficient for your needs? Therefore, says Hume, the promise of rewards and punishments after death has little influence on conduct.

The major defect in this argument, however, is that even if it should succeed in show-

[23]Ibid., pp. 219–220.
[24]Ibid., p. 220.

ing that religion is useful, it fails to establish that it is true. For example, it may be useful for a man who is dying to believe that he will live. He may be happier because he accepts as true something that is indeed false. The belief's utility does not prove its truth. Thus, even if a person's belief that God will punish him after death for his misdeeds in this life should cause him to adhere to the rules of morality, this result of his belief has not the slightest tendency to establish its truth.

Another version of the moral argument asserts a stronger connection between morality and religious belief. It says that if theism were not true, then no one would have any moral obligations whatsoever. Every action would be permitted. The reason is this: The content of morality consists of various commands such as "Thou shalt not kill," "Thou shalt not steal," and so forth. But a command presupposes someone who issues the command. In addition, for a command to be valid or binding, the one who issues it must have the appropriate authority. Thus, assuming that the commands of morality are valid, we can infer the existence of a supreme authority who has issued them, and this authority is God.

One way to criticize this argument is to accept the idea that morality consists of commands but to deny that the existence of God is thereby implied. Thus, Kant argued that each individual is the source of moral law; each person issues commands intended to be binding upon himself and others. (See Chapter Two for a fuller discussion of Kant's position.)

A different and more plausible approach to criticizing this argument is simply to deny that morality must be interpreted as consisting of commands. It is of course true that those whose morality is imparted in a religious context think of moral rules as prescriptions coming from God. And because religion has had such a pervasive influence upon our thought and conduct, we are liable to accept uncritically the command theory of morality. But there are alternative interpretations. For example, moral rules may be construed merely as statements about what people ought to do or refrain from doing (e.g., No one ought to steal). Morality thus consists not of commands but of "ought" statements. And these "ought" statements can be justified not by reference to God's will but by their social value. (See Chapter Two for a discussion of utilitarian ethics.) In any case, it is difficult to establish the truth of personal theism merely through an analysis of the linguistic form that our moral rules may assume.

Arguments against God's Existence

Thus far we have not been successful in finding a sound argument for God's existence. It is not merely that we have been unable to formulate a strict proof. We have not even found sound evidence of the probability that the God of personal theism exists. We shall now examine some arguments that have been offered to disprove God's existence.

GOD AND EVIL

I have heard people say that the destruction of the European Jews under Hitler's regime during World War II persuaded them that there is no God. If there were a God, he would not have allowed so tremendous a calamity to occur. But it did occur. So there is no God. This is a common reaction to the experience of great evil.

It seems as if personal theism is quite vulnerable in this regard. God is defined as a perfectly good, omnipotent, omniscient creator of the universe. But this conception of God implies that our universe is the best of all possible worlds. God, being absolutely good, wishes to create such a world. Being omniscient, he knows how to do it. Being omnipotent, he is able to do it. Therefore, he does it. If you want to do one thing more than anything else, and if you know how to do it and are able to do it, you will do it. Thus, God will create the best world that is possible.

But how can this world be the best one possible? Look at all the suffering that human beings experience. Each person must face his own death. Often death is accompanied by terrible pain. Most people experience the death of some of their loved ones. One's own illnesses cause much suffering. Natural disasters such as earthquakes and floods kill thousands of people each year. The evil that people inflict on one another is immense. Certainly we can imagine a world better than this one. Therefore, the God of personal theism does not exist.

Although this argument may seem to be persuasive, it does not, I think, succeed in proving the truth of atheism. The religious person can show that the existence of any amount of evil is compatible with this world's being the best one possible. To understand this, it is necessary to distinguish between two forms of evil, moral and natural. *Moral evil* consists of the bad things that human beings do to one another of their own free will and for which they must bear the responsibility. A person who has murdered someone or who has stolen what is rightfully another's property is guilty of moral evil. *Natural evil* consists of the bad things that happen that are outside of human control. Floods and earthquakes are examples of natural evil.

Moral evil is caused not by God but by human beings as a result of their own decisions. So God is not directly responsible for the existence of moral evil. But why, it may be asked, didn't God create a world in which there are no beings who are able to inflict moral evil on one another? To this question the theist answers that a world in which there exists beings who are able to exercise choice and to assume responsibility for their actions is better than one in which all agents are merely machines. (See Chapter Five for a discussion of the problem of free will.) The existence of responsible agents is something good in itself. Moral evil is simply the inevitable consequence of the existence of this great good. Thus, what Hitler did to the Jews does not show that there is no God.

But what about the existence of suffering for which the individual is not responsible? This suffering is the consequence of both natural and moral evil. Couldn't we conceive of a world in which there are far fewer victims than in this one? To these questions, theism answers that God will compensate people in some way for their suffering. If there is perfect compensation, then the evil is nullified. For example, at the end of his life, King Priam of Troy witnessed the conquest and burning of his city by the Greeks; before he died, he witnessed the deaths of many of his friends and loved ones. If this is the best of all possible worlds, then God will see to it that King Priam will receive sufficient compensation for his suffering so that it will be nullified.

It is not necessary for the theist to show how God will provide compensation. He can claim that this is beyond what human beings can know. All that he need establish is that it is possible that any evil will be nullified by God's providing a greater good. And if that is possible, then the existence of any amount of evil is compatible with this world's being the best of all possible worlds. As long as it is possible that evil is a part of God's plan according to which the good will ultimately triumph, then this world can be the best one possible. So the attempt to disprove God's existence on the basis of evil in the world fails.

Hume agreed with this conclusion. Nevertheless, he argued that the existence of evil is still a problem for the theist:

> I will allow, that pain or misery in man is *compatible* with infinite power and goodness in the Deity. . . . What are you advanced by all these concessions? A mere possible compatibility is not sufficient. You must *prove* these pure, unmixed, and uncontrollable attributes from the present mixed and confused phenomena, and from these alone. A hopeful undertaking! Were the phenomena ever so pure and unmixed, yet being finite, they would be insufficient for that purpose. How much more, were they are also so jarring and discordant?[25]

Even though the existence of evil does not disprove God's existence, says Hume, it makes it more difficult to prove that God does exist. Any sound proof must be based upon the observed features of the world about us, such as the existence of cause and effect or of adaptive systems. Evil, however, undercuts any such inference, for, given the quantity of evil that is observed, one is not entitled to infer that there exists a perfectly good, omniscient, and omnipotent creator.

GOD AND SCIENCE

We live in a scientific age, and when we wish to find out something, we naturally turn to science. Using its rigorous methods, we are gradually acquiring a profound understanding of nature. Even human life is gradually yielding its secrets to scientific inquiry. Though there are many things that we do not yet know, if we are ever to obtain the knowledge we seek, it will have to be by the repeated application of the scientific method.

How does this bear upon religious belief? Science is often the reason given for rejecting theism. It is said that science has either refuted the belief in God or shown it to be a useless superstition. After the Russians sent their first manned rocket into space, the Soviet dictator Khrushchev concluded that God did not exist because his astronauts did not find him in outer space. If we were to take his argument seriously, it would go something like this. Science investigates objects distant from us in space and time. For example, astronomers study the composition of galaxies millions of light-years away. In addition, science studies objects that are extremely small. It has uncovered many particles that are even smaller than the atom. And in all its investigations, it has not found God. Therefore, there is no God.

The theist would have no difficulty at all in replying to this rather crude argument.

---

[25]Ibid., p. 201.

God is spirit, not matter, he would say. Spiritual beings cannot be observed through the senses nor by means of the devices of the scientist. God is not like a star or an atom whose existence can be ascertained by looking through a telescope or turning on an atom smasher. The fact that you have failed to discover the existence of something using a certain method does not disprove its existence if it is not the sort of thing that can be discovered by that method. For example, suppose you are led to wonder whether there is an elephant in the main reading room of the library. One way of satisfying your curiosity is to go there and look around. If, after a careful search, you fail to come upon an elephant, it is reasonable to conclude that there is none there. This is reasonable because an elephant is the sort of thing that you can find just by looking around. But God is not like that at all. So your failure to find him by looking around has no bearing whatever on whether he does or does not exist.

It is natural for the atheist to ask: If God is not the sort of being who can be discovered by means of scientific method, what method can be used to establish his existence? None of the proofs that we have already studied seems to work. What other methods are there? The appeal to faith, he continues, is not relevant, for faith is not a form of knowledge. To have faith in God is not to *know* that he exists.

MIRACLES

The theist can reply: My faith in God is based upon the ideas expressed in the Bible. My belief in the reliability of the Bible is supported by the numerous miracles that have occurred whose nature establishes the reality of the God of personal theism. A **miracle** is a break in the ordinary pattern of events. It is a violation of the laws of nature. Only if God exists can we understand how the miracles that countless numbers of people have witnessed could have been caused to occur. Almost everyone, for example, knows of someone who has survived a serious illness after prayer and meditation. How else can this be explained except by the fact that there is a God who has heard the prayer and responded by curing the illness?

The most famous discussion of miracles in modern philosophy is contained in a passage by David Hume:

> A miracle is a violation of the laws of nature; and as a firm and unalterable experience has established these laws, the proof against a miracle, from the very nature of the fact, is as entire as any argument from experience can possibly be imagined. Why is it more than probable, that all men must die; that lead cannot, of itself, remain suspended in the air; that fire consumes wood, and is extinguished by water; unless it be, that these events are found agreeable to the laws of nature, and there is required a violation of these laws, or in other words, a miracle to prevent them? Nothing is esteemed a miracle, if it ever happened in the common course of nature. It is no miracle that a man, seemingly in good health, should die on a sudden: because such a kind of death, though more unusual than any other, has yet been frequently observed to happen. But it is a miracle, that a dead man should come to life; because that has never been observed in any age or country. There must, therefore, be a uniform experience against every miraculous event, otherwise the event would not merit that

appelation. And as a uniform experience amounts to a proof, there is here a direct and full *proof,* from the nature of the fact, against the existence of any miracle. . . . The plain consequence is . . . That no testimony is sufficient to establish a miracle, unless the testimony be of such a kind, that its falsehood would be more miraculous, than the fact, which it endeavours to establish.[26]

Hume begins his argument against the existence of miracles by defining a miracle as an event that violates the laws of nature. A dead man's returning to life would be a miracle because it is a law of nature that once one is dead, one is always dead. Next he points out that our belief that something is a law of nature is established by a uniform and unalterable experience. That the dead never do come to life is accepted as a law of nature because we have never observed people who were really dead come to life. Therefore, all the evidence favors the law of nature. It follows, then, that all the evidence is against the occurrence of the miracle. Thus, we can have a great deal of assurance that the alleged miracle never did occur. If someone tells you that he saw a dead man come to life, you can be sure that his report is false. Perhaps he had a reason to spread falsehoods. Perhaps he was mistaken in thinking that the man was really dead. In any case, Hume claims that no reports of a miracle are to be trusted. If Hume's reasoning is correct, then one of the bases for faith in God is seriously undermined.

I think that Hume's attack on the reality of miracles has certain weaknesses. He insists, for example, that the experience that we have favoring the inviolability of the laws of nature is uniform and unalterable. But this begs the question, i.e., it assumes what has to be proved. Someone who claimed to see a dead person rise again would deny that all *his* experience favored the truth of the law that once one was dead, one was always dead. In addition, the observations recorded in science do not usually conform exactly to the laws that the scientist formulates. There is a tendency in scientific research to smooth out the irregularities found in experiments by blaming them on errors in measurement or on defects in the instruments of measurement. The scientist assumes that there are regular laws of nature, but the evidence that he gathers does not establish this beyond all doubt. It is, therefore, at least possible that miracles can occur.

The most that Hume is entitled to conclude is that relative to the existing scientific evidence, the occurrence of a miracle is always improbable. But then it is open to the theist to assert that he has special evidence favoring the occurrence of a particular miracle, evidence that outweighs the evidence against it. The upshot is, I think, that although we are always justified in being skeptical about reports of miracles, we are not entitled to feel completely sure that no miracle has ever occurred.

Hume provides additional arguments against the belief in miracles, all of which are aimed at discrediting those who report the occurrence of a miracle. First, he says,

There is not to be found, in all history, any miracle attested by a sufficient number of men, of such unquestioned good-sense, education, and learning, as to secure us against all delusion in themselves; of such undoubted integrity, as to

---

[26]David Hume,"An Enquiry concerning Human Understanding," in *Hume's Enquiries,* ed. L. A. Selby-Bigge (Oxford: The Clarendon Press, 1972), pp. 114–116.

place them beyond all suspicion of any design to deceive others; of such credit and reputation in the eyes of mankind, as to have a great deal to lose in case of their being detected in any falsehood; and at the same time, attesting facts performed in such a public manner and in so celebrated part of the world, as to render the detection unavoidable.[27]

In addition, says Hume, there is a strong propensity in human nature to believe accounts of marvelous and extraordinary events and to pass them on as if they were undoubtedly true. Also, reports of miracles "are observed to abound chiefly among ignorant and barbarous nations."[28] And finally, different religions are based on different miracles, so these miracles tend to cancel out one another. A miracle that supports one religion casts doubt on all others in disagreement with it.

Even if Hume has overstated his case, the general result of all his arguments is that there is a strong presumption against any report of a miracle being true. This presumption against miracles, however, can be rebutted in particular cases by very strong evidence to the contrary. Do any of you feel convinced that some event you know of was a miracle? Is your evidence strong enough to outweigh Hume's arguments?

THE PROBLEM OF NEGATIVE EXISTENCE STATEMENTS

An atheist can formulate his view by saying that there is no such being as the God of personal theism, or any God at all, for that matter. A statement of the form "There is no such being as . . . " is called in logic a negative existence statement. We have already seen that when a negative existence statement is restricted in its application, it is often possible to find out whether or not it is true. For example, the statement "There is no such being as an elephant in the reading room of the library" can be easily verified just by looking around the reading room. But a negative existence statement can be unrestricted in its formulation. It would then say that there is no such being at all, anywhere at anytime. For example, if I said that there are no blue swans at all, I would certainly have difficulty finding evidence to support my statement. The fact that blue swans have never yet been found does not prove that none exists or have existed or will exist. The atheist's claim is of this unrestricted type. He does not say that God is not to be found in Montana or on the moon. He says that there is no God at all at anytime or any place.

An unrestricted negative existence statement can be confirmed if the existence of something is in conflict with something else that we know to be true. For example, we know that there are no perpetual motion machines anywhere in the universe because their existence would contradict certain well-established principles of physics. Are there any well-established facts that are in conflict with the existence of God? Many atheists have thought that the existence of evil is incompatible with God's existence, but we have seen that this is not necessarily true. Must we then give up the attempt to find an argument against the existence of God?

I think that the search for a conclusive proof of atheism is hopeless. There is, however,

[27]Ibid., pp. 116–117.
[28]Ibid., p. 119.

an argument of a weaker sort that may provide reasonable grounds for atheism. Let me first introduce the idea of a theory's being a reasonable account of the nature of the universe. A theory is reasonable if reasoning and observation better support its statements than alternative statements. Thus, the statement that there is no elephant in my kitchen is better supported than the statement that there is. So the former statement would belong to a reasonable theory. It is the task of science to arrive at reasonable theories about the nature of the universe and its parts. These theories change with time as new laws and facts are discovered and older ones rejected. For example, at one time, it was reasonable to believe that the earth was at the center of the solar system, given the evidence then available. This later became unreasonable to believe as new evidence pointed to the sun's being at the center.

Does the statement that the God of personal theism exists belong to our current reasonable theory of the universe? If we consider the statements that are established by scientific investigation, it is doubtful that it does. One of the things that qualifies a statement to belong to our current reasonable theory is that it is necessary or useful in explaining the existence of some fact, and it explains it better than other statements. But with the growth and development of science, it is difficult to find any facts that God's existence is necessary or useful in explaining. Why the rain falls, why the earth spins, why natural species evolve, why lead is heavier than wood, why people suffer, why economic depressions occur are all susceptible to explanation without reference to God. Whereas in the early stages of scientific development, it was not unusual to refer to supernatural causes in the explanation of natural phenomena, this appears less and less plausible. It would seem, then, that the statement that God exists does not belong to the current reasonable theory of the world.

The final step of the argument is that if a statement does not belong to our current reasonable theory, then we have a good reason not to accept it and a good reason to accept its opposite. Thus, it is reasonable to assert that there is no God, given the current status of scientific theorizing. Of course, this argument is not a proof of the truth of atheism. It is simply a consideration that supports the claim that it is reasonable to deny God's existence.

Can the theist respond to this line of reasoning? He may very well admit that it is not reasonable to believe in God, given what science establishes. But he would insist that an individual's conception of reality should not be dictated by science. There are other ways of gaining access to God than scientific methods. We shall now consider two such ways: mysticism and existentialist theology.

Mysticism

MYSTICAL EXPERIENCE

A person having a **mystical experience** claims to be in direct communication with God or some other supernatural agency. The consciousness of God is provided not by argument or reasoning but by direct acquaintance. A person who has had a mystical experience usually does not feel the need for any arguments or proofs. If you met your friend

WILLIAM JAMES
(1842–1910)

William James was one of America's best-known psychologists and philosophers. He was born in New York City and later studied medicine at Harvard. He joined the Harvard faculty, moving from the teaching of anatomy and physiology to psychology and finally to philosophy. He is best known as one of the founders of pragmatism, a philosophical movement that emphasizes the importance of the practical consequences of our ideas and theories. He came from an interesting and talented family; his brother was the famous novelist Henry James. His book *The Principles of Psychology* has remained a classic in its field. His main works in philosophy are *The Varieties of Religious Experience* (1902), *Pragmatism* (1907), and *Essays in Radical Empiricism* (1912).

on the street and spoke to her for awhile, you would find it absurd for someone else to insist that you provide a proof of her existence. "I do not need any proof or evidence for the existence of someone I have actually met," you may reply. In the same way, the mystic claims to have met with God, and that is sufficient.

In his classic discussion of religion, *The Varieties of Religious Experience,* William James (1842–1910) quotes this report of a mystical experience:

> I have on a number of occasions felt that I had enjoyed a period of intimate communion with the divine. These meetings came unasked and unexpected, and seemed to consist merely in the temporary obliteration of the conventionalities which usually surround and cover my life. . . . Once it was when from the summit of a high mountain I looked over a gashed and corrugated landscape extending to a long convex of ocean that ascended to the horizon, and again from the same point when I could see nothing beneath me but the boundless expanse of white cloud, on the blown surface of which a few high peaks, including the one I was on, seemed plunging about as if they were dragging their anchors. What I felt on these occasions was a temporary loss of my own identity, accompanied by an illumination which revealed to me a deeper significance than I had been wont to attach to life. It is in this that I find my justification for saying that I have enjoyed communication with God.[29]

Experiences of this type can occur when one is moved by a sublime or beautiful natural scene.

---

[29]William James, *The Varieties of Religious Experience* (New York: Longmans, Green, and Co., 1920), p. 70.

James also quotes St. Teresa, thereby illustrating the fact that mystics find it difficult to put their experiences into words:

> One day . . . it was granted to me to perceive in one instant how all things are seen and contained in God. I did not perceive them in their proper form, and nevertheless the view I had of them was of a sovereign clearness, and has remained vividly impressed upon my soul. It is one of the most signal of all the graces which the Lord has granted me. . . . The view was so subtle and delicate that the understanding cannot grasp it.[30]

It is often said that what mystical experiences reveal is beyond the comprehension of our normal capacities. Even though the understanding cannot grasp how all things are contained in God, St. Theresa was convinced that this was so because she saw it. Like all mystics, she may have had difficulty in describing what she had observed, but she did not doubt that she had observed something of great significance.

William James pointed out that mystical-like states can be induced by using drugs or alcoholic beverages or various chemicals. This is a familiar idea today when so many people have experimented with drugs and have reported unusual experiences. After having himself breathed in nitrous oxide, James writes:

> One conclusion was forced upon my mind at that time, and my impression of its truth has ever since remained unshaken. It is that our normal waking consciousness, rational consciousness as we call it, is but one special type of consciousness, whilst all about it, parted from it by the filmiest of screens, there lie potential forms of consciousness entirely different. We may go through life without suspecting their existence; but apply the requisite stimulus, and at a touch they are there in all their completeness, definite types of mentality which probably somewhere have their field of application and adaptation. No account of the universe in its totality can be final which leaves these other forms of consciousness quite disregarded. . . . Looking back on my own experiences, they all converge towards a kind of insight to which I cannot help ascribing some metaphysical significance. The keynote of it is invariably a reconciliation. It is as if the opposites of the world, whose contradictoriness and conflict make all our difficulties and troubles, were melted into unity.[31]

The use of drugs helps create an altered state of consciousness. Some mystics claim that in this altered state, they are able to become conscious of things that the normal waking state conceals. In particular, they become conscious of God.

EVALUATION OF MYSTICISM

To evaluate the claims of the mystic, it is necessary to distinguish two aspects of human experience. In any experience, there is something that is experienced; I shall call it the

---

[30]Ibid., p. 411.
[31]Ibid., p. 388.

ARGUMENTS FOR GOD'S EXISTENCE

The first cause argument
The argument from design
The ontological argument
The moral argument
The argument from miracles
The argument from mystical experience

ARGUMENTS AGAINST GOD'S EXISTENCE

The argument from evil
The arguments from science and scientific explanation

object of the experience. For example, if you catch sight of a cow, then the cow is an object of your experience. If you have a toothache, then the ache is an object of your experience. In addition to the object, there is the *interpretation* that the individual makes of the experience. An interpretation is the individual's opinion about the object experienced. An individual's saying or thinking that it is a cow that he sees is an example of an interpretation. An interpretation can be correct or incorrect. You can mistake a horse for a cow. You can be in error about which tooth it is that aches.

Similarly, we must draw a distinction between object and interpretation in a mystical experience. A mystic may have certain feelings and images—the objects of his experience—that he may then interpret as a vision of God. He is often quite sure of the meaning of his experience. Saint Teresa had no doubt that her experience was one of seeing all things in God. But we are justified in wondering whether her interpretation is correct. We do know that some people have experienced hallucinations that they have mistakenly thought presented an object that really existed. We also know that drugs or excitement or fatigue or stress can induce strange experiences in individuals. Those of us who are not mystics, who have not had mystical experiences, have the right to question the interpretation that the mystic places upon them.

A famous disagreement over the interpretation of mystical experiences concerns that very feeling of unity and oneness that William James mentions as characteristic of the mystical consciousness. In his *Civilization and Its Discontents,* Sigmund Freud (1856–1939), the founder of psychoanalysis, tells of a certain feeling that a friend of his reported. This friend described it as a feeling of eternity, of something unbounded and limitless. Freud called it an oceanic feeling. His friend asserted that this feeling was the source of religion and even intimated that it brought the individual who felt it into contact with God.

Freud said that he himself had never experienced this feeling, but he challenged his friend's interpretation. He did not deny that his friend had had a genuine experience, but he rejected his friend's interpretation that the feeling had put him in touch with the spiritual world. Freud did not accept his friend's view of the object of his experience. Instead, Freud traced the feeling back to our earliest experiences. When a child is first born, he is not yet capable of distinguishing himself from the outer world. His earliest experiences are not divided between self and other. This distinction is learned, and it is only acquired gradually. The oceanic feeling, says Freud, is merely the remnant of this earlier childhood state that existed before the self had distinguished itself from the outer world.[32]

This example shows how the nonmystic is able to adopt a critical attitude toward the experiences of the mystic. Freud did not doubt that the mystic is having an unusual and striking experience. But he did not accept the mystic's interpretation—his claims about the supernatural status of the object of the experience. It would, however, be unreasonable for the nonmystic to dismiss the claims of the mystic dogmatically. There may be a supernatural reality, and altered states of consciousness may be a way of getting in touch with it. Mysticism may very well turn out to be the most persuasive and impressive foundation for personal theism.

Existentialism

THE EMPHASIS ON CHOICE AND DECISION

Existentialism is a philosophical trend of the past century and a half that emphasizes the role of passionate commitment and choice in the search for meaning in life. We cannot yield the responsibility for our decisions to any authority, whether it be religious or scientific or political. Our lives are what we make of them. There is nothing to discover that will decide things for us. For example, suppose you are trying to make up your mind what subject you are going to major in. You discuss the matter with your family and friends. You confer with your teachers and advisers. Perhaps you even take some aptitude tests to ascertain your capabilities. Even after you have done all these things, you must still decide. Decision is unavoidable, and no one can do it for you. If it turns out that you made a mess of things, you have no one to blame but yourself. Even if the choice you made was one that your favorite teacher recommended, he or she cannot be blamed for your failure. After all, you *chose* to take this advice and to reject the advice of others. Attempts to place the blame on others for the consequences of your choices is a form of self-deception in which you hide from yourself the fact that what happened was a consequence of *your* choice.

The turn toward an existentialist approach to religion in the nineteenth century was stimulated by the extremely influential and persuasive criticisms of natural religion included in Hume's *Dialogues concerning Natural Religion* and Kant's *Critique of Pure Reason.* Natural religion attempts to establish the truth of theism by means of argument and evidence instead of relying upon supernatural sources such as biblical revelation or mystical experiences. As we have already seen, the major attempts of natural religion to prove the existence of God have been failures. According to the existentialist approach, this failure was fortunate for religion, because the attempt to establish reli-

---

[32]Sigmund Freud, *Civilization and Its Discontents,* trans. Joan Riviere (London: Hogarth Press, 1953), sect. I. (This book was first published in 1930.)

gion by proving God's existence presupposes an incorrect view of the purpose of religious faith.

KIERKEGAARD'S THEISM

The leading representative of an existentialist approach in religion was the Danish philosopher Søren Kierkegaard (1813–1855). One of the main targets of his criticism is the *objective attitude* characteristic of science, of scholarship, and of much of philosophy. An objective attitude is one in which an individual attempts to discover the truth about some issue and consequently is committed to following the evidence wherever it leads. He adopts an impartial stance; he cares more that his conclusions are reasonable than about what his conclusions actually say. He will not defend a position that he thinks is unreasonable or is contrary to the weight of the evidence.

For Kierkegaard, however, the Christian religion is concerned with an individual's eternal life. Each person has only a brief time allotted to him to decide what his attitude toward Christianity is to be. The objective attitude is not appropriate for arriving at a decision:

> Let the inquiring scholar labor with incessant zeal, even to the extent of shortening his life in the enthusiastic service of science; let the speculative philosopher be sparing neither of time nor of diligence; they are none the less not interested infinitely, personally and passionately, nor could they wish to be. On the contrary, they will seek to cultivate an attitude of objectivity and disinterestedness. And as for the relationship of the subject to the truth when he comes to know it, the assumption is that if only the truth is brought to light, its appropriation is a relatively unimportant matter, something that follows as a

SØREN KIERKEGAARD
(1813–1855)

Kierkegaard was a Danish philosopher and writer on religious subjects. He lived an outwardly uneventful life in Copenhagen, but his inner life was characterized by intense religious and emotional turmoil. He was critical of the worldliness of the church and of the attempt to found religion on metaphysical systems and scientific theories. The important thing, he thought, is the individual's personal commitment to religion. He is considered to be one of the founders of existentialism and has exerted an enormous influence upon European philosophy and theology in the twentieth century. His most important philosophical writings are *Fear and Trembling* (1843), *Philosophical Fragments* (1844), *Concluding Unscientific Postscript* (1846), and *The Sickness unto Death* (1849).

matter of course. And in any case what happens to the individual is in the last analysis a matter of indifference. Herein lies the lofty equanimity of the scholar, and the comic thoughtlessness of his parrot-like echo.[33]

When a person adopts an objective attitude, says Kierkegaard, his interest lies in discovering and proving the truth. He is indifferent about what happens afterward. But leading a religious life is not a matter of merely discovering just one more truth. It is a matter of living one's life so that one's eternal happiness is assured. And this can be accomplished only by making a commitment and abiding by its implications. One can spend one's whole life thinking about whether Christianity is true, but if one has failed to assimilate it, to make it a part of one's feelings and actions, one has lost the chance to attain the good that Christianity promises. The good of religion is won through commitment, not impartial inquiry.

In contrast to the objective standpoint, Kierkegaard recommends a subjective attitude. In adopting a subjective attitude, an existing individual commits himself to Christianity despite the fact that, objectively speaking, Christianity does not have much evidence in its favor.

> Without risk there is no faith. Faith is precisely the contradiction between the infinite passion of the individual's inwardness and the objective uncertainty. If I am capable of grasping God objectively, I do not believe, but precisely because I cannot do this I must believe.[34]

Faith is an existential standpoint in which the human being is deeply concerned about his own fate.

> Christianity proposes to endow the individual with an eternal happiness, a good which is not distributed wholesale, but only to one individual at a time. . . . Christianity protests every form of objectivity; it desires that the subject should be infinitely concerned about himself.[35]

In adopting the objective attitude the individual forgets that he is an individual whose eternal happiness is at stake:

> Alas, while the speculative and worshipful Herr Professor is engaged in explaining the whole of existence, he has in distraction forgotten his own name: namely, that he is a human being, not a fantastic three-eighths of a paragraph.[36]

Kierkegaard here protests against the excessively intellectual and scientific temper of the modern world. A person who is preoccupied with attaining knowledge about the

---

[33]Søren Kierkegaard, *Concluding Unscientific Postscript,* trans. David F. Swenson and Walter Lowrie (Princeton: Princeton University Press, 1968), pp. 23–24. (This book was first published in 1846.)
[34]Ibid., p. 182.
[35]Ibid., p. 116.
[36]Ibid., p. 130.

nature of things may forget that his salvation is at stake. It would be a mistake to put off thinking about one's salvation until later, when one has more time. When the time arrives that you have put aside to consider your eternal happiness, it may be too late. You may have forfeited your eternal happiness by your conduct. Or you may be dead.

Kierkegaard insists that, in a certain sense, Christianity is absurd:

> What now is the absurd? The absurd is—that the eternal truth has come into being in time, that God has come into being, has been born, has grown up, and so forth, precisely like any other individual human being, quite indistinguishable from other individuals.[37]

And just because it is absurd, it is necessary to have faith in it. If Christianity were part of a reasonable theory, then we could adopt the objective attitude, gather evidence, and assess probabilities. But because it is absurd, it is necessary to adopt a subjective attitude:

> The absurd is precisely by its objective repulsion the measure of the intensity of faith in inwardness. Suppose a man who wishes to acquire faith; let the comedy begin. He wishes to have faith, but wishes also to safeguard himself by means of an objective inquiry and its approximation-process. What happens? With the help of the approximation-process the absurd becomes something different; it becomes probable, it becomes increasingly probable, it becomes extremely and emphatically probable. Now he is ready to believe it, and he ventures to claim for himself that he does not believe as shoemakers and tailors and simple folk believe, but only after long deliberation. Now he is ready to believe it; and lo, now it has become precisely impossible to believe it. Anything that is almost probable, or probable, or extremely and emphatically probable, is something he can almost *know*—but it is impossible to *believe*. For the absurd is the object of faith, and the only object that can be believed.[38]

Kierkegaard believes that without faith and risk and commitment, the human being ceases to be an individual. But only a theory that is beyond the possibility of scientific verification, only an absurd theory, can be the object of faith. Kierkegaard thus seems to revel in the absurdity of Christianity. For only through faith in what is absurd can the individual maintain himself as an individual.

The objective attitude is one in which the firmness of one's belief in an idea is determined by the strength of the evidence in its favor. The stronger the evidence, the firmer can one's belief justifiably be. When the evidence approaches certainty, then one's belief passes into knowledge. By adopting the objective attitude, one can at least decide what to believe. *The objective rule of belief* maintains that a person's firmness of belief in any idea should be determined by its degree of probability relative to all the available evidence. When an idea is no more or no less probable than its opposite, then the rule says that one should suspend judgment. For example, according to this rule, if the evidence

[37]Ibid., p. 188.
[38]Ibid., p. 189.

for God's existence is no greater and no less than the evidence against it, then one should be an agnostic.

The problem with the subjective attitude as Kierkegaard explains it is that it does not tell any individual what to believe. Kierkegaard himself opts for Christianity. Does that mean that a Jew should choose Judaism and a Moslem the Islam religion or should both choose Christianity? Should one choose whatever faith is most absurd or least absurd? How can one even begin to measure degrees of absurdity? The subjective attitude does not, of itself, provide any guidance. If one already has reason to become a Christian, then Kierkegaard is able to show what it means to be a committed Christian. But what if one has doubts about Christianity? What if one prefers another religion? What if one questions religion in general? Kierkegaard has no argument to offer to those who start out from a different religious viewpoint.

SARTRE'S ATHEISM

In fact, the existentialist approach can be used by atheists as well as theists. In "Existentialism Is a Humanism," a famous lecture that was first published in French in 1946, Jean-Paul Sartre declared himself to be a representative of atheistic existentialism. A cardinal point of his philosophy is that human individuals define themselves by their actions and choices:

> What do we mean by saying that existence precedes essence? We mean that man first of all exists, encounters himself, surges up in the world—and defines himself afterwards. If man as the existentialist sees him is not definable, it is because to begin with he is nothing. He will not be anything until later, and then he will be what he makes of himself. Thus, there is no human nature, because there is no God to have a conception of it. Man simply is. . . . Man is nothing else but that which he makes of himself. That is the first principle of existentialism.[39]

Even humanity's morality and its values are chosen rather than discovered:

> Man makes himself; he is not found ready-made; he makes himself by the choice of his morality, and he cannot but choose a morality, such is the pressure of circumstances upon him. We define man only in relation to his commitments.[40]

The meaning of an individual's life is created as a consequence of his or her choices. Individuals do not fit into any preestablished plans or patterns but must create their own plans:

> If I have excluded God the Father, there must be somebody to invent values. . . . To say that we invent values means neither more nor less than this; that there is

[39]Jean-Paul Sartre, "Existentialism Is a Humanism," in *Existentialism from Dostoevsky to Sartre,* ed. and trans. Walter Kaufmann (New York: New American Library, 1956), pp. 290–291.
[40]Ibid., p. 306.

no sense in life *a priori*. Life is nothing until it is lived; but it is yours to make sense of, and the value of it is nothing else but the sense that you choose.[41]

We can see from these passages by Sartre that the subjective attitude of passionate commitment can just as easily be used to develop an atheistic as a theistic philosophy. In itself, the subjective attitude does not help the individual who is genuinely puzzled as to what to believe. It is not enough to urge someone to commit himself to this, that, or the other philosophy. One must provide reasons why one philosophy is more worthy of belief than another.

The Right to Believe

In his essay "The Will to Believe," William James attempted to formulate a rule other than the objective rule for determining belief.[42] James tried to formulate a rule that would reconcile the subjective and objective attitudes and would leave room for religious faith. In his discussion, he introduces the notion of a **genuine option.** An option is a decision about what we shall believe. A person who is considering whether or not to believe in God is faced with an option. An option is genuine when it is living, forced, and momentous. Let me explain each of these notions.

Suppose someone says to you, "You should choose between being a Christian and being a Jew." Your choice between these faiths is *living* provided both have some appeal to you and provided both are relevant to your existence as you understand it. If, instead, you were told, "You should choose between the Greek gods and the Egyptian gods," it is unlikely that this option would be living because neither set of gods has much appeal to anyone at this point in human history. Usually the faith in which a person is raised and its rivals are the ones that are living for him.

An option is *forced* when you cannot avoid making a choice. Suppose you are in a building in which there is a dangerous explosive that can detonate at any time. You have a choice between staying and being killed or leaving. Sitting around wondering what you should do is equivalent in its practical effects to staying. However you act, a choice has been made; your decision was forced.

An option is *momentous* when it is unique or significant or irreversible. If you were offered a trip to the moon, your choice whether or not to go would probably be momentous to you. James points out that most scientific questions are not momentous. We can usually afford to wait for the answer. Nothing very important depends upon our knowing the exact temperature of the surface of Jupiter. We can afford to wait a bit longer for the information.

---

[41]Ibid., p. 309.
[42]This essay was first published in 1896.

James now proposes the following rule:

> *Our passional nature not only lawfully may, but must decide an option between propositions, whenever it is a genuine option that cannot by its nature be decided on intellectual grounds.*[43]

Suppose you have a choice whether or not to accept a certain proposition P or another proposition Q. If the option is genuine *and* if it cannot be decided on scientific grounds or by any other rational method, then we are entitled to believe what we want to believe. We have the right to have faith in either one, depending upon our personal preference. Notice that James's rule includes the rule of the objective attitude. For when a choice between competing propositions can be decided by scientific or other rational methods, then our belief ought to be adjusted to the evidence. We are entitled to have faith only in that class of cases in which rational methods fail to settle the issue and in which the choice is living, forced, and momentous.

James points out that the objective rule represents a very cautious approach toward questions of truth and falsehood. Rather than believe a falsehood, we are to suspend our judgment when the evidence is inconclusive. James's rule, on the other hand, is less cautious. It allows us to take a chance on something's being true at the risk of falling into error.

> Our errors are surely not such awfully solemn things. In a world where we are so certain to incur them in spite of all our caution, a certain lightness of heart seems healthier than this excessive nervousness on their behalf.[44]

It was James's view that his rule is particularly important in the question of religious faith.

Let us suppose that a person is faced with the choice of being a Christian or being an atheist. The choice, let us suppose, is living for him. The options seem also to be momentous for, as Kierkegaard emphasized, Christianity offers salvation to the individual. James also claims that the choice is forced because, if one should decide to remain an agnostic and thus refuse to make the choice, one would thereby lose the good that Christianity offers. With respect to that good, agnosticism is equivalent to atheism. For all practical purposes, then, not to choose is to make a choice. Therefore, the choice between Christianity and atheism is a genuine option. And because rational methods do not seem able to yield a definite answer, James concludes that one has the right to believe in Christianity if one wants and to be an atheist if that suits one best.

Notice that James's rule allows the choices that are made to be relative to the individual who makes them. What is living for one person may be dead to another. What is momentous to one may be trivial to another. What one person wants badly to believe may be despised by another. Thus, different persons will have the right to believe quite

[43]William James, *The Will to Believe and Other Essays in Popular Philosophy* (New York: Longman, Green, and Co., 1919), p. 11.
[44]Ibid., p. 19.

different things. One person may be a Christian, another a Moslem, a third a Jew, a fourth an atheist, a fifth a Buddhist, and so forth. Thus, James's rule does not lead to a uniform set of beliefs held by everyone who follows the rule. It has a personal application. In contrast, the objective rule will lead to uniformity of opinion provided the persons who use it agree about the evidence and its import.

The Problem of Belief

Two rules of belief have been discussed. Perhaps you have thought of others that you would like to propose. What is the basis for choosing among them? How does one settle upon an ethics of belief?

James suggests that different rules reflect different personal temperaments. The objective rule represents a cautious, prudent, careful approach, a fear of falling into error. James's rule, on the other hand, allows individuals to take risks, giving them the opportunity to believe something that may be true. Another point made by James is that sometimes faith in an idea is necessary or useful in confirming its truth. Many theists have argued that the evidence for God's existence became apparent to them only after they made the leap of faith. Mystics often say that faith can put us in a frame of mind in which we become receptive to mystical experiences. Perhaps some rules are more effective in revealing new truths just as others are more helpful in avoiding error.

One can also appeal to the actual practice of groups of human beings as support for one or the other rule. For example, it is commonly argued that the objective rule is exemplified by the activities of the scientific community. Do scientists actually follow the objective rule? Are they invariably careful to adjust their beliefs to the evidence? Karl Popper has argued, to the contrary, that dogmatism exists in science and that it has an important use there. "Somebody had to defend a theory against criticism, or it would succumb too easily, and before it had been able to make its contributions to the growth of science."[45] The scientific approach, thinks Popper, is a mixture of a critical attitude that allows nothing to be accepted without its being rigorously tested and a dogmatic attitude that vigorously defends theories and makes sure that they are not rejected without strong evidence against them. Science can combine both attitudes at the same time because each is exemplified by different persons. The person who defends a theory to the last is different from the one who criticizes it vigorously. In any case, even in science the emotions and preferences of the scientist may influence his acceptance or rejection of certain theories.

Perhaps the ultimate argument for a rule of belief is that the rule will permit you to accept just the ideas you want to accept and will allow you to reject just those you want to reject. The individual who is committed to personal theism will likely accept that rule that will allow him to sustain his belief system unimpaired. A tough-minded scientist may be attracted to the rule that requires his beliefs be adjusted strictly to the evidence. As long as a rule does not lead an individual to fall into logical contradictions, it seems

---

[45]Karl R. Popper, *Objective Knowledge* (Oxford: The Clarendon Press, 1973), p. 30.

as if "our passional nature" may lawfully settle our ethics of belief. This does not exempt a person's ethics from criticism. You may find another's method of formulating belief faulty in various ways. It may lead him to neglect certain things that you think should not be neglected; it may have damaging consequences on his life or the lives of others; and so on. And he may be led to change his method upon hearing the criticism.

With regard to personal theism, our long discussion suggests the following conclusion. As a theory, it has not yet been either verified or refuted by arguments that will satisfy an impartial mind. In the absence of proof or evidence a person is entitled to accept personal theism on the basis of faith provided he accepts a rule of belief that allows his passional nature to settle the issue. But someone who accepts personal theism on faith must concede the equal right of the atheist to deny the existence of God in accordance with his passional nature. The question of the existence of God is a matter of personal choice, but it is a choice that is open to criticism.

Naturalism and the Meaning of Life

Both Platonism and personal theism are world views that include a major supernatural component. They both claim that beyond nature, beyond the material world in space and time, there is another world, a spiritual world that includes God and other spirits or, in the case of Plato, the forms or absolutes. For both Plato and personal theism, the supernatural world is prior in reality and in importance to nature. For both, nature depends upon and has its source in the supernatural. And for both, the meaning of human life is to be found through contact with the supernatural realm. For Plato, the purpose of life is to gain knowledge of the forms. For theism, the true purpose of life is to live in accordance with the will of God.

Naturalism is a world view that claims that the only reality is nature. It claims that the meaning of life is to be found in the natural world, not beyond it, and regarding God is either atheistic or agnostic. As a philosophical orientation, naturalism can be found in the writings of such philosophers as Lucretius, Thomas Hobbes, Benedict Spinoza, David Hume, Jeremy Bentham, George Santayana, John Stuart Mill, and John Dewey. The term *naturalism* as used here is of recent vintage and is closely associated with the thought of John Dewey.

But what is nature? In its simplest terms, nature consists of all the physical objects and events that are related to one another in space and time. It is the spatiotemporal physical universe. The God of personal theism does not belong to nature because he is not conceived as being a physical object or as having a particular position in space and time. What exactly is this material world that is spread out in space and time? What is the nature of matter? Contemporary versions of naturalism usually respond that the formation of theories of matter is the purpose of science, not of philosophy. The nature of matter will gradually be revealed by scientific inquiry, especially in physics and chemistry. Reality is disclosed by the rigorous methods of experimental science, not by the armchair reflections of the philosopher.

Both Platonism and theism emphasized changelessness, whether of the world of the forms—which Plato described as having being but not becoming—or of the God of personal theism. It was as if change is in some way inferior, perhaps indicating decay, struggle, and destruction. But naturalism accepts change as an essential and inescapable part of reality. Thus, John Dewey (1859–1952) contrasts older and new approaches to reality as follows:

> Philosophical doctrines which disagreed about virtually everything else were at one in the assumption that their distinctive concern as philosophy was to search for the immutable and ultimate—that which *is*—without respect to the temporal or spatial. Into this state of affairs in natural science as well as in moral standards and principles, there recently entered the discovery that natural science is forced by its own development to abandon the assumption of fixity and to recognize that what for it is actually "universal" is process.[46]

According to Dewey, modern science sees process or change as the primary aspect of reality. The concepts of event, change, process, and becoming better describe the nature of reality than the notions of substance, form, fixity, and permanence. In the twentieth century, an important philosophical orientation called *process philosophy* has emerged. Thinkers like Henri Bergson and Alfred North Whitehead joined Dewey in emphasizing the primacy of process in their theories of reality.

What about life and mind? For naturalism, life and mind are biological phenomena dependent upon physical processes. That certain creatures are alive and that some of these have minds means, for naturalism, that these creatures have certain functions and capacities that can be explained as emerging from the underlying physical and chemical processes. (See the discussion of emergent materialism in Chapter Five.) No mysterious supernatural agents or souls or forces have to be postulated to explain the activities of living and intelligent beings.

How does naturalism cope with the question with which this chapter began, the question of the meaning of life? It cannot offer meaning to the individual in the way that personal theism does. For personal theism, an individual's life has meaning because it is an important part of God's plan. Everything that he does in this life helps determine the life to come. Naturalism cannot offer this type of meaning. For the naturalist, the meaning of life is something to be created by the individual. Of course, no human being lives in a vacuum. Each person starts out with a biological nature that invests him with certain needs, desires, and capacities. The basic biological impulses of sex, hunger, and thirst give his life a certain shape, or agenda. In addition, each human being is born into a particular culture at a particular moment in its history. His culture will impose on him patterns and values in accordance with which he will seek to satisfy his basic needs. But culture also sets new tasks. If human beings were merely creatures of biological impulse, they would have no more need for culture and its components—such as political association, ethics, science, art, and ritual—than the other animals.

The agenda set by the individual's biological nature and his culture constitute the raw materials out of which he must make his life. These raw materials are something given, something he must discover, something that sets limits to what he can accom-

---

[46]John Dewey, *Reconstruction in Philosophy* (New York: The New American Library, 1950), p. 12.

plish. These raw materials, however, do not provide life's meaning. They constitute the stage setting within which each person must work out his or her own life. At this point naturalism agrees with existentialism's emphasis on personal choice; each individual must choose what he shall become. In creating his own destiny each person creates the only meaning and significance his life will have. He is not part of a larger plan. He is like an artist who must design his own plan of life.

What of death? How does naturalism accommodate that great encounter with nothingness? Naturalism has not dwelled at length on the problem of death. But the account of death that is most consistent with the spirit of naturalism would describe death as something natural in the sense that members of all living species sooner or later die. Moreover, death and the finitude of human life give life its value, its zest, and its significance. If life continued indefinitely, we would begin to find it boring. We would feel no urgency to complete any task. Human relationships would become less precious. For naturalism death is an appropriate terminus to a full and satisfying life. An individual can triumph over death by creating things of value for those who will live on after him. There is furthermore the consolation that death brings to an end the struggles and suffering of life.

Perhaps the following story about the Chinese sage Chuang Tzu represents the appropriate response to Tolstoy's tale about Ivan Ilych:

> When Chuang Tzu's wife died, Hui Tzu came to the house to join the rites of mourning. To his surprise he found Chuang Tzu sitting with an inverted bowl on his knees, drumming upon it and singing a song. "After all," said Hui Tzu, "she lived with you, brought up your children, grew old along with you. That you should not mourn for her is bad enough; but to let your friends find you drumming and singing—that is going too far! "You misjudge me," said Chuang Tzu. "When she died, I was in despair, as any man might well be. But soon, pondering on what had happened, I told myself that in death no strange new fate befalls us. In the beginning we lack not life only, but form. Not form only, but spirit. We are blended in the one great featureless indistinguishable mass. Then a time came when the mass evolved spirit, spirit evolved form, form evolved life. And now life in its turn has evolved death. For not nature only but man's being has its seasons, its sequence of spring and autumn, summer and winter. If some one is tired and has gone to lie down, we do not pursue him with shouting and bawling. She whom I have lost has lain down to sleep for a while in the Great Inner Room. To break in upon her rest with the noise of lamentation would but show that I knew nothing of nature's Sovereign Law. That is why I ceased to mourn."[47]

Summary

Does life have any meaning? Is life worth living? Does life have any value? The fact that each of us will die makes us question the value of life. Both Tolstoy and Plato

---

[47]From Arthur Waley, *Three Ways of Thought in Ancient China* (Garden City, N.Y.: Doubleday, 1956), pp. 6–7.

portrayed death as raising doubts about the value of our everyday concerns. Plato argued that death will finally remove the distractions of everyday existence, allowing us to attain a glimpse of the forms, which represented the true nature of things. For personal theism, the meaning of a person's life is determined by its being a part of God's design. Thus, both Platonism and personal theism offer the idea of an afterlife, which may perhaps take the sting out of death. Various arguments for the existence of God have been offered. The first cause argument, the argument from design, and the ontological and moral arguments are all in some way wanting. The arguments used to disprove God's existence are also insufficient. Mysticism seems to be a more promising basis for religious belief than either argument or proof. Nevertheless, whereas the reality of mystical experience seems evident, the claim by mystics that their experience directly reveals God can be questioned.

The existentialism of Kierkegaard is valuable for its emphasis upon the subjective attitude as distinct from the objective, which is thought to be characteristic of science. But the subjective attitude itself does not allow us to determine what faith should be chosen. William James's ethic of belief includes a rule allowing a person to believe what he pleases when faced by a genuine option that cannot be resolved on rational grounds. Given the present state of our knowledge, the question of God's existence is a matter of personal choice—a choice, however, that is susceptible to analysis and criticism and that can be more or less reasonable. Naturalism is modern philosophy's major alternative to theism. It emphasizes nature over spirit, change over the changeless, and this world over the supernatural. Reality is disclosed by scientific investigation, and life's meaning is to be created by the individual in the pursuit of his goals.

Glossary

Agnosticism: A view that there is no evidence or argument that can either justify believing in God's existence or disbelieving in it. The agnostic suspends judgment.

Argument from design: An argument for God's existence based upon the fact that nature exhibits order, design, and adaptation.

Atheism: The belief that there is no God.

Existentialism: A philosophy that emphasizes commitment and personal choice in the search for meaning.

Faith: A belief in God not based upon proof or direct evidence.

Genuine option: For William James, a choice among beliefs that is forced, living, and momentous.

Miracle: An event said to be caused by God that is an exception to the laws of nature.

Mystical experience: An experience said to be of God or of the source of life's meaning.

Naturalism: The view that the only reality is nature and that there is no supernatural realm.

Ontological argument: An argument that tries to prove that God exists by an analysis of what is included in the idea of God.

Theism: Belief in the existence of God.

Further Reading

A good collection of writings on death and the afterlife is Antony Flew (ed.), *Body, Mind, and Death* (New York: Macmillan, 1964).

A brief survey of the philosophical problems of religion is John Hick, *Philosophy of Religion* (Englewood Cliffs, N.J.: Prentice-Hall, 1963). Another collection of writings is Steven M. Cahn (ed.), *Philosophy of Religion* (New York: Harper & Row, 1970).

The Platonic world view is well represented in the dialogues *Phaedo* and *Republic*. A contemporary version of Platonism is defended by Bertrand Russell, *The Problems of Philosophy* (New York: Oxford University Press, 1912).

Important versions of philosophical theism are to be found in St. Thomas Aquinas's *Summa Theologica* and Descartes' *Meditations on First Philosophy*. The major criticisms of philosophical theism are to be found in David Hume's *Dialogues concerning Natural Religion* and Immanuel Kant, *Critique of Pure Reason*. A collection of classical and contemporary sources on the question of God's existence is John Hick (ed.), *The Existence of God* (New York: Macmillan, 1964). There are two collections of papers on the ontological argument: Alvin Plantinga (ed.), *The Ontological Argument* (Garden City, N.Y.: Doubleday, 1965); John H. Hick and Arthur C. McGill (eds.), *The Many-Faced Argument* (New York: Macmillan, 1967). A collection on the design argument is Donald R. Burrill, *The Cosmological Arguments* (Garden City, N.Y.: Doubleday, 1967). Contemporary criticisms of theism are to be found in Bertrand Russell, *Why I Am Not a Christian and Other Essays on Religion and Related Subjects* (New York: Simon and Schuster, 1957).

For further reading in mysticism and religious experience see William James, *The Varieties of Religious Experience* (New York: Longman, Green, and Co., 1920); William Ralph Inge, *Christian Mysticism* (London: Methuen, 1948); and Gershom G. Scholem, *Major Trends in Jewish Mysticism* (New York: Schocken Books, 1961).

Two examples of naturalist approaches to the understanding of reality are John Dewey, *Experience and Nature* (La Salle, Illinois: Open Court, 1925); and George Santayana, *Scepticism and Animal Faith* (New York: Dover, 1955).

For religious existentialism, see Søren Kierkegaard, *Concluding Unscientific Postscript* (Princeton: Princeton University Press, 1941) and *Philosophical Fragments* (Princeton: Princeton University Press, 1936). Jean-Paul Sartre's *Existentialism and Humanism* (London, 1948) is a good example of atheistic existentialism. Martin Heidegger's *Being and Time* (London: SCM Press, 1962) is the most influential work in the existentialist tradition of this century.

Questions for Thought and Discussion

1. Most people fear death and think that it is a great misfortune. Can you describe exactly why it is a misfortune, if it is? If, as Socrates thought, death leads to either a permanent rest or a new and interesting experience in the afterlife, isn't it a blessing rather than a misfortune?

2. Both Tolstoy and Plato think that the inevitability of death decreases the significance and worth of our ordinary experience in life. Do you agree with their evaluation of everyday life? If the soul is immortal, as many versions of theism claim, is the value of everyday life enhanced or diminished?

3. Which of the arguments for God's existence do you find to be the most plausible, if any? Can you defend it against criticisms? Do you think that the case for God's existence is stronger than the case of atheism or agnosticism?

4. Does theism or atheism provide a better account of how and why life has meaning? What is the meaning of "the meaning of life"?

5. Is God's existence compatible with the extraordinary amount of evil and suffering we find in the world and in our own personal lives?

6. Do you have any reason to believe that miracles have occurred? If you do, defend your belief against Hume's arguments against the possibility of miracles.

7. Has science proved that there is no God? Can science prove or disprove God's existence? Do you agree with Kierkegaard's view that the objective or scientific attitude is irrelevant to religious belief?

8. What are the strengths and weaknesses of using mystical experience to bolster one's belief in God?

9. Do you agree with one of the conclusions of this chapter that the question of the existence or nonexistence of God is a matter of personal choice that is still open to rational criticism? Can some personal choices be better than others? How?

10. Are you a naturalist? After reading this chapter, what reasons do you find decisive in determining whether you accept or reject naturalism?

Part III

KNOWLEDGE
AND
REASON

Chapter 7

SENSE PERCEPTION AND THE PHYSICAL WORLD

PREVIEW

We shall begin our discussion of the nature of human knowledge by formulating a definition of what it means to know that something is true. Because sense perception is thought to be the most fundamental source of our knowledge of the world, the remainder of the chapter shall provide a critical account of the most important theories of sense perception in contemporary philosophy: direct realism, the representative theory, and phenomenalism. But is sense perception really the sure source of knowledge that we think it is? At the end of the chapter, we shall consider this question by discussing the view of the skeptic, who doubts that sense perception is a source of knowledge.

The Nature of Human Knowledge

TYPES OF KNOWLEDGE

What does it mean to know something? How is knowledge related to certainty and truth? Do we actually have knowledge of reality? What are the best methods of obtaining knowledge? To begin answering these questions, we must first make some preliminary distinctions. One important distinction is the distinction between **practical knowledge** *(knowing how)* and **factual knowledge** *(knowing that)*. One has practical knowledge when one *knows how* to do something. Knowing how to swim or to ride a bicycle or to write an essay or to repair a leaky faucet are examples of practical knowledge. Anything that a person is able to do or knows how to do or has the capacity to do is an example of practical knowledge.

One has factual knowledge when one *knows that* a given statement is true or is false. If, for example, Peter knows that Erica is living in Detroit, then Peter knows that a certain statement is true—the statement that Erica is living in Detroit. If Arlyne knows that Jim does not have any money in the bank, then Arlyne knows that a certain statement is false—the statement that Jim has money in the bank. The concept of factual knowledge thus entails applying the concepts of truth and falsehood to statements or propositions. In this part, we shall discuss the nature and extent of human factual knowledge. The branch of philosophy that is concerned with this topic is called the theory of knowledge, or **epistemology.**

Another important distinction is the distinction between **empirical knowledge** and **a priori knowledge.** Empirical knowledge is the knowledge you have that is based upon your observation of the world around you. It is knowledge gained through the use of your senses. Most of the information you have about your immediate environment is acquired this way. Because sense perception is so important in the generation of human knowledge, it shall be discussed fully in this chapter. In Chapter Eight, we shall discuss other kinds of knowledge, such as memory and induction, that are based on sense perception.

The knowledge that you have just by thinking, independently of the use of your senses, is called a priori knowledge. For example, just by thinking, you can know that $7 + 12 = 19$. Mathematics is one of the main examples of a priori knowledge. In Chapter Nine, we shall discuss a priori knowledge fully. Before discussing the distinction between empirical and a priori knowledge, we must further explore the notion of factual knowledge in general.

WHAT IS KNOWLEDGE?

Is it possible to formulate a definition of human factual knowledge? Can one state the general conditions under which it would be true to say that someone knows something? From the time of Plato in the fourth century B.C. to the present day, there have been numerous attempts to discover a satisfactory definition of what it means to know that something is true. An adequate definition must clarify the relations between knowledge, certainty, and truth. Let us first consider certainty.

Suppose Peter says the following: "I know that Erica is living in Detroit but I am not sure that she is." This is certainly a strange thing to say. Why is it strange? Because someone who claims to know something is, among other things, implying that he feels sure of it, that he is certain or convinced of its truth. Peter here contradicts himself, for he is at the same time implying that he is sure that Erica is living in Detroit and also that he is not sure. We can, then, affirm that part of what is meant by saying that someone has factual knowledge of the truth of a statement is that he is sure of its truth, that he is certain of it, that he has a strong conviction or belief that it is true.

But feeling sure is not all that there is to knowledge. To see this, let us suppose that Peter is mistaken; Erica is living in Chicago, not Detroit. Although Peter thinks he knows that Erica is living in Detroit, he does not really know it. He has a false belief, not knowledge.

The fact that a person feels sure that something is true, or believes firmly that it is true, is not sufficient to prove that he has knowledge. For what he is sure is true may in fact be false. He may have made an error. Knowing something is a kind of achievement; it is a bit like winning a race. Just as winning a race is more than running it, so knowing something to be true is more than believing that it is true. What more is needed? To have knowledge it appears that your belief must not be in error, that your belief must be true. Knowledge implies the truth of the statement believed to be true. We can sum up our results by saying that a person has knowledge that something is true only if he is sure that it is true and only if it really is true.

But that cannot be all that there is to knowledge. To see this, consider the following example. A man has a strong hunch that a certain horse will win the race; he feels sure of it, sure enough to place a sizable bet on the horse. Lo and behold, the horse does win the race, and the man collects his winnings. The man had a true belief that the horse would win, and yet he could not be said to have *known* that it would win. A strong hunch is not knowledge even if it should turn out to be true.

In general, people can acquire beliefs in many ways: They can guess; they can flip a coin; they can act on hunches or inner feelings; they can consult fortune-tellers or study tea leaves; they can blindly accept whatever some authority tells them to believe. Some of the beliefs thus acquired may turn out to be true. But in none of these cases would it be true to say that the people had knowledge. Guesses, hunches, conjectures, and instances of blind faith are not cases of knowledge even if they should be correct. To have knowledge, you need more than true belief. But what additional element is needed?

Consider the following example. Suppose Jennifer thinks that a man called Shakespeare wrote *Hamlet*. What she believes is obviously true. But suppose the reason she is convinced that it is true is that she thinks that Sir Walter Scott wrote *Hamlet* and that Sir Walter was called "Shakespeare" by his friends. She has true belief, but she does not have knowledge because she believes what is true for the wrong reason. So it seems that having knowledge involves believing what is true for the right reason. But what does it mean to have the right reason? The horseplayer's hunch fell short of knowledge because it was just a hunch and was not based upon evidence. So perhaps having knowledge consists in having a true belief that is based upon evidence.

I do not think that this is quite the correct solution. There are two problems with this definition of knowledge. First, the definition is circular. For when we ask what it means to have evidence for the truth of something, we find that a person has evidence that a statement is true when there are other statements she *knows* to be true that support the truth of the original statement. The idea of having evidence itself includes the concept of knowledge and cannot be used in its definition without circularity.

Second, there are, it would appear, certain things that we can know to be true without any evidence at all. For example, suppose after jogging you realize that you feel a sharp pain in your knee. What is your evidence for this? You will probably be inclined to say that your evidence for the fact that you have a sharp pain in your knee is that you are aware of the very fact itself. Philosophers have called this kind of knowledge where something is "evidence" for itself self-evident or **intuitive knowledge.** But to say something is evidence for itself is to say that you know the fact through the fact itself without any evidence at all, that you do not need any further support for your belief.

What then is it that is present in knowledge that is absent when we fall short of knowledge? In each instance of knowledge, the person is *fully justified* in his belief. Consider the case of a horseplayer who knows that a certain horse will win because he knows that the other horses are drugged. He is fully justified in his conviction that his horse shall triumph. In the example that concerned your jogging, you were fully justified in thinking that you felt a pain in your knee. On the other hand, those whose convictions are based upon hunches or guesses or uncritical appeals to authority or on the wrong reasons lack a full justification for their beliefs. The definition of knowledge that I shall propose, then, is that *knowledge consists of a fully justified true conviction.*

The term *fully* plays an important role in the definition and should not be overlooked. Suppose you have a bag from which you are going to draw a single marble. Suppose you were told that the bag contains three marbles, two of which are red. You predict, quite naturally, that the marble you will draw out will be red. This prediction of yours is justified because it is clearly favored by the evidence. In fact, the probability that you are right is 2 to 3. But although you have a justified belief that the marble you draw out will be red, you do not *know* that it will be red, even if it turns out to be true that it is red. The reason is that, given the evidence, your belief has only a high degree of probability but not that justified certainty that is the hallmark of knowledge. To distinguish knowledge from a true belief that is justified, I have indicated in the definition that the belief must be *fully* justified. This means that the justification must be sufficient to establish your conviction with certainty. Those cases of justified true belief that fall short of knowledge are *probable opinions.*

Our definition of knowledge does not tell us how to determine whether or not any of our convictions are fully justified. That would be too much to expect of a definition. The theory of knowledge as a whole must provide us with a complete account of justification. It is, however, well established that sense perception is one of the sources by which our beliefs are strongly supported. I can, for example, come to know that there is a yellow pencil on my desk just by *seeing* it there. In the remainder of this chapter, we shall study the role of the senses in the generation of human knowledge.

The Human Senses

A normal human being possesses five senses by means of which he acquires information about the physical world external to him. They are the senses of sight, hearing, touch, taste, and smell. Each sense has a sense organ as its physical basis: sight, the eyes; hearing, the ears; touch, the skin; taste, the tongue; and smell, the nose. What is the relation between a sense and the sense organ associated with it?

Suppose we came across a strange animal the likes of which we had never before seen, and suppose that it had various organs protruding from its body. How could we tell which of these organs were eyes, which were ears, and so on? If the animal used a certain organ to become aware of sounds (how we would find this out is an interesting problem), we would call it an ear; if it used another to become aware of light and colors, we would call it an eye; if it used still another to become aware of smells, we would call it a nose, and so on. It seems, then, that our classification of the sense organs is based upon the feature in the environment that it can be used to discriminate. A person who has a certain sense has the capacity to make a certain range of discriminations. Thus, one who has the sense of sight can discriminate among colors; one who has the sense of sound can discriminate among sounds. In general, a **sense** is a capacity to become aware of the physical world by means of the discrimination of certain features or aspects of that world. A sense organ is the physical mechanism by means of which this capacity is realized. Through the use of his sense organs, an individual receives information from his environment by means of which he is able to become aware of various features and aspects of the world about him.

For each of the senses, there is a feature or features of the world that it alone is able to discriminate. Corresponding to sight are light and colors, to hearing sounds, to smell odors, to taste tastes, to touch temperature. Some features of the world can be discriminated by more than one sense. For instance, the shape or motion or size of an object may be detected by both sight and touch. Most of our knowledge of the environment is constructed from our perception of the features of the world that our senses are fitted to discriminate.

Sense Awareness and the Perceptual Judgment

Consider a newborn infant who has opened its eyes and is capable of following the movements of objects as they pass in and out of its field of vision. Suppose that someone holds a bright red rose in front of its eyes. The child, then, *sees* the rose. But it would not be correct to say that the child *sees that* the thing before it is a rose or that it is red. It sees a red rose, to be sure, but seeing a red rose is not the same thing as seeing that it is red and that it is a rose.

In this example, the word *see* is used in two different ways. In "The child sees the rose" it is used as a transitive verb that takes a direct object. In "The child sees that the rose is red" it introduces a clause beginning with the word *that*. The latter statement implies that the child has succeeded in making a judgment about what it sees. In the former statement, however, no judgment is implied. When the child just sees the rose, there is no implication that it sees that the object is a rose. In general, when we say that a person perceives an object, it is implied that the object is present in his perceptual field. If the object is seen, then it is present in one's visual field; if it is heard, then it is present in one's auditory field, and so on. A person has **sense awareness** of an object or feature when it is present in one of his perceptual fields. When the child sees the rose, it has sense awareness of the rose and its bright red color. If the child should be startled by the sound of a door being closed, then it has sense awareness of the door and of the sound. If you respond to the odor of cabbage cooking in the kitchen, then you have sense awareness of the cabbage and its smell.

The reason why the child is not yet able to judge that what it sees is a rose is that it lacks the necessary conceptual skills. An individual has the **concept** of an object if he knows what kind of object it is and if he is able to identify and recognize objects of that kind. Because the child does not yet know what a rose is or what color is or what red is, it cannot judge that what it sees is a rose with the color red. Most of the concepts that we have are acquired as we learn how to speak. True, a young child or an animal may occasionally give evidence through its behavior that it is able to recognize things of a certain sort. But certainly the acquisition of language vastly increases our conceptual skills.

Let us now consider an adult who possesses the necessary concepts and thus not only sees the red rose but also sees it *as* a red rose. In seeing that the rose is red, he has made a judgment or concluded that the rose is red. On the basis of his *sense awareness* of the red rose, he has made the **perceptual judgment** that the rose is red. This type of judgment is called "perceptual" because it is directly founded upon the sense awareness of the object about which the judgment is made. Perceptual judgments formulate information about the external world that is conveyed to us through the senses.

Suppose a color-blind person judges that the red rose is blue. He has made a **perceptual error.** But the error lies in his judgment, not in his sense awareness. His sense awareness—the way that the rose appeared to him—may have caused him to make the error, but what was in error was his judgment. Although he judged that the rose was blue, he did not see that it was blue. He couldn't have seen that it was blue simply because it wasn't blue. Thus, the notion of *seeing that* does not apply just to any perceptual judgment but only to those that embody knowledge and that are thus true. Perceptual judgments that embody genuine knowledge are called **veridical judgments.**

Appearance and Reality

The color-blind man mistakenly judged that the rose was blue. One explanation of the cause of his error is that even though the rose was red, it nevertheless looked blue to him. An object may look or sound or feel or taste or smell differently from the way it really is. In such cases, we can say that its appearance differs from its real nature. An object can easily appear to be different from the way it really is. Something that is cool may feel warm: Just place your hand in some cool water after you have come into the house on a cold day. Something that is round may look elliptical: Tilt a round plate away from you. Something that is straight may look bent: Place a straight stick in water.

One must not, however, exaggerate the differences between appearance and reality that occur in everyday life. We think that in most cases objects appear just the way they are. Things that are red usually look red; things that are cool usually feel cool. Some disagreements between appearance and reality are caused by permanent impairments of the sense organs; color blindness is an example. But sometimes temporary impairments may interfere with veridical perception. Just consider how difficult it is to discriminate tastes and smells when you have a cold. Other errors may be caused by factors in the surrounding environment. Bright sunlight reflected off certain surfaces will make it appear that there is a puddle of water even when there is none. Other errors may be caused by an impairment of the mind, causing one to see or hear things that are not there at all.

If you should see something that is not there at all, then you are having an hallucination. Do you remember Macbeth's hallucination in Shakespeare's play?

> Is this a dagger which I see before me,
> The handle toward my hand? Come, let me clutch thee:
> I have thee not, and yet I see thee still.
> Art thou not, fatal vision, sensible
> To feeling as to sight? or art thou but
> A dagger of the mind, a false creation,
> Proceeding from the heat-oppressed brain?

Suppose that you are watching the color-blind man looking at the red rose that appears blue to him. You can see the rose and you can see him looking at the rose. But that the rose looks blue to him is not a something that you are able to see. The way that something looks to a person seems to be a fact about his mind, a subjective fact that is not publicly observable. We can discover how that thing looks to him only by his telling us or by our making inferences on the basis of his behavior or circumstances. But what kind of fact about the human mind is an appearance?

If we examine the term *appearance* as we use it in everyday life, I think that we shall find it ambiguous. It is used to represent at least two distinct kinds of mental fact. First, the appearance of an object to a person may be just a tentative belief that the person has about the object. Suppose that you are looking at something but because of the dim light you are not sure what color it is. You think that it is blue, you are inclined to believe that it is blue, but you are not quite sure. Instead of asserting that it is blue, you may express your lack of certainty by saying, "It appears blue to me." You are thereby saying that you are inclined to believe that it is blue. In this sense, then, the appearances of objects are those perceptual beliefs we have about them in which we do not have much confidence.

But there is another use for the term *appearance*. Suppose you express a hesitant belief that a certain object is blue. "Why do you hesitate?" your friend asks. You reply, "This thing looks blue to me, but in this light I cannot be sure that things that look blue really are blue." In this case, what you are describing is not your belief; you are explaining why you have the belief you do by mentioning the way the object appears. You are saying that the reason why you are inclined to believe that it is blue is that it appears blue. You are describing the experience or sense awareness on the basis of which you take the thing to be blue. Appearances in this sense I shall call **percepts.** The newborn infant has a percept of the red rose; the red rose appears to it; it is present in its visual field. But it has no belief at all that the rose is red. When we have sense awareness of things and events in nature, we have percepts that consist of the ways these things and events appear to us.[1] In our subsequent discussion of perceptual knowledge, the term *appearance* will be used to mean percept.

[1]Sometimes the word *sensation* is used in psychology where I have used *percept*.

Direct Realism

In our everyday perceptual encounters with the world, there are various things that we take for granted. First, we assume that the objects we perceive are, for the most part, things and events, qualities and relationships in the external physical world. Despite the fact that we occasionally experience illusions and hallucinations, we tend to think that the physical world is directly revealed to us in sense perception. Second, we think that the way things appear to us are usually indicative of the ways things really are. Although we admit that appearance and reality occasionally diverge, we do not think that these divergences are pervasive or permanent except for those people whose sense organs are permanently impaired.

Third, we tend to make a further assumption about time. We think that sense perception reveals to us the world as it exists *now,* at the very moment of perception. Whereas our memories and written records preserve information about the past, perception tells us the way the world is at the present. A fourth assumption is that of independent existence. We think that the objects that we perceive exist independently of our perception of them. Take the pencil that I am now holding in my hand. I can see it and I can see that it is red. I firmly believe that if I should shut my eyes and put the pencil down so that neither I nor anyone else in the room, not even my dog, were to have any perceptions of it, the pencil would still exist and it would still have the red color I saw it to have. In summary, we think that sense perception reveals an independently existing physical world to us, as it really is at the time that we perceive it.

This set of ideas constitutes our commonsense theory of the nature of sense perception and its meaning for human knowledge. This commonsense theory I shall call **direct realism,** and it never occurs to most people to question it. It may, therefore, be a surprise to you to find out that most of the major figures in the history of modern philosophy have not been direct realists. Most of them have argued that there are serious difficulties with the commonsense theory. In the following pages, we shall consider some of these difficulties.

Challenges to Direct Realism

THE FINITE VELOCITY OF LIGHT

According to the accounts of visual perception that have been accepted in science since the seventeenth century, human beings and animals are able to see objects only after light is reflected or emitted from them. The light travels to the eye and causes a change in the retina that itself causes a signal to be sent to the optic nerve and thence to the brain. As a result of what happens in the brain, the perceiver is caused to have a perception of the object. He is then said to see it. Now this process takes time. And some of this time is taken up by the time it takes light to travel from the object to the perceiver. The velocity of light is approximately 186,000 miles per second. It takes about 8 minutes for light from the sun to reach the earth. The light from some visible stars may take many years to reach human eyes. A light-year is the distance that it takes light to travel in 1 year. It takes light over 8 years to travel from Sirius, the brightest of all stars, to the earth. Light from another very bright star, Rigel, takes 650 years to reach the earth.

When we look up into the sky to see a distant star, we *now* see the star. But the star as we now see it existed some time in the past. Thus, we see Sirius as it was 8 years ago, Rigel as it was 650 years ago, and our sun as it was 8 minutes ago. Suppose Rigel explodes right now and is completely destroyed. No one now living will ever know about it. No one will know about it for 650 years!

Of course, the time that it takes for light to travel from nearby objects such as the pencil that I am now holding is much less than the time that it takes for light to travel from distant stars. But the temporal gap exists nevertheless. The signals that convey information about objects in the world and that cause these objects to appear to us travel with a finite velocity; it takes time for them to move from one place to another. Even objects that are quite close to us are perceived as they were in the recent past. The commonsense assumption that sense perception reveals the world as it exists at the very moment of perception is thus wrong. We see objects as they were, not as they are.

Our commonsense assumptions about sense perception were formed well before modern science developed its account of how we perceive. It should cause no surprise that some of these assumptions need to be revised in light of scientific advances in our understanding of nature. Ideas that are deeply entrenched in our everyday view of the world may come into conflict with the results of exact research. For example, it looks to us as if the sun rises in the morning and sets every evening and hence revolves around the earth. But since the seventeenth century, it has been accepted that it is the earth that revolves around the sun. Assumptions that seem obvious to most people may turn out to be wrong nevertheless.

PRIMARY AND SECONDARY QUALITIES

The **sensible qualities** of objects are those features such as color and sound, taste and smell, shape, size, and temperature that can be detected by the use of our senses. In the seventeenth century, a certain theory about the status of these qualities came to be widely accepted among philosophers and scientists. This theory is best represented by John Locke's famous distinction between **primary and secondary qualities.** Because the theory is used to provide a major challenge to direct realism, I shall present it here in his own words:

> Qualities thus considered in bodies are, First, such as are utterly inseparable from the body, in what estate soever it be; such as, in all the alterations and changes it suffers, all the force can be used upon it, it constantly keeps; and such as sense constantly finds in every particle of matter which has bulk enough to be perceived, and the mind finds inseparable from every particle of matter, though less than to make itself singly be perceived by our senses; e.g., take a grain of wheat, divide it into two parts, each part has still solidity, extension, figure, and mobility; divide it again, and it retains still the same qualities: and so divide it on till the parts become insensible, they must retain still each of them all those

JOHN LOCKE
(1632–1704)

John Locke was the first of the great British empiricists. Upon graduating from Oxford University, he became a lecturer there in philosophy and also took up the study of medicine. He became acquainted with the first Earl of Shaftsbury, an important political figure, and left Oxford to join the earl's household as his physician and adviser. After Shaftsbury fell from power, Locke fled to Holland, where he remained until after the English revolution of 1688. While in Holland, he completed his major philosophical works. His famous *Essay concerning Human Understanding* (1690) embodies his empiricist theory of knowledge and has been one of the most influential works in modern philosophy. His *Two Treatises of Government* (1690) contains his famous defense of democracy against tyranny. He argued in favor of religious toleration in *A Letter concerning Toleration* (1689) and wrote an influential work on education, *Some Thoughts concerning Education* (1693).

qualities. For, division . . . can never take away either solidity, extension, figure, or mobility from any body, but only makes two or more distinct separate masses of matter of that which was but one before; all which distinct masses, reckoned as so many distinct bodies, after division, make a certain number. These I call *original* or *primary* qualities of body, . . . solidity, extension, figure, motion or rest, and number.[2]

The main idea is that the primary qualities of a body are those of its sensible qualities that are inseparable from it. These qualities are thus included in the definition of a body; they tell us what it means for something to be a body or a material thing.

Let us take a look at some of these primary qualities. We say that a body has extension because it fills or takes up space. Solidity is the capacity that any body has to resist the entrance of other bodies into the space that it occupies. Figure is simply the shape and size of a body. Mobility is its capacity to move or to remain at rest. To say that something is a body is simply to say that it is extended in space, that it is solid, that it has a shape and size, and that it is capable of motion and rest. The other sensible qualities are not incorporated into the definition of body; they are not inseparable from it. Take color, for example. It is not a primary quality. Even though a body might have a certain color, that it has that color is not implied by the mere fact that it is a physical body.

[2]John Locke, *An Essay concerning Human Understanding* (London: George Routledge and Sons), II. viii. 9.

To better understand this idea, you should realize that Locke believed in an atomic theory of matter. During Locke's lifetime, the atomic theory gained ground and became the dominant conception of nature. According to Locke, the bodies that are visible to us are composed of atoms or corpuscles too minute to be seen. Large bodies are really groups of atoms that cohere together. Of course, Locke did not have the complex conception of an atom that we now have according to which every atom is itself composed of many smaller subatomic particles. If you asked him what an atom is, he would reply that it is a very small body that has the primary qualities alone. Because the other qualities such as color or sound were understood by Locke to be caused by the ability of larger bodies to reflect and emit particles of various kinds, he concluded that an individual atom does not have color and cannot of itself emit a sound. The primary qualities are those features that are common to all bodies, large or small.

As for the secondary qualities, Locke writes:

> Such qualities, which in truth are nothing in the objects themselves, but powers to produce various sensations in us by their primary qualities, i.e. by the bulk, figure, texture, and motion of their insensible parts, as colours, sounds, tastes, etc., these I call *secondary* qualities.[3]

The secondary qualities are colors, sounds, tastes, odors, and temperatures. In this passage, Locke says three important things about them.

First, secondary qualities are powers that objects have to do certain sorts of things. And they are only powers, nothing more. A power is a capability or a disposition. For example, take a lump of sugar and drop it into a cup of hot water. The sugar immediately dissolves. But suppose that instead of placing it in the water, you just hold it in your hand. Even though the sugar does not actually dissolve, it is still true to say that it is soluble in water. This means that it has the capacity to dissolve or the disposition to dissolve when placed in water. Terms such as *soluble, fragile,* and *flammable* indicate powers or **dispositional qualities** of bodies.

Second, Locke tells us what kinds of powers these secondary qualities are. They are powers to produce sensations in us. By a sensation, Locke means the same thing as a percept or appearance. A secondary quality is a power that bodies have to cause percepts to occur in the minds of perceivers. For example, take the color blue. When a normal human being looks at a blue object in daylight, then it will look blue to him. The phrase "looks blue" describes the appearance of the object to the perceiver; it refers to a certain percept that he is caused to have. When we describe as blue not the appearance but the object itself, we are simply referring to the power to cause an appearance of blue in the mind of a normal observer under normal conditions of observation. The words that we use for secondary qualities are ambiguous. As applied to bodies they denote powers. As applied to percepts, they denote the ways that a thing has of appearing to us. For example, in "looks blue" and "looks yellow" the words *blue* and *yellow* describe distinct ways in which bodies appear.

Third, Locke offers an account of why it is that bodies have the secondary qualities

[3]Ibid., par. 10.

that they have. They have them because of the primary qualities of the atoms of which they are composed. For example, the reason why one object is blue and another yellow is due to the differences in their underlying atomic structure. And these differences are themselves differences in primary qualities. This general idea of Locke is well entrenched in modern science. We now tend to explain secondary qualities in terms of the atomic or molecular structure of bodies. For example, the colors of bodies are explained in terms of their powers to reflect, refract, and to emit light, and these powers are themselves explained in terms of their atomic structure. Differences in temperature are explained as the velocities of the molecules of which the bodies are composed.

THE RELATIVITY OF SENSE PERCEPTION

Why should we accept the idea that whereas the primary qualities are real qualities of bodies, the secondary qualities are mere powers? Why aren't the colors of bodies as real as their shapes? Why aren't sounds as real as sizes?

One reason that Locke offers is based upon the relativity of perception. Take a pail of warm water. Put your left hand near a source of heat and your right hand on some ice. Then plunge both hands into the pail of water. The water will feel cold to the left hand and hot to the right. Yet, the water itself cannot be both cold and hot at the same time. So Locke concludes that the temperatures that we feel are not really in the water but in the way that the water appears to us. How objects appear is determined not only by the nature of the objects themselves but also by the circumstances of the perceiver. Changes in the sense organs or feelings or in the mental capacities of human beings can affect how secondary qualities appear to them. The perception of secondary qualities is relative to the perceiver. Because secondary qualities are relative in this way, Locke concluded that they could not be real qualities of bodies.

The trouble with this argument, as one of Locke's major critics, George Berkeley (1685–1753), pointed out, is that primary qualities are just as relative as the secondary ones:

> It is said that heat and cold are affections only of the mind, and not at all patterns of real beings existing in the corporeal substances which excite them, for that the same body which appears cold to one hand seems warm to another. Now, why may we not as well argue that figure and extension are not patterns or resemblances of qualities existing in matter, because to the same eye at different stations, or eyes of a different texture at the same station, they appear various and cannot, therefore, be the images of anything settled and determinate without the mind?[4]

If, says Berkeley, the relativity of perception proves that color is not a real quality of bodies, it also proves that shape is not real either. Locke's argument can be used to criticize his own theory of the distinction of primary and secondary qualities.

But in opposition to the views of both Locke and Berkeley, we should ask why the

---

[4]George Berkeley, *A Treatise concerning the Principles of Human Knowledge,* par. 14.

relativity of perception shows that secondary qualities are not real. The fact that the same thing can feel both hot and cold does not prove as such that temperature is not a real quality. Why can't the water really be warm even though it feels hot to one hand and cold to the other? If a red object looks blue to someone who is color-blind, how does that prevent it from being red? That something can appear to have a quality different from the qualities it really has does not show that the qualities it really has are merely dispositional.

SCIENTIFIC EXPLANATION AND THE STATUS OF SECONDARY QUALITIES

There is another argument that Locke offers that is not so easily defeated.[5] Consider the following example: You stick yourself with a pin and you feel a pain in your finger. The pain is something that is in you, not in the pin. You do not ascribe the pain to the pin as one of its qualities. The pin feels sharp. But now you agree that the sharpness is a feature of the pin, not of you. How can we explain the difference between the way we understand the pain and the sharpness?

The difference can be accounted for in this way. For you to explain why you have a feeling of sharpness when you touch the pin in a certain way, you accept the idea that the pin itself is sharp. That the pin is sharp is necessary to explain why you have the experience of sharpness. We ascribe the sharpness to the pin as one of its features because its having that feature is implied in our account of the experience.

The case is different with the pain. To explain why you feel pain when you touch the pin, it is not at all necessary to assume that the pin has pain in it. Given our general understanding of the causes of bodily sensations, we realize that to explain the pain, we need merely refer to the fact that the pin is sharp and that its point has exerted a strong pressure against your finger. The difference between the two cases is a difference in what is required to explain the two experiences.

In general, to explain our experience of the world, we develop conceptions of how the world works. Some of these conceptions are embodied in our commonsense understanding and some in scientific theories. These conceptions refer to certain objects and features of objects; for example, the atomic theory that Locke accepted referred to the existence of atoms and their primary qualities. The only objects and qualities whose objective reality we are committed to are those referred to by the best conceptions available at any given time of how the world works. Now Locke thought that the atomic hypothesis was in principle sufficient to explain our experience of nature. According to this hypothesis, sense perception is the result of streams of atoms affecting the sense organs. The only qualities that these atoms possess are primary qualities. To explain our experience of secondary qualities there is no need to assume that the atoms themselves possess them. Our experience of color and sound, for example, can be understood by reference to the ways atoms affect our eyes and ears. Therefore, there is no need for Locke to accept the objective reality of secondary qualities. At best they are mere pow-

[5]What follows is an interpretation of Locke's *Essay concerning Human Understanding,* II. viii. 18.

ers of bodies, ways that bodies affect the senses. Secondary qualities are thus similar to bodily sensations such as pain. Both exist in experience, both have a subjective reality, and there is no need to assume they have any objective status (other than as powers) to explain the course of human experience.

On the basis of his overall theory of nature, Locke drew the following conclusion:

> The ideas of primary qualities of bodies are resemblances of them, and their patterns do really exist in the bodies themselves; but the ideas produced in us by these secondary qualities have no resemblance of them at all. There is nothing like our ideas existing in the bodies themselves.[6]

To understand this passage, the term *idea* should be taken to mean percept or appearance. What Locke is saying is that when we perceive an object, the primary qualities that the object appears to have (assuming that no illusions are occurring) it really does have, and it has those qualities in just the way that it appears to have them. For example, when a square object looks square, then it really is square; it really is just the way it looks. Thus, the percepts of primary qualities resemble those qualities as they exist in bodies. But, says Locke, the secondary qualities have no such resemblance. Even though an object may appear blue, it is not really blue except in the dispositional sense of having the power to cause an appearance of blue.

Thus, the way that Locke distinguishes between primary and secondary qualities leads him to challenge one of the main ideas of direct realism, the idea that things usually appear to be the way they really are. For with respect to colors and sounds and all the remaining secondary qualities, for Locke things are quite different from the way that they appear to be. All of our perceptions of nature are thus characterized by a fundamental illusion.

How is it possible for all of us to be victims of this illusion? How is it that we take features that belong only to appearances as real qualities of objects? Locke answers as follows:

> The ideas we receive by sensation are often in grown people altered by the judgment without our taking notice of it. . . . The judgment presently, by an habitual custom, alters the appearances into their causes. . . . We take that for the perception of our sensation which is an idea formed by our judgment.[7]

The way an object appears to us causes us to judge that the object is as it appears. If something looks blue we usually take it to be blue. The judgment then causes the quality accepted in perception to be taken as a quality of the object of perception. Accepted secondary qualities are projected by the mind into nature so that they are taken to be as real and as objective as the primary qualities.

[6]Ibid., par. 15.
[7]Ibid., chap. 9, pars. 8–9.

THE GIVEN IN PERCEPTION

For Locke, there is an even more fundamental difficulty with direct realism.

> It is evident the mind knows not things immediately, but only by the intervention
> of the ideas it has of them. Our knowledge therefore is real only so far as there is
> a conformity between our ideas and the reality of things. But what shall be here
> the criterion? How shall the mind, when it perceives nothing but its own ideas,
> know that they agree with things themselves? . . . Every man's reasoning and
> knowledge is only about the ideas existing in his own mind, which are truly,
> every one of them, particular existences; and our knowledge and reasoning about
> other things are only as they correspond with those our particular ideas.[8]

Locke here argues that what is given to us in perception, what we are really sure about,
are the appearances of things—the ideas we have of them—not the things themselves.
Objects appear to us to have certain sensible qualities. These appearances or percepts
exist in the mind and provide the evidence on the basis of which all our beliefs about
the physical world are founded. According to Locke, the basic idea of direct realism
that sense perception places us in direct contact with nature is mistaken.

The Representative Theory of Perception

The alternative that Locke offers us is a **representative theory of perception.** Its main
idea is that the appearances of things represent the physical world to us and that we
must infer what the world is really like from these appearances. Take the example of
someone seeing a piece of paper that is blue and square. The paper, then, appears blue
and square to her. She becomes aware of the appearances and judges that there really
is a blue and square piece of paper there before her eyes. According to the representative
theory, her perceptual judgment is an interpretation of the appearance. Appearances
are signs or representations of things as they exist independently of our perceptions.

Another way of understanding the representative theory of perception is by using the
concept of *justification.* When someone claims to know of the existence of an object, it
is always appropriate to ask her how she knows it. If she knows it by perception, she
will reply that she saw the object and its qualities. But you may then ask what makes
her so sure that she really saw it; perhaps she was mistaken; illusions are always possible. It would be natural for her to reply by referring to the way the object looks or
appears to her. She may say, "Well, this looks like a piece of paper, and it looks blue
and square, so I take it that it really is a blue and square piece of paper." Here she is
justifying her belief about an object by referring to the way it appears to her. The
representative theory says that we justify our beliefs about objects by reference to the
appearances in our minds. The foundation of natural knowledge is, then, subjective; it
is based upon something that exists in our minds.

[8]Ibid., IV. iv. 3 and IV. xvii. 8.

The representative theory agrees with direct realism that there is a world of physical bodies and events that exists even when no one is actually perceiving it; nature exists independently of our perception of it. It disagrees with direct realism by denying that our access to nature is direct. Instead, it claims our knowledge consists of interpretations of the ways that nature appears to us. An important question is thus raised: How correct are our interpretations, how veridical are our perceptual judgments? For, as we saw in the case of the secondary qualities, many of our perceptual judgments, more than we would like to think, are incorrect.

According to the representative theory, human sense perception is a much more complex affair than it seems at first. Instead of the world's being directly given to the mind, instead of its being directly there, what is there is the way that the world affects the mind. The subjective appearances of things, being signs or representations of the objective world, are like the elements of a language. Sense perception is a process of interpretation in which we read off the meaning of the appearances.

Problems with the Representative Theory

DESCARTES' DOUBT

In the course of arguing for his theory of knowledge, Locke asks this very interesting question: "How shall the mind, when it perceives nothing but its own ideas, know that they agree with things themselves?" If appearances provide the only evidence for our beliefs about the objective world, how can we know what they are evidence of? For example, if something presents me with an appearance of blue, how can I tell that I am justified in taking it to be blue? After all, I cannot directly compare the appearance or percept with the thing itself to prove that my judgment is correct. I have direct access only to my percepts, not to the object as it is in itself.

Locke was made aware of this problem by the philosophical writings of the French philosopher René Descartes (1596–1650). In his *Meditations on First Philosophy,* Descartes asked a number of important questions about the very possibility of human knowledge. At the beginning of the first meditation, he writes:

> Several years have now elapsed since I first became aware that I had accepted, even from my youth, many false opinions for true, and that consequently what I afterwards based on such principles was highly doubtful; and from that time I was convinced of the necessity of undertaking once in my life to rid myself of all the opinions I had adopted, and of commencing anew the work of building from the foundation, if I desired to establish a firm and abiding superstructure in the sciences.[9]

Descartes lived in a time when the dominant philosophical, scientific, and religious views of the medieval world were being vigorously challenged. He was aware how uncertain

[9]Descartes, *Meditations on First Philosophy,* trans. John Veitch, I,.

was the body of received opinion that he had been taught in school or had acquired during the course of his life. To achieve certainty in his opinions, to transform his opinions into knowledge, in this first meditation he proposes to try to doubt all his beliefs, even the ones that seem most obvious to him.

In attempting to carry out this project, he turns first to the case of sense perception:

> All that I have, up to this moment, accepted as possessed of the highest truth and certainty, I received either from or through the senses. I observed, however, that these sometimes misled us; and it is part of prudence not to place absolute confidence in that by which we have even once been deceived.[10]

He suggests here that, given that our perceptual judgments occasionally turn out to be mistaken, it is reasonable to doubt them all. In fact, this is not a reasonable basis for doubt. The reason that we know that some of our perceptions are deceptive is that we compare them to other perceptions that we take to be veridical. For example, we know that the stick that looks bent when it is submerged in water is really straight because when we remove it from the water, we *see* that it is straight. To determine that some of our perceptions are in error, we need to take others as correct. Thus, it is not possible to doubt all our perceptions by means of this argument.

THE ARGUMENT ABOUT DREAMS

Descartes realized that his first argument was not sound, and he did not rely upon it. Instead he discovered that he could bring himself to doubt his senses by reflecting on the fact that he dreamed:

> I am in the habit of sleeping, and representing to myself in dreams those same things, or even sometimes others less probable, which the insane think are presented to them in their waking moments. How often have I dreamt that I was in these familiar circumstances—that I was dressed, and occupied this place by the fire, when I was lying undressed in bed? At the present moment, however, I certainly look upon this paper with eyes wide awake; the head which I now move is not asleep; I extend this hand consciously and with express purpose, and I perceive it; the occurrences in sleep are not so distinct as all this. But I cannot forget that, at other times, I have been deceived in sleep by similar illusions; and, attentively considering those cases, I perceive so clearly that there exist no certain marks by which the state of waking can ever be distinguished from sleep, that I feel greatly astonished; and in amazement I almost persuade myself that I am now dreaming.[11]

This is Descartes' famous dream argument. Let us reflect upon its meaning and significance.

---

[10]Ibid.
[11]Ibid.

In Lewis Carroll's *Through the Looking Glass*, Alice, Tweedledum, and Tweedledee are watching the sleeping Red King:

"He's dreaming now," said Tweedledee: "and what do you think he's dreaming about?"

Alice said, "Nobody can guess that."

"Why, about you!" Tweedledee exclaimed, clapping his hands triumphantly. "And if he left off dreaming about you, where do you suppose you'd be?"

"Where I am now, of course," said Alice.

"Not you!" Tweedledee retorted contemptuously. "You'd be nowhere. Why, you're only a sort of thing in his dream!"

"If that King was to awake," added Tweedledum, "you'd go out—bang—just like a candle!"

The key to understanding the argument lies in Descartes' assertion that "there exist no certain marks by which the state of waking can ever be distinguished from sleep." This may seem quite wrong, for we can do many things to assure ourselves that we are not now dreaming. For example, we can pinch ourselves or run around the room or ask someone to tell us whether we are really wide awake. The problem here, however, is that all the things that we could do to assure ourselves that we are not now dreaming are things that we might be dreaming that we are doing. If I dream that I am pinching myself, then that is just a dream, not an actual case of self-pinching. If I dream that I am running around the room, then I am not really doing any running at all. What I dream happens does not really happen. Because we cannot have a fully justified assurance that we are not now dreaming, it follows that we do not now *know* that we are not dreaming. For all we *know,* we might be asleep and everything that we think is happening may be just a dream. But then any perceptual judgment that I make may, for all I know, be false. At this moment, I think that I see a typewriter on the table before me. But for all I know I may be in my bed sleeping and not really seeing a typewriter at all. I do not *know* any of my perceptual judgments to be true. I am not entitled to rely upon my senses.

Although Descartes began his meditations a skeptic, he did not want to end up a skeptic. His intention was to place human knowledge upon secure foundations. Although I cannot here explain in detail how he went about avoiding the consequences of his initial skepticism, I shall provide a brief summary. His argument is as follows. Even though I can bring myself to doubt sense perception and many other things, there is something that I cannot doubt at all, namely, that I exist. In the act of trying to doubt that I myself exist, I think to myself that perhaps I do not exist. But this very act of thinking proves that I do in fact exist. Only something that exists can think. I think; therefore, I exist.

Descartes then notices that what assures him of the truth of the statement "I think; therefore, I exist" is that it is a thought so clear and distinct, so self-evident that he cannot bring himself to doubt it. Are we then entitled to accept as true any thought that is self-evident to us? But what if there existed an evil and very clever and powerful being who was bent upon deceiving us? He might cause certain falsehoods to be self-evident to us. If, however, instead of this evil being, there existed a completely good and powerful God, then we know that he would not deceive us and that we could trust those of our thoughts that are self-evident.

Descartes' next step, therefore, was to prove that a completely good and powerful God does exist. We shall not discuss the proofs that he offers (but see Chapter Six for one of them, the ontological argument). But assuming that God exists, Descartes concluded that God cannot be responsible for any errors or mistakes in our own thought, for being good, he will not deceive us. Error is the result of our own intellectual and moral imperfections. And if we would just stick to those of our thoughts that are self-evident, we would be able to avoid most errors.

At the very end of his meditations, Descartes returns to the dream argument:

> And I ought to reject all the doubts of those bygone days as hyperbolical and ridiculous, especially the general uncertainty respecting sleep, which I would distinguish from the waking state: for I now find a very marked difference between the two states, in respect that our memory can never connect our dreams with each other and with the course of life, in the way it is in the habit of doing with events that occur when we are awake. And, in truth, if some one, when I am awake, appeared to me all of a sudden and as suddenly disappeared, as do the images I see in sleep, so that I could not observe either whence he came or whither he went, I should, not without reason, esteem it either a spectre or phantom formed in my brain, rather than a real man. But when I perceive objects with regard to which I can distinctly determine both the place whence they come, and that in which they are, and the time at which they appear to me, and when, without interruption, I can connect the perception I have of them with the whole of the other parts of my life, I am perfectly sure that what I thus perceive occurs while I am awake and not during sleep. And I ought not in the least degree to doubt of the truth of those presentations, if, after having called together all my senses, my memory, and my understanding for the purpose of examining them, no deliverance is given by any one of these faculties which is repugnant to that of any other: for since God is no deceiver, it necessarily follows that I am not herein deceived.[12]

In this passage Descartes suggests that there is a way to distinguish dreams from waking states. Dream experiences, he says, lack coherence. In dreams anything can follow from anything. Dreams contain no order or regularity. The experiences that we have when awake fit together in a coherent whole. Because God is not a deceiver, we are entitled to take the presence of coherence as a reliable indication that we are awake. We are also entitled to take the perceptual judgments that we make when awake as being probably true.

I hope that you can grasp from this brief summary how unusual was the argument that Descartes presented in his *Meditations*. It is so striking that from the time that it was first published, it has been studied with care by almost all subsequent philosophers. Hardly any of them, however, have agreed with Descartes' solution to the problem of

[12]Ibid., VI.

skepticism. The basic difficulty is that his line of reasoning seems insufficient to overcome the very powerful skepticism of the first meditation. If our intellectual capacities are as weak and as uncertain as he says they are, then there is no reason at all to trust the proofs that he offers for God's existence. We might be mistaken in thinking that these proofs are sound. But if we are not entitled to accept God's existence on the basis that Descartes provides, then we cannot use the idea that God is not a deceiver to recover the world that we have lost.

The representative theory of perception is thus vulnerable to the skeptic's arguments. If the world is not given to us directly but must be inferred from subjective appearances, then how can we be sure that any of our perceptual judgments are true? We began our discussion of the problem of sense perception with the commonsense view—direct realism. In trying to incorporate the results of science into our commonsense understanding of nature and of perception, we were driven away from direct realism to representative realism. And further reflection drives us on to skepticism.

BERKELEY'S FIRST ARGUMENT AGAINST THE REPRESENTATIVE THEORY

George Berkeley was one of Locke's most severe and profound critics. In two important works, *A Treatise concerning the Principles of Human Knowledge* and *Three Dialogues between Hylas and Philonous,* he not only presented powerful arguments against the representative theory of perception, but he attempted to construct a system of philosophy that would be less vulnerable to the skepticism of Descartes.

GEORGE BERKELEY
(1685–1753)

George Berkeley was one of the three great British empiricists, along with John Locke and David Hume. He was born in Ireland and was educated at Trinity College in Dublin. He was one of those philosophers who arrive at their main ideas at a young age. In 1709 he published a major work on the psychology of vision, *An Essay towards a New Theory of Vision.* His major philosophical work, in which he criticizes materialism and defends immaterialism, is his *A Treatise concerning the Principles of Human Knowledge* (1710). Berkeley published a more readable and popular account of his immaterialism in *Three Dialogues between Hylas and Philonous* (1713). He organized a movement to establish a college in Bermuda to educate the Indians, traveling to Rhode Island to await the promised support and spending several years in America. The support never came, so he returned to England. He became a bishop in 1734.

Two of his arguments against the representative theory are still of great interest. In the first, Berkeley asks how we could know that bodies exist independently of the human mind (or, in his words, "without the mind"):

> But, though it were possible that solid, figured, movable substances may exist without the mind, corresponding to the ideas we have of bodies, yet how is it possible for us to know this? Either we must know it by sense or by reason. As for our senses, by them we have the knowledge only of our sensations, ideas, or those things that are immediately perceived by sense, call them what you will; but they do not inform us that things exist without the mind, or unperceived, like to those which are perceived.... It remains therefore that if we have any knowledge at all of external things, it must be by reason, inferring their existence from what is immediately perceived by sense. But what reason can induce us to believe the existence of bodies without the mind, from what we perceive, since the very patrons of matter themselves do not pretend there is any necessary connection betwixt them and our ideas? I say it is granted on all hands (and what happens in dreams, frenzies, and the like, puts it beyond dispute) that it is possible we might be affected with all the ideas we have now, although no bodies existed without resembling them. Hence it is evident the supposition of external bodies is not necessary for the producing of our ideas.[13]

This argument presents the advocate of the representative theory with a dilemma. How, Berkeley asks, do we know that there are bodies that appear to us? How do we know that our inner percepts have external physical causes? If we can know this, then it must be accomplished either by our scrutinizing our percepts themselves (what Berkeley calls knowledge by sense) or by our making inferences based upon our percepts (what he calls knowledge by reason). But we cannot know of the existence of bodies by sense alone. Because our percepts are separate and distinct from bodies, we cannot know of the existence of bodies merely by examining our percepts. So it must be that reason tells us of the existence of bodies. But reason also fails, for we can have percepts even when there are no bodies.

Let us examine in greater depth the critique of reason that Berkeley offers. Suppose you have two things, A and B. Suppose A is something that you can see or be directly aware of. Under what conditions are you entitled to infer the existence of B from the existence of A? For example, let A be smoke and let B be fire. If you see smoke, are you entitled to infer the existence of fire? Berkeley answers that you are entitled to make the inference only if you could not have A without B, only if B is necessary for A. Thus, if you knew ahead of time that you could not have smoke without fire, then you would be entitled to infer fire from smoke. But if things other than fire could cause smoke, then you would not be entitled to make the inference.

Let us summarize these points by saying that for Berkeley one is entitled to infer B from A only if one knows that B is a necessary condition for A. Berkeley correctly points out that the existence of bodies is not necessary for the existence of our percepts. We

---

[13]Berkeley, *Treatise*, par. 18.

often have percepts without the corresponding bodies, as in dreams and hallucinations. So we cannot infer the existence of bodies from the existence of our percepts.

The advocate of the representative theory may reply as follows. Berkeley's account of inference is much too restrictive, for it excludes those inferences that introduce probabilities. For example, suppose I want to know whether B or C or D is responsible for A, and suppose I also know that none of them is necessary for the existence of A. But suppose I have reason to believe that in the circumstances B is more likely to have caused A than C or D. For instance, if I look out the window and notice that the streets are wet, I may list as possible explanations that it recently rained, that the street cleaners washed the streets, and that a water main has burst. None of these three possibilities is a necessary condition of the street's being wet. But given that a storm cloud is now passing out of sight, I conclude that rain is the most probable explanation. Now the advocate of the representative theory may claim that the existence of bodies is the most probable explanation for the percepts we have. So although the existence of bodies cannot be proved with certainty, the hypothesis that there are bodies is the most probable opinion.

BERKELEY'S SECOND ARGUMENT

This response leads us directly to Berkeley's second argument against the representative theory:

> But though we might possibly have all our sensations without them [bodies], yet perhaps it may be thought easier to conceive and explain the manner of their production by supposing external bodies in their likeness rather than otherwise; and so it might be at least probable there are such things as bodies that excite their ideas in our minds. But neither can this be said, for, though we give the materialists their external bodies, they by their own confession are never the nearer knowing how our ideas are produced, since they own themselves unable to comprehend in what manner body can act upon spirit, or how it is possible it should imprint any idea in the mind. Hence it is evident the production of ideas or sensations in our minds can be no reason why we should suppose matter or corporeal substances, since that is acknowledged to remain equally inexplicable with or without this supposition.[14]

The problem that Berkeley here raises has been of major significance in the history of philosophy. It is the problem of trying to understand the interaction between the physical and mental aspects of human nature. (See Chapter Five for a full discussion of the mind–body problem.) Consider the following example. Suppose you see that there is a glass of milk on the table before you. This means that you have made the perceptual judgment that there is a glass of milk. On the basis of the theories that we now accept, we would explain the occurrence of this judgment by reference to the light that is

---

[14]Ibid., par. 19.

reflected from the milk, which enters the eyes and causes a nerve impulse to travel from the optic nerve to the brain. This chain of physical events then causes the occurrence of something in the mind, namely, the judgment that there is a glass of milk out there. It is now generally thought that mental activity is directly caused by events that happen in the brain. Now suppose that you feel like drinking a glass of milk. Because you see that one is there on the table, you reach out your arm, pick it up, and drink it. In this case, a certain judgment—that there is a glass of milk there—and a desire to drink milk, both events in the mind, arouse certain events in the brain and nervous system that cause your arm to reach for the milk. So certain physical effects can be the result of mental activity.

Many of the philosophers whom Berkeley called materialists, Locke among them, had confessed that they did not understand either how physical activity can induce changes in the mind or how mental activity can induce changes in the body. How can things that are so unlike each other as the mind and the body possibly interact? Most of these philosophers accepted a representative account of perception, and we have seen that this theory does assume that mind and body are able to interact. But Berkeley rejected the representative theory on the grounds that it assumes something totally unintelligible, mind–body interaction.

THE PROBLEM OF CAUSATION

As we look back upon the debate, we can see that the issue partly hinges upon the notion of intelligibility. According to Berkeley, to accept that a certain type of event A causes another type of event B, the causal relation between A and B must be intelligible or explainable. On the other hand, the defenders of the representative theory claimed that even if we cannot understand *how* A causes B, in some cases we can at least know *that* A causes B.

David Hume (1711–1776), who wrote in full knowledge of this debate, added a wholly new dimension to the issue with his theory of causality. According to Hume, all that is implied by A's being the cause of B is that A and B are correlated. In Hume's terms, this means that A and B are constantly conjoined.[15] No deeper understanding is involved or presupposed. We know, for example, that fire causes smoke because, whenever fire occurs, so does smoke. Defenders of the representative theory can use Hume's definition of causality to escape Berkeley's criticism. They would say that Berkeley is assuming an unacceptable account of causality. He is supposing that whenever there is a causal connection between two events, there must be a relation between them in addition to constant conjunction. But, says Hume, no further relation is required.

From the above, you can see how different philosophical issues become intertwined. Questions about the nature of perceptual knowledge lead us to consider further questions about the nature of the relation between mind and body and the nature of causality.

---

[15]David Hume, "An Enquiry concerning Human Understanding," in *Hume's Enquiries,* ed. L. A. Selby-Bigge (Oxford: The Clarendon Press, 1972), sect. 7.

Phenomenalism and Idealism

PHENOMENALISM

Though he criticized the representative theory, Berkeley was not a skeptic. Indeed, he thought that the major fault of the theory was that it led directly to skepticism. According to his critique, the representative theory created an unbridgeable gap between what we are aware of in sense perception and the physical bodies that we think we know. Berkeley's own positive account of perception has come to be known as **phenomenalism.** He argued that there really is no gap to bridge. Physical bodies are not things whose existence we need to infer; they are directly given to us by our senses. Both Berkeley and Locke agreed that what is directly given by our senses are appearances, or percepts. They also agreed that these percepts exist only in that they are perceived by someone; their existence depends upon the mind. As Berkeley sees it, the existence of a percept or idea consists in its being perceived. He bases his solution to the problem of perception upon the thought that the physical bodies that we believe we are in contact with in daily life are merely groups of percepts. After all, we are not usually conscious of making inferences to the existence of bodies. We think we see bodies directly. But if what we really see are percepts or ideas or appearances, then a body is just the sum total of the percepts we are aware of when we see the body. What we mean by body, "what every plain, ordinary person means by that word," is "that which is immediately seen and felt, which is only a combination of sensible qualities or ideas."[16]

Berkeley thus presents himself as a defender of common sense against skepticism. Yet his phenomenalism appears to have a consequence that is directly contrary to common sense. It seems to imply that because bodies are collections of percepts whose existence depends upon the mind or minds perceiving them, then they exist only when they are being perceived by some mind. There are no unperceived bodies. But this is an absurd consequence. Consider the pencil that I am now observing. I can see that no one else is now looking at it. Now I shut my eyes, and I am sure that no one is perceiving it at all. Does Berkeley mean to say that it goes out of existence at that moment?

Berkeley offers two responses to this difficulty. One, which is suggested by the following passage, became widely adopted by contemporary phenomenalists:

> The table I write on I say exists, that is, I see and feel it; and if I were out of my study I should say it existed—meaning thereby that if I was in my study I might perceive it, or that some other spirit actually does perceive it.[17]

According to this passage, it would be incorrect to say that unperceived objects do not exist. They do exist in the sense that they *might* be perceived. An object is thus a possibility of perception. To say that a certain body exists merely means that if someone were in the right position, he would be able to perceive it.

An apparent difficulty with thinking of bodies as potential objects of perception is

---

[16]Berkeley, *Treatise,* par. 95.
[17]Ibid., par. 3.

that we are left with the question: How can we explain the course of our experience? If the only items in nature that actually exist are appearances, there seems nothing left to explain why certain appearances occur rather than others. Both direct realism and the representative theory can explain the course of human experience because both accept the idea that there are independently existing bodies that affect human sense organs. But this solution is not open to phenomenalism. The way that certain contemporary phenomenalists tried to handle this problem is to argue that the occurrence of a given percept can be explained by reference to other percepts. In this view, causality obtains among items that we experience, not between bodies and percepts. For example, if I see smoke and find a fire burning, the fire as it appears is the cause of the smoke as it appears. No independently existing causes are needed. But this solution won't work. Its fault is that the actual causes of our percepts do not always show themselves in experience. If I receive a shock upon touching a wire, there is nothing that I see that explains it. To understand what happened, one needs to turn to the scientific theory of electricity, which postulates that the shock was caused by an electric current moving through the wire. We seem to be driven to postulate unseen causes because experience gives us an incomplete causal order.

A related problem stems from the fact that certain processes continue to occur even when they are not being perceived. I light a fire in the fireplace, leave the room, and when I return, the log is completely consumed. I explain why it was consumed by saying that an actually existing fire was going on in my absence. A mere potential fire cannot consume an actual log. Thus, to fill in the gaps in our experience, we postulate unperceived processes. Because experience is not self-explanatory, because in both science and everyday life we must refer to objects and processes that are both unperceived and actually existing to construct a coherent representation of nature, this version of phenomenalism must be rejected.

IDEALISM

Berkeley sensed these difficulties and proposed an alternative solution. Because he was convinced that matter could not intelligibly be used to explain the course of human experience—to give it the requisite coherence—he proposed a nonmaterialist answer. When an object or process is not being perceived by any human being, it is still being perceived by God and hence continues to exist. Berkeley thus introduces God as an hypothesis to explain how objects and processes continue to exist when unperceived by

---

PHILOSOPHICAL THEORIES OF SENSE PERCEPTION

Direct Realism: An independent physical world is directly perceived.
Representative Theory: An independent physical world is indirectly perceived by means of percepts that are directly perceived.
Phenomenalism: Only percepts are directly perceived; physical bodies are bundles of percepts.

human beings. An unperceived object exists as an idea in the mind of God. For Berkeley, God is an infinite mind or spirit, whereas human beings are finite minds or spirits. The only things that exist are minds and their ideas. This view of reality is commonly called **idealism** (though it was called **immaterialism** by Berkeley). According to Berkeley's idealism, human experience occurs in a coherent and orderly manner because God exists. When there are gaps in experience Berkeley refers to God to explain how they can be bridged. God sustains nature as a system of ideas that exist in his mind and in the minds of finite spirits.

Locke proposed that the world of atoms best explains human experience. Berkeley relies instead on God. In Berkeley's time, his solution was backed by the prestige of religion. In our times, the atomic solution is backed by the prestige of science. There is no easy way to choose between them. But there is an argument that tends to establish the superiority of Locke's view.

LOCKE VERSUS BERKELEY

The argument supporting Locke rests on the strength of his explanation compared to that of Berkeley's. To understand this point, consider the case in which you are looking at a blue object that also appears blue to you. Why does it look blue rather than yellow or red or any other color? The question is, Why this *rather than* that? The only answer that Berkeley can offer is that God brought it about that you see blue rather than some other color. And if you should ask why God brought it about, there is no answer except to say that that is the way he wanted it. But according to Locke's atomic theory, the reason why you see blue rather than some other color is explained by the specific internal nature of the object (what Locke calls its **real essence**) and the circumstances in which it is placed. The object reflects certain sorts of atoms (or, as we would say today, light of a certain wavelength), and it is seen as blue when it is illuminated by sunlight. Different perceptions are correlated with different real essences. Blue, yellow, and red objects have slightly different physical natures that explain why they appear different to human observers.

Locke's theory as well as the theories of modern physical science has a greater *differential explanatory force* than does Berkeley's. Even though Berkeley's idealism is equipped to explain why anything happens (God wanted it that way), it does not give us a deep understanding of why one thing occurs *rather than* some other thing. Scientific theories tend to provide differential explanations. Normally when we ask for an explanation of some natural phenomenon, we want an understanding sufficiently specific to enable us to predict the occurrence of that phenomenon. A theory that says of every natural phenomenon that God caused it does not help us to make predictions or to understand the specific character of our experience. That is why most people who accept the existence of God do not, as did Berkeley, doubt the existence of an independently existing natural world.

Both versions of phenomenalism are unacceptable because both fail to render the course of human experience intelligible. Contemporary phenomenalism fails because it does not provide a representation of nature as a coherent causal order. The natural world that it proposed is full of gaps. Berkeley's idealism fails for a different reason. It does not leave any gaps, but it fills in the gaps in a way that fails to provide illuminating explanations.

The Representative Theory and Contemporary Criticism

In our examination of theories of perceptual knowledge in early modern philosophy, we have found that there are three main views to contend with. Most theories of perception are variations of direct realism, the representative theory, or phenomenalism. We have found that direct realism cannot withstand arguments that make use of scientific findings and that phenomenalism has serious deficiencies. We seem left with the representative theory. In this section, I shall discuss certain problems of the representative theory that have been explored in contemporary thought.

THEORIES OF THE PERCEPT

The first problem concerns the nature of appearance. As we saw, an object's appearing to someone consists of a percept in his mind. But what is a percept? What sort of thing is a percept, or appearance, in the mind? The most common theory of the percept is the **sense datum theory.** Suppose something looks red to you. Then, according to the sense datum theory, the red percept is something that really is red. Qualities that bodies appear to have are really possessed by the appearances, or the sense data. Sense data are items that are directly perceived and that possess sensible qualities, both primary and secondary. They are remarkably similar to physical objects with this difference: Sense data are alleged to be private rather than public objects. They exist only in the minds of perceivers.

The sense datum theory has a serious difficulty. Suppose you are directly aware of a sense datum that is blue and square. According to the theory, you will be aware of this whenever something appears blue and square to you. It is an obvious question how something that is blue and square, as our sense datum is supposed to be, can exist in the mind. Whatever the mind is, whether it is identified with the brain or understood as a nonphysical spiritual principle (see Chapter Five for a discussion of the nature of the mind), it is not clear how something that is both blue and square can exist in it. Suppose you identify the mind with the soul, a nonphysical principle that does not take up space, as bodies do. Then something that is blue and square, being extended and hence taking up space, cannot be something that takes up no space. Now suppose you identify the mind with the brain. But when you see a sense datum that is blue and square, we have no reason to think that there is something both blue and square somewhere in your brain. Being private, sense data do not occupy the physical world outside of the perceiver. But there does not seem to be a place "within" the perceiver for them to exist. There seems to be no room in mind or brain for sense data. They are mythical creatures that have no place in any plausible account of sense perception.

A different and more promising theory of the percept has recently been developed. It may be called the **adverbial theory.** When we describe something as appearing blue or appearing square, the terms *blue* and *square* are used to say something about our percepts. But they do not represent qualities of the percepts, as the sense datum theory says. They indicate the manner in which objects are presented to us. Thus, terms describing our percepts function more like adverbs than like adjectives or nouns. To understand this, consider the difference between "He is holding a book" and "He is dancing a waltz." In the first case, the term *book* designates a distinct object. But in the second case, the term *waltz* does not represent an object distinct from the dancing. It indicates the way he is dancing, not the object of his dance. Particular dances are *ways* that people dance. Similarly, the terms used to describe appearances are interpreted by the adverbial theory as representing the *ways* in which objects affect people. They do not describe distinct objects of awareness in their own right. Thus, when something appears blue to someone, it is not necessary to try to locate an item that really is blue in his mind or brain. The representative theory of perception can accept the adverbial account of the percept and avoid the difficulties of the sense datum theory.

WHAT WE PERCEIVE

In adopting the adverbial account of the percept, we are led to another problem. According to the representative theory, our knowledge of the physical world is indirect. It is mediated by and based upon our percepts. As a result of having percepts, we are able to form reliable beliefs about nature. It would seem, then, that in perception, we are first aware of our percepts and then make judgments about the external world. But the adverbial theory disrupts this picture of human knowledge. According to the adverbial theory, percepts are not objects somehow related to a subject; they are the way that external bodies affect the mind. Instead of being things of which we are aware of on their own account, percepts are ways in which awareness occurs, just as a waltz is a way in which a particular dance occurs. When a red object looks red to me, that is just the way in which I become aware of it and its color. It seems that in sense perception, then, we are directly aware of bodies themselves. This leads us back to direct realism.

In most normal cases of perception, we are directly attentive to objects in the physical world and inattentive to how they appear. It is usually much easier to tell how bodies are than how they look or sound or taste. I do not mean to imply that we are always unaware of the appearances of things or that these appearances are inaccessible to us; painters, for example, are often more interested in the visual appearance of things than in their objective features. And sometimes when we are unsure of what it is that we are seeing (the light may be dim), or hearing (the source may be distant), we may attend to our percepts for clues. It requires, however, a special effort of mind to attend to appearances. It involves a shift from the attitude we normally have when attending to objects to a special attitude that lets us attend to how objects are given. But if I do not normally attend to appearances, then how can they provide evidence for the existence and qualities of bodies?

This line of argument has led some philosophers to deny that percepts invariably occur in sense perception. Perhaps we need percepts to explain how illusions and hallucinations are possible. But just because they are there in abnormal cases, it doesn't follow that they are present in every case, normal or abnormal. If a straight stick immersed in water looks bent, then in this case we can admit that there is a percept present because we know that there is a difference between the stick's actual shape and the one that it appears to have. But when there is no disagreement between appearance and reality, then there is no reason to think that there are two distinct items, one the appearance and the other the reality. Again, we seem led back to direct realism, at least for cases of normal perception.

I think, however, that a case can be made for percepts even in normal perception. First, we can always ask whether an object appears to have the properties that it really does have. "Did that red object look red?" Whether we answer "yes" or "no" to this question, we seem to be admitting that there are appearances or percepts. When appearance and reality coincide, we seldom have need to attend to or to mention the appearance. But our lack of interest in something doesn't prove that it isn't there. Moreover, in both normal veridical perception and perceptual illusion, the mechanism of perception is the same. Whether the stick looks bent or straight, the same type of retinal stimulation and brain activity occur. But if this stimulation and brain activity cause percepts to occur when the stick looks bent, then they would be sufficient to arouse percepts even when the stick looks the way it really is. There is a final point favoring percepts. When a straight stick looks bent, then it looks the way that sticks that are bent normally appear. And when a blue object looks red, then it looks the way that red objects normally appear. So the way we talk about cases of perceptual illusion seems to presuppose that percepts occur in normal veridical perception. Thus, the case against percepts is not convincing.

THE FUNCTION OF PERCEPTS

If percepts are not objects that we are aware of, what role do they play in perception? Let us reconsider the distinction between sense awareness and perceptual judgment. When someone sees that a rose is red, she has sense awareness of the red rose and forms the perceptual judgment that that is a red rose. Percepts have a role to play in each of these aspects of sense perception. Let us first consider sense awareness. Suppose that you close your eyes and merely think of the red rose. Now you open them, and the rose is present in your visual field. In both cases, you were aware of the rose, but only in the second case was the awareness sense awareness. How can we explain the difference between the kind of awareness we have of things when we are merely thinking of them and that vivid presentness of objects we have in sense perception? Here is where percepts enter the picture. In sense perception, things appear to the perceiver, arousing percepts in him, whereas in mere thought, percepts do not occur. The occurrence of percepts explains the difference between sense perception and thought. In sense awareness, the object causes or arouses a percept in the mind of the perceiver.

Consider a mechanism that is sensitive to and hence reacts to various forms of physical stimulation. For example, there are doors that open automatically when someone approaches them. But the automatic door does not see the people approaching it. Although the door reacts to objects, these objects do not appear to it. The occurrence of percepts is what distinguishes that human and animal form of reaction to objects that we call sense perception from the types of reaction characteristic of mindless mechanisms.

Let us now consider perceptual judgments. Because appearances are not themselves things we are generally aware of, we can no longer think of the process of arriving at a perceptual judgment as an inference from the percept to the object. Percepts are not usually premises from which judgments are inferred. What, then, is the relation between percepts and judgments? The answer is that percepts cause or arouse judgments. What distinguishes perceptual judgments from other kinds of judgments is that they are caused by something's appearing to a perceiver. For example, the percept of a red rose causes one to judge that one is seeing a red rose. In certain cases, a percept may provide evidence for the judgment as well as causing it. For example, if the light is dim, I may be unsure of the color of the object I am looking at. I may think to myself, "Something that looks like that in light like this is probably blue." In this case, the percept or look of the object functions as a premise that helps me arrive at a conclusion.

Where does the representative theory of perception stand in light of this account of the percept? Either the representative theory needs to be modified in the direction of direct realism or direct realism needs to be modified in the direction of the representative theory. Either way, we end up with an account of sense perception that lies between direct realism and the representative theory. Our final theory differs from direct realism in admitting that there are percepts that function as intermediaries between the object and the perceiver. But it also differs from the representative theory in its acceptance of the idea that in sense perception we are directly aware of physical objects. Perceptual consciousness is not normally doubled; we are not first aware of percepts and then of objects. There is usually only a single consciousness of the physical object and its features. Percepts represent objects to us by being present in sense perception, by causing perceptual judgments, and by being potential premises for the confirmation of perceptual judgments. But they do not normally function as actual premises. They are not representations in just the way that the traditional representative theory understood them to be.

Skepticism and Sense Perception

SOLIPSISM

Both Berkeley and Descartes raised the issue of **skepticism** with regard to the representative theory. If all that we are aware of are appearances, how can we establish the existence of an external world? This form of skepticism does not apply to the modified version of the representative theory just outlined. For according to this version, we are normally conscious of the external world, not of appearances. Yet we cannot so easily free ourselves of the doubts that the skeptic raises. First, any given perceptual judgment might be in error. I may think that I am aware of a physical object when in fact I am experiencing an hallucination or having a dream. Perceptual belief is thus *corrigible*. This means that no matter how firm my perceptual assurance may be, it is always possible that future experience will provide new evidence that will require me to correct my former belief.

Second, as Berkeley argued, it is possible that we have all our percepts without there being an external world at all. Perhaps, as Descartes suggested, we are the playthings of an evil genius bent upon deceiving us.

The skeptic does not merely say that we cannot have absolute certainty about the existence of an external world. If that were all that he was saying, then we could reply that we will be satisfied with probability. But the skeptic also denies that probability can be attained. For example, I am now looking at a yellow pencil. I feel quite sure that there is a yellow pencil there before my eyes. The skeptic argues: "You have no right to feel absolutely sure of the existence of a pencil. After all, in the next moment you may awake from a dream and be willing to admit that there is no pencil there at all." Suppose I reply that it is at least very probable that I am seeing a yellow pencil. The skeptic then answers: "What makes you think that it is even probable that you are seeing a yellow pencil? What is the evidence that is supposed to make it probable? Nothing is entitled to be called probable unless the evidence favors it. But what is your evidence?" I reply that it seems to me that I am seeing a yellow pencil. The way things appear provides me with all the evidence I need. But the skeptic answers: "The fact that it appears to you that a yellow pencil is there is not evidence of a yellow pencil's being there unless you have some reason to think that when you have such an appearance, then a yellow pencil is usually there. But you have no reason to accept this. You can know what usually accompanies your percepts only if you know in particular cases what object accompanies a particular percept. But your ability to know that is what is in question. I challenge you to show me in just one case that there is any likelihood at all that something is as it appears to be."

If we consistently develop this skeptical line of argument, the solid, reliable world of everyday life gradually dissolves. Not only does each of us lack any reason to believe in the existence of an external world, the very existence of the past is challenged by doubts about the reliability of memory. Nor is the future very likely. And now I must switch into the first person. For I am led to doubt the existence of you, dear reader. After all, it is sense perception that provides me with reasons for thinking that there are others besides myself. Once sense perception is called into question, then for all I know, I am alone in the universe. I have no reason to think that anyone will ever read these words that I am writing. I am left alone with my experiences of the present moment. I can know that I exist and that I am now having these experiences. But that is all that I can know or even reasonably conjecture. This result is called **solipsism.** Were I a solipsist, I would declare that for all I know I am the only thinking being. No matter how reasonable I think that solipsism is, I cannot recommend it to you, dear reader, for I have no reason to think that there is a *you* to recommend it to. Of course, if there is a *you*, then you know that you exist. But you have no reason to think that *I* who am writing these words exist.

HUME'S WAY OUT

Skepticism challenges us to discover a way out of this solipsistic view and to return to the solid world of everyday life. Descartes thought that he could make this journey by proving that God exists and is not a deceiver. David Hume, who explored skepticism and its consequences more deeply than any other modern philosopher, did not find Descartes' solution plausible:

> To have recourse to the veracity of the supreme Being, in order to prove the veracity of our senses, is surely making a very unexpected circuit. If his veracity were at all concerned in this matter, our senses would be entirely infallible; because it is not possible that he can ever deceive. Not to mention, that, if the external world be once called in question, we shall be at a loss to find arguments, by which we may prove the existence of that Being or any of his attributes.[18]

Descartes' project, Hume thinks, cannot be completed because his skepticism is so extreme that it undercuts the very arguments he needs to establish God's existence. Hume denied that the arguments of the extreme skeptic can be refuted. We are unable to transcend solipsism through argument.

According to Hume, the arguments of the skeptic *"admit of no answer and produce no conviction."*[19] Skepticism is of theoretical interest only, for the doubts that it engenders are theoretical rather than practical. No one in his right mind can actually live as a solipsist. Even the philosophical skeptic must accept the world of common sense in his everyday life. Skepticism is not a theory that can be lived:

> The great subverter of . . . the excessive principles of skepticism is action, and employment, and the occupations of common life. These principles may flourish and triumph in the schools; where it is, indeed, difficult, if not impossible, to refute them. But as soon as they leave the shade, and by the presence of the real objects, which actuate our passions and sentiments, are put in opposition to the more powerful principles of our nature, they vanish like smoke, and leave the most determined skeptic in the same condition as other mortals.[20]

In a famous passage, Hume indicates how "the more powerful principles of our nature" operate:

> Most fortunately it happens, that since reason is incapable of dispelling these clouds, nature herself suffices to that purpose, and cures me of this philosophical melancholy and delirium, either by relaxing this bent of mind, or by some avocation, and lively impression of my senses, which obliterate all these chimeras. I dine, I play a game of backgammon, I converse, and am merry with my friends; and when after three or four hours' amusement, I would return to these speculations, they appear so cold, and strain'd, and ridiculous, that I cannot find in my heart to enter them any farther.[21]

[18]Hume, "Enquiry," p. 153.
[19]Ibid., p. 155n.
[20]Ibid., pp. 158–159.
[21]David Hume, *A Treatise of Human Nature,* ed. L. A. Selby-Bigge (Oxford: The Clarendon Press, 1968), p. 269.

Hume claims that skepticism can neither be refuted nor believed. It arises in one's philosophical thoughts when one notices that certain arguments admit of no conclusive refutation. But these philosophical thoughts cannot be translated into action. To live and to act, one must take for granted that there is a world in which to live and act.

PEIRCE'S THEORY OF DOUBT

The American philosopher Charles S. Peirce (1839–1914) argued against Descartes' use of doubt as a method of restructuring one's beliefs:

> We cannot begin with complete doubt. We must begin with all the prejudices which we actually have when we enter upon the study of philosophy. These prejudices are not to be dispelled by a maxim, for they are things which it does not occur to us *can* be questioned. Hence this initial skepticism will be a mere self-deception, and not real doubt; and no one who follows the Cartesian method will ever be satisfied until he has formally recovered all those beliefs which in form he has given up. It is, therefore, as useless a preliminary as going to the North Pole would be in order to get to Constantinople by coming down regularly upon a meridian. A person may, it is true, in the course of his studies, find reason to doubt what he began by believing; but in that case he doubts because he has a

---

CHARLES SANDERS PEIRCE
(1839–1914)

The American philosopher Charles Sanders Peirce is best known as one of the founders of pragmatism and as its profoundest advocate. He was the son of Benjamin Peirce, a leading mathematician, and throughout his life maintained an interest in mathematics and logic. Unable to gain a permanent academic appointment, he worked for many years in government service for the Geodetic Survey. Peirce never published a philosophical book. His published essays and his unpublished fragments were gathered together in his *Collected Papers* (8 vols., 1931–1958). His criticisms of Descartes are contained in two papers "Questions concerning Certain Faculties Claimed for Man" and "Some Consequences of Four Incapacities." His pragmatic interpretation of science is represented by "The Fixation of Belief," "How to Make Our Ideas Clear," and "What Pragmatism Is." His theory of signs is contained in "Letters to Lady Welby." A good one-volume selection of his essays is Charles S. Peirce, *Selected Essays,* ed. Philip Wiener (New York: Dover, 1966).

---

positive reason for it, and not on account of the Cartesian maxim. Let us not pretend to doubt in philosophy what we do not doubt in our hearts.[22]

In this important passage, Peirce criticizes Descartes' method of philosophizing, that is, his profound doubt. Doubt that is based only upon general philosophical grounds is not really doubt at all. Real doubt must be based upon specific reasons appropriate to the case at hand and not upon the general considerations that Descartes and other skeptics have offered. For example, it may be reasonable to doubt that there is a pencil on my desk because, when I reach out to pick it up, I cannot feel it. But, says Peirce, it would not be reasonable to doubt that the pencil is there simply because my senses might be deceptive or I might be dreaming. As an alternative method of philosophizing, Peirce proposes that we begin with all the beliefs that we actually do have and that we try to understand how we came by them. Philosophy offers explanations of the structure of our considered opinions. In Hume's words, "philosophical decisions are nothing but the reflections of common life, methodized and corrected."[23]

What neither Hume nor Peirce seems to realize is that Descartes' method of doubt may be quite useful in methodizing and correcting the reflections of everyday life. For example, in attempting to develop a theory of the nature of perceptual knowledge, we are interested in whether our perceptual judgments are reliable and in what evidence we have for them. Even if we do not actually doubt these judgments, we want to understand why we have a right to rely upon them. We also want to understand their connection with experience on the one hand and with our more complex theoretical judgments on the other. The method of doubt may be useful in investigating these issues. Hume and Peirce criticized the method because, as used by Descartes, it led to a philosophical dead end. But if skeptical criticism is moderated by the kind of warning that Hume and Peirce offer, it may be a useful way of deepening our understanding of the structure of our beliefs.

HEIDEGGER AND BEING-IN-THE-WORLD

The main problem with the skepticism of Descartes is its leaving the impression that each human being is an isolated mind entitled to believe that it lives alongside other beings only after it is able to provide a proof of the existence of the external world. Descartes suggests that without such proof, we are required to embrace solipsism. In opposition to this, the contemporary German philosopher Martin Heidegger (1889–1976) claims that humans are beings whose nature it is to dwell alongside other beings. The existence of the world is not established by proof. That there is a world is something already given in the structure of human consciousness. In the following passage, Heidegger uses the German word *Dasein* to denote the human person:

> When Dasein directs itself towards something and grasps it, it does not somehow first get out of an inner sphere in which it has been proximally encapsulated, but

---

[22]*Collected Papers of Charles Sanders Peirce,* ed. Charles Harshorne and Paul Weiss (Cambridge: Harvard University Press, 1934), vol. V, par. 265.
[23]Hume, "Enquiry," p. 162.

its primary kind of Being is such that it is always "outside" alongside entities which it encounters and which belong to a world already discovered. Nor is any inner sphere abandoned when Dasein dwells alongside the entity to be known, and determines its character; but even in this "Being-outside" alongside the object, Dasein is still "inside," if we understand this in the correct sense; that is to say, it is itself "inside" as a Being-in-the-world which knows. And furthermore, the perceiving of what is known is not a process of returning with one's booty to the "cabinet" of consciousness after one has gone out and grasped it; even in perceiving, retaining, and preserving, the Dasein which knows *remains outside,* and it does so *as Dasein.*[24]

For Heidegger, the important problem is to understand Dasein. And if we should achieve such an understanding, we would no longer find it important to prove the reality of an external world.

> The question of whether there is a world at all and whether its Being can be proved, makes no sense if it is raised by Dasein as Being-in-the-world; and who else would raise it? . . .
> If Dasein is understood correctly, it defies such proofs, because, in its Being, it already *is* what subsequent proofs deem necessary to demonstrate for it.[25]

The important philosophical task is not to prove that solipsism is mistaken. Probably such a proof cannot be found. What is important is to understand Dasein and to investigate the ways in which human individuals exist alongside other beings.

Summary

To understand the nature of knowledge, we need first to make a distinction between practical knowledge (knowing how) and factual knowledge (knowing that). Factual knowledge, with which philosophers are primarily concerned, entails knowing whether a statement is true or false. Ultimately, it may be defined as fully justified true conviction.

Sense perception is the primary source of our knowledge of the world. Each of our five senses is a capacity to discriminate certain features of the world, e.g., hearing is the capacity to detect sounds. Sense perception is a complex affair in which it is necessary to distinguish sense awareness of an object and its characteristics from the perceptual judgment that the object is what it is.

The appearances of things—the percepts that things cause in us—do not always accurately represent the way things really are; illusions, hallucinations, and other sources of perceptual error must be contended with. Nevertheless, direct realism claims that for the most part sense perception reveals to us an independently existing external

---

[24]Martin Heidegger, *Being and Time,* trans. John Macquarrie and Edward Robinson (London: SCM Press, 1962), p. 89.
[25]Ibid., pp. 246–247, 249.

world as it really is at this moment. Powerful challenges to direct realism have been based upon the finite velocity of light (which shows us that our perceptions are always of the past, however recent), the relativity of perception, and the distinction between primary and secondary qualities. Accordingly, many philosophers have argued for a different theory of perception that says that the external world is not directly given but is represented to us by means of our percepts.

This representative theory of perception seems to lead to extreme skepticism. According to Descartes' method of doubt, we do not have any reason to think that our percepts actually correspond to reality. Berkeley also wondered how our percepts could correspond to reality, which led him to criticize Locke's distinction between primary and secondary qualities. Though Locke had argued that primary qualities are inseparable from the object, secondary qualities are only powers or dispositional qualities. Berkeley pointed out that primary qualities are just as relative as secondary qualities. To overcome this difficulty, he developed a phenomenalist account of perception according to which bodies are interpreted as bundles of actual or possible percepts. The drawback to Berkeley's system is that it fails to provide us with a coherent representation of our experience.

The most plausible account of sense perception is a compromise between direct realism and the representative theory. Although percepts are not normally objects of perception, as the representative theory claims, they function to distinguish sense awareness from mere thinking and to cause perceptual judgments about the external world. Percepts are best understood not as objects in relation to a subject but as ways in which physical objects appear to subjects.

It is doubtful that extreme skepticism or solipsism can be conclusively refuted by argument. For Hume, skepticism dissolves in the course of living one's life. Peirce argued against the use of skepticism as a method of philosophizing. We should only doubt something, he claims, if we have a specific positive reason to do so. Heidegger responded to the claims of skepticism by saying that the important task is not to prove the existence of the external world but to understand that each of us exists alongside others in a world already given to us.

Glossary

Adverbial theory: The view that percepts are ways that bodies appear rather than objects of awareness in their own right.

A priori knowledge: Knowledge that is independent of observation; knowledge acquired solely through the use of reason.

Concept: One has a concept of an object if one can identify it, classify it, and recognize it.

Direct realism: Our commonsense theory of sense perception according to which an external, public, physical reality is directly given to the senses as it really is.

Dispositional quality: A power or capacity of an object such as the disposition that a lump of sugar has to dissolve in water.

Empirical knowledge: Knowledge based upon observation or sense perception; knowledge gained through the senses.

Epistemology: The theory of knowledge; the philosophical account of the nature, extent, and foundations of human knowledge.

Factual knowledge: The knowledge that something is true; knowledge of facts or propositions, such as knowing that the cat is on the mat.

Idealism: The view that the only things that exist are minds and their ideas. Berkeley, its leading exponent, called it immaterialism.

Immaterialism: See **Idealism.**

Intuitive knowledge: Knowledge that is self-evident, that implies a direct awareness of the thing that is known.

Percept: The way an object appears in sense perception.

Perceptual error: The result of a perceptual judgment's being false or mistaken.

Perceptual judgment: A judgment based upon the sense awareness of an object.

Phenomenalism: The view that bodies are nothing but actual or possible percepts or appearances.

Practical knowledge: Knowing how to do something, such as knowing how to swim.

Primary quality: A quality that, according to Locke, is inseparable from an object, such as size, shape, extension, and solidity.

Real essence: What an object really is, for Locke; that part of an object that explains why it behaves in the way it does.

Representative theory of perception: The idea that the external world is not perceived directly but is represented through the percepts or appearances that bodies cause in the minds of the perceivers.

Secondary quality: A power in bodies to arouse percepts in the mind such as percepts of color and sound.

Sense: A capacity to become aware of some aspect of the world; for example, the sense of sight or of hearing.

Sense awareness: Awareness of something that is present in one's perceptual field or that presents itself as an appearance to a perceiver.

Sense datum theory: The view that percepts are private mental items that possess both primary and secondary qualities.

Sensible quality: A quality of a body that can be detected by means of the senses, such as a color or a sound.

Skepticism: A skeptic is one who doubts; in philosophy, this generally refers to whether sense perception really does provide knowledge of the external world.

Solipsism: The view that no one has any reason to believe in the existence of anything except himself and his thoughts.

Veridical judgment: A perceptual judgment that is true or correct.

Further Reading

For the distinction between factual and practical knowledge (or knowing that and knowing how) see Gilbert Ryle, *The Concept of Mind* (London: Hutchinson's University Library, 1952), chap. 2. A good discussion of the definition of factual knowledge is provided by A. J. Ayer, *The Problem of Knowledge* (Penguin Books, 1956), chap. 1.

The development of theories of sense perception in modern philosophy can be traced by reading the following works: John Locke, *An Essay concerning Human Understanding,* book II; René Descartes, *Meditations on First Philosophy;* George Berkeley, *A Treatise on the Principles of Human Knowledge;* David Hume, *A Treatise of Human Nature,* book I; and Immanuel Kant, *Critique of Pure Reason.* Thomas Reid, a contemporary of Hume, presents a critique of the general approach initiated by Locke and Descartes in his *Essays on the Intellectual Powers of Man* in *Philosophical Works,* ed. Sir William Hamilton, vol. I.

There are many discussions of perception in twentieth-century philosophy. Among the most influential are A. J. Ayer, *The Foundations of Empirical Knowledge* (London: Macmillan and Co., 1963); D. M. Armstrong, *Perception and the Physical World* (London: Routledge and Kegan Paul, 1961); J. L. Austin, *Sense and Sensibilia* (Oxford: The Clarendon Press, 1962); Roderick Chisholm, *Perceiving: A Philosophical Study* (Ithaca, N.Y.: Cornell University Press, 1957); Arthur Lovejoy, *The Revolt against Dualism* (La Salle, Illinois: Open Court, 1955); and Ryle, *The Concept of Mind,* chap. 7.

Questions for Thought and Discussion

1. How is knowledge to be distinguished from a mere opinion that something is true?

2. What reasons can be given for doubting our commonsense theory of sense perception, the theory called direct realism in this chapter?

3. What is the significance of Locke's distinction between primary and secondary qualities for the theory of perceptual knowledge? What does it mean to say that secondary qualities are dispositional? Does the way he explains this distinction tend to support the representative theory of perception?

4. Do you agree with Descartes that the fact that we dream provides us with a good reason for doubting the existence of bodies, including our own body?

5. Both direct realism and Berkeley's phenomenalism try to be consistent with common sense. Which do you think accords better with common sense? Is it important for a theory of perception to accord with common sense?

6. Do you agree with Berkeley's criticism of the representative theory? Do the difficulties with the representative theory and with phenomenalism make direct realism the only plausible alternative?

7. Explain how percepts or appearances function in our knowledge of bodies.

8. Is there a way to avoid the outcome of skepticism, e.g., solipsism? Is our belief in the existence of bodies something that can be substantiated by reason and argument?

Chapter 8

THE STRUCTURE OF HUMAN KNOWLEDGE

PREVIEW

There are two main approaches to the problem of knowledge in the history of Western philosophy: empiricism and rationalism. Empiricism emphasizes the role of the senses and of observation in providing a foundation for human knowledge, whereas rationalism emphasizes the role of the mind. After discussing some of the main issues that divide empiricists and rationalists, we shall examine the claims of empiricism by studying the various methods we use to fix our beliefs about the world. We shall find that certain formulations of empiricism, including verificationism, fail to provide an adequate account of the complexity and variety of human knowledge. Finally, we shall discuss the problem of the nature of truth and the relation of truth to verification.

Rationalism and Empiricism

Our discussion of human knowledge began in Chapter Seven with a consideration of the nature and the objects of sense perception. This emphasis on perception is justified by the importance of the senses in the generation of human knowledge. According to **empiricism,** sense awareness is the foundation of knowledge; all factual belief is based upon sense experience. Locke, Berkeley, and Hume, some of whose ideas were discussed in the preceding chapter, have been classified as the British empiricists because each tried in his own way to show how the senses furnish the basic materials of knowledge. **Rationalism,** which is represented most fully by Plato and Descartes, is a tradition opposed to empiricism. Rationalists claim that human knowledge is based on reason as well as on sense perception. For the rationalist, human reason has an independent and crucial role to play in the formation of justified belief.

THE ORIGIN OF IDEAS: RATIONALISM

In early modern philosophy, the main issue on which the debate between rationalism and empiricism focused was the question of the origin of ideas. Do all our ideas come from the senses or are they in some way innate, originating in the human mind? Descartes claimed that some ideas are innate. For example, in speaking of the idea or concept of God, he says:

> I have not drawn it from the senses. . . . It is not even a pure production or fiction of my mind, for it is not in my power to take from or add to it; and consequently there but remains the alternative that it is innate, in the same way as is the idea of myself.[1]

According to Descartes, if an idea is not learned from sense experience and if it is not created by the human imagination, then it must be innate. If a person has an idea or concept of something, then he knows what that something is. For example, to have an idea of God is to know what God is; to have an idea of an elephant is to know what an elephant is; to have an idea of red is to know which color red is. Let us call this kind of knowledge **conceptual knowledge.** An innate idea is a form of conceptual knowledge that is not acquired through the senses but is possessed from birth. It is not something that we had occasion to learn.

In a similar vein, the German philosopher Gottfried Leibniz (1646–1716) writes:

> There are some ideas and some principles which do not come to us from the senses, and which we find in ourselves without forming them, although the senses give us occasion to perceive them.[2]

To the objection that we do not always find in ourselves the ideas that he classifies as innate, Leibniz replies that "one possesses many things without knowing it."[3] For the rationalist, innate ideas often assume the form of unconscious or tacit knowledge. We are unaware of this knowledge until there arises an occasion to make use of it. The mind comes already stored with ideas, and it has the power to organize these ideas into theories that it uses to interpret the impressions of the senses. The rationalist thus emphasizes the contribution that the mind makes to human knowledge.

---

[1]René Descartes, *Meditations on First Philosophy,* trans. John Veitch, iii.
[2]Gottfried Wilhelm Leibniz, *New Essays concerning Human Understanding,* trans. A. G. Langley (La Salle, Illinois: Open Court, 1949), p. 70.
[3]Ibid., p. 74.

THE ORIGIN OF IDEAS: EMPIRICISM

The empiricist, on the contrary, declares that the human mind comes into existence without any ideas at all. Ideas are furnished solely by sense experience. In the words of Locke,

> Let us then suppose the mind to be, as we say, white paper, void of all characters, without any ideas; how comes it to be furnished? Whence comes it by that vast store, which the busy and boundless fancy of man has painted on it with an almost endless variety? Whence has it all the materials of reason and knowledge? To this I answer, in one word, From experience: in that all our knowledge is founded.[4]

Locke then points out that experience includes two distinct sources of ideas:

> Our observation, employed either about external sensible objects, or about the internal operations of our minds, perceived and reflected on by ourselves, is that which supplies our understandings with all the materials of thinking. These two are the fountains of knowledge, from whence all the ideas we have, or can naturally have, do spring.[5]

The first source of ideas is our sense awareness of the external world. The second source, which Locke calls *reflection* and which later came to be known as *introspection,* is the mind's awareness of its own operations. Some of the operations of which it can be aware are thinking, perceiving, reasoning, choosing, and comparing.

A later representative of empiricism, David Hume, gave the following explanation of the difference between sense experience (or, as he called it, impressions of sensation) and the ideas or concepts that the mind abstracts from its impressions. Suppose I am looking at a yellow pencil. Then I close my eyes and think of it. The only difference between the sense impression and the thought or idea is that the latter is less vivid or lively than the former. An idea, for Hume, is merely a mental image that copies the corresponding impression. For Hume and for many subsequent philosophers and psychologists, thinking is just a succession of images in the mind. There is no fundamental difference between thought and sense experience.

We are of course able to form ideas of things that we have never perceived. We can form the idea of a mermaid or of a golden mountain, although no one has ever seen either thing. Thinking seems to have an "unbounded liberty"; it does not seem to be limited to what is given in sense perception. But Hume explains that this liberty is an illusion:

> But though our thought seems to possess this unbounded liberty, we shall find, upon a nearer examination, that it is really confined within very narrow limits,

---

[4]John Locke, *An Essay concerning Human Understanding* (London: George Routledge and Sons) II. i. 2.
[5]Ibid.

and that all this creative power of the mind amounts to no more than the faculty of compounding, transposing, augmenting, or diminishing the materials afforded us by the senses and experience. When we think of a golden mountain, we only join two consistent ideas, *gold,* and *mountain,* with which we were formerly acquainted. . . . In short, all the materials of our thinking are derived either from our outward or inward sentiment: the mixture and composition of these belongs alone to the mind and will.[6]

In this passage, Hume introduces a very important distinction between the materials of thinking—the ideas that the mind abstracts from sense experience—and the activities of the mind, which organizes these materials in various ways. The mind compounds, transposes, augments, and diminishes the ideas that come from sense and reflection. For example, we can form the idea of a mermaid by joining or compounding the idea of a fish with the idea of a woman. We can form the idea of a giant by augmenting the idea we have of a normal human being. According to Hume, the mind has a structure, a fixed way of organizing the materials given to it in sense perception.

TWO MAIN ISSUES

We are now in a position to see that the traditional debate between rationalism and empiricism involves two different issues. The first issue concerns the origin of conceptual knowledge. How do human beings acquire concepts or ideas? We know that some animal behavior is unlearned or instinctive. For example, children come into the world able to suck and swallow; no one has to teach them how to do these things. It is possible that some conceptual knowledge is likewise unlearned. But most of it is learned. How is it learned? What is the mechanism by which we acquire the ability to employ concepts, an ability made apparent in such activities as recognition, identification, and language use? In contemporary thought, these questions have been most fruitfully pursued by psychology. Just as psychologists apply their experimental techniques to understanding and explaining the difference between learned and instinctive behavior, so it is by the experimental study of behavior and its underlying mechanisms in the nervous system that the source of conceptual knowledge will be discovered.

The second issue concerns the structure of the mind, the way that the mind organizes its ideas and its knowledge. According to traditional empiricism, the mind is limited to arranging and rearranging the materials given in sense awareness. A different approach to the issue was provided by the German philosopher Immanuel Kant (1724–1804) in his *Critique of Pure Reason.* Countering the empiricists, he argued that the mind is not limited to merely arranging given materials but introduces its own order or structure into sense experience. According to Kant, the mind imposes on the content provided by experience such relations as the spatiotemporal disposition of observed objects, the causal order of events, and the relation of a thing to its qualities. Human knowledge is thus a product of the mind's working upon the materials of sense to create an intelligible

---

[6]David Hume, "An Enquiry concerning Human Understanding," in *Hume's Enquiries,* ed. L. A. Selby-Bigge (Oxford: The Clarendon Press, 1972), p. 19.

structure. For Kant, empiricism is correct to the extent that it insists upon the importance of sense experience in providing the content of knowledge, and rationalism is correct in its emphasis upon the mind's providing the structure for experience. Kant's *Critique of Pure Reason* was a monumental attempt to bring together into one system of thought the major contributions of traditional empiricism and traditional rationalism.

Two main issues in the debate between empiricism and rationalism:

1. How do human beings obtain ideas?
   Empiricism: All ideas are acquired from experience.
   Rationalism: Some ideas are innate.
2. How is human knowledge organized?
   Empiricism: The mind arranges and stores materials that are given in experience.
   Rationalism: The mind introduces new principles of order into experience drawn from its own nature.

As a result of the Kantian synthesis, the debate between rationalism and empiricism shifted away from the question about the origin of conceptual knowledge. This question was seen as a question of fact to be decided by scientific investigation. The new question was one of *justification:* Given that human beings accept various statements as true and that they invent theories, what, if anything, justifies or establishes the right to believe such statements and theories? This is a question not for psychology but for epistemology or the theory of knowledge. Modern empiricists claim that only experience *justifies* our accepting these statements and theories as true. Rationalists find this answer unsatisfactory and incomplete. They insist that reason has an independent role to play.

EMPIRICAL AND A PRIORI KNOWLEDGE

With regard to the question about how our beliefs are to be justified, David Hume introduced an important distinction between relations of ideas and matters of fact:

> All the objects of human reason or enquiry may naturally be divided into two kinds, to wit, *Relations of Ideas,* and *Matters of Fact.* Of the first kind are the sciences of Geometry, Algebra, and Arithmetic; and in short, every affirmation which is either intuitively or demonstratively certain. *That the square of the hypotenuse is equal to the square of the two sides,* is a proposition which expresss a relation between these figues. *That three times five is equal to the half of thirty,* expresses a relation between these numbers. Propositions of this kind are discoverable by the mere operation of thought, without dependence on what is anywhere existent in the universe. Though there never were a circle or a triangle in nature, the truths demonstrated by Euclid would for ever retain their certainty and evidence.[7]

[7]Ibid., p. 25.

The most prominent statements formulating relations of ideas are those belonging to mathematics. Hume's point is that the truth of these statements is determined by "the mere operation of thought." Following Kant, it is common today to call statements known by the mere operation of thought independently of observation *a priori statements*. Statements that are based upon observation are called *empirical* or *a posteriori statements*. It appears, then, that there are two methods of verification: One involves the mere operation of thought and the other observation, that is, the use of sense experience and introspection. The discussion of **a priori knowledge** is reserved for the following chapter. In this chapter we shall concentrate on our knowledge of matters of fact and its basis in observation.

Verificationism

THEORY AND OBSERVATION

The major claim of empiricism is that all our knowledge of matters of fact is based upon observation. If we are to have justified belief about the natural world, we cannot sit in an armchair just thinking about it. We must actively intervene in nature through experiment and by recording the observations that experiment makes possible. There is no a priori knowledge of matters of fact, says the empiricist.

Let us consider, for a moment, the whole edifice of our commonsense and scientific knowledge of the world. This system of knowledge contains various kinds of statements that we take to be true. For example, it contains a variety of singular statements. These are statements about particular things, such as "The moon is the only satellite of the earth." It contains numerous general statements expressing laws of nature; such statements include the law of gravitation, which says that every body in the universe attracts every other body with a force proportional to the product of their masses and inversely proportional to the square of their distances. It contains statements about objects that are very distant in space, such as stars that are thousands of light-years away. It contains statements about things distant in time, such as events that occurred hundreds of years ago in human history. It contains statements about things that can be observed only with the help of instruments such as microscopes and telescopes and about things that cannot be observed at all because they are so minute. According to empiricism, the ultimate reason for accepting any of these statements as true is that they are verified or confirmed by statements that formulate the result of observation. We shall call such statements **observation statements.** An observation statement records what a person sees or hears or discovers by means of his senses or by introspection. All other statements, all those statements established by means of observation statements, are called **theoretical statements.** Empiricism claims that the whole structure of human theoretical knowledge is based upon a foundation of observation statements. The verification of any theoretical statement consists in showing how that statement can be justified or made probable by reference to observation statements.

THE VERIFIABILITY CRITERION

This approach to the problem of the basis of human knowledge was developed in detail in this century by a group of empiricists who called themselves *logical positivists*. The positivists developed a method that they called the **verifiability theory of meaning.** Consider the sentence "The cat is on the mat." We know that it has meaning because we understand what statement a person who utters it is making. Not every string of words constitutes a meaningful sentence. Some strings such as "On is mat the cat" are just ungrammatical and say nothing. But even if a string is grammatical, meaning is not guaranteed. What can possibly be meant by "The massive red number flew mightily over the longest word in the apple's sum"? Nonsense sentences need not be ungrammatical. To be meaningful, a sentence must be both grammatical and make a statement that we can understand.

The traditional empiricists, Locke and Hume in particular, imposed a further condition upon meaningful sentences. Certain of the words that appear in sentences are **descriptive;** this means that they are used to describe or characterize the things to which they apply. For example, in "The cat is on the mat," the words *cat* and *mat* are descriptive because they tell us something about the features of the objects they name. According to traditional empiricists, for a sentence to be meaningful, all the descriptive words in it must ultimately be definable by observation, by our pointing to things that can be experienced. After all, there are only two ways in which you can explain to someone the meaning of a descriptive word. You can explain it by using other words. Thus, you can define the word *triangle* by saying that a triangle is an enclosed plane figure with three straight sides. But suppose some of the words in this definition are not understood. You can use other words, of course. But somewhere there must be an escape from the circle of words, for people do learn language from scratch. Ultimately, the meanings of words must be learned by pointing to items that are experienced. Ways of explaining word meanings by pointing to the observed features of things are called **ostensive definitions.** For Locke and Hume, the meaning of a word is an idea, and all ideas come from experience. So all descriptive words must be definable in terms of words that are capable of ostensive definition. Thus, children are taught the meanings of color words such as *red* and *blue* by an adult's uttering the words while pointing to a red or a blue object.

But this requirement of traditional empiricism was not sufficient for the logical positivists. They noticed that even a sentence that is grammatical and whose descriptive words can all be given ostensive definition could be unverifiable. Take the statement "Everything in the universe doubled in size last night." Normally we can tell when an object increases in size by comparing it with something that has stayed the same. Thus, if someone says to me that my pen doubled in length last night, I can verify the truth of what he says by measuring it with a ruler. If all objects, however, including rulers and our own bodies double in size, then we have no method of comparison and no way of telling whether or not this mysterious doubling really occurred. Thus, we have no way of verifying the statement.

For the logical positivists, this conclusion was unacceptable. The logical positivists were committed to science and to a scientific approach to understanding the world. They wanted to formulate a way of distinguishing scientific theories and the scientific uses of language from the nonscientific, the mystical, and the superstitious. They argued that for a statement to be scientific, it must at least be verifiable; there must be some way of finding out whether or not it is true. If a statement is not verifiable, if no observations that we could possibly make could tell us whether or not it is true, then for logical positivists the statement is meaningless, for our ability to understand language depends upon relating it to what we can observe. Although unverifiable sentences appear to say something, they really do not say anything at all. They lack cognitive significance, or **cognitive meaning.** In the words of one of the most eloquent of the positivists, A. J. Ayer:

> The criterion which we use to test the genuineness of apparent statements of fact is the criterion of verifiability. We say that a sentence is factually significant to any given person, if, and only if, he knows how to verify the proposition which it purports to express—that is, if he knows what observations would lead him, under certain conditions, to accept the proposition as being true, or reject it as being false. If, on the other hand, the putative proposition is of such a character that the assumption of its truth, or falsehood, is consistent with any assumption whatsoever concerning the nature of his future experience, then, as far as he is concerned, it is, if not a tautology, a mere pseudo-proposition. The sentence expressing it may be emotionally significant to him; but it is not literally significant.[8]

One of the consequences of this verifiability criterion of cognitive significance is that many of the sentences used to formulate religious and ethical ideas are meaningless. If I have no way of telling by observation that God exists or that honesty is better than cheating, then such statements have no cognitive significance. Of course, they seem to say something, and often they have a strong effect upon our emotions. People who utter the words "There is a God" are said to be expressing certain optimistic feelings about the world. People who say that honesty is better than cheating are expressing their approbation of honesty and their disapprobation of cheating. The positivists admitted that these sentences have a certain kind of meaning. They called it **emotive meaning.** It is akin to the kind of meaning expressed in poetry. A sentence that seems to have cognitive meaning may, upon analysis, turn out to have emotive meaning only.

According to the verifiability criterion of meaning, the meaning of a sentence is provided by formulating all the evidence drawn from observation that would establish its truth or its falsity. If I understand a given statement, then I know which possible observations would convince me that it is true or false. Consider the statement that water boils at one hundred degrees centigrade. If I heat a pot of water to one hundred degrees and observe it boil, then I have confirmed the statement. If, on the other hand, it did not boil when heated to that temperature, then the statement would be disconfirmed or falsified. The verifiability theory says that the meaning of a statement consists in all the

[8]A. J. Ayer, *Language, Truth and Logic* (London: Victor Gollancz, Ltd., 1946), p. 35.

possible observations of this sort, both those that would confirm it and those that would falsify it.

Contemporary empiricism as embodied in logical positivism makes two basic claims about human knowledge. First, it says that all our knowledge of matters of fact is based upon observation. Second, it asserts that the very meaning of the statements formulating matters of fact is based upon observation. Thus, the very observations that serve to establish that we have knowledge also serve to determine the meaning of our knowledge. In the following sections, we shall delve more deeply into the relation between theory and observation to determine for ourselves whether contemporary empiricism is capable of supporting these major claims about knowledge and meaning.

Observation

Observation includes both sense perception and introspection. Sense perception, as we learned in Chapter Seven, is one way we become aware of the objects and events in nature. Sense awareness in itself is not a form of knowledge. Factual knowledge arises when we form judgments about what is given in sense awareness. The perceptual judgment is one form that knowledge can assume. When expressed in words, it is an observation statement.

Let us examine a particular case. I look carefully at a cat and observe that the cat is on the mat. This seems simple enough but it is really quite complex. The observation is really a judgment that I have made on the basis of sense awareness. The cat and the mat appeared to me in some way, and these appearances led me to make the judgment that the cat is on the mat. We have seen that the ability to judge presupposes a certain amount of conceptual knowledge. I must know what a cat is and what a mat is to judge that the cat is on the mat. In addition, I need to know what it is for one thing to be on another thing; I must possess the idea of the relation *on*. But possessing these concepts is not enough. For the judgment to occur, I must bring them together in thought or in speech. In making the judgment, I am thus using quite a bit of conceptual knowledge. Every step of the way, error is possible. Perhaps it is not a cat, or a mat. Perhaps the mat is on the cat rather than the other way around. I have no absolute guarantee that my judgment is correct.

Most of our conceptual knowledge presupposes the ability to use language. I am not saying that there are no concepts without language. Before a child learns to speak, she is able to distinguish many objects—her mother, her rattle, and so forth. But the ability to classify and to become aware of facts of any complexity rests upon learning the names and descriptions of things. Thus, the simple judgment that the cat is on the mat may very well make use of certain linguistic skills that allowed the relevant conceptual knowledge to be realized.

There is, then, no definite answer to the question, what can I observe? The answer depends in part upon the conceptual knowledge and linguistic skills that I happen to possess. Moreover, culture is important in determining the observational capacities of an individual. Someone who comes from a primitive culture may be unable to judge that something is an automobile or a lawnmower.

In addition, my ability to observe certain things depends upon the preexisting factual knowledge that I happen to possess. Because I know that an X-ray machine is able to take pictures of internal bodily organs, I may realize that what I see is a picture of someone's lungs. Because I know various facts about a television set, I may realize that I am actually looking at the president of the United States as he reads a speech. I use the facts that I already know to interpret my experience and to make judgments about the objects of my sense awareness.

These points may be summarized by saying that no sharp line can be drawn between theory and observation. The perceptual judgment and the observation statement that records it result not merely from my awareness of objects but from what I already know and what theories I already accept. Observation statements differ in the degree to which they presuppose and employ preexisting knowledge and capability. "That is red" presupposes less than "That giraffe is taller than any mouse." The ratio of the factors contributed by the senses to those contributed by preexisting knowledge varies from one judgment to another. But the need for preexisting knowledge never vanishes altogether. Furthermore, a judgment that is perceptual for one person may not be so for another. Hence, we simply cannot take a set of statements and say, once and for all, "These and these alone are observational statements." A judgment, observational or not, always goes beyond the immediate experience. This close link between observation and theory casts doubt upon the verifiability criterion of meaning proposed by the logical positivists. For that criterion assumes that there is a clear-cut set of observational statements that gives meaning to theoretical judgments. It assumes a definite separation of theory and observation that does not exist in fact.

Memory

Once made, a perceptual judgment is no longer perceptual. The occasion of sense awareness that aroused it has faded into the past, and the judgment remains in the mind as a memory. I no longer see the giraffe that I saw five minutes ago, but I remember seeing it. Sometimes my memories are in error. I may have a completely false memory belief that I once saw or did something. Errors in memory can be caused by previous errors in observation. I think I see a lion but it is really a tiger. Thus, the error in my memory belief that it was a lion I saw is a consequence of faulty observation. But memory may mislead me on its own. I may think that I telephoned you last week when it was really six months ago. There is a well-known phenomenon called *déjà vu,* in which a person has the strong impression of having previously visited a certain place that he has never visited at all.

The trust that I now have in the correctness of my memory beliefs is no longer based upon the original observation, for that is now in the past and is irrecoverable. If you say, "I saw Judy the giraffe at the zoo yesterday" and I ask what makes you think that you actually did see her, your reply will naturally be "I remember seeing her." But if I then ask what makes you so sure that your memory belief is true—what makes you so sure that you really remember seeing her—it is difficult to know how to answer. Nothing that you presently observe can prove that you saw her yesterday.

If someone calls one of your memories into question, there are some things that you can do to confirm or to falsify it. Suppose I remember putting my pen into my desk drawer yesterday. Finding the pen in the drawer today would provide some support for my memory. But it does not provide conclusive proof, for there are many other ways for the pen to have been placed in my drawer other than my putting it there yesterday. My failing to find it in the drawer tends to show that my memory is in error. But that does not provide conclusive falsification, for it may have been removed after I had put it there. In addition, in evaluating my memory, I rely upon beliefs that I already have. Thus, if I think that no one has been near my desk since yesterday except me, then finding my pen in the drawer would provide rather strong support for my memory. But if I think that many people had the opportunity of placing it in the drawer, then my finding it there provides less support.

Memory beliefs are similar to perceptual judgments because both usually arise spontaneously in the mind without forethought or deliberation. We have a natural instinct to accept what is given to us by our senses and by our memory. Memory and perceptual beliefs have an initial credibility; we trust them unless we have some reason not to; they are innocent until proved guilty. Their initial credibility may be increased or diminished by new observations and by other beliefs that we take to be reliable. If a memory fits in or coheres with our other beliefs, its credibility is thus increased. If it clashes with some of them, its credibility is diminished.

Can one remember the future? The White Queen in Lewis Carroll's *Through the Looking Glass* thinks one can:

"That's the effect of living backwards," the Queen said kindly: *"it always makes one a little giddy at first—"*

"Living backwards!" Alice repeated in great astonishment. *"I never heard of such a thing!"*

"—but there's one great advantage in it, that one's memory works both ways."

"I'm sure mine *only works one way,"* Alice remarked. *"I can't remember things before they happen."*

"It's a poor sort of memory that only works backwards," the Queen remarked.

"What sort of things do you remember best?" Alice ventured to ask.

"Oh things that happened the week after next," the Queen replied in a careless tone.

To make this clear, consider the following example. I think I remember seeing a building on the corner of Lexington Avenue and East 68th Street last month. I now pass the corner and find an empty lot. Is my memory mistaken? Because I know that buildings don't just come and go, my present observation tends to reduce the credibility of the recollection. But I now meet someone who tells me that a serious fire occurred on that corner three weeks ago. Assuming that the witness is trustworthy, I can explain the absence of the building in a way that does not cast doubt upon my memory. There are other possibilities. When I first see the empty lot, I may feel so sure of my memory that I may judge that my senses are now deceiving me. Or perhaps I may give up my belief about the relative permanence of buildings. In any case, the credibility of a memory is increased or diminished by its cohering or failing to cohere with what we already believe. It is this coherence applied to an assumed initial credibility or plausibility that provides the basis of our trust in memory.

Testimony and Authority

In checking the reliability of my memory belief that a building stood at Lexington Avenue and East 68th Street last month, I relied on someone's report that the building burned down three weeks ago. The witness remembered seeing the fire; I trust his report because I trust the memory and senses of others in general. I also assume that he is honest, that he is not deceiving me on purpose. In general, then, reliance upon the testimony of others is a major source of our beliefs. But using the reports of others to build up our own system of knowledge requires our assuming that they are reliable.

We should not underestimate the importance of testimony to our understanding of the world. Think how little we would know if all we had to go on were our own observations and our memory of them. We would lack knowledge of everything except what we have personally observed. We would, for instance, lack scientific knowledge. Science is a cooperative endeavor spanning centuries of time and incorporating the findings of countless numbers of researchers. Reliance upon the scientific enterprise entails relying upon the word of others. So does our conception of human history. When modern historians write that Columbus discovered America in 1492, they are ultimately relying upon documents that were written by eyewitnesses or by persons who interviewed eyewitnesses. Every time we accept something we read in a book, we are relying upon someone's testimony. Thus, what I know of my world is built upon the experiences of countless other human beings, some of which becomes incorporated into books, documents, and other records of time past. Descartes wished to build his system of knowledge upon his own thought alone; he was engaged upon an impossible task.

In general, when we rely upon the word of another, we take for granted that he arrived at his own beliefs by reliable methods and that he is honest. Both of these assumptions can be challenged in particular cases. If I discover that someone's prediction that there will be an eclipse of the sun tomorrow was based upon his looking into a crystal ball, I will not take him seriously. If I think that he has reason to deceive me or that he has a reputation for dishonesty, I also will not rely upon his judgment. When I use the testimony of others, I must make use of what I already know to evaluate their assertions. I am more likely to accept someone's testimony if what he says and the way he has established his report coheres with my own established beliefs and methods. If I have found crystal balls trustworthy, then I am more likely to accept a prediction based on looking into one. If someone tells me of something that he has read in the newspaper, I must evaluate his reliability—Did he really read it?—as well as the newspaper's. Almost anything I know about the world may become relevant in assessing the testimony of others.

In some cases, I rely upon someone's word because he or she is an expert authority. When I accept what the author of a physics or a history textbook writes, for example, I assume that this person can be trusted because he or she is an authority in this field. We live in a period of human history in which knowledge has become specialized and technical. It is becoming more and more difficult for any one person, no matter how intelligent, to check personally the findings of specialists in fields other than his or her own. Thus, we find ourselves relying more and more on authorities to settle our beliefs about the world.

It is often a controversial matter to determine who is an authority. In some cases, of course, there may be no controversy. If a person has received an advanced degree in physics from a major university after years of study, then I will be willing to rely upon his or her exposition of Einstein's theory of relativity. This does not mean that experts are infallible. They occasionally go wrong, and there are matters about which the experts disagree. Therefore, we need to develop a critical attitude toward the claims of experts. In addition, experts can often be bought. Pharmaceutical companies will employ chemists to testify to the reliability of drugs that they wish to market. Defense attorneys hire psychiatrists to testify that their clients are insane. Manufacturers employ engineers and physicians to testify to the safety of their products and their factories. It is an old saying that every man has his price. This should be kept in mind in deciding whether or not to rely upon the judgment of an authority.

Another reason for adopting a critical attitude toward an authority is that a person who claims to provide an authoritative view of some topic may not be an authority at all. There are outright frauds. And there are people who may be authorities in their own fields who use their prestige to influence people on matters about which they have no expertise at all. It is not uncommon, for example, to find movie stars on television talk shows telling people who to vote for and what to think on a whole variety of matters having nothing to do with the film industry. And then there are those who claim to be authorities on topics about which no authoritative pronouncement is possible. Consider the religious leader who tries to influence people by telling them what God really wants them to do. But how can any human being actually know what God really and truly wants? As we saw in Chapter Six, there is a question whether there even is a God. And if there is a God, there are many competing views about his nature and attitudes. People who claim to be experts on what God wants disagree among themselves. Some say, for example, that abortion is murder and others say that there is nothing wrong with it. Some say that you must attend this church to attain salvation and others say that you should go to that one. And when one inquires about the basis of their presumed authority, one is told that one must have faith in the words written in some book or passed on in some tradition. But faith is not knowledge, and a genuine authority or expert is one who knows or at least has a belief that can be shown to be reliable or based upon valid methods of investigation.

When a person claims to be an authority in some field, it is always reasonable and proper to ask for his or her credentials. If someone claims to be able to cure diseases or to be an expert in ancient history, we are entitled to know the basis of this expertise. Where has he or she studied? Under whom? What examinations has he or she passed? What degrees earned? What books written? How is he or she regarded by other experts? There is a kind of coherence test for authority. If other physicians agree with my doctor's diagnosis, my confidence in his or her judgment increases. When authorities agree, this tends to support the judgment of any one of them. But if they disagree, I cannot rely upon them to the same extent. I am then thrown back on my own judgment.

I must find some reason to prefer the views of one of them or, if that is not possible, I must become an expert myself and serve as my own authority. And even where the authorities agree, we must not surrender our critical attitude. Remember that at one time most astronomers believed that the sun revolved around the earth. The agreement of authorities is no guarantee of truth.

Induction and Sampling

INDUCTIVE GENERALIZATION

Our system of beliefs not only includes singular statements about particular objects but also a large variety of generalizations. **Universal generalizations** are statements about all things of a certain kind, such as "All crows are black."

> *. . . general Truths, which are themselves a sort of Elements and Agents, Under-powers, Subordinate helpers of the living mind.*
> from Wordsworth's *Prelude*

Universal generalizations can be formulated in other ways than the pattern "All As are Bs." We can say "Water freezes when the temperature drops below thirty-two degrees Fahrenheit," and "If water is heated above 212 degrees Fahrenheit, then it boils." This last statement is of the conditional or hypothetical form.

In addition to universal generalizations, there are **statistical generalizations** of the form "m/n of the As are Bs." For example, "Nine out of ten swans are white" and "One out of every three voters is a registered Republican." When we do not know the precise fraction of As that are Bs, we use terms that indicate a ratio in a purposefully vague way, such as "Most swans are white," "Some voters are Republicans," and "Many lemons are yellow."

To establish that a generalization is true, we examine instances that fall under it. To establish that water freezes below thirty-two degrees Fahrenheit, we examine instances of water at various temperatures. If in all the instances we have examined, we have observed that water has frozen below thirty-two degrees and in no case has it frozen above thirty-two degrees, we take the generalization to be confirmed. A generalization confirmed by its instances is an **inductive generalization.** The term **induction** is often used to describe the process of confirming a generalization by examining its instances.

A universal generalization is confirmed *to a certain extent* by positive instances. A negative instance falsifies it, that is, it proves conclusively that it is false. Thus, the assertion that all swans are white is definitely refuted by finding one black swan. But, a statistical generalization is not refuted by one negative instance. By finding one or a few black swans, I do not falsify my belief that many swans are white.

In certain cases, a generalization can be verified by examining all the instances that fall under it. This is called *induction by complete enumeration*. For example, if I say to one of my classes that all the students in the room are matriculated at Hunter College, I am in a position to verify this conclusively by examining each and every student in the room. Complete enumeration is possible only where there is a relatively small number of instances and where they are all accessible. In many cases, however, the inductive class is very large, or, even if it is not large, we cannot be sure that we have examined all of them. For example, there are not many eagles left in the United States, but a complete enumeration would be very difficult because we can never be sure that we have observed all that remain. In such cases, we must be content with a partial enumeration, or a *sample*.

A familiar example of taking a sample is a poll. Polls are often used to predict the results of elections. How many voters intend to vote for candidate X in the forthcoming election? In a national or state election, no attempt is made to ask all the voters. Usually a rather small sample is considered to be sufficient provided it is selected in the proper way. There are certain conditions that a sample must satisfy to be reliable. First, it must be of a certain minimum size. A sample of just three voters is insufficient to predict how many will vote for X. Exactly how large the sample should be is a matter of experience to be determined by the outcomes of previous polls. Second, the sample must not be biased. If only Republicans or only Democrats are asked their opinion, the generalization will not be correct. In particular, we know that various characteristics of citizens are relevant in determining their voting habits and political preferences. Not only political party, but age, geographical location, religion, race, and economic class influence how people vote. To be reliable, a sample must be fairly distributed among all the relevant classes of voters. Thus, the ratio of northerners to southerners in a sample for a national election must reflect accurately the ratio of northerners to southerners in the population at large.

The results of an election poll can be directly checked at election time. If we judge that three out of five will vote for X on the basis of our sample, and three out of five do vote for X, then we have a direct confirmation of the validity of the poll. But in most cases, we never achieve this type of confirmation. Thus, we believe that the water molecule contains two atoms of hydrogen and one of oxygen, but no one will examine anything more than a minute fraction of all the water molecules there are. As long as all the water molecules we bother to examine exemplify this structure, we retain confidence in the generalization.

THE INDUCTIVE LEAP

In many cases, therefore, we make judgments about whole classes of objects, many of which have never been and never will be observed or studied. In such cases, there is an *inductive leap*. To understand this leap, consider the difference between an inductive and a deductive inference. Here is a deductive inference:

> All the students in this room are matriculated at Hunter College.
> John Jones is a student in this room.
> Therefore, John Jones is matriculated at Hunter College.

In a deductive inference, if the premises are true, then it is established conclusively that the conclusion is true. But an inductive inference is different:

> This swan is white.
> That swan is white.
> Those swans over there are white.
> Therefore, all swans are white.

Even if the premises are all true, the conclusion is not conclusively established. At best one can say that it is very probable that all swans are white, or that it is confirmed to a certain degree that all swans are white. But it remains logically possible that we will come across a swan that is not white, thus upsetting our conclusion. In a valid deduction, there is no logical gap between the premises and the conclusion. But in induction by partial enumeration, there always remains a gap, and hence certainty cannot be attained.

In induction, then, we employ our past experience of the world to establish generalizations. Often these generalizations deal not only with objects that have existed in the past but with things that will appear in the future. If I have observed only white swans, then I am likely to think that the next swan I observe will also be white.[9] So in induction we use past experience to inform us not only of the general makeup of the inductive class but also of what particular observations we will make in the future. Induction is thus used to predict particular events.

HUME'S SKEPTICISM ABOUT INDUCTION

David Hume raised the question why we are entitled to make this inference from the past to the future:

> As to past *Experience,* it can be allowed to give *direct* and *certain* information of those precise objects only, and that precise period of time, which fell under its cognizance: but why this experience should be extended to future times, and to other objects, which for aught we know, may be only in appearance similar; this is the main question on which I would insist. The bread which I formerly ate, nourished me; that is, a body of such sensible qualities was, at that time, endued with such secret powers: but does it follow, that other bread must also nourish me at another time, and that like sensible qualities must always be attended with like secret powers? The consequence seems nowise necessary.[10]

Because the inference from the past to the future is not deductive, there is no logical connection between statements about what has been observed and statements about unobserved instances in the future. What connects the statements in a way that justifies our inferring the future from the past? Hume thinks that "no one will be ever able to

---

[9]The reader who is becoming weary of swans should note that there are black swans which are native to Australia.
[10]Hume, *Enquiry,* pp. 33–34.

discover any connecting proposition or intermediate step, which supports the understanding in this conclusion."[11]

Perhaps a connection can be established by the following argument. If I infer that the next swan that I observe will be white because all previously observed swans have been white, then I am taking for granted the fact that the future will be like the past. I assume that I am entitled to project into the future the uniformities that I have already discovered. This projection, the argument runs, can be justified as follows. In the past, the future has always turned out to be like the past. All past futures—that is, all times past that were once in the future but have by now become the past—have been observed to resemble the past. So I conclude that the actual future that awaits me will also turn out to resemble the past.

Hume points out that the preceding argument is fallacious because it assumes what has to be proved:

> All our experimental conclusions proceed upon the supposition that the future
> will be conformable to the past. To endeavour, therefore, the proof of this last
> supposition by probable arguments, or arguments regarding existence, must be
> evidently going in a circle, and taking for granted, which is the very point in
> question.[12]

If to make an inference from the past to the future, I need to assume that "the future will be conformable to the past," then my inference from past futures to the future also assumes this. But that "the future will be conformable to the past" is the very thought that I was trying to establish by the inference from past futures to the future. This argument begs the question; it assumes exactly what was to be proved.

At this point, you may be inclined to argue that Hume's skepticism regarding induction is purely academic. After all, we have used induction to establish most of our scientific theories, and we have used these theories for many practical purposes. Using science, we build tall buildings, we create nuclear power plants, we manufacture computers and copying machines, we cure diseases, and so forth. Induction, it may be said, has proved its reliability by its practical value. Yet this pragmatic argument is no better than the preceding argument. For the fact that induction has proved itself to be a practical success is nothing in its favor unless we have a reason to think that it will continue to be a practical success. But the inference from past to future success is itself an inductive inference. So the pragmatic argument also presupposes what it set out to prove.

One might argue that Hume and all other sceptics take induction for granted in their daily life. Hume conceded this point:

> My practice, you say, refutes my doubts. But you mistake the purport of my
> question. As an agent, I am quite satisfied in the point; but as a philosopher, who
> has some share of curiosity, I will not say scepticism, I want to learn the
> foundation of this inference.[13]

[11]Ibid., p. 34.
[12]Ibid., pp. 35–36.
[13]Ibid., p. 38.

It is no good to reply to Hume that what he has shown is merely that induction does not have the same degree of certainty as deduction. For Hume thinks that his argument raises doubts about whether induction provides any probability at all. How does the fact that all the swans that I have ever seen were white make it even probable that the next swan that I see will be white? It is probable only if it is likely that the future will resemble the past. But even to establish the probability that the future will resemble the past, one needs to *assume* that the future will resemble the past. And we have not yet found a way to establish that.

Hume says that it is a characteristic of human nature that when things go together in our experience, we form the expectation that they will continue to go together. My experience of seeing only white swans leads me to form the habit of expecting only white swans in the future. Hume concludes that the basic principle in human nature regulating our inductive inferences is not reason, but habit or custom.

> Custom, then, is the great guide of human life. It is that principle alone which renders our experience useful to us, and makes us expect, for the future, a similar train of events with those which have appeared in the past. Without the influence of custom, we should be entirely ignorant of every matter of fact beyond what is immediately present to the memory and senses. We should never know how to adjust means to ends, or to employ our natural powers in the production of any effect. There would be an end at once of all action, as well as of the chief part of speculation.[14]

According to Hume, the acceptance of induction as a method of fixing our beliefs is not founded upon any rational basis. Induction cannot be justified either by experience or by reason. The pattern of inductive argument cannot be shown to yield either certainty or probability. Nevertheless, the inductive method is built into the structure of the human mind. It is a fundamental characteristic of the mind that it uses past experience to form expectations about the future. Because this characteristic cannot be justified, it is called custom rather than reason.

CAN INDUCTION BE JUSTIFIED?

Some contemporary philosophers have tried to refute Hume's skepticism regarding induction by claiming that it is based upon an incorrect use of such terms as *reasonable* and *rational*. Consider, for example, an inductive generalization based upon a reliable and soundly established sample. In the sample, we find that three out of every five voters intend to vote for candidate X. So we conclude that in the election, X will gather 60 percent of the votes. According to Hume's critics, inductive reasoning of this sort is rational by definition:

> The rationality of induction . . . is not a fact about the constitution of the world.
> It is a matter of what we mean by the word "rational" in its application to any

[14]Ibid., pp. 44–45.

procedure for forming opinions about what lies outside our observations or that of available witnesses. For to have good reasons for any such opinion is to have good inductive support for it.[15]

According to this view, the meaning of the word *rational* is fixed by our practice of applying it to certain methods used to form our beliefs. One of these methods is induction. Induction is therefore rational, given the meaning of this term. To say, as does Hume, that induction is not based upon reason is like saying that a triangle does not have three angles. It has three angles because that is part of what is meant by *triangle*. Induction is rational because that is part of what is meant by *rational*.

This argument against Hume threatens to turn the issue into a verbal battle. Does it all depend upon what we mean by *rational?* We do call inductive inferences based upon reliable samples rational, and we call some other methods of fixing belief such as consulting a fortune-teller, irrational. When we call some methods rational and others irrational, we have in mind some criterion that the first satisfy but that the second do not.

A person is rational to the extent that he chooses means adequate to his ends. For example, if it is very important to you to pass an examination, then it is rational for you to study hard and irrational for you to fritter away your time in frivolous activities. If we think of the methods of forming beliefs as means of achieving certain ends, then a method's suitability for an end can be used as a criterion for separating rational from irrational methods. Now when we believe a statement, what we really believe is that the statement is *true*. Truth is the goal that we hope to achieve by the various methods of fixing belief. The person who consults a fortune-teller hopes that what he is told is true. What is wrong with relying upon a fortune-teller is that in the light of what we know of the world, this method is not likely to result in true belief. If Peter wants to find out whether Jane loves him, he is more likely to obtain the truth by talking to Jane and observing her behavior toward him than by looking into a crystal ball or reading a horoscope.

On this analysis, the challenge of Hume cannot be dismissed by calling it a verbal error about the meaning of the word *rational*. The issue is whether induction satisfies the basic criterion for rational belief. Is induction a procedure that will, in the long run, tend to produce true beliefs about matters of fact? Hume claims that we have no rational assurance, no proof, no good argument that it will. Although philosophers have produced a variety of solutions to the problem that Hume raised, none has won general acceptance. The problem of induction remains a problem.

Theoretical Inference

In our discussion of cognitive methods, we have thus far emphasized those methods that produce beliefs about observable features of the world. It is, however, characteristic of human thinking and of science to try to explain observable phenomena by reference to what is unobservable. The atomic theory of modern physics is one of the prime examples

[15]P. F. Strawson, *Introduction to Logical Theory* (London: Methuen and Co., 1952), pp. 261–262.

of the use of unobservables to make sense of phenomena available to our senses. The theories of science often refer to unobservable entities. **Theoretical inference** is the method of attempting to establish the truth of such theories and the existence of the unobservables to which the theories refer.

Consider a common phenomenon such as the evaporation of water. After it rains, for example, the puddles of water formed in the streets soon disappear. How can this disappearance be explained? Among superstitious peoples, it might be thought to be a kind of magic. But according to the atomic theory of modern science, the water is composed of very small particles—molecules—themselves composed of smaller particles—atoms. Each water molecule consists of two atoms of hydrogen and one of oxygen. It is thought that the molecules are in continuous motion and are knocking against one another. Occasionally a water molecule that lies on the surface of the puddle will be knocked away, and then another and another. Finally, they will all have been knocked away and the water will have disappeared. We say that it has evaporated.

This example illustrates the process of theoretical inference in a very simple way. We start with something observable that we wish to understand. In some cases, the event to be explained can be understood by reference to other observable events. For example, we can explain the breaking of Mr. Smith's window by pointing out that Peter threw a brick at it. But nothing we can actually see accounts for the evaporation of the water. So we try to imagine what the water is made of. If it is made of moving particles that are being continuously knocked about and occasionally even knocked away, we can predict that evaporation will occur. We ask whether the event to be explained would occur if the theory were true. If the answer is "yes," then the theory is confirmed to some extent. If the answer is "no," then it is disconfirmed.

It would be perfectly arbitrary to suppose that only water is made up of unseen particles and perfectly natural to suppose that other substances, perhaps all substances, are made of atoms and of their molecular combinations. But the fact that an atomic theory of matter can account for the evaporation of water is not itself a sufficient reason for accepting it. A theory as broad and sweeping as the atomic theory becomes acceptable only if it can explain a wide variety of phenomena. The atomic theory of matter has in fact been proved to have great explanatory power. As developed in modern science, it explains such things as the difference between solids, liquids, and gases. It is the basis of our understanding of chemical combinations. It is used to account for radiation, heat, light, energy, sense perception, and countless other phenomena. The theoretical inference that serves to confirm the atomic theory of matter is a complex intellectual activity extending over a period of time during which the theory proves its worth by being used to explain numerous processes occurring in nature.

Another well-known example of the occurrence of unobservables in a scientific theory is Freud's hypothesis of unconscious mental processes and states.[16] Freud's theory of the unconscious can be summarized as the claim that many phenomena in mental life and

---

[16]The Freudian theory is much more controversial among psychologists than is the atomic theory among scientists. The discussion of theoretical inference does not assume that the theories taken as examples are true or are the last word on the topic.

human behavior can be understood on the hypothesis that human beings have goals and intentions and purposes of which they are unaware. Take a common phenomenon like a slip of the tongue. An example given by Freud is the case of a person who, in declaring a session of Parliament to be open, says, "Gentlemen: I take notice that a full quorum of members is present and herewith declare the sitting *closed!*"[17] Freud believes that many such slips are caused by unconscious desires.[18] The person calling the meeting to order evidently desired that it never take place. According to Freud, his slip was caused by this desire. Of slips of the tongue in general, Freud writes,

> I almost invariably discover a disturbing influence . . . which comes from something *outside* the intended utterance; and the disturbing element is either a single thought that has remained unconscious, which manifests itself in the slip of the tongue and which can often be brought to consciousness only by means of searching analysis, or it is a more general psychical motive force which is directed against the entire utterance.[19]

Slips of the tongue are examples of a wide variety of phenomena that appear to be accidental but that are, according to Freud, purposive and intentional. Other examples discussed by Freud in *The Psychopathology of Everyday Life* are the forgetting of names and other words, misreadings and slips of the pen, bungled actions, and superstition. In all these examples, Freud finds a meaning that is deeper than can be found if we confine our attention to what the agent is aware of. We must, he argues, postulate that a part of the mind is unobservable even by the person whose mind it is.

The theory of the unconscious would not have achieved the standing it presently has if it were limited to explaining everyday errors and mistakes. Freud developed his theory further, giving it great explanatory power. He felt that such major aspects of human life as dreams, character formation, neurotic behavior, sexuality, ethics, wit, art, and religion can be explained by his theory. As he extended the theory to more and more phenomena, he felt that it achieved greater confirmation.

The feature that gives the atomic theory and the theory of the unconscious such great explanatory power is that they are able to explain much more than just those phenomena they were originally designed to explain. They give our system of knowledge unity and coherence by bringing together a large number of diverse and puzzling phenomena under a single system of explanation. Through theoretical inference, an enormous variety of observable phenomena can be shown to be the outcome of a relatively small number of laws, forces, and events. Observation displays the variety of nature; theory shows the unity underlying the variety.

---

[17]Sigmund Freud, *The Psychopathology of Everyday Life,* trans. Alan Tyson (New York: Norton, 1965), p. 59.

[18]When I first typed this page, the word *slips* came out as *slops.* Could this have been an expression of my unconscious feelings about Freud's theory?

[19]Freud, *Psychopathology,* p. 61.

> **SOURCES OF HUMAN KNOWLEDGE**
>
> Observation
>   Sense perception
>   Introspection
> Memory
> Testimony and authority
> Induction
> Theoretical inference

Problems with Empiricism

Our survey of the sources of human knowledge has revealed that our beliefs are not merely reproductions of materials given to the senses. It has also revealed to us new grounds for skepticism. Judgments based upon observation make use of preexistent knowledge and are liable to error. The use of memory increases the possibility of error. When we add the beliefs of others to our system of beliefs through testimony, all the errors that others have made are transmitted to us. Induction extends our beliefs into the distant past and the remote future and is thus vulnerable to the skepticism so well stated by Hume. Theoretical inference carries us even further away from observable phenomena. Each step of the way, what we claim to know extends far beyond what is given in sense awareness and introspection.

PROBLEMS OF THEORY SELECTION

Another important point needs to be mentioned. Let us suppose that there are several theories that explain the same facts. In trying to choose among them, it turns out that observation does not always determine which theory is the most acceptable. This may be illustrated by the following example. Suppose you are performing a laboratory experiment in which you are trying to ascertain the relationship between two characteristics of some substance. Call these characteristics C and D. The method you adopt is to change C and observe how D changes as a consequence. You discover that you always have twice as many units of D as of C. You then record the results of your experiment as follows:

Units of C	Units of D
1	2
2	4
3	6
4	8

This chart shows that in the four cases in which you have compared C and D, you have found twice as much D as C. Using the method of induction, you are likely to conclude that all occurrences of C are accompanied by twice as many units of D. This can be represented in the equation $D = 2C$. It is common to plot the results of an experiment on a graph. In constructing the graph, each of the points represents one of the four observations that you have made:

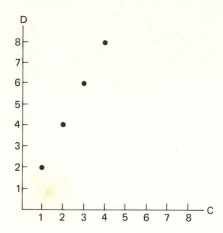

The next step in constructing the graph is to connect the four points with a straight line:

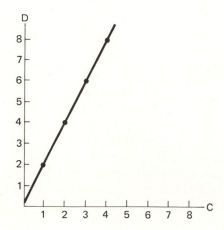

One may ask why you used a straight line rather than a line like this:

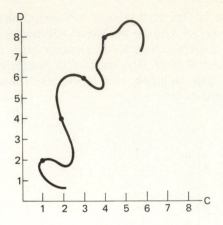

Or one like this:

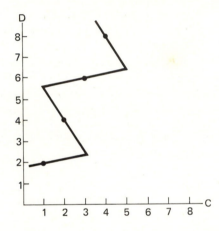

The straight line seems natural and right whereas the other lines seem artificial and absurd. But what makes the straight line correct? Each of the three lines represents a different inductive generalization. Each is compatible with the four observations you have made because each goes through the four points. Remember that between the four points, or between any finite number of points for that matter, it is mathematically possible to draw an infinite number of lines that connect all the points. This means that there is an infinite number of inductive generalizations compatible with the four observations. Why is the generalization represented by the straight line to be preferred to all the others? You might be inclined to reply that you can test your choice of a straight line by conducting a further experiment. Suppose you find that 5 units of C produce 10 units of D. Doesn't that prove that the straight line is correct and that the others are mistaken? The answer is that although this result does establish that the other two lines are mistaken, it does not prove that the straight line is correct. After all, you now have a graph with five points on it, and there are an infinite number of lines connecting all five points. So you are still left with an infinite number of inductive generalizations that fit your data.

A common explanation of why the straight line is chosen is that it is the simplest of the lines, the simplest both mathematically and aesthetically. In general, to specify which theory is acceptable, it is not sufficient to select one that fits all the data because too many fit all the data. One also needs a *rule of simplicity* that says that of all the theories that fit, the simplest one should be selected.[20]

On the basis of this discussion, the claim made by traditional empiricism that all our statements about matters of fact are based upon observation becomes implausible. Even if observation is required to provide the data used in selecting theories, more than observation is required to yield a unique selection. Moreover, it is difficult to maintain any strong version of the verifiability criterion of cognitive significance. According to that criterion, the meaning of a scientific theory is determined by its observational consequences. Take all the observational data that serve to confirm or to disconfirm a theory. The meaning of the theory is supposed to be completely given by the data. But because theories go way beyond the data and because observation is not sufficient to determine what theories are acceptable, our theories have an excess of meaning that is not reducible to experience.

A weaker version of empiricism says that for a statement to be meaningful, observation must be relevant to confirming or disconfirming it. Although observation is not sufficient to select the equation $D = 2C$, it is relevant to it. To be acceptable, a theory must be compatible with all the data. But this weak version of empiricism does not conflict with that part of the rationalist tradition that emphasizes the role of nonobservational factors in theory construction. If empiricism says merely that observation counts in verifying theories, then it is consistent with the claim of rationalism that more than observation is required.

PRAGMATISM

An idea that some empiricists have adopted to avoid these unwelcome results is that theories that go beyond the observational data are not to be understood as assertions about what the world is really like but rather as instruments designed to achieve certain of our ends. According to this *instrumentalist* or *pragmatic* account of science, the purpose of the scientific endeavor is to enable us to predict the future and to control natural processes for the purpose of enhancing satisfaction. The importance of science lies in the technology that it produces. Theories are merely devices enabling us to predict and to control the course of natural events.[21]

Instrumentalism is certainly correct in its claims that the theories of science are used

---

[20]The rule of simplicity is often called Occam's Razor after the fourteenth-century philosopher William of Occam, who formulated a version of it.

[21]The American pragmatists—William James, Charles Peirce, and John Dewey—have been responsible for developing a conception of knowledge that supports this instrumentalist view of science.

to predict and to control nature and that they are the basis of our recent technological advances. That theories are used as instruments of prediction and control does not, however, prove that they are not also statements of matters of fact. If it is now daytime, then from the statement of fact that night follows day, I can predict that it will soon be night.

Another difficulty with instrumentalism is that its claims are difficult to reconcile with the way that scientists understand their theories. When Newton describes his atomic theory of matter, for example, it sounds as if he is trying to tell us what the world is really like:

> God in the Beginning form'd Matter in solid, massy, hard, impenetrable, moveable Particles, of such Sizes and Figures, and with such other Properties, and in such Proportion to Space, as most conduced to the End for which he form'd them; and . . . these primitive Particles being Solids, are incomparably harder than any porous Bodies compounded of them; even so very hard, as never to wear or break in pieces; no ordinary power being able to divide what God himself made one in the first Creation. While the particles continue entire, they may compose Bodies of one and the same Nature and Texture in all Ages: But should they wear away, or break in pieces, the Nature of Things depending on them, would be changed. Water and Earth, composed of old worn Particles and Fragments of Particles, would not be of the same Nature and Texture now, with Water and Earth composed of entire Particles in the Beginning. And therefore, that Nature may be lasting, the changes of corporeal Things are to be placed only in the various Separations and new Associations and Motion of these permanent Particles.[22]

The intention of most scientific writing is to provide a description of the world or of some portion of it to gain an understanding of natural phenomena. It is this understanding that is the goal of scientific inquiry. Prediction is just a way that scientists have to test whether their understanding is correct. According to this *realist* account of science, one should not confuse science with technology. Technology uses the theories of pure science to create products that satisfy human purposes. But pure science exists to satisfy our curiosity about the nature of things. If one accepts **scientific realism,** it is difficult to maintain at the same time the severe version of empiricism embodied in the verifiability theory of meaning.

The Problem of Truth

The concept of truth has played an important role in both this chapter and the preceding one. It is now appropriate to ask, "What is truth?". This question, however, is ambiguous. It may be interpreted as a request to determine what particular things are true: Does God exist? Are there unconscious mental events? Is the atomic theory of matter true? This is not the interpretation that shall occupy our attention for the remainder of

---

[22]Sir Isaac Newton, *Opticks* (New York: Dover, 1952), p. 400.

this chapter. Rather, the question is interpreted as follows: What do we mean when we say that some statement is true? What does truth consist of? How can truth generally be defined? This question should not be confused with the related question of verification: How do we find out what is true? Although there is a close association between truth and verification, they are not the same. Verification presupposes the concept of truth. In verifying a statement, we try to find out whether or not it is true. But truth does not presuppose the concept of verification. There are truths that have not yet been and perhaps never will be verified.

TRUTH AND CORRESPONDENCE

According to the **correspondence theory of truth,** to say that a statement is true means that it corresponds with the facts. If the statement that the cat is on the mat is true, then there exists a fact—the cat's being on the mat—to which it corresponds. If it is false, then there is no such fact. Statements imply or presuppose the existence of facts. The statement that the cat is on the mat implies or asserts that there exists the fact of the cat's being on the mat. It is because it implies this fact that its truth consists in its correspondence to this fact.

According to some versions of the correspondence theory, the relation of correspondence is understood as a kind of picturing.[23] Statements are like pictures of facts. Just as the fact that the cat is on the mat consists of three items—the cat, the mat, and the relation *on*—so the sentence "The cat is on the mat" contains terms that refer to each of these three items, namely *the cat, the mat,* and *on.* In the fact that the cat is on the mat, the three items fit together in a particular way. They so fit together that it is the cat that is on the mat rather than the mat's being on the cat. In the sentence, the three terms are so arranged as to represent the way the items in the fact are arranged. In other versions of the theory, correspondence is understood more simply: A statement corresponds to a fact just in case there exists the fact that the statement says exists.

There are various difficulties with the correspondence theory. The most serious problem is that, according to many of its critics, it has unacceptable ontological or metaphysical implications. **Ontology** and **metaphysics** are terms that are used to refer to that part of philosophy which tries to answer the question: What exists? In other words, what kinds of being are there in the world? The ontological implications of a theory are those of its implications, which assert the existence of various kinds of things. For example, the statement that the cat is on the mat implies or presupposes the existence of the cat and the mat. Thus, the existence of the cat and the mat are among its ontological implications. The basic ontological implication of the correspondence theory of truth is the existence of facts. For, according to the theory, to say that a statement is true implies that there exists a fact to which it corresponds. Many critics have claimed that it is unreasonable to think that in addition to things such as the cat and the mat, there are facts such as the fact of the cat's being on the mat. There is a metaphysical theory called **nominalism** according to which the only items that exist are concrete particular

---

[23]The idea that statements picture facts was developed by Ludwig Wittgenstein in his *Tractatus Logico-Philosophicus,* trans. D. F. Pears and B. F. McGuinness (London: Routledge and Kegan Paul, 1963).

individuals—*particulars* for short—such as the cat and the mat. There are no entities such as facts. These critics would prefer a theory of truth that does not imply the existence of anything except particulars.

Another criticism focuses upon the ontological implications of certain types of statements. Even if there is a fact to which the statement that the cat is on the mat corresponds, what about the statement that the cat is *not* on the mat? Is there a fact of the cat's not being on the mat? If so, what item in the fact does the word *not* refer to? Is there really something in the world referred to by *not*? These questions indicate skepticism about the existence of negative facts. And what about general statements such as "All crows are black"? Are there general facts in addition to such singular facts as the cat's being on the mat? Does there exist the fact of all crows being black? Once we admit such rather noncontroversial facts as the fact that the cat is on the mat, there seems to be no way to prevent the introduction of such metaphysical oddities as negative and general facts.

A further criticism of the correspondence theory is founded upon an additional feature that facts are alleged to have. In the statement "The cat is green," the term *green* is interpreted by the advocates of facts as referring to one constituent of the fact and the term *the cat* is interpreted as referring to another. The fact consists of two constituents: the cat and the color green. But what ties the two constituents together into one fact? After all, other things than this cat are green. And this cat has properties other than its being green. How is the cat related to its color in such a way that it succeeds in being green? The advocates of facts have usually answered this question by saying that there is a special relation that ties various items together to form a fact. In the sentence "The cat is green," the word *is* is interpreted as naming this special relation. It has been called by various names. Plato (427–347 B.C.) called it participation. In contemporary philosophy it has often been called predication or exemplification. Critics point out that a theory calling for the existence of facts becomes committed to the existence of such unusual relations as predication. Thus, in addition to such ordinary relations as *on, under, above, below, before, after, father, mother,* and so forth, other more unusual relations are required by the correspondence theory.

We can sum up these criticisms of the correspondence theory of truth by saying that the theory requires an unnecessarily complex and implausible ontology. Of course, for the nominalist to substantiate his case, he must present an alternative theory of truth that is committed to the existence of particulars only.

TRUTH AND CONSEQUENCES

Another definition of truth, developed by the American *pragmatists,* is that a statement or an idea is true provided that it is successful. People adopt ideas to find their way successfully in the world. Those ideas are true that have successful consequences. Those are false that fail to solve the problems for which they were adopted. Because ideas are instruments for dealing with the world, those ideas are true that have good consequences and those are false whose consequences are bad. According to the **pragmatic theory of truth,** an idea is true or agrees with reality just to the extent that it is successful.

William James (1842–1910) explains the pragmatic concept of truth as follows:

> The essential thing [for truth] is the process of being guided. Any idea that helps us to *deal,* whether practically or intellectually, with either the reality or its belongings, that doesn't entangle our progress in frustrations, that *fits,* in fact, and adapts our life to the reality's whole setting, will agree sufficiently to meet the requirement. It will hold true of that reality.[24]

An initial problem with James's approach is that an idea that may have good consequences in a person's life or be useful in some way may also turn out to be false. Suppose, for example, that John Jones is willing to undertake a difficult project for his employer because he thinks that when he completes it he will be promoted. But when he is finished, to his disappointment, he is not promoted after all. His belief was completely false. Yet it was useful, at least to his employer, because it spurred Jones on to do his best. The true and the useful are not exactly the same.

James's reply stresses the long-term consequences of our ideas:

> *"The true," to put it very briefly, is only the expedient in the way of our thinking, just as "the right" is only the expedient in the way of our behaving.* Expedient in almost any fashion; and expedient in the long run and on the whole of course; for what meets expediently all the experience in sight won't necessarily meet all farther experiences equally satisfactorily. Experience, as we know, has ways of *boiling over,* and making us correct our present formulas. The "absolutely" true, meaning what no farther experience will ever alter, is that ideal vanishing-point towards which we imagine that all our temporary truths will some day converge.[25]

An idea is true provided it works well in the long run. If it should work well forever, then it would be absolutely or unconditionally true.

There is, however, an ambiguity in James's presentation that he fails to clear up satisfactorily. An idea can have good consequences in two distinct ways. In one, if a person accepts an idea and uses it to guide his actions, then what he does may have good consequences for himself and for others. These *personal consequences* are the results of the actions he chooses because of his acceptance of the idea. It is difficult to imagine that truth consists in the goodness of an idea's personal consequences or of its *personal utility.* If a person leads a satisfied life because of his religious faith, that does not prove his faith to be true. People with different and incompatible faiths may be happy. But if their faiths are incompatible, they cannot all be true. Moreover, ideas can have personal utility for reasons other than their being true. John Jones's belief that he would be promoted provided him with an incentive for action. That is why it had utility. But it was not true.

---

[24]William James, *Pragmatism: A New Name for Some Old Ways of Thinking* (New York: Longman, Green, and Co., 1949), p. 213.
[25]Ibid., pp. 222–223.

In addition to personal consequences, an idea can have *logical consequences* or *logical utility*. Given some idea or statement or theory, I can develop its logical implications. Thus, from the atomic theory of matter, I can predict which elements will combine with each other; I can predict that under certain conditions water will evaporate; and so on. If these logical consequences are confirmed in human experience, then the idea has logical utility; it is confirmed or verified by observation. In abstract terms, if a theory T implies an observation statement 0, and if we find that 0 is true by observation, then T is confirmed or partially verified. In the words of another pragmatist, John Dewey (1859–1952), T is a warranted assertion. Now if T is continuously confirmed in this way, and if no observation conflicts with it, then we are justified in accepting it as true. Thus, an idea's logical utility can be a reason for accepting it as true.

We are not, however, entitled to identify truth with logical utility or verification. First, an idea that is verified by many observations may in the end turn out to be false. We may make an observation that conflicts with it. Second, verification is relative to persons and times: An idea is verified by a particular person or persons at a particular time or times. But truth does not imply any such relation to persons and times. An idea might be true even if no one ever has or ever will think of it. So truth does not consist in verification. And finally, the idea that truth consists in logical utility means that the idea is true provided we can observe that its logical consequences *are true*. But what does it mean to say that its logical consequences are true? That an observation statement is true does not mean that it has been verified by its logical consequences, for it is tested by a direct comparison with the facts. Thus, on neither interpretation is James's pragmatic theory plausible.

TRUTH AND COHERENCE

Another alternative to the correspondence theory of truth is the **coherence theory.** It was developed by a group of philosophers who were influenced by the German philosopher G. W. F. Hegel (1770–1831). The clearest exposition of the coherence theory is to be found in the writings of the American philosopher Brand Blanshard.[26] Blanshard's argument contains two major steps. In the first step, he argues that the basic test of whether a theory or idea or belief is true is whether it is coherent. In the second step, he concludes that if coherence gives us the test of truth, then it also gives us the nature of truth.

Before I explain this argument further, let me say a word about the meaning of coherence. To say that one idea A coheres with another idea B means roughly that A tends to support or to confirm or to justify B, or at minimum that A does not contradict B. Because there are many ways in which ideas may support one another, the term *coherence* stands for a variety of logical relationships. For example, if A logically implies B so that B is deducible from A, then if A is true, B must be true. In that case, A provides the strongest sort of support for B. For example, that all swans have hearts and that this bird before me now is a swan implies that this bird has a heart. This is a case in

[26]Brand Blanshard, *The Nature of Thought* (London: George Allen and Unwin, 1939), vol. II, chaps. 25–27.

which the premises conclusively prove the truth of what they logically imply, provided of course that they themselves are true. For Blanshard, the ideal of coherence is a system of beliefs all of whose elements are deducible from one another. But in practice, Blanshard concedes, we are willing to accept far less than this; we settle for types of support weaker than deduction.[27] An example of a weaker type of support is induction, which we have already discussed. In induction, particular instances are used to confirm a generalization; we infer, for instance, that all crows are black from our observation of just a few crows.

In the first step of his argument, Blanshard states that the test of truth is coherence. This means that whenever we are justified in accepting an idea as true, our justification consists in its being supported or confirmed in some way by other ideas. Blanshard is correct in those cases in which an idea is accepted on the basis of evidence or argument. For in such cases, the evidence or argument consists of other ideas that provide justificatory support. But what about the case where we test a truth by observation, where we just see that something is true? Is it not implausible to say that perceptual judgments are tested by their coherence with other judgments? Are they not tested directly by observing their correspondence with facts? Blanshard denies that they are.

> Now, plausible as this argument is, it goes to pieces on inspection. It assumes that, corresponding to our judgment, there is some solid chunk of fact, directly presented to sense and beyond all question, to which thought must adjust itself. And this "solid fact" is a fiction. What the theory takes as fact and actually uses as such is another judgment or set of judgments, and what provides the verification is the coherence between the initial judgment and these.[28]

According to Blanshard, it is wrong to interpret sense perception as a process in which a fact is given to us by the senses. Perception is best understood as a process of interpretation prompted by sense experience. Thus, there are no brute, given facts. Any perceptual judgment may be mistaken. And if a perceptual judgment fails to fit into our system of beliefs, we are prepared to reject it as an illusion. Blanshard draws the conclusion that coherence and not correspondence is the test of truth.

The second stage of the argument tries to show that if we accept coherence as the test of truth, we must also accept it as giving us the nature or definition of truth. For suppose we accept correspondence as giving us the nature of truth but agree with Blanshard that we test all truth by reference to coherence. Blanshard argues that in that case we would never have any reason to believe that any statement is true. We would be forced into skepticism. For how can we be assured that any of our ideas corresponds to a reality beyond our ideas—as the correspondence theory claims—if, when we test for their truth, we remain confined within our ideas? If ideas are always verified by reference to other ideas and judgments, then there is no assurance at all that any idea corresponds with fact. Therefore, we have no choice but to consider coherence as giving us the nature of truth.[29]

[27]Ibid., pp. 264–266.
[28]Ibid., p. 228.
[29]Ibid., pp. 261–269.

The major achievement of the coherence theory of truth has been to bring to our attention the importance of the interrelationships of ideas in our accepting or rejecting beliefs. If a new idea is proposed to me, one of the first things I must do is to determine how well it fits in with the structure of my existing beliefs. If it coheres with my beliefs, I have reason to accept it. If it conflicts with them, then it is less acceptable. Even in the case of conflict, I may still accept the new idea, provided I reject the old ideas that contradict it. The coherence theory is correct when it points out that the process of verification involves the adjusting and readjusting of our system of beliefs to meet challenges posed by new theories and claims. Thus, the coherence theory reveals a major difficulty with strong forms of empiricism. For empiricism has usually emphasized that stage of verification in which our ideas are compared directly with experienced items. The coherence theory provides a corrective to the one-sidedness of empiricism by pointing out that observation itself must meet the test of coherence.

The coherence theory has a most important point to make about the trust that we place in our senses. If we were to ask why we trust our senses to the extent that we do, part of the reason that we would give is that our theories about the nature of sense perception provide some basis for its reliability. We think of sense perception as the result of the impact of various forms of energy upon our sense organs. This energy is emitted by objects in the world that exist independently of sense awareness. Using this understanding of the place of sense perception in nature, we can make some estimate of its reliability. In the discussion of primary and secondary qualities in Chapter Seven, we saw that scientific theory may itself lead to new judgments about perception's reliability. So we not only use perception to test our theories, we use our theories to evaluate perception. There is an interplay between theory and observation that is better explained by the coherence theory of verification than by traditional empiricism.

In the end, however, Blanshard's defense of the coherence theory fails. The reason that it fails is that it goes too far in reducing the role of observation. To understand this, consider how Blanshard deals with the perceptual judgment, "That bird is a cardinal."

> Consider the cardinal. This is supposed to be fact, unadulterated brute fact, given directly to our senses and providing a solid reality to which our thought is to correspond. But no bird is a mere sense datum, or even a collection of sense data. . . . To recognize a cardinal is a considerable intellectual achievement, for to do it one must grasp, implicitly but none the less really, the *concept* of cardinal, and this can only be done by a leap far out of the given into ideal classification. . . . The idea of living organisms, the thought of the bird kingdom and its outstanding characteristics, the notion of flight and a peculiar song and a determinate color—these and many other notions are so bound up with the identification that our thought would lose its character with the removal of any one of them. . . . And these essential elements, at least at the time and for the most part, are not given in sense at all.[30]

[30]Ibid., pp. 228–229.

In this passage, Blanshard quite rightly emphasizes the importance of our preexisting knowledge in the making of a perceptual judgment. To see a bird as a cardinal, it is necessary to employ a large amount of conceptual knowledge and perhaps some factual knowledge as well. We use our established ideas and beliefs to arrive at the new belief that it is a cardinal that I see.

Yet the coherence theory does not maintain merely that we use our preexisting beliefs and ideas to verify the new idea. It also maintains that that is *all* that we use. We are confined within our ideas, and we can never break free of them to an independent reality. The difficulty with this view is that the preexisting ideas and beliefs to which we are confined are not sufficient to justify our accepting that that bird is a cardinal. Merely knowing what a bird is, what a cardinal is, that there are cardinals in the neighborhood, that many birds are cardinals, and so forth does not provide support that that bird over there is a cardinal. My sense awareness of the cardinal is just as important as my preexisting beliefs in supporting my perceptual judgment. It is through sense awareness that we break out of our ideas and come into contact with the natural world. In fact, it is one of our ideas that there is a world independent of our ideas. Thus, our belief system itself demands that we find a way of achieving contact with that independent world. According to our belief system, sense awareness provides that contact. Without sense awareness, our system of ideas would be "hanging upon air." We would be unable to distinguish a valid system of beliefs from the ravings of a lunatic.

Another way of making this point is to realize that one idea is able to support another only if the first is itself worthy of belief. A statement A can be a reason for my accepting another statement B only if I have a reason for accepting A. But what can be my reason for accepting A? Perhaps it is still another statement C. But what can justify C? For each belief we can ask for its justification. If each of our beliefs was justified by another belief on the condition that it was justified by another belief, and so on ad infinitum, then none of them would be justified. Sooner or later we must come upon beliefs that are justified through our contact with the world. Justification must come to an end sooner or later. It is sense awareness that provides that contact according to our own conception of the mind's place in nature.

Thus, our perceptual judgments are justified because they arise out of sense awareness. And it is by relations of support to our perceptual judgments that our other beliefs about matters of fact become worthy of acceptance. Despite its deficiencies, empiricism is correct in emphasizing that sense experience is indispensable for human knowledge. But the coherence theory also has an important point to make. Traditional empiricism claims that as a method of verification, observation is independent of theory—that regarding different and competing theories about the world, it is neutral. Yet in supporting empiricism's claim that sense awareness is central to our acquiring knowledge, I have argued that according to *our existing theory of the world,* there is a world independent of our beliefs that is revealed in sense awareness. So the centrality of sense perception is itself an idea that belongs to our existing belief system, and our reliance upon observation is necessary if we are to form our beliefs in the manner required by what we already believe about the world.

TRUTH AND MEANING

None of the three classical theories of truth has been able to withstand criticism; each has a major flaw. Although the correspondence theory is intuitively plausible, it leads to a problematic ontology. The pragmatic theory confuses truth with utility. The coherence theory fails to provide an adequate account of the role of observation and sense awareness. There is another approach to the problem of truth developed in recent logical research. Its founder, Alfred Tarski, calls it the **semantic conception of truth.**[31]

The semantic conception has two aspects that contribute to the resolution of our problem about the nature of truth. First, consider the following pair of statements:

> *(a)* The cat is green.
> *(b)* "The cat is green" is true.

Tarski noticed that (a) and (b), as well as any pair of statements like (a) and (b), imply each other. If the cat is green, then "The cat is green" is true. And if "The cat is green" is true, then the cat is green. This relationship between (a) and (b) is summed up by:

> *(c)* "The cat is green" is true if and only if the cat is green.

Statements that imply each other, as do (a) and (b), are *logically equivalent*. Statements that are logically equivalent, it is argued, say the same thing. So (b) says the same thing as (a).

It appears, then, that in many of its uses, the concept of truth is not even needed. I never need to say of some given statement that it is true. For example, I never need to say of "The cat is green" that it is true. If I want to say that, all that I need to say is that the cat is green. I do not need to use the concept of truth. When we have two ways of saying the same thing, and one way enables us to do without a given word, then in a sense we have defined that word. Because (a) and (b) say the same thing, then (a) gives the meaning of (b). Consider now all the pairs of sentences in English like (a) and (b). The first member of each pair is an indicative sentence. The second member is a sentence that says that the first member is true. The second member could always be replaced by the first wherever it occurs. Thus, speakers of English seldom or never need to use the term *true*. All those pairs of sentences taken together provide a definition of the word *true*.

This approach avoids the problems of the three classical conceptions of truth. Unlike the correspondence theory, it is ontologically neutral. It does not imply or assert the existence of facts. But it does seem to capture what is plausible in the correspondence theory: the idea that a statement is true if what it says about the world is so. Thus, the statement "The cat is green" is true provided that what it says is so, that is, provided that the cat is green. And unlike both the pragmatic and coherence theories, the seman-

---

[31]A nontechnical presentation of this theory is provided by Tarski in "The Semantic Conception of Truth" in *Readings in Philosophical Analysis,* eds. Herbert Feigl and Wilfrid Sellars (New York: Appleton-Century-Crofts, 1949).

tic conception does not depend upon any particular account of verification, of how we find out that a given statement is true.

One may, nevertheless, feel dissatisfied. One may feel that something important is left out that is required for an adequate understanding of truth. After all, the statements uttered by human beings are distinct from the items in the world that they are used to describe. Language is one thing; the world is another. We use language to talk about the world. Saying what is true is different from saying what is false. This suggests that true statements have a different relationship to the world than do false statements. If the cat is indeed green, then the sentence "The cat is green" must be differently related to the world than if it were not green. A theory of truth should capture and explain these differences.

This brings us to the second aspect of the semantic conception of truth. It is the idea that the relations of words to the world must be studied if we are to understand how statements that are built up in various ways out of words and out of simpler statements can be true or false. The conditions under which statements of various types are true or false are called *truth conditions*. That branch of logic that studies the truth conditions of statements is called *semantics,* or *the theory of meaning.* By studying the truth conditions of various statements, we come to understand in a piecemeal fashion how words are related to the world and how true statements differ from false ones.

For example, "The cat is green" is composed of four words. This statement is true provided that the item that is denoted by the phrase *the cat* belongs to the class of items to which the word *green* applies. One way that a word or phrase can be related to the world is *denotation;* a word or phrase can denote, or name, a particular object. Another relation is that of *application.* A word can apply to, or be true of, a given set of objects. So *green* is true of all green objects just as *red* is true of all red objects.

Now consider the simple sentences "The cat is green" and "The cat is on the mat." Using them, we can form various compound sentences such as "The cat is green *and* the cat is on the mat," "The cat is green *or* the cat is on the mat," and "*If* the cat is green, *then* the cat is on the mat." Semantics provides an account of the truth conditions of compound sentences. For example, "The cat is green and the cat is on the mat," is true provided both components are true. "The cat is green or the cat is on the mat," is true provided at least one of the components is true. The presentation of semantics can become quite a technical affair, so it will not be pursued here any further. The point is that whereas the classical theories of truth try to provide a broad and sweeping formula intended to apply to all cases, the semantic conception sees its task as understanding

---

THEORIES OF TRUTH

Correspondence theory: Truth is what corresponds to the facts.
Pragmatic theory: Truth is what works, what is useful.
Coherence theory: Truth is what fits in logically with established belief.
Semantic conception of truth: Truth is explained by reference to the truth conditions of statements.

how words relate to the world in a step-by-step fashion using concepts that can be clearly explained and that can be applied to a wide variety of sentences. The semantic conception shifts the emphasis from truth in some overall sense to the truth conditions of linguistic expressions.

Summary

Rationalism and empiricism are the major traditions in the theory of knowledge. The debate between them involves two main issues. In early modern philosophy, the main issue was that of the origin of ideas. Rationalists claimed that many of our most important ideas are innate, whereas empiricists asserted that all ideas come from experience. After Kant, the issue became one of showing how our beliefs and theories can be justified. Empiricists claimed that the justification of all statements about matters of fact is founded upon experience, whereas rationalists asserted that some knowledge of matters of fact is a priori and based upon reason. The logical positivists were radical empiricists who developed a verifiability theory of cognitive signficance according to which statements that cannot be verified through observation are meaningless.

There are various methods of fixing our beliefs: sense perception, memory, testimony, induction, and theoretical inference. Traditional empiricism fails to give an adequate account of the fact that in all these methods, we go beyond the observed data; there is no clear line between theory and observation. The rationalists are thus correct in thinking that nonobservational factors such as simplicity and coherence are relevant in fixing our beliefs.

The three classical accounts of truth—the correspondence, coherence, and pragmatic theories—are all subject to serious difficulties. The correspondence theory has dubious ontological implications. The difficulty with the pragmatic account is that a successful idea can nevertheless be false. The coherence theory fails because, if we cannot base our ideas upon an independent source of justification, then none of our ideas is credible. A more plausible approach is provided by the semantic conception of truth according to which truth is explained by elucidating the truth conditions of statements.

Glossary

A posteriori knowledge: See **Empirical knowledge.**

A priori knowledge: Knowledge based upon the mere operation of thought; knowledge that is independent of sense experience.

Cognitive meaning: A statement has cognitive meaning if it is capable of expressing factual knowledge, that is, if it is capable of being either true or false.

Coherence theory of truth: The view that a statement is true to the extent that it is supported by our beliefs and theories.

Conceptual knowledge: Having an idea of something or knowing what something is, for instance, knowing what an elephant or a triangle is.

Correspondence theory of truth: The claim that a statement is true if it corresponds to the facts.

Descriptive word: A word such as *blue* or *triangle* or *elephant* that is used to describe or classify some object.

Emotive meaning: A sentence has emotive meaning to the extent that it is capable of expressing the speaker's feelings or emotions or attitudes.

Empirical knowledge: Knowledge that is based upon observation or experience.

Empiricism: The theory that all factual knowledge is founded upon observation or sense experience.

Induction: A method of verifying general statements by observing particular instances that fall under them.

Inductive generalization: A general statement arrived at by induction.

Metaphysics: The branch of philosophy that discusses the types of things that exist or that have some kind of reality.

Nominalism: A metaphysical theory that says that only particulars exist.

Observation statement: A statement that records what someone sees, hears, or otherwise observes.

Ontology: See **Metaphysics.**

Ostensive definition: An explanation of the meaning of a word by pointing to something to which the word applies.

Pragmatic theory of truth: The view that a statement is true if it is useful in helping individuals attain their goals.

Rationalism: The claim that some human knowledge is based upon reason independently of experience; the claim that there is a priori knowledge of matters of fact.

Scientific realism: The view that scientific theories are to be taken at face value as descriptions of the world and are not merely instruments to predict the future.

Semantic conception of truth: A theory that explains truth by reference to the truth conditions of statements.

Statistical generalization: A statement that a certain proportion of a class has a certain property, such as "Nine out of ten swans are white."

Theoretical inference: The method of verifying the truth of theories that refer to unobservables.

Theoretical statement: A statement about things that are unobservable in contrast to an observation statement.

Universal generalization: A general statement about all the objects of a certain type, usually of the form "All As are Bs."

Verifiability theory of cognitive significance: The claim that for a statement to have cognitive meaning, it must be verifiable or falsifiable by observation.

Further Reading

The main writings of the classical empiricists are John Locke, *An Essay concerning Human Understanding;* George Berkeley, *A Treatise concerning the Principles of Human Knowledge;* and David Hume, *A Treatise of Human Nature,* book I and *An*

Enquiry concerning Human Understanding. For classical rationalism see Descartes, *Meditations on First Philosophy* and *A Discourse on Method;* Spinoza, *Ethics;* Leibniz, *New Essays concerning Human Understanding.* Kant's contribution to the theory of knowledge is provided by *The Critique of Pure Reason,* a briefer version of which is his *Prolegomena to Any Future Metaphysics.*

For the tradition of American pragmatism see Charles S. Peirce, *Selected Writings,* ed. Philip Wiener (New York: Dover, 1966); William James, *Pragmatism: A New Name for Some Old Ways of Thinking* (New York: Longman, Green, and Co., 1949); and John Dewey, *The Quest for Certainty* (New York: Minton, Balch, and Co., 1929).

A lucid account of logical positivism and verificationism is provided by A. J. Ayer, *Language, Truth and Logic* (New York: Dover, 1952). For problems and changes in the verifiability theory of meaning see Carl G. Hempel, *Aspects of Scientific Explanation* (New York: The Free Press, 1965), part II.

A reliable and readable account of scientific knowledge is Ernest Nagel, *The Structure of Science* (New York: Harcourt, Brace and World, 1961). Two recent readable surveys of the theory of knowledge are Israel Scheffler, *Science and Subjectivity* (Indianapolis: Bobbs-Merrill, 1967) and W. V. Quine and J. S. Ullian, *The Web of Belief* (New York: Random House, 1978).

For a statement of the correspondence theory of truth and for criticisms of the pragmatic and coherence theories see Bertrand Russell, *Philosophical Essays* (New York: Simon and Schuster, 1968). Tarski's semantic conception of truth is clearly explained in W. V. Quine, *Philosophy of Logic* (Englewood Cliffs, New Jersey: Prentice-Hall, 1970).

Questions for Thought and Discussion

1. Explain the main issues concerning human knowledge that distinguish rationalism from empiricism.

2. Can empiricists explain how we obtain ideas of things we have not experienced? For example, how could we obtain the idea of God from experience?

3. Show how the verifiability criterion of cognitive significance was used by the logical positivists to bolster an empiricist theory of knowledge. According to the verifiability criterion, what is the status of the statement that God does *not* exist?

4. How much of your knowledge of the world would remain if you subtracted the amount you owe to the testimony and authority of others? To what extent are you entitled to rely on testimony in building up your picture of reality?

5. Why does Hume think that there is a problem in justifying induction? Are you convinced by any of the arguments that attempt to justify it?

6. What overall verdict about empiricism do you think is justified by the survey of knowledge conducted in this chapter?

7. "A statement is true just to the extent that it represents or fits the facts." Do you agree?

Chapter 9

TRUTHS OF REASON

PREVIEW

Some philosophers have claimed that human beings have a special capacity (based on reason) to know certain things without having to rely upon experience. The main example of these truths of reason is mathematical knowledge. This chapter explores the case for and against the existence of truths of reason and hence for and against the existence of this capacity for **a priori knowledge.**

The basic framework for discussing truths of reason was established by Kant's asking, "How is synthetic a priori knowledge possible?". We shall see how rationalists answered this question. We shall also see on what grounds empiricists denied the existence of synthetic a priori knowledge. The chapter will end with doubts recently expressed about the very framework in which rationalism and empiricism have conducted their debate.

The Problem of A Priori Knowledge

THE A PRIORI

David Hume (1711–1776) distinguished between matters of fact, which he said were known through experience, and relations of ideas, which "are discoverable by the mere operation of thought." The former are called empirical statements, the latter a priori statements. In the history of philosophy, the truths drawn from mathematics have been the chief examples offered of a priori statements. Such statements of arithmetic and geometry as "2 + 3 = 5" and "The shortest distance between two points is a straight line" have often been considered examples of knowledge that can be obtained merely by thinking without the aid of experience. Some philosophers have also claimed that the basic statements of ethics and religion, such as "Promises ought to be kept" and "There is a God," can also be known a priori. There is another class of propositions—Locke called them trifling propositions—that are alleged to be knowable a priori. Examples of these are "Red is not green," "Whatever is square is not triangular," and so on.

A priori knowledge has represented a problem from the very dawn of philosophy in ancient Greece. How is it possible for human beings to attain knowledge of the world without observation? How is it possible to learn new facts about reality just by thinking? In his dialogue *Phaedo,* Plato (428–348 B.C.) speculated that a priori knowledge is acquired by the human soul before its birth. Plato thought that the existence of a priori knowledge proved that there is a difference between the soul and the body and that the soul existed in a life previous to this one. But this conjecture is no solution at all. Even if there is a soul that exists before the present life, we still need to know how it managed to obtain its a priori knowledge in its previous existence. Plato has nothing to say on this matter that really explains the acquisition of a priori knowledge. But one of his ideas was widely adopted in early modern philosophy. Plato said that the awareness of a priori knowledge is a form of recollection. The soul remembers ideas that it already possesses. Thus, the soul is stocked with innate ideas. In the thought of Descartes, Leibniz, and other rationalists, a priori knowledge was explained by the theory of innate ideas. The mind or soul is stocked with certain ideas at birth; various experiences help to remind it of what it already knows or possesses. Thus, Plato's theory of recollection led to the theory of innate ideas offered by some modern philosophers.

INTUITIVE KNOWLEDGE

You may remember from the previous chapter that John Locke (1632–1704) was the most important and influential modern critic of the theory of innate ideas. He claimed that all ideas arose from experience, from sensation and reflection. Even though Locke thought that all ideas or concepts are empirical, he realized that when we bring them together into propositions, we find that some propositions are knowable a priori. Thus, although the ideas of red and green are drawn from sense experience, the proposition that red is not green formed from these ideas is knowable a priori. Some of these a priori propositions are self-evidently or intuitively true. This means that we can grasp their truth just by understanding the meaning of the terms that make up these propositions. Take "Red is not green" as an example. If I understand the meanings of the terms *red* and *green,* then I immediately grasp that the proposition is true. According to Locke, a priori knowledge is knowledge based upon the meanings of terms that occur in propositions or statements.

Locke did not stop there. He attempted to explain how this kind of knowledge is possible. Here is his explanation:

> Knowledge then seems to me to be nothing but the perception of the connection and agreement, or disagreement and repugnancy, of any of our ideas. In this alone it consists. Where this perception is, there is knowledge; and where it is not, there, though we may fancy, guess, or believe, yet we always come short of knowledge. For, when we know that white is not black, what do we else but perceive that these two ideas do not agree?[1]

[1]John Locke, *An Essay concerning Human Understanding* (London: George Routledge and Sons), IV. i. 2.

Locke claims here that the mind has the power to perceive or become aware of the relations among ideas or concepts that enter into a proposition. He said that all these relations are examples of either the agreement or disagreement of concepts. Some concepts agree with each other. For example, we can grasp that the idea expressed by the equation $3 + 2$ agrees with or is equal to the idea expressed by 5. Other concepts disagree with each other. For example, the concepts of red and green disagree, that is, they exclude one another. By perceiving their disagreement, we come to learn that red is not green.

Of course, this form of perception is not sense perception. Concepts are not items that we can see or hear or apprehend by means of sense awareness. The awareness of a concept is nonsensory. According to Locke, we can have a nonsensory awareness or intuition of concepts and their relationships. A priori knowledge is possible because the mind has the power of acquiring **intuitive knowledge.**

DEMONSTRATIVE KNOWLEDGE

Locke distinguished between intuitive and **demonstrative**, or deductive, **knowledge**. In intuitive knowledge, the mind directly perceives certain conceptual relations:

> For if we will reflect on our own ways of thinking, we shall find that sometimes the mind perceives the agreement or disagreement of two ideas immediately by themselves, without the intervention of any other: and this, I think, we may call "intuitive knowledge." For in this the mind is at no pains of proving or examining, but perceives the truth, as the eye doth light, only by being directed towards it. Thus, the mind perceives that white is not black, that a circle is not a triangle, that three are more than two, and equal to one and two. Such kind of truths the mind perceives at the first sight of the ideas together, by bare intuition, without the intervention of any other idea; and this kind of knowledge is the clearest and most certain that human frailty is capable of. This part of knowledge is irresistible, and, like bright sunshine, forces itself immediately to be perceived as soon as ever the mind turns its view that way; and leaves no room for hesitation, doubt, or examination, but the mind is presently filled with the clear light of it. It is on this intuition that depends all the certainty and evidence of all our knowledge.[2]

We have demonstrative knowledge in those cases in which the mind perceives a conceptual connection by the use of intermediate ideas:

> In this case then, when the mind cannot so bring its ideas together as, by their immediate comparison and, as it were, juxtaposition or application one to another, to perceive their agreement or disagreement, it is fain, by the intervention of other ideas (one or more, as it happens), to discover the agreement or disagreement which it searches; and this is that which we call "reasoning."[3]

[2] Ibid., IV. ii. 1.
[3] Ibid., IV. ii. 2.

An example of demonstrative knowledge arrived at by reasoning rather than by intuition is represented by the following argument:

> The number 2 is smaller than the number 3.
> The number 3 is smaller than the number 4.
> Therefore, the number 2 is smaller than the number 4.

In this argument, instead of establishing that 2 is smaller than 4 by a direct comparison of these two numbers, we first compare 2 to 3 and 3 to 4 and then *conclude* that 2 is smaller than 4. The number 3 functions as an intermediary idea that enables the mind to relate 2 to 4.

Many of you are familiar with the mathematics of plane geometry. Geometry is usually presented in a systematic way known as the **axiomatic method.** In a geometrical system, certain statements are classified as **axioms** or **postulates.** Axioms are those statements that function as first principles and are not given any proof in the system. Those statements that are proved by deducing them from the axioms are called **theorems.**

Today many systems of thought other than geometry are organized according to the axiomatic method. If we use this method, then we can say that we learn the truth of the theorems, supposing that they are true, by deducing them from the axioms using the rules of logic. These deductions yield what Locke calls demonstrative knowledge. But how do we learn the truth of the axioms? If the axioms are examples of a priori knowledge, then according to Plato, they were learned by the soul before birth. According to Descartes and Leibniz, the axioms are a type of innate knowledge. And according to Locke, they are self-evident, intuitive truths.

Necessity and the Distinction between the Analytic and the Synthetic

NECESSARY TRUTH

The next important contribution to the discussion of the sources of a priori knowledge is contained in Immanuel Kant's *Critique of Pure Reason.* Kant (1724–1804) attempted to discover a criterion of the a priori. How can we tell whether or not a given statement can be known a priori? For Kant, *necessity* is the criterion:

> Experience teaches us that a thing is so and so, but not that it cannot be otherwise. First, then, if we have a proposition which in being thought is thought as *necessary,* it is an *a priori* judgment.[4]

---

[4]Immanuel Kant, *Critique of Pure Reason,* trans. Norman Kemp Smith (London: Macmillan, 1950), B3. (First published in 1781.)

A judgment is necessarily true if it is impossible for it to be false. For example, under no conceivable circumstances could the judgment that a triangle has three sides be false. But the statement that the cat is green might be false; the cat might be gray instead of green. A **necessary truth** is a statement that is true in every possible world, under every conceivable circumstance. A **contingent truth** is one that is true of the world as actually constituted but might have been false. Thus, although it is true that I now have a mustache, it might not have been true. I might never have decided to grow one; I might have shaved it off yesterday. So it is a contingent truth. But if I think that I have a mustache, then "I exist" is not contingent. It could not possibly be false that if a person thinks something, then he exists, for only existing persons can actually think. Kant argues that necessary propositions are a priori.[5] The reason he gives is that although experience can tell me that a certain statement is true, it cannot tell me that it is necessarily true. Necessity is not an observable feature of matters of fact. Experience gives me knowledge only of what is contingent.

To find out that a given statement is necessarily true, we must find out two things about it: that it is true and that it is necessary. One might very well learn from experience that a certain necessarily true proposition is true. For example, a child may learn that 2 + 3 = 5 by counting piles of blocks. She has one pile in which she counts two blocks, and another pile in which she counts three. And when she counts them both together, she discovers that there are five. According to Kant, however, even though experience will awaken her to the truth of certain arithmetical statements, it will not establish that they are necessary.

ANALYTIC AND SYNTHETIC JUDGMENTS

Kant introduced another and different distinction between two kinds of judgment. A **synthetic judgment** is one that formulates a matter of fact, such as "The cat is on the mat" or "Columbus discovered America in 1492." There is another class of judgments, however, whose truth is not based upon fact but upon definitions or word meanings. The truth of "A triangle has three angles" is based upon the fact that the term *triangle* is defined to mean a certain kind of figure with three angles. Examples of the same sort are "A square has four equal sides" and "A bachelor is an unmarried man." These judgments tell us nothing about the world or about matters of fact. Their truth is a direct consequence of the meanings of the words that make them up. Kant called this type of judgment **analytic.**

The statement "A triangle has three angles" is of the subject-predicate form. The phrase "a triangle" is the subject and "has three angles" the predicate. Kant defined an analytic statement as one in which the meaning or concept of the predicate is contained in the meaning or concept of the subject.[6] Having three angles is contained in or

---

[5]Recently, Saul Kripke has argued that some necessary propositions are not knowable a priori or not completely a priori. An example of an empirical necessity that he provides is "Heat is the motion of molecules." See his "Identity and Necessity," in *Identity and Individuation,* ed. Milton Munitz (New York: New York University Press, 1971).

[6]Kant, *Critique of Pure Reason,* B10.

included in the meaning of "a triangle." Having four sides is included in the meaning of "a square." Being unmarried is part of the meaning of "bachelor."

This definition of an analytic statement turns out to be too narrow because some statements whose truth depends upon the meanings of their terms are not of the subject-predicate form. An example is "If A is the father of B, then B is a child of A." It is part of the meanings of the words *father* and *child* that a person is a child of his or her own father. We can, however, revise the definition of analyticity to take care of this problem. Consider the statement:

(*a*) All bachelors are unmarried.

The word *bachelor* means unmarrried man. When two phrases mean the same thing, they can replace one another in discourse. By a replacement we arrive at

(*b*) All unmarried men are unmarried.

We can derive (b) from (a) by replacing the word *bachelor* in (a) with the term *unmarried man,* which has the same meaning. The operation by means of which we derive (b) from (a) is called *replacing synonyms by synonyms.* Now the pattern of (b) can be represented as follows:

(*c*) All As who are Bs are As.

Thus, (b) can be reformulated as "All unmarried persons who are men are unmarried." Now (c) is a logical truth; this means that no matter which expressions are used to replace A and B, you end up with a true statement.

Working backward, we can derive (a) from (c). First, in (c) replace A with *unmarried person* and B with *men.* We then have:

(*d*) All unmarried persons who are men are unmarried.

Then by the rule that allows us to replace synonyms by synonyms, we replace *unmarried persons who are men* with *bachelor* and we arrive back at (a). This procedure illustrates the idea that we can define an analytic truth as a true statement that can be derived from logical truths by the process of replacing synonyms by synonyms.[7] According to this definition, there is no requirement that analytic truths be of the subject-predicate form.

KANT'S CLASSIFICATION

According to Kant, there are two methods of classifying statements. First, every statement is either a priori (necessary) or empirical (contingent). Second, every statement

[7]W. V. Quine, *From a Logical Point of View* (New York: Harper & Row, 1963), pp. 20–23.

is either analytic or synthetic. When we try to combine these classifications, we obtain the following possibilities:

> Analytic empirical statements
> Analytic a priori statements
> Synthetic empirical statements
> Synthetic a priori statements

Kant urges that there are no statements that are both analytic and empirical:

> Judgments of experience, as such, are one and all synthetic. For it would be absurd to found an analytic judgment on experience. Since, in framing the judgment, I must not go outside my concept, there is no need to appeal to the testimony of experience in its support.[8]

Because an analytic statement is one whose truth can be ascertained by reflecting on the meanings of its terms, it is unnecessary to turn to observation to verify it. One does not have to conduct research on bachelors to discover that they are one and all unmarried. Moreover, analytic statements are necessary; they could not be false. Therefore, according to Kant's criterion, they are all a priori.

Thus we are left with these three cases:

> Analytic a priori statements
> Synthetic empirical statements
> Synthetic a priori statements

Statements that are analytic and a priori are those whose truth depends upon the meanings of their component terms. Those that are synthetic and empirical are statements of matters of fact that presuppose observation in their verification; the discussion of knowledge in Chapter Eight was concerned mainly with this type of statement. Finally, statements that are both synthetic and a priori are those that represent matters of fact that can be known by the mere operation of thought.

HOW IS SYNTHETIC A PRIORI KNOWLEDGE POSSIBLE?

For Kant, the main problem in understanding the structure of human knowledge is represented by the question, How is synthetic a priori knowledge possible? How is it possible to achieve knowledge of the world in the absence of observation by the use of reason alone? According to Kant, synthetic a priori judgments are central to human knowledge. For example, as Kant points out, *"All mathematic judgments, without exception, are synthetic."* In a well-known passage, he considers the statement that 7 + 5 = 12.

---

[8]Kant, *Critique of Pure Reason,* B11.

> We might, indeed, at first suppose that the proposition 7 + 5 = 12 is a merely analytic proposition, and follows by the principle of contradiction from the concept of a sum of 7 and 5. But if we look more closely we find that the concept of the sum of 7 and 5 contains nothing save the union of the two numbers into one, and in this no thought is being taken as to what that single number may be which combines both. The concept of 12 is by no means already thought in merely thinking this union of 7 and 5; and I may analyse my concept of such a possible sum as long as I please, still I shall never find the 12 in it.[9]

Kant is here arguing that it is not part of the meaning of "7 + 5" that the sum of these two numbers equals 12. Using our definition of analytic statements, we can see that 7 + 5 = 12 cannot be derived from logic by replacing synonyms by synonyms. In particular, the symbols "12" and "7 + 5" are not synonymous. Thus, the statement is not true merely in virtue of the meanings of its terms.

In Chapter Eight, we discussed the traditional opposition between rationalism and empiricism. At the very beginning of modern philosophy, the rationalist defended and the empiricist criticized the theory of innate ideas and innate knowledge. But since the time of Kant, the issue has changed. The question has become, Is there synthetic a priori knowledge? Is there knowledge of matters of fact that is based upon reason and is independent of observation? Kant thought that there is. But for the modern empiricist, all knowledge of matters of fact is empirical. Thus, empiricism must deny that there is any knowledge that is synthetic and a priori; if there are any a priori statements, they are one and all analytic.

The Two Strategies of Modern Empiricism

If empiricism is to develop a satisfactory answer to Kant, it must formulate a philosophy of mathematics that does not presuppose that mathematical statements are synthetic a priori. Empiricists are committed to the view that the only kinds of statements are those that are analytic a priori and those that are synthetic empirical. Therefore, two strategies are open to empiricism. Either it could assert that mathematical statements—in fact all statements that appear to be a priori—are really empirical and contingent, or it could claim that mathematical statements are really a priori and analytic. The first strategy was adopted by John Stuart Mill (1806–1873) and the second by logical positivism.

MILL'S THEORY OF MATHEMATICS

According to Mill, mathematical statements are

> experimental truths; generalizations from observation. The proposition, Two straight lines cannot enclose a space . . . is an induction from the evidence of our senses.[10]

[9]Ibid., B15.
[10]John Stuart Mill, *A System of Logic,* book II, chap. 5, par. 4.

The propositions of arithmetic and geometry are inductive generalizations founded upon observation. It is an error to think that they are necessary truths, that no possible experience could falsify them. The source of this error is the extraordinary certainty that mathematics possesses. But, for Mill, the source of this certainty is the fact that the truths of mathematics are confirmed over and over again by observation.

Mill does briefly consider the view that mathematical statements are analytic, that they merely express relationships among word meanings and hence do not apply to the actual world. But he quickly dismisses it:

> There is in every step of arithmetic or algebraic calculation a real induction, a real inference of facts from facts; and . . . what disguises the induction is simply its comprehensive nature and the consequent extreme generality of the language. All numbers must be numbers of something; there are no such things as numbers in the abstract. *Ten* must mean ten bodies, or ten sounds, or ten beatings of the pulse. But though numbers must be numbers of something, they may be numbers of anything. Propositions, therefore, concerning numbers have the remarkable peculiarity that they are all propositions concerning all things whatever; all objects, all existences of every kind known to our experience.[11]

Mathematical truths are statements about matters of fact. When I assert that seven sounds of a bell plus three sounds are equal to ten sounds, I am making a factual judgment. What I say could possibly be false. It is a contingent, not a necessary truth, and hence not a priori. The feeling we have that such elementary equations of arithmetic are self-evident results from the fact that they are frequently confirmed by observation and that we consequently become so habituated to them that we could not believe or even conceive how they could turn out to be false.

One of the traditional arguments used by rationalists to prove that mathematical truths are necessary is that we are unable to conceive of their being false. No matter how hard I try, it is inconceivable to me that $2 + 1 \neq 3$. I cannot even imagine a case in which I have two objects of a certain kind and one other object of that kind but do not have three objects of that kind. In response, Mill asserts that this appeal to what is inconceivable to us is irrelevant:

> Now I cannot wonder that so much stress should be laid on the circumstance of inconceivableness, when there is such ample experience to show that our capacity or incapacity of conceiving a thing has very little to do with the possibility of the thing in itself, but is in truth very much an affair of accident and depends on the past history and habits of our own minds. . . . Inconceivableness is an accidental thing, not inherent in the phenomenon itself, but dependent on the mental history of the person who tries to conceive it.[12]

Mill here argues that appealing to the fact that one cannot conceive or imagine how "2 + 1 = 3" could possibly be false as evidence that it is a necessary truth is appealing

[11]Ibid., chap. 6, par. 2.
[12]Ibid., chap. 5, par. 6.

to a psychological fact about a given person. But instead of taking a rationalist approach, we should, says Mill, be content to explain such facts by reference to the psychological law that once we become habituated to thinking that something is true because of numerous observations that confirm it, we form a firm belief that cannot easily be shaken.

Mill's empiricist solution to the problem of the nature of mathematical truth has not been widely accepted by subsequent philosophers. There is a profound difficulty in his assertion that the truths of arithmetic are continuously confirmed by observation. The difficulty is that if we relied on observation as the basis of arithmetic, we would have to reject it as false. For example, take the proposition $3 + 2 = 5$:

> We place some microbes on a slide, putting down first three of them and then another two. Afterwards we count all the microbes to test whether in this instance 3 and 2 actually added up to 5. Suppose now that we counted 6 microbes altogether. Would we consider this an empirical disconfirmation of the given proposition, or at least as a proof that it does not apply to microbes? Clearly not; rather, we would assume that we had made a mistake in counting or that one of the microbes had split in two between the first and second count. But under no circumstances could the phenomenon just described invalidate the arithmetical proposition in question; for the latter asserts nothing whatever about the behavior of microbes.[13]

We do not always obtain the results that arithmetical propositions require when we actually count objects. Two male rabbits placed in a cage with two female rabbits will sooner or later yield more than four rabbits. This does not mean that two plus two does not equal four.

According to the German logician Gottlob Frege (1848–1925), Mill's error lies in confusing propositions of pure arithmetic with applications of these propositions to physical fact. For example, if in the proposition $2 + 3 = 5$, we interpret the plus sign as representing a physical relation between things—for example, the relation that results when you put two microbes next to three microbes—then because you don't always obtain five things, the equation seems to be false. But interpreting the plus sign as standing for a physical relation is an error. It is a relation of arithmetic, a relation among numbers and not one holding among physical things.[14]

Because of Frege's and others' criticisms of Mill, most subsequent empiricists have adopted the solution that the truths of arithmetic are analytic and hence do not formulate matters of fact. Let us consider this approach.

ARE ALL A PRIORI TRUTHS ANALYTIC?

Consider the sentence "The cat is on the mat." To determine whether or not it expresses a truth, I first have to find out what the words of which it is composed mean. But that

---

[13]C. G. Hempel, "On the Nature of Mathematical Truth," in *Readings in Philosophical Analysis,* ed. Herbert Feigl and Wilfrid Sellars (New York: Appleton-Century-Crofts, 1949), pp. 223–224.
[14]Gottlob Frege, *The Foundations of Arithmetic,* trans. J. L. Austin (Oxford: Basil Blackwell, 1953), pp. 12–14. (This book was first published in 1884.)

is not sufficient. I must also look and see whether the cat is on the mat. So some sentences express truths both because of what they mean *and* because of observable reality. But I can determine the truth of "All bachelors are unmarried" just by knowing what the words mean. I do not have to consult observable reality to determine its truth. Thus, some sentences express truth because of the features of language and the features of observable reality, and other statements express truth because of language alone. The latter class consists of analytic statements, those statements whose truth follows from the meanings of the component words. The question is whether all a priori statements, including the truths of mathematics, are analytic.

To understand the issues at stake, I shall focus upon a particular example that has often been discussed. All of you know what a cube is, and it does not require much reflection to realize that the surface of a cube is divided into six squares of equal size. The straight lines that separate the squares are called edges. Ask yourself how many edges a cube has. Before you read any farther, try to answer the question yourself. Just think about it for a while. Perhaps you need to imagine a cube and count its imagined edges. If you judge that a cube has twelve edges, then you have the right answer.

For the statement that a cube has twelve edges to be analytic, it is necessary that the notion of having twelve edges be included in the meaning of the word *cube*. We agree on the fact of a cube's having twelve edges. The problem is to determine the status of that fact. Is it a fact about meaning or a fact about reality?

Perhaps your first impulse is to argue that the statement is really empirical. Its truth was determined by our recalling cubes that we have observed in the past. After all, cubes are familiar objects. Children play frequently with cubical blocks. Lumps of sugar are often cubical in shape. It seems plausible to say that the notion that cubes have twelve edges has been verified by observation.

This is not, however, correct. Let me assume that although you know what cubes are, you never actually before counted the number of edges of a cube. So the statement that a cube has twelve edges was news to you. You discovered its truth by imagining a cube on the basis of your memory and counting its edges. Now the fact that you counted the edges of an imaginary cube does not imply that the proposition is empirical. For an empirical proposition cannot be verified merely by the use of the imagination. For example, you all know what the president of the United States looks like. Suppose I ask you to imagine him and on the basis of your imagination to describe the garments he is now wearing—his real garments, not merely imaginary ones. You would properly reply that you couldn't do it. One cannot ascertain a matter of fact just by picturing things in one's mind. It is necessary to make observations of reality. Similarly, you could not now prove that a cube has twelve edges by counting imaginary edges if its having twelve edges were an empirical statement.

It seems, then, that the statement is a priori and necessary. But is it analytic? A rationalist would claim that it is synthetic by citing the following facts. Even though you already know what a cube is, that it has twelve edges is new information to you and thus cannot be included in the meaning of the word *cube*. For if it were included in its meaning, then you could not have known what a cube is without already knowing that it has twelve edges.

The empiricist, however, would reject this argument, claiming that something can be included in the meaning of a word either explicitly or implicitly. Something is included explicitly if it is mentioned in the definition. For example, because *bachelor* is defined as meaning unmarried man, then being unmarried is included explicitly in the meaning of *bachelor*. Something is included implicitly when, even though it is not mentioned in the definition, it is implied or entailed by it. For example, being human is included implicitly in the definition of *bachelor* because it is implied by the notion of being a man, which is part of the definition. The standard definition of *cube* is a regular solid of six equal square sides, so having twelve edges is not included explicitly in the definition. The empiricist, however, claims that having twelve edges is included implicitly in its meaning. Therefore, that a cube has twelve edges is an analytic statement. The fact that this statement contains information that is new to you is the result of our not always being aware of what is implied or entailed by the meanings of words.

ENTAILMENT

To explain the reply of the rationalist to this argument, I must say something about the notion of **implication,** or **entailment.** A statement A implies or entails a statement B provided that if A is true, then B *must* be true. Another way of saying this is that it is necessary that if A is true, then B is true. Thus, "No apples are oranges" entails "No oranges are apples." But "It is raining" does not entail "The streets are wet" because the latter does not follow from the former by logical necessity. We must distinguish between physical necessity, by which one event causes the existence of another event, and logical necessity, by which one statement entails another statement.

The rationalist claims that there are two forms of entailment. The first form is *analytic entailment*. Statement A analytically entails statement B provided that B follows from A according to the rules of logic and the definitions of terms alone. For example, "No apples are oranges" analytically entails "No oranges are apples" because the latter follows from the former according to the rule of logic that if no M are N, then no N are M, no matter what M and N are. Also, "This is a cube" analytically entails "This has six sides" because the latter follows from the former according to the definition of *cube* and certain rules of logic. The second form is *synthetic entailment*. Statement A synthetically entails statement B provided A entails B but B does not follow from A merely by logic and the definitions of words. According to the rationalist, the statement "X is red" synthetically entails "X is not green" because something's being not green does not follow from its being red just by reference to the meanings of words.

Rationalists have no difficulty admitting that having twelve edges is entailed by something's being a cube. But they claim that the entailment is synthetic, not analytic, and hence does not follow from the meaning of the word *cube*. You cannot extract the having of twelve edges from the mere knowledge of what a cube is. In addition, an insight into the relationship between the property of being a cube and the entirely distinct property of having twelve edges is required.

Rationalists claim that the human mind is so constructed as to have the ability to have a *rational insight* or *intuition* into various relationships among the properties of things. We are able to see with "the eye of the soul" that being a cube necessitates having twelve edges, that being red excludes being green, that being the sum of 7 and

5 is the same as being 12, and so forth. The empiricist replies that the only kind of seeing available to human beings is the kind accomplished with the eyes of the body. There is no such thing as a rational intuition into connections among properties. The scientific study of the human mind has not brought to light any mechanism that would account for rational intuition.

Conventionalism

Certain of the philosophers who claim that all a priori propositions are analytic believe that it follows that all a priori propositions are true by convention. They argue as follows. An analytic statement is true by virtue of the meanings of the words that constitute it. But the meaning of a word is a matter of convention, not a natural fact. The meaning of a word consists in the way it is used. For example, the word *red* could have meant anything. That it means a certain color is a consequence of the fact that human beings deliberately used it to name or designate that color. Think of the difference between "The word 'red' means the color red" and "Smoke means [is a sign of] fire." The connection between smoke and fire is independent of human choice; it is a natural relationship. But there is no natural connection between the word *red* and the color red. That *red* means red is due to human usage. Moreover, the meaning of *red* can be altered by human beings. If we changed our usage, using *red* to represent the color yellow, then it would come to mean yellow. But the natural connection between smoke and fire is not alterable by anything that human beings can do. If word meanings are based upon human convention, then analytic statements, whose truth is based upon word meaning, are true by convention.

Here is a typical formulation of **conventionalism:**

> We have already explained how it is that these analytic propositions are
> necessary and certain. We saw that the reason why they cannot be confuted in
> experience is that they do not make any assertion about the empirical world.
> They simply record our determination to use words in a certain fashion. We
> cannot deny them without infringing the conventions which are presupposed by
> our very denial, and so falling into self-contradiction. And this is the sole ground
> of their necessity. . . . It is perfectly conceivable that we should have employed
> different linguistic conventions from those which we actually do employ. But
> whatever these conventions might be, the tautologies in which we recorded them
> would always be necessary. For any denial of them would be self-stultifying. We
> see, then, that there is nothing mysterious about the . . . certainty of logic and
> mathematics. Our knowledge that no observation can ever confute the
> proposition "7 + 5 = 12" depends simply on the fact that the symbolic
> expression "7 + 5" is synonymous with "12," just as our knowledge that every
> oculist is an eye-doctor depends on the fact that the symbol "eye-doctor" is
> synonymous with "oculist." And the same explanation holds good for every other
> a priori truth.[15]

[15]A. J. Ayer, *Language, Truth and Logic* (London: Victor Gollancz, Ltd., 1946), pp. 84–85.

Conventionalism in mathematics is sometimes called **formalism.** According to the formalist, mathematics is like a game played with symbols. Certain symbols are invented, such as 7 and 12 and + and =. Then, as in a game, rules are made up for manipulating the symbols, rules that resemble the rules for moving the pieces in a game. Thus, in the "game" of mathematics, there is a rule that the symbol 7 + 5 may be replaced by the symbol 12. The equation 7 + 5 = 12 is merely a way of recording this rule.

Here is how Humpty Dumpty in Lewis Carroll's *Through the Looking Glass* explains the conventional character of word meaning:

"When I use a word," Humpty Dumpty said, in rather a scornful tone, *"it means just what I choose it to mean—neither more nor less."*
"The question is," said Alice, *"whether you can make words mean so many different things."*
"The question is," said Humpty Dumpty, *"which is to be master—that's all."*

A main problem with conventionalism stems from the fact that if a priori statements are true by convention, then a change in convention should lead to a change in their truth. If, as Ayer says, analytic propositions merely "record our determination to use words in a certain fashion," then, if we change the use of words, we should be able to turn a true proposition into a false one. Thus, if the word *cube* comes to have the same meaning as the word *elephant* has now, then the statement "A cube has six sides" would appear to be false. But if we can change a true a priori statement into a false one just by changing the meaning of words, then how can a priori statements be necessary? Ayer seems to have adopted Kant's idea that all a priori statements are necessary truths. And a necessary truth is one that could not under any conceivable circumstance be false. So the truth of a necessary proposition cannot depend upon linguistic conventions.

The existence of a linguistic convention, moreover, is discovered by observing the verbal usages of people speaking a given language. It is by such observation, for example, that we find that the English word *red* and the German word *rot* have the same meaning. So a statement that records a linguistic convention is a type of empirical statement. Conventionalism seems to have the consequence that there are no a priori propositions at all.

As formulated by Ayer, conventionalism seems to be self-contradictory, for it has the implication that statements that are necessary and a priori are neither necessary nor a priori. But conventionalism can be reformulated to avoid this inconsistency. The conventionalist can simply say that those statements that other philosophers had thought to be necessary and a priori are neither; they are instead truths based upon linguistic convention, truths that can be altered by a change of convention.

There is, however, a further difficulty that seems fatal to conventionalism: Conventionalism confuses sentences with the statements that sentences are used to make. To understand this difficulty, consider the following example. People who speak English will use the sentence "The cat is on the mat" to make the statement that the cat is on the mat. But people who speak only French or German will not use that sentence. They will use a sentence consisting of words from their own language. That the same statement can be expressed by different sentences establishes the fact that sentences and statements are not to be identified. Moreover, a sentence just by itself is neither true nor false. Just by examining the sentence, one cannot tell whether "The cat is on the mat" is true. One would need to know who uttered it, what cat and what mat he had in mind, and when it was uttered. It is what people say with the sentences that they utter that has truth value.

The linguistic conventions that govern the use of words in "The cat is on the mat" determine the type of statement that it can be used to make. Because we understand these conventions, when a person utters the sentence "The cat is on the mat" we can interpret him to be making the statement that the cat is on the mat. If we should change the convention, we can alter the statement that the sentence is used to make. Thus, if *cat* comes to have the same meaning as *elephant,* then the sentence "The cat is on the mat" can no longer be used to say that the cat is on the mat but can be used to say that the elephant is on the mat. Although a change of convention can thus alter the statement that is made, it cannot affect the truth of whatever statement is made. If indeed the cat is on the mat, no change in the meanings of words will turn the truth of the statement that the cat is on the mat into a falsehood. The only effect that a change in meaning has is to make it impossible to use certain words to make that statement.

The same remarks apply to cases of a priori knowledge. It is a linguistic convention that *cube* means a regular solid of six equal square sides. Because of this convention, we are able to use the sentence "A cube has six sides" to state that a cube has six sides. But if we change the convention so that *cube* comes to mean a solid with eight sides, then we cannot use that sentence to state that a cube has six sides. But this change does not affect the truth of the statement in the slightest. It merely affects the form of words we use to state it. So in the end conventionalism fails.

Formalism in mathematics has analogous difficulties. The idea that mathematical statements are merely expressions of rules for the arbitrary manipulation of symbols ignores the fact that mathematical symbols have acquired definite meanings as a result of their being used in acts of counting and measuring. If I say that there are three apples on the table, what I say has definite meaning and is either true or false. There are either three apples or more than three or less than three. Of course, if I change the meanings of the symbols so that 3 comes to mean what I now mean by 2, then I cannot use the sentence "There are three apples on the table" to state that there are three apples on the table. But I cannot modify the actual number of apples just by changing the meaning of a symbol.

Rational Intuition

If we agree that an analytic proposition, such as the statement that a cube has six sides, does not depend upon linguistic conventions for its truth, then there are two questions that it is natural to ask. In what does its truth consist? How can we come to learn that

297

it is true a priori? To discuss one of the traditional answers to these questions, let me introduce here the distinction between a *thing* and the various *characteristics* or *properties* that it has. Consider a child's building block. It is a physical thing that has the following characteristics or properties: It is solid, it is cubical, it has six sides, it has twelve edges, it is blue, and it is wooden. These characteristics are represented in language by such general terms as *solid, six-sided, twelve-edged, cubical, blue,* and *wooden.* A characteristic such as the color blue is a quality. But other characteristics, such as being of such and such a size or having so many sides, are quantities. Still others, such as being next to that block, are relationships. Still others are kinds or types, such as being a block.

The statement that a cube has six sides expresses a relationship between two characteristics: the characteristic of being a cube and the characteristic of having six sides. The relationship itself consists in the fact that having six sides is a part of or is included in the characteristic of being a cube. We can think of the characteristic of being a cube as being formed of the conjunction of various characteristics, such as being a regular solid, having square sides, having sides of equal size, and having six sides. We can see that having six sides is one of the characteristics that make up being a cube. The truth of

(*a*) A cube has six sides.

consists in the fact that the following is true:

(*b*) The characteristic of having six sides is included in the characteristic of being a cube.

Thus, we can explain the truth of certain analytic statements as consisting in the fact that certain characteristics are included in other characteristics.

The second question is, How do we learn a priori that (a) is true? We can learn that it is true because we are capable of discovering that (b) is true. But how do we manage that? One way of doing so is to reflect upon the meaning of the word *cube.* We begin by thinking of the various characteristics that cubes have in common and considering whether any of them is part of the definition or nature of a cube. Would I classify something as a cube if it did not have six sides? I would not, so having six sides is part of what a cube is. Would I classify something as a cube if it were not blue? Of course I would, provided it was a regular solid having six sides. So being blue is not a defining or essential characteristic. I determine what is and what is not included in the characteristic of being a cube by thinking about what I mean, by determining what characteristics I have in mind when I classify something as a cube. Perhaps I can never achieve absolute certainty in this matter. Many philosophers have thought that our insight into the contents of our own meanings could never be mistaken. I believe that they are wrong; wherever there is judgment, there is room for error. But the main point is that the human mind has the power to think about the characteristics it expresses in discourse and to determine that certain characteristics are included in others.

Earlier, I pointed out that for Locke the human mind possesses the power of acquiring intuitive knowledge of the relations among its ideas. For example, we can know intuitively that red is not green because the mind can become aware of the fact that red excludes green, that nothing can be both red and green at the same time and in the same respect. We also saw that rationalism has claimed that the mind can attain rational insight into the relationships among the characteristics of things. The ability of the mind to gain the knowledge that one characteristic is included in another—the ability to learn the truth of certain analytic statements—is a form of intuitive knowledge or rational insight.

The fact that rational insight is needed to verify analytic statements suggests an apparent victory for rationalism in its continuing debate with empiricism. For if the mind has the power of rational insight into the connections among the characteristics of things, then we can answer Kant's question, How are synthetic a priori statements possible. Such statements are possible because we can verify them through our power of rational insight. For if the mind has the power of grasping that one characteristic is included in another, then it may also have the power of grasping other relationships, such as the ones that form the basis of synthetic a priori knowledge.

For example, let us consider what is involved in knowing a priori that if something is red, then it cannot be green at the same time and in the same respect. First, this does not appear to be an analytic statement because the characteristic of not being green is not included in the characteristic of being red. A person may very well know what the color red is without knowing what the color green is and that red is other than green. Second, just as the human mind has the power to grasp that certain characteristics include others, so it has the power to grasp that certain characteristics exclude others and in particular that red excludes green. The power to grasp inclusions is the same sort of power as the power to grasp exclusions, and a person who has the one may very well have the other. He may thus have the power to grasp all sorts of relationships, including those that constitute the basis of synthetic a priori statements.

In sum, the rationalist claims that if we can come to know the truth of analytic statements, then the mind has the power of rational insight. And if it has the power of rational insight, then the mind can use it to know the truth of synthetic a priori statements. Thus, rationalists confirm the possibility of synthetic a priori knowledge referring to two facts. The first is that there are necessary connections among the characteristics of things. The second is that the mind has the power of becoming aware of these connections.

Numbers and Universals

WHAT IS A NUMBER?

If we should apply the rationalist theory of rational insight to the case of mathematical truth, then we would have to say that the truths of mathematics are known by means of rational insight or by deduction from truths known by rational insight. If it is asked how we know that $2 + 1 = 3$, the answer is that we have insight into relationships among numbers. But what is a number anyway? What sort of thing is the number 3, for example?

We must be careful not to confuse a number with the numeral that is used as its name. We need to distinguish between the number 3 and the numeral *3* that names the number. In most cases, we are not likely to confuse names with the things named. No one in his right mind would identify Paris with the word *Paris* or Plato with the name *Plato*. But because numbers are things whose nature is difficult to understand, it is tempting to say that a number is just a symbol for a group of things.

Consider the group of three apples on my kitchen table. According to the view that numbers are just symbols, the number 3 is the name for this group of apples. But if 3 is the name of the group of apples, then it is not the name of the group of three pencils on my desk. So the number 3 is not the name of a particular group. But perhaps it is the name of all groups with three members. Consider what all groups with three members have in common. It is the number 3, not the name. The number 3 has many names; there are numerals such as *3* and *III*. There are words such as *three* and *trois*. If 3 were a name, which of these various names would it be? Is it the word *three?* But this implies the absurdity that the number 3 consists of five letters.

UNIVERSALS

But if a number is not a word or a symbol, what sort of object is it? Is it a physical object like a stone or a table? Physical objects always have a definite location in time and space. We can always ask where a certain object is. Where is my pen? Where is Mt. Everest? And we can also ask for the period of time during which an object has existed. When was my pen made? How long will it last? But these questions do not seem to apply to numbers. "Where is the number 3?" and "How much longer will the number 3 last?" appear to be absurd questions. It is implausible to think that numbers are physical objects located in space and time. Nor are they items that are perceptible to the senses. Although I can see the apples on the table, I cannot see the number 3. For if a number were something that I could see, then it would have a color. But is the number 3 blue? If it were something that I could hear, then it would emit sounds. But what sound does 3 make?

A line of reasoning such as this provoked St. Augustine (354–430) to write:

> Whatever I may experience with my bodily senses, such as this air and earth and whatever corporeal matter they contain, I cannot know how long it will endure. But seven and three are ten, not only now but forever.... Therefore, I have said that the truth of number is incorruptible and common to all who think.... Numbers themselves are not drawn from the bodily senses.... Anyone who really thinks about the number one realizes that he cannot perceive it through the bodily senses, for whatever we experience through a sense is proven to be many, not one.... No one perceives all the numbers by any bodily sense, for they are innumerable. How do we know that this is true for all numbers? Through what ... vision do we discern so confidently the firm truth of number throughout

the whole innumerable series, unless by some inner light unknown to bodily sense?[16]

This conception of the nature of number is sometimes called Platonic because of its association with the Greek philosopher Plato. According to the Platonic view, there are two types of objects of thought that the human mind can grasp. The first type consists of physical objects in space and time. Sense perception is the basis of our knowledge of these objects. The second type consists of nonphysical objects that do not occupy space or time, that do not change or come into being or pass out of being. Plato called these objects *forms* or *ideas.* In medieval philosophy, it became customary to call them **universals.** They do not exist just within the human mind; they are not ideas in the psychological sense. They are as independent of the mind as are physical objects. But they belong to a world of their own, known through rational insight, not sense perception.

BERTRAND RUSSELL
(1872–1970)

Bertrand Russell is the most influential British philosopher of the twentieth century. He was educated at Cambridge University and remained there as a member of the faculty. He was briefly imprisoned during World War I because of an antiwar publication. He later taught at various universities in the United States, and in a famous incident, his appointment to teach at the City College of New York was canceled because of his liberal views on divorce and sexual ethics. In 1950, he won the Nobel prize for literature. During his final years, he organized demonstrations against nuclear weapons and joined the opponents of the Vietnam War. Most of his early writings centered on issues in mathematics and logic. With Alfred North Whitehead, he wrote *Principia Mathematica* (1910–1913), one of the most important contributions to symbolic logic. His greatest subsequent influence was in the areas of the theory of knowledge and metaphysics. His main philosophical books are *Our Knowledge of the External World* (1914), *Mysticism and Logic* (1918), *Analysis of Mind* (1921), *Analysis of Matter* (1927), and *An Inquiry into Meaning and Truth* (1940).

One of the most prominent of modern philosophers, Bertrand Russell, describes the world of universals as follows:

We shall find it convenient only to speak of things *existing* when they are in time, that is to say, when we can point to some time *at* which they exist. . . . Thus

---

[16]St. Augustine, *On Free Choice of the Will,* trans. Anna S. Benjamin and L. H. Hackstaff (Indianapolis: Bobbs-Merrill, 1964), pp. 54–56.

thoughts and feelings, minds and physical objects *exist*. But universals do not exist in this sense; we shall say that they *subsist* or *have being,* where "being" is opposed to "existence" as being timeless. The world of universals, therefore, may also be described as the world of being. The world of being is unchangeable, rigid, exact, delightful to the mathematician, the logician, the builder of metaphysical systems, and all who love perfection more than life. The world of existence is fleeting, vague, without sharp boundaries, without any clear plan or arrangement, but it contains all thoughts and feelings, all the data of sense, and all physical objects, everything that can do either good or harm, everything that makes any difference to the value of life and the world. According to our temperaments, we shall prefer the contemplation of the one or of the other.[17]

According to the Platonist, numbers are universals and belong to the world of being. Characteristics have also been thought to be universals as well. The world of existence, the world of objects and events in space and time, consists of particulars. According to Plato, many different particulars can participate in the same universal. For example, many different particular things may be cubical in shape. This means that they all participate in the universal cube.

THE NATURE OF NUMBER

To say that a number is a universal is not yet to say precisely what numbers are. The dominant contemporary account of the nature of number is due to the logical researches of Frege and Russell. To understand their contribution, let us think about these two statements:

>   (*a*) There are red apples on the table.
>   (*b*) There are three apples on the table.

Although the surface grammar of these sentences is the same, they are really quite different in logical structure. From (a) it follows that each of the apples on the table is red. But obviously it does not follow from (b) that each of the apples is three. The difference is that whereas a characteristic like red applies to a group of things by belonging to each member of the group, a number belongs to the group as a whole rather than to its members. In a dozen eggs, the number 12 applies to the whole set of eggs, not to the eggs taken individually. No single egg is a dozen.

We can say, then, that whatever numbers are, they are things that belong to groups or sets of objects rather than individual members of those groups. This thought is again confirmed when we notice that to ask a definite question about number, we first have to specify which set of objects we are asking about. For example, suppose that I have ten bags of marbles on a table, each bag containing ten marbles. If I point to the items on the table and ask, "How many?", the question is ambiguous. Do I mean, "How many

---

[17]Bertrand Russell, *The Problems of Philosophy* (Oxford: Oxford University Press, 1951), pp. 99–100.

bags?" or do I mean, "How many marbles?" If I meant the bags, the answer is ten; if I meant the marbles, the answer is one hundred. We are not in a position to count objects until we have first classified them and identified the sets to which they belong.

Numbers, then, belong to sets of objects. Take the number 3 as an example. It belongs to any group of three things. Let us call a group of three things a trio. The number 3 belongs to each and every trio. What, then, is the number 3? It is what all trios have in common. But what is that? What do they all have in common? After all, trios can differ from one another in many ways. What do three apples, three elephants, three stars, and three electrons have in common? The answer is obvious. They are each one of them a trio. That is, each of them belongs to the set of trios. Take all the trios in the universe. Take all the groups of things that have just three members. All these trios taken together is the set of all trios. So what each trio has in common with every other trio, no matter how unlike their members are from one another, is that each trio is a member of the set of all trios.

Russell summarizes this line of thinking as follows:

> A particular number is not identical with any collection of terms having that number: the number 3 is not identical with the trio consisting of Brown, Jones, and Robinson. The number 3 is something which all trios have in common, and which distinguishes them from other collections. A number is something that characterises certain collections, namely those that have that number.[18]

If the number 3 is what is common to all trios, and if all trios have in common the fact that each belongs to the set of all trios, then it is natural to identify the number 3 with the set of all trios. Numbers are just the sets that are common to sets of objects that have the same number. If two sets have the same number of objects in them, then they are said to be *similar* to each other. A number, then, is a class or set or group of similar sets. The number 2 is the set of all couples; the number 4 is the set of all quadruples; and the number 5 is the set of all quintuples; and so forth.

Russell explains his identification of numbers with sets of similar sets as follows:

> We naturally think that the class of couples (for example) is something different from the number 2. But there is no doubt about the class of couples: it is indubitable and not difficult to define, whereas the number 2, in any other sense, is a metaphysical entity about which we can never feel sure that it exists or that we have tracked it down. It is therefore more prudent to content ourselves with the class of couples, which we are sure of, then to hunt for a problematical number 2 which must always remain elusive. Accordingly we set up the following definition:—*The number of a class is the class of all those classes that are similar to it.* Thus the number of a couple will be the class of all couples. In fact, the class of all couples will *be* the number 2, according to our definition.[19]

[18]Bertrand Russell, *Introduction to Mathematical Philosophy* (London: George Allen and Unwin, 1953), pp. 11–12.
[19]Ibid., p. 18.

Russell's argument may be understood as an attempt to lessen the mystery of numbers by identifying the more mysterious with the less mysterious. There appears to be no mystery about sets or classes. That there is a set of all couples Russell does not doubt. But the number 2, for instance, seems to be a mysterious and elusive thing, something that is not in space and time, something that cannot be perceived. So Russell proposes that numbers be construed as sets. Moreover, sets can serve as numbers for mathematical purposes. Just as numbers can be added to one another, so can sets. For example, take a set with three members and another set with two members. Then, assuming that these sets have no members in common, the set that consists of the three objects of the first and the two objects of the second will have five members. So this combined set, sometimes called the union of the two sets, will be a set that belongs to the class of all quintuples, that is, it will have the number 5.

If you have been able to follow Russell's argument thus far, you may be wondering about the numbers 0 and 1. With what sets can these be identified? If we were to continue the line of reasoning that Russell started, then the number 1 would be identified with the set of all sets with one member, and 0 would be identified with the set of all sets with no members. But are there such sets? Thus far in our thinking about sets, we have been content to identify them with the groups or collections of objects of everyday life. We have spoken about groups of apples and pencils and stars. For most purposes, there is nothing wrong with thinking of sets as groups. But mathematicians have developed a theory called *set theory* in which sets become differentiated to some extent from the groups of everyday life. In set theory there can be sets with only one member in it. For instance, the set of all the satellites of the earth has only one member in it, namely, the moon. Although we would not normally think of such a set as a group because groups must have several members, nevertheless, according to set theory, there are sets with only one member. These are called *unit sets*. The number 1 is to be identified with the set of all unit sets. Now consider the set of all mermaids. Because there are no mermaids, according to set theory, the set of all mermaids will have no members. It is an empty set. According to our commonsense view of groups, there cannot be a group with nothing in it. But there are sets with no members. Because sets are the same when their members are the same, there is only one set with no members in it. It is called the empty set or the null set. The number 0 is identified with the set whose only member is the empty set.

We are now in a position to see that there is a connection between Platonism and rationalism. Rationalists have tended to be Platonists and vice versa. The rationalist says that there is synthetic a priori knowledge as well as analytic knowledge and that we learn the truth of a priori statements through a process of rational insight. The Platonist adds that what the mind apprehends through rational insight are connections of various sorts among universals, including characteristics, numbers, and sets. In the following passage, Russell combines rationalism and Platonism:

> Let us revert to the proposition "two and two are four." It is fairly obvious . . . that this proposition states a relation between the universal "two" and the universal "four." This suggests a proposition which we shall now endeavour to establish: namely, *All a priori knowledge deals exclusively with the relations of*

universals. . . . Thus the statement "two and two are four" deals exclusively with universals, and therefore may be known by anybody who is acquainted with the universals concerned and can perceive the relation between them which the statement asserts. It must be taken as a fact, discovered by reflecting upon our knowledge, that we have the power of sometimes perceiving such relations between universals, and therefore of sometimes knowing general *a priori* propositions such as those of arithmetic and logic.[20]

Logical Truth

After our discussion of the nature of numbers and universals, there still remains the question whether or not arithmetic is to be interpreted as analytic, as the modern empiricist claims, or as synthetic, as Kant claims. Does Russell's account of the nature of number throw any light upon this issue?

In 1910, Russell published a major work in logic entitled *Principia Mathematica,* written in collaboration with Alfred North Whitehead. Using a number of ideas that were first developed by Frege a generation earlier, Russell and Whitehead tried to demonstrate that the truths of arithmetic can be deduced from logic. We saw how Russell showed that the truths of arithmetic were part of set theory. If we regard set theory as a part of logic, then arithmetic becomes a part of logic. You remember that an analytic statement was earlier defined as a statement that follows from logic alone, plus the definition of terms. So if the ideas of Frege, Russell, and Whitehead are correct, it would follow that the truths of arithmetic are analytic. This is sometimes called the **logistic thesis.**

But what is logic? What is a truth of logic? Are logical truths analytic or synthetic? Are logical truths themselves known a priori? It is time to say a few words about the nature of logic.

Logical theory was introduced by the philosophers of ancient Greece and given its first systematic presentation in the writings of Aristotle. His chief work in formal logic, the *Prior Analytics,* presents his account of inference. As it was developed by Aristotle and subsequent thinkers to the present day, logic is the study of inference or argument. When we reason about something and draw a conclusion, we can usually present our reasoning in the form of an inference or an argument. An argument has two parts. One part is the *conclusion* that we infer. The other part consists of the *premises,* those statements from which we draw the conclusion. Here is an example of an argument with two premises.

> (*a*) All Athenians are Greeks.
> Plato was an Athenian.
> Therefore, Plato was a Greek.

The main question of logic is to determine whether or not an argument is *valid,* that is, whether or not the conclusion really does follow from the premises. Logical theory is

---

[20]Russell, *Problems*, pp. 103–105.

concerned with developing methods for evaluating and criticizing arguments. Thus, logicians as such are not interested in specific arguments such as (a). They wish to develop a system of general rules that applies to large classes of arguments. They proceed as follows. Argument (a) is of a certain form or pattern. We can represent the general pattern exemplified by (a) by replacing the descriptive terms with letters:

> (*b*) All M are N.
> X is an M.
> Therefore, X is an N.

The letters are called variables. Using variables, the logician is able to represent the logical form of any argument. Another example is

> (*c*) No vegetables are animals.
> All carrots are vegetables.
> Therefore, no carrots are animals.

This is of the logical form:

> (*d*) No M are N.
> All O are M.
> Therefore, no O are N.

It turns out that all arguments of the forms (b) and (d) are valid. This means that in all such arguments the conclusion follows from the premises. And when the conclusion follows, then if the premises are true, the conclusion must be true. In a valid argument, you can't have true premises and a false conclusion. A valid argument with true premises is sometimes called a *proof* because it proves the truth of its conclusion.

We can now understand why logic is sometimes described as being *formal*. It is formal because the logician wants to study the forms or patterns of arguments. Since the further development of logic in the nineteenth and twentieth centuries, it has become common to call formal logic *symbolic* or *mathematical logic*.

In modern presentations of logic, it is customary to formulate the rules of valid inference as if they were statements. For example, (b) can be formulated as

> (*e*) If all M are N, and X is an M, then X is an N.

And (d) becomes

> (*f*) If no M are N, and all O are M, then no O are N.

Examples (e) and (f) are not actually statements but become statements when the variables are replaced by descriptive words. For this reason they are more properly called *statement forms*.

Most of the truths of logic are the statement forms corresponding to valid arguments such as (e) and (f). Logical truths have two characteristics that distinguish them from truths of other kinds, such as truths of biology or physics or history. First, a logical truth remains true no matter what terms are used to replace the variables. No matter what words replace the letters M, N, and X in (e) or the letters M, N, and O in (f), we end up with a true statement. This means that those statement forms which express truths of logic remain true under all interpretations. *Being true under all interpretations* is the most important characteristic of logical truth.

Second, logicians want to develop a theory of valid argument that applies to all arguments, no matter what they are about. They want a theory that applies to all cases, to the work of the biologist, the mathematician, the historian, and to the arguments of everyday life. Therefore, the truths that they try to formulate are neutral regarding subject matter. Biologists study living beings, but logicians do not. Mathematicians study numbers, but logicians do not. Physicists study matter in motion, but logicians do not. What then do logicians study? They study those patterns of inference that can be used in reasoning about anything whatever. In a sense, then, they study everything, because they study those forms of language in which anything can be represented. Thus, the second major feature of logical truths is that they are *neutral regarding subject matter*.

Doubts about the Distinction between the Analytic and the Synthetic

THE PROBLEM OF DEFINITION

Our discussion thus far has presupposed the distinction that Kant made between analytic and synthetic statements and between a priori and empirical statements. The contemporary debate between rationalism and empiricism is based on the question, Is there any synthetic a priori knowledge? The question of the nature of mathematical truth has been couched in Kant's terms: Are the truths of arithmetic analytic or synthetic? Are they empirical or a priori?

Recently, doubts have been raised whether the very terms by means of which these questions have been raised are acceptable. In particular, doubts have been raised about the distinction between the analytic and the synthetic. Can we really make the distinction as confidently as Kant? Even if we can in some cases, perhaps it is not universally applicable to all cases, as Kant thought. In this section, I will present some of the reasons for the present controversy and will give some indication of contemporary thought on the problem of truths of reason.

First, an analytic statement was defined as a statement that is deducible from the laws of logic if you allow synonyms to be replaced by synonyms. This is the sense in which "All bachelors are unmarried" and "All triangles have three angles" are analytic. But what about the laws of logic themselves? Take the famous law of noncontradiction. It says that given any object X and any property A, X cannot both have A and not have A. Is this analytic or synthetic? In one sense the answer is easy. There is a law of logic that says that any statement is deducible from itself. Thus, the laws of logic are deducible from the laws of logic because they are deducible from themselves. This makes them analytic, according to our definition. But they are analytic in a very trivial and uninteresting sense. Their being analytic does not explain the nature of logical truth.

The basic idea of the distinction between the analytic and the synthetic is that some statements are true because of the way the world is—the synthetic statements—and others are true because of their meaning—the analytic statements. There are thus two sources of truth: matters of fact and meaning. But we cannot always distinguish these sources so easily. For example, suppose that someone claims that the equation $5 = 3 + 2$ is analytic because it can be proved to be true using certain definitions plus certain laws of logic alone. The definitions are as follows:

$$D1: 2 = 1 + 1$$
$$D2: 3 = 2 + 1$$
$$D3: 4 = 3 + 1$$
$$D4: 5 = 4 + 1$$

Using these definitions and substituting synonymous terms freely for one another, we can construct the following proof:

$$5 = 5 \text{ (the law of identity)}$$
$$5 = 4 + 1 \text{ (D4)}$$
$$5 = 3 + 1 + 1 \text{ (D3)}$$
$$5 = 3 + 2 \text{ (D1)}$$

Does this proof establish that the equation is analytic? Kant and his followers would answer "No." They would immediately point out that to call D1 through D4 definitions assumes the very point at issue. According to Kant's theory, these are not definitions at all. They are synthetic statements. Thus, the fact that $5 = 3 + 2$ can be derived from them does not establish that it is an analytic proposition. So the disagreement between rationalism and empiricism as to whether certain statements are analytic or synthetic spills over into a disagreement as to whether certain statements are or are not definitions. It is often difficult to distinguish meaning from matters of fact.

THE MEANING OF MEANING

Because of persistent disagreements over what is and what is not a matter of meaning, some philosophers have even questioned the concept of meaning. Frege made a very important distinction between the meaning or sense of a word and its reference.[21] He noticed that there can be pairs of words or phrases that have different meanings and yet refer to the same things. For example, the phrases "the Morning Star" and "the Evening Star" name the same planet, Venus, but have different meanings or senses.

---

[21]Gottlob Frege, "On Sense and Reference," in *Translations from the Philosophical Writings of Gottlob Frege* (Oxford: Basil Blackwell, 1952).

The same holds true for the terms "the author of *Ivanhoe*" and "the author of *Waverley*." Both terms refer to Sir Walter Scott, but they each mean something different. Now there is no problem in principle about the reference of words. Their references are just the objects or things in the world that they name. But what is the meaning of meaning? What kind of thing is the meaning of a word?

One answer that has often been advanced is that the meaning of a word or phrase is the characteristic or property that anything must have in order that that word or phrase refer to it. Thus, the reference of "the author of *Ivanhoe*" is Sir Walter Scott and its meaning is the characteristic of having written *Ivanhoe*. In this view, to verify the statement "All bachelors are unmarried," one must grasp that the characteristic of being unmarried is included within the characteristic of being a bachelor. This conception of the nature of meaning leads to the by-now-familiar view of Plato that a split exists between the world of empirical particulars and the world of universals. A nominalist, who rejects the world of universals, would be unable to accept this account of meaning and will try to make do with a purely referential account of the way that language applies to the world.

QUINE'S SKEPTICISM ABOUT MEANING

According to W. V. Quine, this account of meaning fails for another reason. To admit objects into our ontology or world view, says Quine, we need to have ways of telling whether we have one or two such objects. We need a criterion of identity. If I have no way of telling whether X and Y are the same or different, then I have a reason for doubting whether there really is anything named by *X* and *Y*. What is the criterion of identity for meanings? If two words are synonymous, then they have the same meaning. So we can use synonymy as the criterion of identity that we are looking for. To determine whether the meanings expressed by *X* and *Y* are the same or different, just find out whether or not they are synonymous. But, argues Quine, there is no valid test for synonymy. We had best drop this Platonist theory of meaning and develop the theory of reference.[22] Plato's two worlds are just a myth.

Quine concludes that the distinction between analytic and synthetic cannot be justified:

> It is obvious that truth in general depends both on language and extralinguistic fact. The statement "Brutus killed Caesar" would be false if the world had been different in certain ways, but it would also be false if the word "killed" happened rather to have the sense of "begat." Thus one is tempted to suppose in general that the truth of a statement is somehow analyzable into a linguistic component and a factual component. Given this supposition, it next seems reasonable that in some statements the factual component should be null; and these are the analytic statements. But, for all its a priori reasonableness, a boundary between analytic and synthetic statements simply has not been drawn. That there is such a

[22]Quine's essays "On What There Is" and "Two Dogmas of Empiricism" in *From a Logical Point of View* (Cambridge: Harvard University Press, 1961) develop this argument in detail.

distinction to be drawn at all is an unempirical dogma of empiricists, a metaphysical article of faith.[23]

Quine rejects both the distinction between analytic and synthetic and that between a priori and empirical. The rationalist would respond by pointing out that there is a clear difference between "There is a penny in the drawer" and "3 + 2 = 5." If I open the drawer and find no penny, then the former statement is refuted. But no observations will lead me to reject the latter. Thus, the former is empirical and the latter is a priori. Quine would reply that although there is a difference between the two statements, it is not at all captured or explained by the Kantian distinctions.

Quine develops an alternative type of explanation based upon a coherence conception of verification like the one we discussed in Chapter Eight.

> The totality of our so-called knowledge or beliefs, from the most casual matters of geography and history to the profoundest laws of atomic physics or even of pure mathematics and logic, is a man-made fabric which impinges on experience only along the edges. . . . A conflict with experience at the periphery occasions readjustment in the interior of the field. Truth values have to be redistributed over some of our statements. Reevaluation of some statements entails reevaluation of others, because of their logical inter-connections—the logical laws being in turn simply certain further statements of the system. . . . But the total field is so underdetermined by . . . experience, that there is much latitude of choice as to what statements to reevaluate in the light of any single contrary experience.[24]

According to Quine, even if an experience leads to a conflict with our belief system, we nevertheless have a choice regarding which of our beliefs we are going to revise. Quine claims that statements differ from one another by reference to how easily they are to be given up in the face of a conflicting experience:

> But such choice of what to revise is subject to a vague scheme of priorities. Some statements about physical objects, e.g., "My pen is in my hand," "The mercury is at 80°," are in some sense closer to possible experience than others; and such statements must be guarded pretty jealously once the appropriate experiences have appeared. Should revision of the system become necessary, other statements than these are to suffer. . . . There is also, however, another and somewhat opposite priority: the more fundamental a law is to our conceptual scheme, the less likely we are to choose it for revision. When some revision of our system of statements is called for, we prefer, other things being equal, a revision which disturbs the system least.[25]

This idea that certain statements are so fundamental to our system of beliefs that a change in them would lead to a widespread change throughout the whole system is the

---

[23]Quine, *Logical Point of View,* pp. 36–37.
[24]Ibid., pp. 42–43.
[25]W. V. Quine, *Methods of Logic* (New York: Holt, Rinehart and Winston, 1964), pp. xii–xiii.

basis of Quine's approach to the truths of logic and mathematics. Because logic and mathematics are so central to our belief systems, they are unlikely to be revised. But revision is not completely excluded as an option:

> Mathematics and logic, central as they are to the conceptual scheme, tend to be accorded such immunity, in view of our conservative preference for revisions which disturb the system least; and herein, perhaps, lies the "necessity" which the laws of mathematics and logic are felt to enjoy. . . . Mathematical and logical laws themselves are not immune to revision if it is found that essential simplifications of our whole conceptual scheme will ensue.[26]

According to the dominant traditional accounts, logic and mathematics were considered a priori because, being fundamental to our systems of belief, it was thought that they were immune from revision. Quine agrees that they are fundamental, but he does not conclude that they are therefore a priori and immune from revision by experience. Systematic considerations of simplicity may make it prudent to change logic and mathematics. At least that possibility must not be excluded. For Quine, the only sense in which the laws of logic are necessary is that they are central to our system. Because centrality is a matter of degree, there is no sharp distinction to be drawn between necessary and contingent statements. The whole Kantian apparatus is thereby swept away.

Quine's views represent a partial return to Mill's version of empiricism. Logic and mathematics are part of a system of beliefs that is susceptible to empirical revision. The major difference between the older empiricism of Mill and the new version represented by Quine is that the latter is more appreciative of the systematic interconnections among our beliefs. Whereas the older empiricism thought that our ideas can be tested individually by referring them to sense experience one by one, the newer version claims that experience does not affect ideas individually but only in their systematic interconnection.

According to Quine's view, the Kantian distinctions represent an incorrect explanation of a phenomenon whose existence he admits. The phenomenon is the fact that some beliefs are less likely to be revised than others, that some feel intuitively more sure. But Quine rejects the notions of a priori truth, rational insight, and the world of universals that were a part of traditional accounts. In its place he proposes a coherence theory of knowledge according to which some beliefs are more likely to be revised than others in light of conflicting experience.

The issue between rationalism and the new empiricism represented by Quine focuses on the question of the existence of characteristics or universals. Rationalism claims that there are universals, that general words mean universals, and that the mind has the power of rational insight into necessary connections among universals. Empiricism rejects all of these claims. It insists that we can develop a referential account of meaning that does not presuppose the existence of universals. It denies the existence of the kind of necessity that rationalism accepts. And it refuses to accept rational insight as one of the powers of the mind. These are the terms in which philosophers are now discussing the great question of truths of reason.

[26]Ibid., pp. xiii–xiv.

Summary

From the time of Plato in ancient Athens to the present day, the question of a priori knowledge has been a major philosophical issue. Rationalists have tended to explain it as a form of innate knowledge. For the empiricist Locke, once the mind is stocked with ideas drawn from experience, it is able to acquire an intuitive grasp of relations among them. Kant argued that necessity is the basic criterion of the a priori. For Kant there is both analytic and synthetic a priori knowledge. Since Kant, rationalists have claimed that there are truths that are synthetic a priori, whereas empiricism claims that if there is any a priori knowledge at all, it is analytic.

In recent philosophy, the status of mathematics has been the chief issue in discussions of a priori knowledge. John Stuart Mill argued that mathematical statements assert well-confirmed empirical matters of fact. But most contemporary empiricists have claimed that mathematical truths are analytic. The conventionalist account—which claims that all a priori propositions are true by convention—fails because it confuses statements with the sentences that are used to express them. Rationalism asserts that a priori knowledge is acquired by means of the mind's power of rational insight into connections among characteristics or universals.

Empiricism in the twentieth century has tended to rely on the logistic thesis, which says that mathematics is a branch of logic. But the thesis depends upon a controversial theory of the nature of logic. Recently, Quine has enlivened the debate by calling into question a certain assumption common to both empiricism and rationalism, namely, that a sharp distinction can be drawn between statements that are analytic and those that are synthetic. The new empiricism, as represented by Quine, rejects the traditional notions of a priori truths, universals, and rational insight.

Glossary

Analytic statement: A statement that is true in virtue of the meanings of its terms.

A priori knowledge: Knowledge that is independent of experience; knowledge that is based upon reason.

Axiom: See **Axiomatic method.**

Axiomatic method: A way of organizing mathematical ideas into a system consisting of axioms or postulates that are not proved in the system and theorems that are proved by deducing them from the axioms.

Contingent truth: A true statement that might have been false, one whose falsehood is conceivable.

Conventionalism: The idea that a priori statements are true by virtue of linguistic conventions.

Demonstrative knowledge: Knowledge gained by means of deductive reasoning from true premises.

Empirical knowledge: Knowledge based upon experience.

Entailment: See **Implication.**

Formalism: Conventionalism as applied to mathematics; in particular, the idea that mathematical truths are really rules for manipulating symbols.

Implication: A statement A implies a statement B when, if A is true, then B must be true.

Intuitive knowledge: Knowledge gained by direct awareness of the thing known.

Logistic thesis: The theory that the truths of arithmetic can be deduced from truths of logic.

Necessary truth: A true statement that could not have been false under any circumstances; a statement that is true in all possible worlds.

Postulate: See **Axiomatic method.**

Synthetic statement: A statement that formulates a matter of fact; a statement that is true because of the facts and not only because of its meaning.

Theorem: See **Axiomatic method.**

Universals: Entities such as properties, classes, and numbers that can be exemplified by many particulars.

Further Reading

One can trace the question of truths of reason in the history of philosophy by reading Plato, *Meno* and *Phaedo;* Aristotle, *Posterior Analytics;* Descartes, *Meditations;* John Locke, *An Essay concerning Human Understanding,* parts I and IV; Leibniz, *New Essays concerning Human Understanding,* parts I and IV; and Kant, *Critique of Pure Reason.*

Elementary and authoritative presentations of the logistic thesis are included in Gottlob Frege, *The Foundations of Arithmetic,* trans. J. L. Austin (Oxford: Basil Blackwell, 1953); and Bertrand Russell, *Introduction to Mathematical Philosophy* (London: George Allen and Unwin, 1919). The approach of W. V. Quine is contained in his *From a Logical Point of View* (Cambridge: Harvard University Press, 1953) and *Word and Object* (Cambridge: MIT Press, 1960).

For Kripke's revision of Kant's framework see his "Naming and Necessity" in Donald Davidson and Gilbert Harmon (eds.), *Semantics of Natural Language* (Dordrecht: D. Reidel, 1972); a briefer account of Kripke's views is in his "Identity and Necessity," in Milton Munitz (ed.), *Identity and Individuation* (New York: New York University Press, 1971). For the topic of universals, a number of important contemporary papers are reprinted in Charles Landesman (ed.), *The Problem of Universals* (New York: Basic Books, 1971). A good starting point for recent work in the philosophy of mathematics is the anthology *The Philosophy of Mathematics,* ed. Paul Benacerraf and Hilary Putnam (Englewood Cliffs, N.J.: Prentice-Hall, 1964).

Questions for Thought and Discussion

1. Some philosophers have claimed that not everything that is known can be proved, so that some statements are intuitive or self-evident. Do you agree that not everything

that is known can be proved? Why does this claim support the idea that there is self-evident truth?

2. Why for Kant is there such a close connection between a truth's being necessary and its being knowable a priori?

3. Explain the meaning of the question, "How is synthetic a priori knowledge possible?" How is this question relevant to the disagreement between empiricists and rationalists?

4. Compare Kant's and Mill's accounts of mathematical truth. Do you agree with either? With neither? Or do you think that the truths of arithmetic are mere conventions? Or only analytic statements?

5. Do numbers have any characteristics that show that they cannot be plausibly classified as physical things? For example, can numbers be observed? Do numbers occupy space and time?

6. Show how Quine's rejection of the distinction between analytic and synthetic that Kant introduced leads him to adopt a coherence theory of knowing.

APPENDIX ONE

The Basic Ideas of Logic

REASONING AND ARGUMENT

The study of logic has been an integral part of philosophy ever since Aristotle began to develop it systematically in the fourth century B.C. The main purpose of logic is to develop methods that enable us to criticize and to evaluate reasoning. We use reasoning to form our beliefs about the world and to decide what lines of conduct are best to pursue. If our reasoning is good, then there is a chance that our beliefs will be true and our conduct successful. Poor reasoning often leads to disaster. Thus, logic can make an important contribution to the improvement of human life by enabling us to distinguish good from bad reasoning.

When we express our reasoning in words, the result is an *argument*. An example of a simple argument is

      (a) (1) It is very cloudy outside.
             (2) So, it will soon rain.

From statement (1), the speaker draws the *conclusion* (2). He uses (1) to support his conclusion. The statement or statements that are used in an argument to support the conclusion are called the *premises*. An argument consists of one or more premises and a conclusion.

It is common for us to state our arguments incompletely. We do not often formulate explicitly all our premises. Take the argument "You should take your umbrella because it is going to rain." From the premise, "It is going to rain" I have drawn the conclusion "You should take an umbrella." But my conclusion is justified only if I am assuming various things that I have not said. For example, I am assuming that you do not want to get wet and that an umbrella will prevent you from getting wet. A fuller statement of the argument is

      (b) It is going to rain.
           You do not want to get wet.
           An umbrella will prevent you from getting wet.
           Therefore, you should take an umbrella.

One reason why we often fail to include all the premises is that, as in this example, they are obvious and do not need to be stated. In other cases, however, the things we fail to say may be very doubtful, and we may be entirely unaware that we are taking for granted something of which we should be critical. When we try to analyze or evaluate the logical structure of an argument, it is customary to formulate all the premises that are needed to support the conclusion.

ARGUMENTS THAT ARE VALID AND SOUND

A good argument is one in which the premises support its conclusion. Two conditions are necessary for an argument to provide support: The argument must be *valid* and it must be *sound*.

An argument is *valid* when the premises would make it reasonable to accept the conclusion provided they are true. Thus, it would be reasonable to accept the conclusion of

(c) All animals that have mammary glands to feed their young are mammals.
All whales are animals that have mammary glands to
feed their young.
Therefore, all whales are mammals.

provided both premises are true.

An argument is *sound* when it is valid and the premises are indeed true. Thus, (c) is sound as well as valid because both premises are true. You must not think, however, that all valid arguments are sound. Consider this example:

(d) All dogs are cats.
All cats are elephants.
Therefore, all dogs are elephants.

According to this argument, it would be reasonable to believe that all dogs are elephants provided the premises were true. But they are not true. So, although (d) is valid, it is not sound.

DEDUCTIVE AND INDUCTIVE LOGIC

Certain arguments are intended to be conclusive. Thus, (c) proves conclusively that all whales are mammals. A conclusive argument is one in which the conclusion follows logically or necessarily from the premises. It is an argument in which if the premises are true, then the conclusion *must* be true. Another way of putting this point is to say that in a conclusive argument the premises *logically imply* or *entail* the conclusion. *Deductive logic* is the theory of conclusive arguments. A conclusive or deductive argument is sometimes called a *proof*.

Some arguments fail to be conclusive. For example, (a) does not prove conclusively that it will soon rain, for clouds are not always or necessarily followed by rain. This argument belongs to a class of sound arguments that do not prove their conclusions but nevertheless endow them with a degree of probability. Thus, (a) shows that it is likely or probable to some extent that it will soon rain. In an *inductive argument* like this one, the intention is for the premises to provide a degree of support or evidence for the conclusion or to show that the conclusion is more probable than not. *Inductive logic* (sometimes called the theory of probability or the theory of statistical reasoning) is the study of inductive arguments. In this appendix, we will be concerned with the ideas of deductive logic.

DEDUCTIVE VALIDITY

When a conclusive argument is valid, we say that it has *deductive validity*. A deductively valid argument can have true premises and a true conclusion, as does (c). In that case, it is sound as well. It can also have false premises and a false conclusion, as in (d). It can even have false premises and a true conclusion, as in

> (e) All apples are cats.
> All cats are fruits.
> Therefore, all apples are fruits.

In these three cases, the conclusion follows logically from the premises, that is, the conclusion is logically implied or entailed by the premises. But there *cannot* be a valid deductive argument whose premises are true and whose conclusion is false. A deductively valid argument is one in which, if the premises are true, then the conclusion *must* be true. This account of deductive validity clearly excludes the possibility of having true premises and a false conclusion.

It is because a valid argument preserves the truth of the premises that we wish to construct valid arguments and detect invalid ones. An invalid argument cannot be trusted because it may not preserve the truth of the premises. Reasoning that starts with truths and ends with falsehoods is bad reasoning that can lead to faulty decisions and wrong actions.

ARGUMENTS

i. An argument consists of a *premise* or *premises* and a *conclusion*. The premises are *statements* that provide *support* for the conclusion. Statements can be either *true* or *false*.

ii. A *valid argument* is one in which the premises make it reasonable to accept the conclusion, provided the premises are true. A *sound argument* is one that is valid *and* has true premises.

iii. A *valid deductive argument* is an argument whose premises logically imply the conclusion. A *valid inductive argument* is an argument whose premises provide a degree of support for the conclusion but do not logically imply the conclusion.

FORMAL LOGIC

Deductive logic is often called formal logic. The reason is that logic studies the form or pattern or structure of arguments. A formal approach to the study of reasoning began with Aristotle's *Prior Analytics* in the fourth century B.C. In that work, Aristotle developed a theory of a type of argument called the *syllogism*. Arguments (c), (d), and (e) are all syllogisms.

Aristotle was not content to present particular examples of the syllogism. He wanted, instead, to classify syllogistic arguments into various types and to find general tests for the validity of these types. His basic strategy was to replace certain of the words in a syllogism by letters. For example, if in (e) we replace *apples* by *A* and *cats* by *B* and *fruits* by *C,* we arrive at the following.

> (f) All A are B.
> All B are C.
> Therefore, all A are C.

This argument represents the general logical form of (e). We can see that we can easily derive particular syllogisms of that form by substituting words for the letters. The letters are called *variables*. Following the example of Aristotle, it has become the practice of logicians to represent the form of arguments by the use of variables.

The advantage of this procedure may be grasped by noticing that every argument of the form (f) is deductively valid. Thus, (f) provides one pattern of valid argumentation. The use of variables, then, enables the logician to formulate general laws of logic. For example, it is a general law of logic that any argument that assumes the form (f) is deductively valid.

There can also be laws pertaining to arguments that are deductively invalid. For example, from the fact that all whales are mammals, it does not follow that all mammals are whales. The form of this example of invalid reasoning is

> (g) All A are B.
> Therefore, all B are A.

It is a general law of logic that (g) represents an invalid argument. It is invalid because it allows for arguments with true premises and a false conclusion.

The branch of logic that Aristotle studied most deeply is the theory of the logical relations among statements of the following forms:

> All A are B.
> No A are B.
> Some A are B.
> Some A are not B.

In modern logic, words such as *all, no,* and *some* are called *quantifiers*. Using this modern terminology, we can say that in the *Prior Analytics* Aristotle initiated the study of *quantificational logic*.

SENTENTIAL LOGIC

The Stoic philosophers of the ancient world began the study of a branch of logic that is today called *sentential logic*. Consider, for example, the following argument:

(h) If you are going to leave the house without
your umbrella, then you will get wet.
You are going to leave the house without your
umbrella.
Therefore, you will get wet.

The general pattern on which the validity of this argument depends is determined by the relations among the sentences. To see this, replace "You are going to leave the house without your umbrella" by "P" and "You will get wet" by "Q." This yields

(i) If P, then Q.
P.
Therefore, Q.

The letters *P* and *Q* are called *sentential variables*. Any argument of this form is valid. In sentential logic, the relations among sentences of the following forms are studied.

P. (affirmative sentence)
It is not the case that P. (negative sentence)
If P, then Q. (conditional sentence)
P and Q. (conjunction)
P or Q. (disjunction)
P if and only if Q. (biconditional)

SYMBOLIC LOGIC

During the past one hundred years, there have been many advances in logical theory. The German logician Gottlob Frege combined and systematized sentential and quantification logic. In their *Principia Mathematica,* Bertrand Russell and Alfred North Whitehead extended the work of Frege and developed a system of symbolism that is still in use. The idea of a logical system has been deeply explored, and a field of study has been developed call *metamathematics,* which studies the general properties of logical systems. New kinds of logic have been invented and studied. Logic has become one of the most flourishing and interesting fields of philosophy, and it has deeply influenced the methods used in the other fields.

These contemporary developments are often collectively called *symbolic logic* because they tend to employ a special symbolism or language to represent arguments and items of discourse in place of ordinary language. It is customary to represent the types of sentence studied by sentential logic by the following symbolism:

P (affirmative sentence)
−P (negative sentence)
P ⊃ Q (conditional sentence)
P ● Q (conjunction)
PvQ (disjunction)
P ≡ Q (equivalence)

FALLACIES

A fallacy is an error in reasoning. The interest in fallacies is as old as philosophy itself. In his dialogue *Euthydemus*, Plato portrays two sophists who purposely use fallacies to mislead, defeat, or humiliate their opponents. An example of a fallacy given in the dialogue is the following:

> Is this your dog? Yes.
> Does your dog have puppies? Yes.
> So, your dog is a father, and he is yours, so
> the dog is your father, and you are the brother of
> the puppies.

This argument is fallacious because the premises could be true while the conclusion is clearly false. But some fallacies are not so obvious. Consider the following:

> (j) If it doesn't rain, then the plants will die.
> The plants died.
> Therefore, it did not rain.

One is not entitled to infer that it did not rain from these premises because there might have been other reasons why the plants died. A formal fallacy such as (j) is an argument that is intended to be conclusive but whose conclusion does not follow from the premises.

One way of detecting a formal fallacy is by the *method of counterexample*. The logical form of (j) is

> (k) If P, then Q.
> Q.
> Therefore, P.

If we can find an instance of (k) whose premises are true and whose conclusion is false, then we have established that (k) is not a valid argument form. For example, suppose you are walking in a dark forest and you think you see a tiger before you, but in reality it is a lion. Then the following premises are true:

> If that is a tiger, then I am in great danger.
> I am in great danger.

But the conclusion is

> That is a tiger.

Clearly, the conclusion is false. By showing that it is possible for (k) to have true premises and a false conclusion, it follows that (k) is not a valid argument form, and this is a reason to suspect the validity of (j).[1]

There are a number of *informal fallacies* that are useful to know because of their frequent occurrence. The fallacy of *begging the question (petitio principii)* occurs when one uses the very conclusion that one is trying to prove as one of the premises. For example, suppose that you are trying to prove that the witness to an accident is reliable and that his word can be trusted. But suppose the only evidence that he is trustworthy is that he has said so. So to use that evidence, one must assume that he is trustworthy, the very conclusion that you are trying to establish. Begging the question is an example of *arguing in a circle.*

In an *ad hominem argument,* one attempts to discredit something that someone says by discrediting the person who says it. This is a fallacy when the characteristics imputed to the person to discredit him are irrelevant to the question at issue. For example, it would be fallacious to try to discredit Darwin's theory of evolution by pointing out that some of the scientists who favor it were also supporters of former President Nixon. But some uses of the ad hominem argument are not fallacious. A lawyer who is cross-examining a witness may justifiably try to throw doubt on his testimony by mentioning that he was once convicted of perjury.

The fallacy of *post hoc ergo propter hoc* consists in inferring that because one event is followed by another event, the first must be the cause of the second. Thus, the fact that the price of automobiles rose immediately after the auto workers were given a wage increase does not prove that the price increase was caused by the wage increase. The price might have increased even in the absence of a wage increase. That one event is succeeded by another may lead you to suspect that the first caused the second, but it does not prove it.

A person commits the fallacy of *ignoratio elenchi* or *irrelevant conclusion* when he tries to prove or refute a conclusion different from the one that his opponent claims to have refuted or proved. For example, if a prosecuting attorney has a very weak case against a defendant accused of murder, he may try to prove that the defendant was guilty of habitual adultery. This may succeed in diverting the jury's attention from the real issue and allow him to win his case. This fallacy is often committed unintentionally when one of the parties to a dispute misinterprets the views of the other party. For example, authors often complain that their critics fail to understand what they are saying and that their criticisms are therefore irrelevant.

The *fallacy of ambiguity* occurs when one draws an incorrect conclusion because of the ambiguity or plurality of meanings of a word or phrase. For example, many dictatorial regimes describe their political systems as democratic, meaning thereby that they

---

[1] The fact that an argument exemplifies an invalid form does not prove conclusively that it is an invalid argument. For example,

P
Therefore, Q,

is an invalid form. Yet every argument, valid as well as invalid, exemplifies it.

rule on behalf of the people. If one should conclude from this description that an election in one of these countries was really a free election, one would have made an error based on the ambiguity of the word *democracy*.

CONTRADICTION AND INCONSISTENCY

It is important to avoid self-contradiction or inconsistency in one's thought and speech. The reason is that when one contradicts oneself, one has said something false. Two statements *contradict* each other when it is impossible for both of them to be true and both of them to be false—one must be true and the other false. For example, consider the statements

> 3 is the smallest prime number.
> 3 is not the smallest prime number.

These statements contradict each other. Two statements are *contraries* when they cannot both be true although they may both be false. Thus

> All swans are white.
> No swans are white.

These statements are contraries because they cannot both be true and, if some swans are white and some are black, they are both false.

A person is guilty of a *logical inconsistency* when something that he believes or says implies either a contradictory or a contrary pair of statements. For instance, someone who believes that whales are mammals and that whales are fish and that no fish are mammals is guilty of an inconsistency because what he believes implies that whales are and are not mammals.

THE LAWS OF THOUGHT

In the traditional logic inspired by the work of Aristotle, three logical laws were given special status. They were called the laws of thought. *The law of noncontradiction* says that a statement and its contradictory or negation cannot both be true. If P is any statement, then its negation can be represented by *not-P*. Thus, the negation of "3 is the smallest prime number" can be written as "not-3 is the smallest prime number" instead of "3 is not the smallest prime number." The law of noncontradiction can be formulated as follows: It is not the case that both P and not-P. *The law of excluded middle* says that any statement must be either true or false; there is no middle ground. With symbols, this is written as P or not-P. *The law of identity* asserts that each thing is identical with itself. With symbols, this is written as A = A. Although the standard systems of symbolic logic retain these laws, they are no longer singled out for special status. In certain nonstandard logical systems, the law of excluded middle does not occur, and there are controversies about the proper way to interpret and apply all three.

REDUCTIO AD ABSURDUM (RAA)

This is a type of argument that occurs frequently in philosophy, in mathematics, and in everyday life. To prove a conclusion P by the method of RAA, one assumes that P is false. This means that one assumes as a premise the negation of P, that is, not-P. If one can then deduce from not-P an inconsistency or some other type of absurdity, one has shown that P is true. For example, the following is an attempt to use RAA to prove that God exists. Assume that God does not exist. Then it follows that the universe has always existed (because there is no God to create a beginning of existence) and that it has never existed (because there is no God to give it existence). But that the universe has always existed and has never existed is an inconsistent statement. So that God does not exist implies an inconsistency and hence is false. So God must exist. Do you think that this is a successful use of RAA?

Further Reading

An excellent elementary survey of contemporary symbolic logic is in Alfred Tarski, *Introduction to Logic* (New York: Oxford University Press, 1963). There are many textbooks that can be used to master the fundamentals of symbolic logic. Three of the best are Albert E. Blumberg, *Logic: A First Course* (New York: Alfred A. Knopf, 1976); Howard Kahane, *Logic and Philosophy* (Belmont, California: Wadsworth, 1969); and Benson Mates, *Elementary Logic* (New York: Oxford University Press, 1965). The traditional Aristotelian approach to logic is presented in H. W. B. Joseph, *An Introduction to Logic* (Oxford: The Clarendon Press, 1946). An advanced text in symbolic logic that requires some mathematical background is Stephen Cole Kleene, *Introduction to Metamathematics* (Princeton: D. Van Nostrand Co., 1952).

APPENDIX TWO

Philosophical Research and Writing

REASONS FOR WRITING A PHILOSOPHY PAPER

There are several reasons for writing a paper on a philosophical subject. One of them is that writing about an idea is one of the best ways to come to an understanding of it. By attempting to express an idea in your own words, you gain a much greater understanding of its meaning and implications than if you merely confined yourself to reading the words of others. A beginning student in philosophy usually writes papers for this reason. Another reason is to develop a new idea of your own to present it to others for their comments and criticisms. One can discover how defensible one's ideas are only by exposing them to the criticisms of others. A student who has mastered the elements of philosophy and is beginning to form his or her own views on philosophical topics will write papers for this reason.

TYPES OF PAPERS

There are various kinds of papers that you can write. The type you select will depend upon your own interests and your assignment.

1. *Statement and interpretation of a theory.* You may wish to put into your own words a theory that some philosopher has developed. For example, take John Stuart Mill's idea that that action is right which brings about the greatest happiness for the greatest number. You may try to state his idea clearly in your own words, and you may attempt to identify the arguments that he gives for it. You should remember that the reasons a philosopher gives for his theory are an integral part of that theory. Remember also that a philosopher's reasons are often arguments against opposing views. Moreover, you may find that there are problems in interpreting Mill's meaning. What does he mean, for example, by *happiness* and *greatest happiness?* Perhaps there are different plausible interpretations of his meaning. Thus, your statement of his ideas may include an interpretation of them as well. An interpretation of an idea is a theory about what the idea means and implies. In presenting your interpretation, you should try to present your reasons for preferring it to alternative interpretations.

2. *Philosophical criticism.* In the course of formulating someone else's ideas, you may find reason to criticize them. In dealing critically with an idea, you are trying to find out whether it is true or false, right or wrong. You may end by rejecting the idea. Thus,

you may feel inclined to reject Mill's view that the greatest happiness for the greatest number is the criterion of right action because you think it is simply untrue or because you think that his arguments fail to prove it. Your criticism may also take the form of defending an idea against the criticism of others. You may, for example, show that Mill could have replied successfully to certain of the criticisms that have been directed against his ethical theory. Your criticism or defense of an idea should be accompanied by your reasons for the stand that you take. Philosophical thinking is essentially a rational activity. The process of giving reasons for your views is not a luxury you may dispense with.

3. *A topical paper.* Instead of beginning with the ideas of a particular philosopher as presented in a specific text, you may wish to master a more general topic and read those texts that shed light on it. For example, the topic you select may be the idea of happiness. What is happiness? What have various philosophers said about it? You may find yourself reading works by Mill and Bentham, by Aristotle and Epicurus. A topical paper involves organizing material taken from a variety of sources. In addition to stating and interpreting the ideas of various philosophers, you may wish to criticize them. A topical paper may very well include your own view. For example, what do you think happiness consists of?

4. *An independent inquiry.* Instead of organizing your paper around the ideas of others, you may wish to make an independent presentation of your own views on a certain issue. You may have, for example, your own theory of happiness that you wish to explain and defend. Such an inquiry could include references to the ideas of others; this is a common, though not invariable, practice of philosophers. For example, although Mill's theory of right conduct in his *Utilitarianism* is an independent inquiry, he does discuss the ideas of Kant and Bentham in the course of his own presentation. But Mill does not undertake a systematic survey of the ideas of others, for his main purpose is to present his own views.

5. *A book review.* Your paper may take the form of interpreting a book as a whole rather than just one idea in it. In that case, you have the responsibility for explaining the main themes and ideas contained in it and for showing how well or how badly they are organized and developed. A book review may contain your critical judgment about the philosophical significance and value of the book, and it may include a comparison with other books on the same topic.

6. *An historical topic.* Instead of emphasizing the criticism of ideas or the presentation of a new idea, you may wish to examine a philosophical idea in its historical context. Often, an historical paper examines the philosophical influences upon a particular text. For example, a paper can consider the extent of Bentham's influence upon Mill's ethical theory. Or it can consider the influence that a particular text has had: What effect, for instance, did Mill's *Utilitarianism* have upon the course of British ethics in the nineteenth century? A paper of this sort may study an idea in the context of the author's biography. What were the particular circumstances under which Mill wrote *Utilitarianism?* Finally, an historical paper may attempt to relate a philosophical idea to various historical trends and events. For example, it may try to show how Mill's political philosophy expressed the problems of a mass society with growing literacy among the working classes.

FINDING A TOPIC

The topic you select should be one that interests you. It should also be one that you want to learn more about, for that is one of the main purposes of writing a paper in the first place. At first you may have only a very general or vague idea in mind: "I want to do something with Plato's ethics." The next step is to narrow down the topic to something more manageable and definite. To accomplish this, you should engage in some preliminary reading. You might read some of Plato's more important writings. You might look at a brief account of Plato's life and thought in a history of philosophy or in the *Encyclopedia of Philosophy*. Suppose you have decided that you will write on Plato's theory of justice as presented in the *Republic*. At this point, it is a good idea to formulate your topic as a question. A research project can always be interpreted as an attempt to answer a question. By phrasing your topic as a question, you will be able to think of what you are doing as an attempt to discover something. Your subsequent reading and thinking can then be guided and controlled by a specific purpose instead of being aimless. What do you want to find out about Plato's theory of justice? Perhaps your question is, "How does Plato relate justice to the other moral virtues?" With a question in mind as specific as this, you can continue your work, confident that you know what you are doing.

PHILOSOPHICAL RESEARCH

Once you have settled upon a topic, you should then plan your research. The extent of your research depends upon several particular circumstances: the nature of the topic, your instructor's requirements, the availability of books and periodicals, the amount of time you have, how advanced you are in philosophy, and the audience for the paper.

The first step in your plan of research is to make a preliminary list of items that you wish to read. Your bibliography should be divided into primary and secondary sources. For example, if your topic is Plato's theory of justice in the *Republic,* then your primary sources will consist of the *Republic* and other relevant writings of Plato, and your secondary sources will consist of various books and articles by scholars who have discussed and analyzed Plato's theory of justice. This preliminary list may be gathered in various ways. The articles or chapters in histories of philosophy and in encyclopedias such as the *Encyclopedia of Philosophy* usually include a list of basic sources. You can also use the card catalogue in your library to find a recent book on your topic. It will very likely include a bibliography that you can use. You can then extend your list by adding items that are mentioned in the books and articles that you already have available. The periodical *The Philosopher's Index* is a guide to the articles that are published in philosophy journals.

If you are just beginning the study of philosophy, it is best to emphasize primary sources and to examine only a few of the most important secondary sources. The articles that are printed in philosophy journals and periodicals often presuppose more than you are likely to understand at the outset. As you gain more experience in philosophy, you will be able to use the journals with greater profit. A graduate student who is preparing a doctoral dissertation or a philosophy professor writing a book is obliged to be familiar with the entire range of relevant primary and secondary sources.

Unlike research in some other fields of study, philosophical research is not usually a matter of amassing a large amount of information but of deepening your understanding of a philosophical problem or of an important text. For this reason, it is better to read a few things slowly and carefully and thoughtfully than to read many things superficially. You should take notes to retain the results of your reading and thinking. It is customary to use index cards to record items of information relevant to your topic. But you should also keep a notebook for jotting down ideas and thoughts that occur during reading and reflection.

WRITING THE PAPER

A philosophy paper usually deals with general ideas and their logical relations to one another. It is important, therefore, that it be logically organized. Its parts and paragraphs must all be relevant to the point you are trying to make or to the question you are trying to answer.

A typical paper may exemplify the following pattern:

Beginning:
1. A full statement of the problem you are investigating or the question you are proposing to answer.
2. A statement of how you propose to answer the question.
3. A preliminary statement of your answer.

Middle:
4. A detailed formulation of your ideas presented in a logical order.
5. Reasons and arguments supporting your ideas and interpretations.
6. A consideration of alternative views.

End:
7. A brief summary and review of what you have accomplished and what remains to be accomplished.

Of course, other patterns are possible and are often desirable. You should not think of this pattern as one to which you should rigidly adhere but as a suggestion that may be varied at your convenience. As you gain in experience and self-confidence, you will develop your own style and method of organization.

Because philosophy addresses itself to general ideas and makes subtle and intricate conceptual distinctions, the particular form of expression that is used is essential to the success of your paper. For this reason, you will need to write more than one draft. The first draft is an opportunity to set your ideas down on paper so that you can more easily think about them without fear of forgetting them. Further drafts are needed to refine your language and organization. You want your writing to express your intentions exactly in a clear, precise, and rigorous way.

For the sake of ease of communication and personal self-respect, you should pay attention to style, grammar, sentence structure, and spelling. A paper that is seriously deficient in any of these areas indicates that you have not thought well enough of your project or of your contribution to put it into respectable shape. Deficiencies in these areas interfere seriously with your efforts at communication, and they constitute an unjustified burden on the time, energy, and good will of your readers.

Your paper should be self-contained. This means that it should not assume that the reader has any specific knowledge of the topic. It should include any information and background ideas essential to understanding what you have written. Even though your only audience might be a philosophy teacher who already knows a great deal about your topic, you should not assume any special knowledge on his or her part. After all, the purpose of writing a paper is to learn something. Part of learning about a subject is the acquisition of the ability to discriminate the essential from the inessential, the important from the trivial. It involves becoming aware of assumptions and prejudices that may interfere with a fair treatment of the topic. It involves becoming aware of what you do not yet know and of what you need to know to gain an adequate understanding of a topic. The requirement that the paper be self-contained forces you to make the necessary distinctions and to confront your assumptions. It also facilitates communication, especially when the audience consists of a variety of readers with different backgrounds and experience.

DOCUMENTATION

Documentation in the form of reference footnotes is indispensable in most philosophy papers. A reference footnote mentions the place in the book or article or manuscript that contains the quotation or idea that you are using. There are two main reasons for the use of reference footnotes. First, they embody evidence for the claims that you are making in your paper. For example, suppose you assert that Plato rejected the idea that might makes right. You need a footnote to indicate where Plato made or implied this statement. If you neglect to include a footnote, you have failed to support your interpretation of Plato. The footnote allows readers to decide for themselves how well you have supported your assertion about Plato. Second, reference footnotes are needed for the sake of fairness. It is unfair to use someone else's words and ideas as if they were your own. Simple justice requires that you acknowledge what you have taken from the work of others. The failure to acknowledge your sources is called *plagiarism*.

The following items should normally receive a footnote:

1. Direct quotations
2. Summaries, paraphrases, and interpretations of texts
3. The use of ideas, opinions, theories, and arguments of others
4. The use of facts and information uncovered by others
5. The use of unpublished manuscripts, papers, documents, lectures, letters, and personal communications

When I have explained these requirements to my students, they have usually felt them to be excessive. "Then everything must be footnoted," they groan. I answer, "Not everything. Ideas that are genuinely your own as well as matters of common knowledge do not require reference footnotes." For what is the alternative? If you neglect to include a footnote where one is needed, this means that you are either claiming as your own the work of another or leaving some claim of yours unsupported by evidence. In my experience, students tend to use too few reference footnotes.

BIBLIOGRAPHY

It is common to place a bibliography at the end of a paper. A bibliography may not be necessary if you have used very few sources and if they are footnoted in the body of the paper. If you decide to include one, it may be more or less extensive, depending upon the requirements of your instructor, the needs of your audience, the purpose of the paper, and so forth. Bibliographies may consist of

1. A list of all those works cited in the reference footnotes
2. A list of all those works cited in the reference footnotes or consulted in the preparation of the paper
3. A list of the most important works on your topic
4. An extensive list of all the works on the topic known to the writer

For a beginning student of philosophy, either the first or second type of bibliography is usually sufficient.

There are various methods that can be used for writing reference footnotes and bibliographical entries. There are many manuals and books of style that have been prepared for writers and students that are available in bookstores and libraries. One of the most widely used is Kate L. Turabian, *Student's Guide for Writing College Papers,* 2nd ed., rev. (Chicago: University of Chicago Press, 1970). You should always select one of the standard methods, and you should use the same method consistently throughout the paper. The reference footnotes should contain enough information for the reader to be able to find the passage being cited, and the bibliographical entry should contain enough information to identify precisely the source being listed.

INDEX